CONTEMPORARY

BUSINESS

REPORT

WRITING

Iris I. Varner
Illinois State University

The Dryden Press
Chicago   Fort Worth   San Francisco
Philadelphia   Montreal   Toronto
London   Sydney   Tokyo

To my husband, Carson

Acquisitions Editor: Mary Fischer
Developmental Editor: Penny Gaffney
Project Editor: Karen Vertovec
Design Supervisor: Jeanne Calabrese
Production Manager: Mary Jarvis
Permissions Editor: Cindy Lombardo
Director of Editing, Design, and Production: Jane Perkins

Text and Cover Design: Vargas/Williams Design
Copy Editor: Jean Berry
Indexer: Leoni McVey
Compositor: The Clarinda Company
Text Type: 10/12 ITC Berkeley Oldstyle

Library of Congress Cataloging-in-Publication Data

Varner, Iris I.
    Contemporary business report writing.

    Includes index.
    1. Business report writing.   I. Title.
HF5719.V37 1987   808'.066651   86-2104
ISBN 0-03-069584-8

Printed in the United States of America
789-039-9876543

Address orders:
The Dryden Press
Orlando, FL 32887

Address editorial correspondence:
The Dryden Press
908 N. Elm St.
Hinsdale, IL 60521

The Dryden Press
Holt, Rinehart and Winston
Saunders College Publishing

PREFACE

Writing successful reports is a challenge, an art, and an exciting task. It is an integral part of effective communication. Many businesspeople, including managers, marketing analysts, financial consultants, and accountants, communicate by writing reports. This textbook will help students to become better communicators—to solve problems, to present ideas persuasively, and to evaluate alternatives.

Contemporary Business Report Writing is not a typical handbook on writing. Handbooks may be useful for checking references and finding quick answers. This book, however, covers all aspects of report writing, including planning, research, data analysis, and organizing information.

ORGANIZATION

Each chapter begins with a list of learning objectives that provides a framework for study. At the end of each chapter a summary of the learning objectives enables students to review chapter material. End-of-chapter questions and problems not only test students' knowledge but also encourage further discussion and application of content.

The first four chapters lay the groundwork for writing good reports. Chapter One discusses the role of reports within the context of the organization. Chapter Two focuses on the principles of the communication process to enhance students' understanding of the characteristics of written reports. Chapter Three examines the elements of effective writing, and Chapter Four presents various types and formats of reports.

Chapter Five focuses on short reports and special reports. It can be covered either before or after Chapters Six through Fifteen, which take students step-by-step through the process of preparing a long report: planning (Chapter Six); secondary research (Chapter Seven); documentation (Chapter Eight); primary research (Chapters Nine and Ten); analysis of results (Chapters Eleven and Twelve); visual presentation of data (Chapter Thirteen); organizing and outlining (Chapter Fourteen); and presentation (Chapter Fifteen).

Managers often are asked to present oral reports. To prepare students for that task, Chapter Sixteen discusses the preparation, delivery, and evaluation of oral reports.

The last three chapters in the book address contemporary business issues that have an impact on report writing. New technology has transformed the traditional workplace. Today, many businesses expect their managers to be experienced in using the tools of computer technology—word processors and microcomputers. Chapter Seventeen prepares students to write reports in the modern business environment. Unique to this text are the chapters on the ethical and international dimensions of report writing. Report writers must function within the environment of their organizations. Because many firms operate worldwide, report writers should also be able to communicate with clients and suppliers of different cultures. Chapter Eighteen discusses the problems and challenges of international communication.

Business ethics is becoming an increasingly important concern for all companies. Managers are being held accountable for their actions—and their words. Chapter Nineteen points out the ethical issues that influence the writing of reports. The technical, ethical, and international issues are woven throughout this textbook. These chapters may be studied as separate units, or professors may choose to integrate parts of these chapters throughout the course.

The cases at the end of the book cover many types of business situations. They require a basic knowledge in the functional areas of business, and they challenge students to consider both ethical and international dimensions.

This textbook has been classroom tested successfully. Years of experience in teaching business report writing have helped to make this a book that works in the classroom and can be applied in the workplace. Numerous examples from actual business situations bring the reality of corporate report writing into the classroom.

Reading each chapter carefully and completing each assignment will prepare students for the report-writing tasks they will perform in the real world of business. It's often difficult for students to translate the study of a subject into a realistic application. To help students make the transition from completing academic exercises to performing on-the-job tasks, instructors may ask students to view each classroom assignment from a working experience perspective. The instructor becomes the boss; the student, the employee. Students, then, approach assignments from instructors as if they were instructions from their boss at work. They have a job to do, and it is in their best interest to do it well.

To help professors plan for the teaching of this course, the *Instructor's Manual* that accompanies this textbook provides sample syllabi, suggestions for approaching each chapter, test questions, and transparency masters.

ACKNOWLEDGMENTS

Many people have helped me develop and produce this textbook. I want to express my appreciation to all those who encouraged me along the way. Thanks to my husband, Carson, and my children, Katrin and Eric, without whose understanding I would have never finished. Thanks to my colleague, Patricia Marcum-Grogg, who critically read and classroom tested the manuscript. Thanks to Paula Pomerenke, who proofed and classroom-tested the text, and to Beth Tanton, who was always available to encourage me and read. I want to thank my friends from business and industry who contributed report examples: Jim Kehias, Gordon Varner, Sonja Reese, Sharon Sullivan, and Patti Gahr.

A special thanks to the reviewers of the manuscript. I appreciate their detailed comments and all their suggestions for improvements.

William J. Buchholz
Bentley College, Massachusetts

Earl A. Dvorak
Indiana University, Bloomington

Jeanette W. Gilsdorf
Arizona State University

Lorita S. Langdon
Columbus Technical Institute

Alexa North
Georgia State University

Peter Porosky
University of Maryland

Robert S. Rudolph
University of Toledo

Margaret Vota
City College of San Francisco

Jean Voyles
Georgia State University

I thank the people at The Dryden Press—Joan Resler, Mary Fischer, Penny Gaffney, Jeanne Calabrese, and Karen Vertovec. Their understanding and care were particularly helpful when things were rough. Last, but not least, I thank my students, who were willing to try it out and give me feedback.

Iris I. Varner
Illinois State University
July 1986

THE DRYDEN PRESS SERIES
IN BUSINESS COMMUNICATION

CONTENTS

CHAPTER SEVEN
SECONDARY RESEARCH

CHAPTER EIGHT
DOCUMENTATION OF SOURCES

CHAPTER NINE
PRIMARY RESEARCH

CONTEMPORARY

BUSINESS

REPORT

WRITING

CHAPTER ONE

ORIENTATION

TO

BUSINESS

REPORTS

LEARNING OBJECTIVES

- To understand the role of reports in modern business organizations.
- To examine and define the basic characteristics of business reports.
- To become aware of the differences between business reports and term papers.
- To recognize the importance of good report-writing skills in career development.

THE ROLE OF REPORTS IN ORGANIZATIONS

WHY DO BUSINESSES NEED REPORTS?

Report writing has been important to business since writing began. During the 1970s archaeologists unearthed clay tablets in Syria that are among the oldest written documents discovered so far. Most of these tablets are tax records, inventory accounts, and records of business transactions. Similarly, many reports today, such as balance sheets and income statements, provide historical data and records; but, increasingly, modern reports also help in planning and decision making.

Every year American businesses, government agencies, and nonprofit organizations produce thousands of reports. These reports are expensive to write, duplicate, and file, yet their number is increasing. This growth is a direct result of changes in the size of businesses, government requirements, technology, and legal considerations.

Business Size. In a small business much less need exists for written reports than in a large business. Let us assume Greta Hillstrom has a small tailoring business in Pleasant Hills, Illinois. She employs five women as seamstresses. Greta herself keeps the books, distributes the work, and meets with customers. When necessary, she will also help with the sewing.

In this environment Greta will communicate directly with her employees. If Mrs. Perry brings in material for a new suit, Greta will discuss the project with her. She may take Mrs. Perry to a particular seamstress for details, or she may jot down basic instructions, but most communication in this environment is oral. If Susan starts the work on Mrs. Perry's suit and later Natasha finishes it, Susan will most likely give oral instructions to Natasha. The environment is informal, and the owner–manager is easily accessible.

As the small business expands into a factory, the personal contact between the owner and the workers changes. To guarantee a smooth and efficient production process, Greta must hire supervisors and managers for finance, personnel, marketing, and production. The factory is divided into smaller manageable units. Now Greta will communicate directly with the heads of the various areas, and her direct contact with the seamstresses will decrease. Much of the communication will be indirect, and much of it will be in written form.

As Exhibits 1.1 and 1.2 illustrate, the need for written reports increases as the company grows. As layers are added to the organizational structure, the direct contact between upper management and workers diminishes. The workers know their supervisors, and they may occasionally talk to the department head, but they will rarely see the person above that level.

If a company has operations in several locations, written reports save time. If the officers of a steel company need information on the production process in the foundry, they could go directly to the foundry, but that would be time consuming, especially if the foundry is in another part of town. Requesting a written report from the foundry might be much more efficient.

Reports help to improve company performance. Let us assume upper management has decided that improving competitiveness is a major goal for the coming year. Before it can be improved, management must have current information on competitors, equipment, price of raw materials, production costs, and customer satisfaction. Obtaining this information would involve visiting a number of areas in the company and talking to many people. Although a personal visit may eventually be necessary, the time such a visit would require might not be spent effectively on a preliminary report. At the

Exhibit 1.1   **Direct Communication**

Exhibit 1.2   **Communication in a Large Organization**

```
                                Greta
         ┌──────────────┬──────────┴──────────┬──────────────┐
    Marketing        Production            Finance        Personnel
                ┌────────┴────────┐
             Cutting            Sewing
      ┌─────┬──┴──┬─────┐   ┌─────┬─────┬─────┬─────┬─────┐
    Team  Team  Team  Team Team  Team  Team  Team  Team  Team
     1     2     3     4    1     2     3     4     5     6
```

beginning management can request a report from the production department. The production manager in turn can contact the other appropriate
departments. Each department can ask the people who are most knowledgeable to prepare a report.

Good reports contribute to efficiency. They provide management with
the information necessary to make appropriate decisions.

Government Requirements. The government requires reports in order to
make certain that businesses obey the law. Business people file numerous
reports with the Occupational Safety and Health Administration (OSHA), the
Internal Revenue Service, the Environmental Protection Agency, the Equal
Employment Opportunity Commission, the Security and Exchange Commission, and many other agencies. Government reports require much detail and
supporting information.

Charles Cecil, the president of a medium-sized canning factory, com-
plains frequently about all the reporting he has to do. In his opinion he could
cut down the number of clerks and accountants he employs if he did not
have to file so many reports. The types of reports he must submit include
tax and income reports to the IRS. He also has to make certain that his
company keeps detailed records on the hiring and promotion of employees
to prove that the company follows affirmative action guidelines. OSHA representatives come regularly for plant inspections, and he must have reports
ready to show that the plant meets safety regulations. For workmen's compensation he has to prepare additional reports.

When the plant was expanded a few years ago, Cecil had to furnish an
environmental impact study to show that the plant did not disturb a wildlife

refuge close by. At this point he is thinking of using a new canning process. The process will have to be approved by authorities and thus will involve more reports. In addition the company has to file reports with local and state authorities. Charles Cecil's grandfather, who founded the company, would be surprised to see the amount of paperwork involved in running a canning factory.

Technology. Technology is a modern ally in the communication process. When the Egyptians prepared business reports, clerks wrote on papyrus rolls. Reports were handwritten until Gutenberg developed the modern printing press in the middle of the 15th century, revolutionizing written communication. The 19th century gave us modern record systems and the typewriter. Our century has given us the ability to transmit messages, not only by pen and paper and the U.S. postal service, but also by telephone, telegraph, satellite, modem, and computer.

Beginning with the typewriter in 1868, improvements in technology have contributed to the proliferation of business reports. Computers and duplicating machines have made it easy to provide copies of every report to all employees in a company. Managers may find stacks of reports on their desks that they often do not have time to read, let alone comprehend. In order to maximize the use and effectiveness of reports, a good company will write only necessary reports and send them only to those people who need them. The effect of technology on the writing process is discussed in detail in Chapter 18.

Legal Considerations. It is not enough to say "I called in an order on the 15th." You should also have a written record of the order signed by both parties. Price, terms, and method of payment must be in writing. A handshake agreement will not be sufficient if you have trouble with delivery. You can find a more detailed discussion of legal aspects of writing in Chapter 19.

WHO WRITES REPORTS?

Everyone writes reports. The typical business person spends 9% of the business day writing, 16% reading, 30% speaking, and 45% listening. Although these figures seem to indicate that writing is of no great importance, writing comprises a permanent record. Writing may provide the background for discussions, serve as the only source of information for other managers, or become the foundation for major decisions. Writing must be effective.

The type of reports a manager writes will change with career level and experience. For example, at the beginning of his career, a business person may write mostly short reports, and most of these reports will deal with aspects of his immediate department. As an example, John Grawe, who is the newly hired supervisor of a production line for dog food, will prepare reports relating to operations in his area, including production reports, personnel reports, and accident reports. At this stage in his career, John Grawe will not be asked to write reports that analyze broad company issues and policies. His contribution to those reports will be limited to factual information about his area of work.

For less complex situations people in beginning management positions may analyze information. If the production area for dog food wants to rearrange the office space, production can gather the information, analyze it, and make recommendations. John Grawe, for example, may be asked to examine such possibilities and recommend a solution.

As John Grawe advances to middle management, his reports will change. He will be fitting together pieces of information that he collects from lower-level management and supervisors. He will then synthesize the information into one report and make recommendations. He can examine the productivity of the entire dog-food production area and work on coordination with sales and marketing.

As John Grawe reaches upper management, he increasingly will find that he is a user of reports written by others. He will base complex and far-reaching production decisions on the information he receives. Sometimes he may ask for recommendations; sometimes he may want only the analysis. At this stage in his career he does not collect information himself; he uses information.

As managers' jobs widen and their responsibilities grow, their reporting functions grow also.

WHO REQUESTS REPORTS?

Most report requests come from superiors because they need information to make decisions. The finished reports in that case go up in the organization.

Not all reports, however, are written because of a specific request. Policies, instructions, and announcements are usually sent down in the organization. These reports, which are often distributed in pamphlets, in handbooks, and on bulletin boards, are to inform employees of decisions made at higher levels.

Some unrequested reports may go up in the organization. For example, if you have noticed that the production process is not set up very efficiently and that with a few changes production could be improved, you may want to write a report. Since nobody asked for that report, you have to take great pains to sell your idea. You must support your recommendation with facts. You must provide figures on what it costs the company to keep the old process and how much the company could save by adopting your suggestion. Since others have not recognized the problem, you must describe the problem in great detail. This type of report is called a justification report. It is discussed in detail in Chapter 5, "Common Short Reports."

Sometimes reports are requested by a person who is at the same level in the organization as the sender. For example, the marketing department and the collection department may exchange reports on a regular basis. If marketing would like to expand the number of credit card holders in order to increase sales, the collection area should be informed. As the number of credit card holders increases, the number of people who do not pay or pay late will probably increase also. Marketing and collections must cooperate by sharing plans and decisions through reports.

DEFINITION OF BUSINESS REPORTS

 All good business reports share certain characteristics. They must be:

1. Functional
   Many of the points we discuss in this text also apply to reports in science and the humanities, but the focus of this book is on the writing of useful business reports.

   A business report should help business people to make good decisions. It may simply provide the information for decisions, or it can analyze the information, draw conclusions, and make recommendations. In each case the report should help the company to become more productive and efficient.

2. Factual
   Business decisions are based on facts, not on feelings. You must be able to substantiate your conclusions and recommendations. You may find the facts in company records; you may talk to fellow employees; you may do a survey or conduct an experiment. Your assumptions must be supported by correct and complete facts. If the facts are accurate and you have experience, you can make intelligent decisions and judgments. If you provide incorrect information, on the other hand, your company may lose thousands of dollars.

   For example, if you are asked to recommend the purchase of new equipment, you will compare the cost of equipment. Based on your research, you may find that Machine A costs $10,500, Machine B costs $15,000, and Machine C costs $16,000. Just based on those figures, you may lean towards Machine A. But let us assume that the price for Machine A does not include installation costs, delivery costs, and first-year maintenance. Those items are, however, included in the price for Machines B and C. Once you add those costs to Machine A, the price may be higher than that for Machines B and C. The facts as first presented are not complete and therefore not correct.

3. Objective
   A report must be objective in its presentation. Bias can creep in at many stages of the report-writing process. Before even starting the report the writer may have decided what the outcome should be. Such gross bias may be rare; more frequent are subtler biases. The writer may read research data selectively and subconsciously block

out information that does not fit his bias. The writer may use vague or emotional words that will change the climate of the text. For example, the writer may use words such as *tremendous, great, fast, inferior,* and *superior* to describe products or business actions without substantiating the terms. Those words create a frame of reference in the mind of the reader that in some cases may not match the actual figures. A report that "production increased by one percent in June" will create a different impression from one that "production increased by a tremendous one percent in only one month."

4. Precise

"The cost is fairly high." "The new machinery will be needed soon." "The production quality improved quite a bit during last month." All of these are examples of vague writing or lack of precision. The reader does not know the meaning of *fairly high, soon,* or *quite a bit.* The writer should give specific numbers and dates. For example, the writer might say: "Machine X costs $25,000. This is $3,000 higher than was estimated six months ago." "The new machine will be needed by the end of March. The mechanics estimate that the current equipment will not last longer than two more months. Any repairs to the current machine are no longer cost effective. In addition, the machinery is outdated." "During the last month the rejection rate of products from Department B dropped from five percent to three percent." The specific examples not only provide numbers but also put them in perspective.

5. Well Organized

Good organization helps in reading. Logical presentation and development of material will help the reader to understand the report and to use the information in it. The organization you choose will depend on the purpose of your report and the needs of the reader.

6. Clear

The reader must understand a report after one reading. A writer can achieve clarity by using concrete words and correct sentence structure. A report that is not clear does not get its message across effectively and may cause the reader to simply give up before finishing it.

7. Concise

Business people are busy. They do not want to waste valuable time reading useless information. Reports should give the necessary information in as few words as possible. Conciseness and brevity are not necessarily the same, of course. For example, the preceding illustrations of precise writing are all longer than the vague ones. What many managers refuse to read is rambling reports.

8. Attractive in Appearance

Before the reader reads the report, he sees the report. A report which is visually appealing will give the impression of being well done. Although the reader may later decide that, despite the good appearance, the clear print, and the visual aids, the report is not well done, the reader initially approaches it with a positive attitude and reads at least part of it. A sloppy looking report may not generate the same goodwill at the beginning. In extreme cases it may not be read at all. Appearance is important, and modern office technology will help to set up reports, draw clear visual aids, and organize page layout.

A specific definition of business reports can be synthesized from these eight characteristics.

A business report is an organized and objective presentation of facts needed to make effective business decisions.

COMPARISON OF BUSINESS REPORTS AND TERM PAPERS

During your years in school and college, you have probably written a number of term papers.

Although the skills necessary to write a good term paper are prerequisites for writing a good business report, the two have different purposes. In traditional term papers the student writes to demonstrate what he has learned. The term paper shows that the student understands the material, that he can use and/or apply it. The student strives to demonstrate an ability to analyze information, to think critically, to collect and organize data, and to express ideas. In short, a term paper is a testimony to the student's knowledge and abilities.

A business report has a different objective. It has a practical purpose and is to help business in the decision-making process by providing pertinent data. The emphasis is on the usefulness of the message and not on the learning experience of the writer. The reader of the report, unlike the reader of the term paper, does not primarily use the report to judge the writer; he uses the information in the report to make business decisions. This purpose influences the presentation of the report. Business reports use headings, illustrations, and itemization to help the reader understand and remember the content.

IMPORTANCE OF REPORTS IN CAREER SUCCESS

The reports you write are important to the company you work for, the advancement of fellow employees, and your own career. The most important consideration is the usefulness of your reports to the company, of course. If the information and the analysis of material are clear, correct, and convincing, management can make appropriate decisions, and, as a result, the company may prosper.

As you advance in your career, you may be asked to prepare personnel reports, recommendation reports, and evaluations of employees you know and have worked with. Your reports can influence the advancement of subordinates. If your recommendation is written well, your opinion will carry more weight. A well-organized and knowledgeable evaluation of the employee will be credible. A disorganized and poorly written report may not.

Well-written reports will not only benefit subordinates but will also reflect favorably on you. Even though the purpose of a report is not to demonstrate your writing ability, good reports will "silently" work for you. They may tell more about you than any verbal statements could. It pays to write good business reports. You receive satisfaction from doing a good job, and you may also obtain direct personal benefits.

The following examples illustrate how well-written business reports can help a corporation and advance the career of an individual.

ALFRED SLOAN

Alfred P. Sloan's great contribution to management was the concept of running a large, diversified company, such as General Motors, through decentralization. What is often overlooked is that in 1919, early in his career at GM, Sloan wrote down his ideas in a memorandum. This memorandum, called "The Organization Study," clearly and concisely laid out the concept of decentralization. After much discussion, the Board of Directors asked him to implement his ideas. Sloan was enormously successful in his more than 20 years as chief executive officer at GM. No matter how good his ideas were, they would never have attracted the directors' attention without that memo.

HARRY B. CUNNINGHAM

Harry B. Cunningham took two years away from his operating responsibilities at S.S. Kresge Company (now K-Mart Corporation) in 1957 and 1958 to see what could be done to reverse the downward trend in Kresge's profitability. Kresge stores were historically located in downtown areas. They sold low-priced, low-margin items. Cunningham recommended in a comprehensive report that S.S. Kresge take advantage of the affluent suburban areas that had developed after World War II by shifting its strategy from the downtown stores to large, self-service discount department stores called K-Marts. After much deliberation by the Board of Directors, Cunningham's report won support for his plans. Like Sloan, Cunningham was entrusted with the job of implementing his profit-generating K-Mart strategy.

An essential ingredient in the extraordinary business success of both Sloan and Cunningham was their ability to express complex ideas so well in writing.

SUMMARY OF LEARNING OBJECTIVES

To Understand the Role of Reports in Modern Business Organizations.
How does the size of the company relate to the number of business reports written?
Reports help in planning and decision making. They also provide records of transactions and agreements. The number of reports increases as the business expands or diversifies. As layers of organization are added in a company, the personal contact between upper and lower management decreases. Reports are needed for communication between the various levels in an organization.

How does career advancement affect report writing?
The types of reports will change as the writer advances in the company. At the beginning, reports will provide mostly information for upper managers; later, as a middle manager the writer will synthesize information and analyze it; finally, as an executive the writer will become mostly a user of reports.

Who requests reports? Who writes reports?
Report requests tend to travel down in the organization, while most reports travel up. All business persons write reports.

To Examine and Define the Basic Characteristics of Business Reports.
A business report should be clear, precise, concise, well organized, factual, objective, attractive in appearance, and business oriented.

To Become Aware of the Differences between Business Reports and Term Papers.
In a term paper the writer's goal is to show the reader that he has mastered the material of the course. In the business report the emphasis is on the content and usefulness of the report rather than on the achievements of the writer.

To Recognize the Importance of Good Report Writing Skills in Career Development.
Business reports benefit the business for which they are written. Recommendations made by the writer can influence the advancement of fellow employees. Good business reports work "silently" for the writer, bringing direct personal benefits.

QUESTIONS AND PROBLEMS

1. Discuss how the growth of business has influenced business reports.
2. Discuss some of the possible reasons why improvements in technology have led to an increase rather than a decrease in the number of reports businesses produce.
3. What types of reports can you expect to write at various levels in your career?

4. What are the characteristics of a good business report?
5. What are some of the major differences between business reports and term papers?
6. What roles do reports play in business careers?
7. Who requests business reports?
8. Obtain a copy of a business report from a local company and analyze it according to the characteristics of good reports.
9. Discuss the direction of reports. What kinds of reports go up, down, or laterally in an organization?

CHAPTER TWO

REPORTS

AND THE

COMMUNICATION

PROCESS

LEARNING OBJECTIVES

- To explore the communication process and understand the importance of reader adaptation in effective communication.
- To become familiar with readability formulas and understand their place in business writing.

To write effective business reports and to deliver convincing oral reports, it is helpful to understand the communication process. Communication can be written, oral, or nonverbal through gestures, appearance, and facial expressions.

EFFECTIVE COMMUNICATION

Communication
Communication transfers meaning.

Effective **communication** achieves transfer of meaning. Effective and ineffective communication, communication problems, communication improvements, and miscommunication are popular terms today.

For example, if a manager and a secretary do not work well together, someone may say, "They sure have communication problems." A recruiter may say after an employment interview, "Well, a good academic record, but poor communication skills." Often we interpret problems in human interaction as communication problems. This viewpoint is not always correct. People may communicate quite well; however, they simply disagree. Two political candidates from opposing parties, for example, may understand each other very well, but they may never agree on foreign policy, domestic issues, or the role of the government in the economy.

Communication in its broadest sense does not require agreement, but in business communication that is often the goal. The business writer has a special goal: the understanding and the acceptance of the report by the reader. The purpose of the report is to transfer meaning to the reader and to elicit agreement. For example, when assigned the task of analyzing the company's personnel policies, Beth Stone expects her superior to accept her conclusions and recommendations. If Beth and her boss have similar philosophies and if both know the personnel goals of the company, the likelihood of agreement increases. Any changes in personnel policy would need to be communicated to all employees, who may view policies from different perspectives and reach different conclusions. This is particularly likely if they are not familiar with the facts and the long-range goals of the company.

Employees at different levels of the organization are not equally aware of the organizational goals and financial situation. A study by the Opinion Research Corporation revealed that information generated at the top of organizations did not filter down to workers. In a large metal industry plant, 91 percent of top-level management knew about the company's declining profit margin, but only 5 percent of front-line supervisors knew this. Other studies have shown that management usually believes that lower level employees know more than they actually do.

A number of factors may account for this problem. Apparently organization members prefer to communicate with those whom they perceive as having higher status than themselves. They may not communicate readily with those whom they perceive to be of lower status. Yet effective communication requires that all employees have access to data relating to the organization.

In order to understand the relationship between people who communicate, let us examine how communication works.

ENCODING AND DECODING OF MESSAGES

Communication theorists have developed various models to depict the communication process. While communication models are excellent vehicles for the discussion of the process, they can never present the total reality because the models cannot account for all of the variables affecting communication.

Often the communication process is presented in a diagram similar to the one in Exhibit 2.1.

A sender (writer or speaker) sends a message to a receiver (reader or listener). The receiver then provides **feedback** to the sender. Feedback is the response to the message. Feedback can be positive, negative, or neutral. Feedback does not necessarily mean agreement with the sender.

Feedback
The receiver's answer to the sender is called feedback.

Exhibit 2.1   **Basic Communication Model**

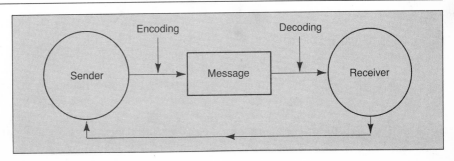

Cycle
Sending a message and receiving an answer form a cycle.

In Exhibit 2.1 the communication process is depicted as a **cycle**, a two-way process in which both the sender and receiver are involved. In written communication the sender of a message often waits for a response before sending another message. When the original sender receives the feedback, a communication cycle has been completed. The feedback to a report or a speech can be oral, written, or nonverbal in form. Not to answer a question may provide feedback. This "silent" feedback can have a variety of meanings, such as "I did not hear the message"; "I don't know what to say"; "I agree with you"; "I disagree with you"; "I am undecided." Nonverbal clues may help to decipher the feedback, but the important point is that a refusal to answer is a message in itself.

Encode
The sender transforms an idea into words.

Let us look at the parts of the process. In all communication the sender has an idea he wants to share with someone. Before he can communicate this idea, he has to transform the idea into words; he has to **encode** the message. Let us assume a manager must explain a new inventory ordering and maintenance system to the inventory clerks. He and other managers have worked together on complicated formulas to keep stockouts at a minimum while at the same time cutting down on inventory-carrying cost. The manager who wrote the proposal for upper management spent hours over old records, research material on inventory control, and computer printouts. The proposal was accepted by upper management; now, in order to communicate the decision to the clerks, the manager must encode the message so that they will understand it.

Decode
The receiver gives meanings to words.

When the inventory clerks receive the message, they must **decode** it. They have to figure out what the new system is and how it will function. In order to work with the new system, they must understand how it differs from the old one. They can ask the manager questions. The feedback they provide will help the manager to determine whether he has communicated effectively. Ideally, the manager will explain the system, and the clerks will be ready to use it without any problems. In reality, the manager may have to explain it several times before it functions well.

AUDIENCE ADAPTATION

How can the painless switch to the new inventory system be achieved? The manager encoding the message has to think of the inventory clerks. How much do they have to know? What is their background? He then **adapts** the message to his audience.

Adapt
The sender encodes the message with the reader in mind.

The manager understands the formulas and intricate calculations underlying the new system and might be tempted to simply send the clerks a copy of the proposal prepared for upper management. This approach would save time. However, if he uses the document that he prepared to persuade upper management, the clerks might not understand the information. In that case they might simply put the document aside and continue with the old system. If they do not understand the message, they cannot decode it.

To communicate successfully, the manager must be able to answer the following questions:

What do the clerks know?

What do they *need* to know?

What is the work background of the clerks?

The clerks probably have never worked with inventory models and inventory formulas, and they may not be interested. There is no need for them to understand the mathematical foundation of the new system. All they need to know is what they are expected to do under the new system. The manager must explain to them when and how to order products. They need to know which forms to fill out, how to fill them out, and how to enter receipts. The manager may want to tell the clerks why the system was changed, but rather than going into great detail, it may be enough to point out how much money the new system will save the company every year or how much easier their jobs will be.

☆ Audience adaptation requires the sender to encode the message in view of the background and experiences of the reader. The receiver, on the other hand, must decode the message in view of the background and experiences of the sender. In the inventory example, the clerks must understand what the manager wants them to do. The decoding and interpretation of the message depend not only on the facts but also on the perceptions of the receiver. Communication researchers estimate that 80 percent of what is communicated is influenced by personal perception of the receiver.

Considering that communication is the transfer of meaning, that meaning is influenced by perception, and that perception is influenced by experience, education, emotions, and mood, it is understandable that many communications do not result in common understanding.

☆ People give different meanings to messages because they do not use all words in the same way. Although dictionaries provide definitions, words have many more meanings than those listed. People from different backgrounds may interpret the same word differently. For example, let us look at the word *make:*

Chevy is my favorite *make* of car. (*Make* in this context means *brand.*)

I hate to get up and *make* breakfast. (*Make* here means prepare.)

What do you *make* of her attitude? (*Make* is used in the sense of think.)

How did you *make* out on the exam? (In this context *make* stands for score.)

A person who is not familiar with the various meanings of *make* may have difficulties understanding or at least may wonder at the use of the verb. Foreigners, since they rely more on the dictionary meaning, may be at a loss and not understand at all.

Problems in the encoding and decoding process include the following:

1. The sender may not have the idea clearly in his own mind. He may, therefore, have difficulty formulating his idea into words.

2. The sender may have difficulty in adapting the message to the receiver because he does not know anything about the receiver or is not familiar with the technical vocabulary that the receiver uses.

3. The receiver may not understand the special vocabulary the sender uses.

4. The receiver may not know the sender very well and thus misinterpret the message.

5. Communication may be hindered because sender and receiver are not aware that they use common words differently. Each may have given a very personal meaning to certain words or connect certain associations with words.

COMMUNICATION CLIMATES

The more the sender and the receiver know about each other, the more successful they will be in communicating effectively. Exhibit 2.2 illustrates the communication process when communication takes place in an area of common experiences.

Two people who discuss a project they have been working on for some time may be able to cut misunderstandings to a minimum in that particular area. They have a common background. The same two people may have more difficulty discussing subjects which are not related to their project.

Let us assume Larry Reed and Chip Stuart have worked together on a production evaluation project for several weeks. They meet regularly for they

Exhibit 2.2 **Communication between People of Common Backgrounds**

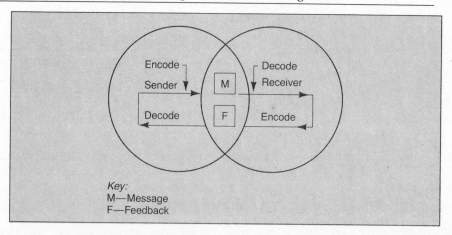

Key:
M—Message
F—Feedback

have to discuss the project, write reports, and present their findings to upper management. They work well together.

Their personal interests are entirely different, however. Larry Reed loves college football. He follows the ratings closely and watches every game shown on television. Chip Stuart, on the other hand, has no interest in sports or the outdoors. He likes theater and concerts. These two men have a lot in common as long as they talk about their work, but they may have a hard time communicating about anything not work related. In fact, they may be so different that they just give up talking about anything outside work.

A perfect overlap of experiences would be possible only with cloning. In reality, there are always differences in backgrounds, experiences, preferences, and outlook on life, resulting in the constant danger of miscommunication. The less two people have in common, the more likely it is that communication problems will arise.

So far, we have talked about communication between two people who work for the same company and who both come from the same cultural background. You can imagine that the communication problems mushroom as soon as we enter the field of international business.

Let us assume Paul Craig from the United States and Kyofumi Katsuki from Japan are negotiating a business deal. Their cultural backgrounds are different. Negotiation styles are different, and contracts have different meanings in both cultures. Mr. Craig is a goal oriented and efficient American manager who hates to waste time. Mr. Katsuki has the patience of the Orient; he wants to do business with a friend. To him business is an extension of personal relationships; he refuses to do business with strangers. Because Mr. Craig speaks only English and Mr. Katsuki speaks only Japanese, they need an interpreter.

You will understand the formidable challenge they face in their negotiations. Exhibit 2.3 illustrates the communication process in this situation. The only overlap, which is their interest in doing business with each other, is overshadowed by cultural differences and linguistic hurdles. The interpreter functions as middleman. This means that Mr. Craig encodes the message, the interpreter decodes Mr. Craig's message and then encodes it for Mr. Katsuki, and finally Mr. Katsuki decodes the message.

Verbal communication is not the only problem. Mr. Craig's and Mr. Katsuki's nonverbal communication is so different that they have difficulty using nonverbal signals to interpret the verbal message. If the interpreter is not knowledgeable about their special area of business, the communication process becomes even more complex. The language competency and the nationality of the interpreter will also influence the success of the negotiations.

To experience cultural problems in communications, you do not have to go to Japan or China. Many different cultural groups exist in the United States. To communicate effectively with Mexican-Americans, Italian-Americans, Blacks, American Indians, Japanese-Americans, or Chinese-Americans, an understanding of their particular cultural backgrounds is helpful. Chapter 18 discusses the problems of international communication in more detail.

Exhibit 2.3   **Communicating through an Interpreter**

Key:
M—Message
F—Feedback

COMPARISON OF WRITTEN AND ORAL COMMUNICATION

The problems discussed so far apply to both oral and written communications, but there are also differences. In written communication the process is linear. The sender sends the message; the receiver then reads the message and provides feedback. The communication cycle is completed before the next one is started. Written communication offers a special challenge because the sender does not have any immediate feedback but must wait for another message in the form of eye contact, facial expression, or body language.

In oral communication the process resembles a spiral. The sender, in this case the speaker, encodes the message. From the beginning, the listener provides immediate feedback either verbally or nonverbally. The speaker can immediately change the message by reencoding it. This process continues until the end of the discussion, presentation, or conversation.

Telephone communication introduces additional challenges to the communication process. The sender has less time to plan the message than in written communication and has no nonverbal feedback. Because much business is conducted over the telephone, many businesses are training their employees to become effective telephone communicators.

PRINCIPLES OF COMMUNICATION

Based on our discussion so far, we can draw the following conclusions:

1.   Communication is never perfect.
2.   Common experiences increase the chance of effective communication.
3.   Written communication tends to have complete cycles, whereas oral communication resembles a spiral. In oral communication the sender

can adapt and readapt the message in response to feedback. Often a new cycle is started before the old one has been completed.

4. The success of communication is influenced by the perceptions, the background, and the experiences of the sender and the receiver.

5. Successful communication requires adaptation to the audience.

6. The sender must be aware of the differences between written and oral communications in order to choose the most effective means for communicating a particular message.

MEASUREMENTS OF COMMUNICATION LEVELS

Good reports are written at a level appropriate to the background and needs of the reader. If the report is too difficult, the reader may have to read it twice. If it is too simple, the reader may feel insulted. Many factors determine the level of difficulty of a text. Among them are word choice, sentence length, sentence structure, paragraph length, paragraph structure, organization of material, logical development of material, difficulty of material, use of headings, page layout, typeface, and the number of illustrations. Most of these criteria are impossible to measure. We may agree that the organization of a report is good or weak, but we will probably never agree on a certain grade or numerical value for the organization. The same is true for measuring the difficulty of material, the complexity of sentence structure, the organization of paragraphs, page layout, illustrations, difficulty of words, use of headings, and print.

Readability Formulas
Readability formulas measure the level of difficulty of a text.

Despite these problems, researchers have developed **readability formulas** for measuring difficulty. In the effort to quantify the level of difficulty, many of the criteria mentioned had to be discarded. All formulas that measure readability concentrate on word length and sentence length because they produce clear and undebatable numbers.

THE GUNNING FOG INDEX

Gunning Fog Index
The Gunning Fog Index measures text difficulty in grade levels.

One of the most widely used readability measures is **the Gunning Fog Index,** which measures the grade equivalent of a text. For example, if the readability measure is 10, the text is appropriate reading for someone in tenth grade. Examination of the following passage will demonstrate how the index works:

> The human resource manager plays an important role in selecting employees. The recruitment and selection process results from human resource planning and is based on the philosophy, "Don't fit a square peg into a round hole!" Adding new employees is an expensive process. Recruitment costs alone are high. Various interviews and tests are often conducted before new employees are selected. Medical ex-

aminations (at company expense) are often required for applicants. Training new people is also costly, and an inefficient worker wastes money. The human resource manager must ensure that potential employees have the necessary qualifications for the job and that they either possess future skill needs or are capable of learning them.[1]

The first step is to count words, sentences, and difficult words:

Number of Words	112
Number of Sentences	8
Number of Difficult Words	24

These figures are then used in two equations:

$$\text{Average Sentence Length} = \frac{\text{Number of Words}}{\text{Number of Sentences}} = \frac{112}{8} = 14$$

$$\text{Percentage of Difficult Words} = \frac{\text{Number of Difficult Words}}{\text{Number of Words in Sample}}$$
$$= \frac{24}{112} = .2143 \text{ or } 21.43\%$$

The final calculations are as follows:

Average Sentence Length	14.00
+ Percentage of Difficult Words	21.43
	35.43
× Multiplier of .4	.40
Readability Level	14.17

The text has a readability level of 14.17. It should be appropriate reading for sophomores in college. When determining the percentage of difficult words, these rules must be followed precisely:

1. Words with three or more syllables are considered difficult words.

2. A word that appears twice is counted twice.

3. Exceptions:
   a. Words of three syllables that are compounds of two simple words are not considered difficult. Examples: typewriter, lawnmower.
   b. Simple verbs that become difficult by adding *-es, -ed,* or *-ing* are not counted. Examples: repeated, conducted.
   c. Proper names are never counted as difficult words.

The difficult words are *manager, important, employees, recruitment, selection, philosophy, employees, expensive, recruitment, various, interviews, employees, medical, examinations, company, required, applicants, inefficient, manager, potential, employees, necessary, qualifications, capable.*

The calculation was rather tedious, and a longer document would require several samples. Today, the readability level of a text can be calculated by a computer. The Gunning Fog calculation is possible with special software packages. Rather than spend your time counting syllables and words, you can spend the time rewriting your report and let the computer do the drudgery.

USE OF READABILITY MEASURES

Insurance companies use readability measures to comply with government requirements for readable and understandable policies. Financial institutions may use them to explain financial data more clearly to customers. Newspapers and magazines use them to see whether the readability level of their publications is appropriate for the target market.

The readability level you choose depends on the purpose of the text. Many business people read newspapers on the way to or from work and understandably do not want to have to use a dictionary. They read for fast information; therefore, newspapers are usually written below the readability level of the readers. Because *The Wall Street Journal* is read mostly by college graduates, the majority of its readers should be able to read at a level of 16, yet it has an average readability level of about 12. *Time* and *Newsweek* have levels of 8 to 10. Magazines such as *Sports Illustrated* and *Better Homes and Gardens* tend to have levels of about 6 to 8.

CONSIDERATIONS FOR USING READABILITY FORMULAS

Readability formulas are only one aspect of measuring the difficulty of a text. Other aspects less easily measured include familiar word choice, familiarity with subject matter, sentence structure, and illustrations. Mechanically following readability formulas will not guarantee that a text is actually readable. They must be used with caution, but they can be helpful in identifying the general level of the text. Furthermore, readability formulas are language specific.

The Gunning Fog Index cannot be used in languages other than English. Difficult words are culture specific. German words, for example, tend to have more syllables than English words. As a result, even an easy text will have a higher percentage of long words than an English text. The following example illustrates the point.

	German	English	
	Textverarbeitung	Word Processing	
Number of Syllables	5	1	3
	Autoreparaturwerkstatt	Garage	
	8	2	
	Gabelstaplerfahrer	Forklift Driver	
	6	2	2

Based on the Gunning definition of difficult words, all of these German words are difficult; in English none is difficult. (Processing falls under exception 3b.) Japanese or Chinese words are not written as letters grouped into syllables, so that the measure of difficulty would have to be based on different criteria altogether.

SUMMARY OF LEARNING OBJECTIVES

To Explore the Communication Process and Understand the Importance of Reader Adaptation in Effective Communication.
The sender of a message must encode the message; the receiver must decode it. The receiver gives feedback to the originator of the message. The encoding and decoding of the message depend on the complexity of the message as well as the educational background, the needs, and the experience of both the sender and the receiver.

The more the communicators have in common, the better they can communicate with each other.

Communication is never perfect.

To Become Familiar with Readability Formulas and Understand Their Place in Business Writing.
Readability measures are an attempt to determine how well a text is adapted to the level of a particular reader or group of readers.

The Gunning Fog Index measures readability according to grade level. It is based on word length and sentence length. Fog indexes should be used with caution because they are culture specific and represent only one aspect of readability.

QUESTIONS AND PROBLEMS

1. Discuss and compare the different communication models presented in this chapter.
2. Define the term *feedback*.
3. Compare written and oral communication processes.
4. What role does perception play in the communication process?
5. Define the terms *encoding* and *decoding*.
6. What elements of a text determine whether it is easy or difficult to read?
7. Discuss the use of readability formulas.
8. Why are most readability formulas based on word length and sentence length?

9. Select passages in several textbooks and calculate the Gunning Fog Index for each.
10. Rewrite at least one of the samples for which you calculated the Gunning Fog Index. First raise and then lower the readability level. The revised passages should be at least two levels above and two levels below the original. Discuss the results. What did you do to achieve the change?

NOTES

[1] Louis E. Boone and David L. Kurtz, *Contemporary Business*, 4th ed. (Hinsdale, IL: The Dryden Press, 1985) 175. Copyright © 1985 by CBS College Publishing.

CHAPTER THREE

PRINCIPLES OF

EFFECTIVE

WRITING

LEARNING OBJECTIVES

- To write with clarity and precision.
- To examine the use of business jargon.
- To use action verbs to make writing more interesting and lively.
- To master correct sentence structure.
- To review the rules of punctuation.
- To write concisely.
- To organize material logically.

As we have seen in the previous chapter, we can measure the difficulty of writing with formulas. We have also seen, however, that the readability formulas are of limited value because it is impossible to develop a perfect quantitative measure of qualitative aspects of writing.

Writers impress readers, either positively or negatively, by writing correctly or incorrectly. A positive impression results not only from writing with clarity and using good grammar, but also from meeting the reader's expectations. The calculation of the readability formulas allows for a quick measure of overall reader adaptation, but there are additional factors that have to be considered in good writing. In this chapter we will examine these factors.

CLARITY AND PRECISION

CLEAR TERMS AND PHRASES

"This tax measure will be good for the middle income family, but it will hurt the poor," a candidate for political office may argue. "The new subsidiary of Company X will bring many new jobs to town and result in a sizable boost to the local economy," you may read in the newspaper. Both of these sentences are vague. What is the definition of a middle-income family? What is poor, well off, rich? The government has an official definition of these terms, but most people do not know it. That problem becomes apparent as soon as you ask people to define (1) the income necessary for a family of four to be above the poverty level, (2) the income for a family of four to qualify as middle income, and (3) the income for a family of four to qualify as rich. You will find that there is little agreement on the categories. What some may consider as middle income, others may consider as poor or even rich.

If you use words such as *poor, middle income*, or *rich* in a report, you must define the terms so that the reader knows exactly what you are talking about. The reader need not absolutely agree with your definition, but it is important that the reader know what your definition is.

The two examples would be more meaningful if they read:

This tax measure will help the family of four in the $20,000 to $30,000 income range, but it will definitely hurt families with incomes below $9,000.

The new subsidiary of Company X will bring 500 jobs to town and add $1,000,000 to the local economy.

The following examples further illustrate how you can add clarity to your writing by substituting a precise expression for a vague one:

Vague	**Precise**
A sizable profit	A profit of $500,000 last year compared to $200,000 the year before
The equipment will be needed very soon.	The equipment will be needed by April 1, 19XX.
He was the leading salesman.	He sold $300,000 worth of merchandise in one month, $50,000 more than the second best salesman.
This is a work-saving machine.	This machine will do the work of ten people.
The new production process will result in significant savings.	The new production process will save the company $20,000 over a period of three months.

All the rewritten versions are longer than the original ones, but they are also more precise and descriptive. The business manager who must decide whether to buy the new equipment wants to know how much money the new machine will save and when the old equipment will be worn out and have to be replaced. Terms such as *work saving* and *soon* will not help in the decision-making process.

Difficult Words
The perception of difficulty depends on the background of the reader.

SIMPLE AND DIFFICULT WORDS

Reports that use **difficult words** will be more difficult to read. Moreover, a word that may be easy for one person may be difficult for another. For example, *consolidated income statements, cost accounting, depreciation,* and *good-*

will may be easy words for accountants but difficult for the layperson. A marketing person knows what *advertising copy* is, but a chemist may never have heard the words. Theory X and Theory Y are common terms in management, but how many assembly-line workers could define them? We are familiar with the technical vocabulary in our area and may, therefore, assume that those words are simple.

The origin of words also influences the difficulty level. In English many words of Latin and French origin are considered difficult. Think of the language part of the SAT test. Most of the word definitions you had trouble with were probably of French origin.

The Gunning Fog Index, which uses the number of syllables as the criterion of word difficulty, does not take into account familiarity and frequency of usage. In business, for example, much of the technical vocabulary—management, assembly, depreciation—has three or more syllables. Even though the words are long, the business person who uses them frequently does not necessarily consider them difficult.

In your business reports you should strive to use words that are easy to understand. In many cases a simpler word can be substituted for a more difficult one:

Difficult	**Simple**
alleviate	solve
commence	begin
ameliorate	improve
finalize	end
incorporate	include
utilize	use
promulgate	publish
ascertain	find out
endeavor	try
exacerbate	make worse
interrogate	ask
capable of	can

Although the simple word can often replace the difficult one, word pairs are not interchangeable in all contexts. For example, the verb *interrogate* is not only stronger than the verb *ask,* but it is also more negative. (You are welcome to ask me, but please don't interrogate me.) People trying to *find out* something might be judged snoopy; *ascertain* is a word with fewer negative connotations. To *alleviate* a problem is to relieve it in some way, which is not the same as *solving* it. *Promulgate* has a broader meaning than *publish.* Before you substitute any words, you should make certain that the new word clearly communicates the meaning you intend it to communicate.

Difficulty is not determined by word choice alone. The concept and the subject matter of a discipline may be difficult to grasp for people from outside the discipline; therefore, audience analysis and audience adaptation are crucial. For example, if your field is production, then a report on quality-control problems in production is easier for you to understand than for someone whose expertise is music. If, on the other hand, you are a cost accounting specialist and are asked to read a report on the application of rhetorical principles to business communication, you may not feel very motivated to go ahead with the reading.

The perception of difficulty, interest, and boredom will influence whether or not the report will be easy or difficult to understand. Writers must consider the needs and the fears of the reader and adapt the material to the reader as much as possible. A marine biologist, for example, may be lost if asked to read an article in a professional journal on econometrics. This same biologist may have no problem reading an article on econometrics in *Time* or *Newsweek* because these magazines adapt the material to a more general audience.

CORRECT USAGE OF WORDS

The English language has a very rich vocabulary. Since English has readily incorporated words from many foreign languages, the writer has many different ways of expressing ideas. At the same time this wealth of words and possibilities can also lead to confusion. Many words that appear to be similar may have entirely different meanings. The good writer uses words correctly. Some of the words many people have difficulty with are given below.

Accept/Except

Accept:	To take something that is offered. *I accepted the reward with great pride.*
Except:	Something left out or excluded. *All employees except John Jones went to the picnic.*

Adapt/Adept/Adopt

Adapt:	To make suitable. *He adapted his speech to the audience.*
Adept:	Highly trained, very good, proficient. *She was adept at explaining new processes to workers.*
Adopt:	To take into possession, to take into a loose relationship. *The company adopted the new strategy without much discussion.*

Affect/Effect

Affect:	To have an impact on, to influence. *The storm affected the delivery schedule.*

Effect: As verb: to result in, to bring about.
The committee effected a change in the procedures.

As noun: result.
The new procedures had a positive effect on production.

Appraise/Apprise

Appraise: To estimate.
The realtor appraised the property.

Apprise: To inform.
The manager apprised him of the new policy.

As/As if/Like

As: As conjunction.
As he predicted, the meeting was very long.

As if: As conjunction.
He acted as if he had not understood the instructions.

Like: As preposition.
The company needs people like you.

Assure/Ensure/Insure

Assure: To promise.
He assured her that the goods had been shipped yesterday.

Ensure: To make certain.
By adding personnel he ensured that the crowded train could leave on time.

Insure: To protect against loss.
The company was insured against theft.

Biannual/Biennial

Biannual: Twice a year.
The report is issued on a biannual basis, January and July.

Biennial: Every two years.
The production plans are examined on a biennial basis.

Cite/Site/Sight

Cite: To quote.
He cited seven sources in his report.

Site: Location.
They visited the new construction site.

Sight: Vision.
His sight was deteriorating.

Complement/Compliment

Complement: To go well with.
The team members complemented each other.

Compliment: As verb: to praise.
She complimented him on his good presentation.

As noun: a word of praise.
She paid him a compliment.

Continual/Continuous

Continual: Regular but interrupted.
She studied continually for the exam.

Continuous: Uninterrupted.
The continuous noise from the street below made him nervous.

Council/Counsel

Council: A group of people who give advice.
The Board appointed a special council.

Counsel: As verb: to give advice.
The professor counsels the student.

As noun: advice.
The professor's counsel was to go to summer school.

As noun: lawyer.
He was represented by counsel.

Precede/Proceed

Precede: To come before something else.
The dinner will precede the address of the guest speaker.

Proceed: To continue, to go on.
After a brief explanation the speaker proceeded to the next point.

Principal/Principle

Principal: The most important.
His principal task was to edit reports.

The chief administrator of a primary or secondary school.
Mr. Stuart was appointed principal of Green Bay High School.

A capital sum invested at interest or due as a debt.
Alex Green used the interest income to pay for his vacation; he did not touch the principal.

Principle: Basic truth, belief.
His actions were based on sound ethical principles.

Stationary/Stationery

Stationary: Not moving, fixed.
He bought a stationary bike.

Stationery: Writing paper.
The company ordered new stationery.

BUSINESS JARGON

Almost every profession has words, terms, and phrases that are peculiar to it. Business people talk about computers, the economy, production, management techniques, and marketing. The technical language which a business person uses is not necessarily easy to understand for an outsider.

Jargon
Jargon is the technical language of a field.

Every field has its **jargon**. Jargon is acceptable as long as both the sender and the receiver of the communication understand it. If the receiver does not understand it, then the sender will miscommunicate using jargon.

Computer experts are known for the use of such jargon as *access a program* and *input material*. Many other people have begun to use *access* and *input* as verbs because they want to appear up-to-date. Computer jargon is fairly new but spreading rapidly.

A different kind of jargon consists of old-fashioned business clichés. Many business people still use them in letters and reports. Some people believe that these clichés are more courteous and polite than the direct style, which they interpret as being pushy. Some people copy the clichés from old reports when writing their own reports, without thinking of what they actually mean. The clichés that follow lack conciseness and directness; the revisions are much more to the point and, therefore, clearer.

Poor: *It has been brought to my attention...*
Better: *I have noticed...*

Poor: *Per your request...*
Better: *As you requested...*

Poor: *Enclosed herewith please find the following material.*
Better: *The enclosed material further demonstrates the benefits of the program.*

Poor: *Kindly be advised that the bill is due by the end of the month.*
Better: *The bill is due at the end of the month.*

Poor: *I thank you in advance for your efforts.*
Better: *I appreciate your efforts.*

Poor: *Attached herewith is the pamphlet you requested.*
Better: *The attached pamphlet answers your questions.*

USE OF NUMBERS

Business people use many numbers, and you, as a business writer, will have to know how to communicate numbers clearly. The following rules for writing numbers are general guidelines. In your reports you may have to modify them to meet special needs.

1. Spell out numbers from one to ten.
   If a sentence has several numbers, spell them out if the majority of numbers is under ten and use numerals if the majority is above ten.

   Mr. Fernandez has been with the company for 15 years. Ms. Alvarez sold three cars in one day.

2. When a sentence has two sets of numbers, spell out the set with the smaller numbers.

   Ten students had scores of 93; five students had scores of 85.

3. Write out numbers in legal documents. The figure can follow or precede the word.

   The finished product will be delivered at a price of $5,000 (five thousand dollars).

   The finished product will be delivered at a price of five thousand dollars ($5,000).

4. Spell out numbers at the beginning of a sentence. If possible, you should avoid numbers at the beginning of sentences.

   Five hundred employees took advantage of the investment plan.

USE OF VERBS

Verbs denote action; they describe what the subject of the sentence does. Each of the following sentences has a slightly different meaning.

He went to the office.

He strolled to the office.

He ran to the office.

He walked to the office.

He jogged to the office.

He rushed to the office.

The careful choice of verbs adds precision to the sentence. Verbs create a certain mood. Unfortunately, in everyday language we have a tendency to overuse weak or nondescriptive verbs such as forms of *to get, to have,* and *to be.* Look at the verbs in the following paragraph:

Because the material did not get in until yesterday afternoon, we couldn't get started on the project till this morning. This delay will be a problem in getting the work finished on time.

Changing the verbs makes the writing more lively.

Because the material did not arrive until yesterday afternoon, we could not start the project earlier. This delay will postpone the completion of the work.

ACTIVE VERSUS PASSIVE VOICE

Active Voice
The verb carries the action.

Passive Voice
The verb is deemphasized.

In the **active voice** the action is in the verb, whereas in the **passive voice** the action is in a form of *to be* and a past participle. As a result, the action is weaker as the following example illustrates:

Passive: The business use of personal computers shall be approved by the regional executive officers and corporate department heads. All hardware will be purchased by the Computer Products Administration Unit of General Administrative Services. A list of tested and approved items will be made available from that source, and all requisitions should be channeled through them. Centralized purchasing is important so that volume discounts can be taken and new programs and developments in the computer field can be disseminated.

Active: Regional executive officers and corporate department heads shall approve the business use of personal computers. The Computer Products Administration Unit of General Administrative Services will purchase all hardware and software. That unit will send a list of tested and approved items to all offices. Centralized purchasing will ensure us of volume discounts; it will also help in the dissemination of new programs and developments in the computer field.

The first example uses mainly passive voice, the second one active voice. The active voice has several advantages over the passive voice:

1. The active voice is more concise. In the example the active paragraph has 68 words; the passive paragraph has 78 words.

2. In the active sentence the subject is the actor, performing the action that the verb designates. In the passive sentence the subject is acted upon. In the active example the officers approve the use of computers. In the passive example the use is approved by the officers.

3. Active writing is more direct, more interesting, and easier to read.

The following examples further illustrate the differences between the active and passive voices:

Passive: *After the report was finished by the secretary, it was sent to the customer.*

Active: *After the secretary had finished the report, she mailed it to the customer.*

Passive: *The office was informed by the insurance company of the change in policy.*

Active: *The insurance company informed the office of the change in policy.*

Passive: *A copy of the results will be sent to all offices by Mr. James.*

Active: *Mr. James will send a copy of the results to all offices.*

Even though the active voice is preferable, in some cases the passive voice is more appropriate. If you do not want to emphasize the actor or if you want to keep the sentence vague on purpose, you may prefer the passive voice.

Let us assume that one of your customers bought a waffle iron. The instructions clearly said not to put the iron into water. The waffle iron fails to heat, and the unhappy customer demands a replacement. As you examine the iron, you find that it was submerged in water. If you say, "You put the iron into water even though the instructions clearly said not to. . ." you will probably alienate the customer. You might prefer to say, "A careful examination of the iron shows that it was put in water. . . ." This sentence does not directly accuse the customer of doing something wrong; the damage simply "occurred."

In some cases you may not want the emphasis on the actor. For example, the sentence, "Mr. Smith wrote this report," puts the emphasis on Mr. Smith. You may want to emphasize that *this* report was written by Mr. Smith, whereas *that* report was written by Mr. James. In such a case the passive voice may be more appropriate.

In your writing you must weigh whether the active or the passive voice is more effective. The goal is not to eliminate the passive voice completely but to use the most appropriate form and to avoid slipping routinely or accidentally into the passive voice.

The computer, with the help of style-evaluation software, can help determine the number of passive phrases used in a report. The software will not change the sentence from passive to active for you; it simply flags the passive constructions. As the cursor stops at each passive construction, you can decide which voice to use.

CAMOUFLAGED VERBS

Because verbs indicate action more effectively than any other sentence element can, they should carry the action. If the action is hidden in another word, usually a noun, the verb then used in the sentence tends to be a weak one.

Hidden Verb: *It was Cathy's decision to sign up for the new training course.*

Cathy's action is hidden in the noun *decision.* The verb *was,* a form of *to be,* is much weaker than the verb *to decide.* The sentence can easily be rewritten as follows:

Action Verb: *Cathy decided to sign up for the training course.*

In the rewritten version the actor and the verb are close together. The sentence is more concise, clear, and lively.

Camouflaged Verbs
The active verb is changed into a noun.

When action is hidden in a noun, the verb is **camouflaged**. Bureaucratic styles tend to emphasize nouns because nouns are perceived to carry more authority than verbs. A text with many camouflaged verbs may seem more impressive but is less action oriented and less interesting. Camouflaged verbs may have their place if you want to deemphasize an idea or the action, but you should use them sparingly. The following examples further illustrate how camouflaged verbs weaken the action:

Camouflaged Verb: *It is my understanding that the meeting was cancelled.*

Action Verb: *I understand the meeting was cancelled.*

Camouflaged Verb: *Mr. Hurtado can be of great help to the organization.*

Action Verb: *Mr. Hurtado may help the organization greatly.*

Camouflaged Verb: *Completion of the project should be accomplished by May 1.*

Action Verb: *You should complete the project by May 1.*

Camouflaged Verb: *The department is undergoing a reorganization.*

Action Verb: *The department is reorganizing.*

The action-oriented sentences are more direct and thus easier to read and understand.

SENTENCE CONSTRUCTION

SENTENCE LENGTH

Short sentences are easier to read than long ones. As a general rule, the average sentence in a business report should be about 16 to 20 words long. Some sentences will be much shorter and some much longer than this average. Of course, the sentence difficulty is measured not only by length but also by the complexity of the sentence structure. A sentence with many relative clauses and appositives is more difficult to understand than a simple sentence or series of simple sentences.

This sentence with complex relationship between parts:

> Kathy Wood, a personnel manager, who had been with Smith Robertson, an accounting firm, for three years, was very concerned about her future with the company—that was not surprising because the office had been full of takeover rumors for weeks—and she decided to look for another job.

can be rewritten as more than one sentence to clarify the relationships:

> Kathy Wood, a personnel manager, had been with the accounting firm Smith Robertson for three years. She was very concerned about her future with the company because of strong takeover rumors. Finally she decided to look for another job.

On the other hand, a series of short sentences can be more difficult to understand than long ones if the short sentences are not clearly related. When subordination or coordination is needed to show relationships between ideas, the resulting sentences may be longer, but the message may be clearer. A series of short sentences, such as these:

> The personal robot came on the market in 1982. Optimists predicted tremendous sales. Consumers soon realized the limitations of the robot. Sales fell short of predictions. Consultants still think there is much potential. Right now manufacturers are cautious.

can be rewritten to show the connection between the ideas and thus improve clarity:

> When the personal robot came on the market in 1982, optimists predicted tremendous sales. Consumers, however, soon realized the limitations of the robots, and as a result sales fell short of predictions. Today manufacturers are cautious even though consultants still think there is much potential.

In the second example the writer used *however, when, as a result,* and *even though* to relate the ideas in the paragraph to each other. As a result, ideas are not isolated and are easier to comprehend.

PARALLELISM

When a sentence contains a list of items or a series, the items or the series must be grammatically and logically parallel. If one part in a series is an adjective, the other parts must be adjectives. If one is a noun phrase, the others must be noun phrases. Contrasting ideas must also be expressed in parallel phrasing.

The following examples illustrate parallel structure:

Wrong: *He is either a capable programmer or someone whose program designs are lucky.*

The parts following either and or must be parallel.

Correct: *He is either a capable or a lucky programmer.*

Wrong: *Not only has he been promoted, but also a cash award was given to him.*

Correct: *Not only has he been promoted, but he was also given a cash award.*

Wrong: *He decided that dictating a letter was better than to call the customer.*

Correct: *He decided that to dictate a letter was better than to call the customer.*
or
He decided that dictating a letter was better than calling the customer.

Wrong: *Executives living abroad need bodyguards, security devices for their homes, and to follow carefully common-sense rules for living abroad.*

Correct: *Executives living abroad need bodyguards, security devices for their homes, and sensible rules for everyday life in a strange environment.*

Wrong: *The company's new office building was modern, functional, and incorporated the latest technology on energy use.*

Correct: *The company's new office building was modern, functional, and energy efficient.*

SUBJECT-VERB AGREEMENT

If the subject is singular, the verb must be singular; if the subject is plural, the verb must also be plural.

Mary writes the weekly sales report.
Mary and John write the weekly sales report.

A series of problems *is* slowing the production line.
Each manager needs training on the new computer.

In most cases it is easy to determine whether or not the subject is singular or plural, but some words can be used as either:

The faculty have worked hard.

or

The faculty has worked hard.

In the first sentence the writer thinks of the faculty as a collection of individuals; in the second sentence the writer considers the faculty as a single unit. Other nouns that can be used as both plural and singular include

Board	Faculty
Army	Group
Committee	Team
Class	

Once you have decided to use one of these nouns as either singular or plural, you have to be consistent within the sentence. It is incorrect to say

The committee publishes their report.

You may say:

The committee publishes its report.

or

The committee publish their report.

To avoid awkward expressions, writers sometimes add *members* to collective nouns so as to use them as plurals. For example, the writer may say

The committee has ranked job applicants.

or

The committee members have ranked job applicants.
The Board meets every month.

or

The Board members meet every month.
The team gets along well.

or

The team members get along well.

Many writers have difficulty maintaining correct subject-verb agreement when the subject is separated from the verb by intervening modifiers.

Wrong:	*The problem with having too many workers are that our sales cannot cover their pay.*
Correct:	*The problem with having too many workers is that our sales cannot cover their pay.*
Wrong:	*There is far too many details to cover in one meeting.*
Correct:	*There are far too many details to cover in one meeting.*

PRONOUN-ANTECEDENT AGREEMENT

A personal pronoun must refer to a specific noun or pronoun. If the reference is not clear, a sentence becomes more difficult to understand. The reference to a particular person, as in the following sentences, usually presents no problem:

> Mary finished her report.
> John finished his work early.
> John and Mary finished their report.

Pronouns are more difficult to keep in agreement when the nouns to which they refer are not specific persons:

Wrong:	*Each* of the workers cleaned *their* work area.
Correct:	*Each* of the workers cleaned *his* or *her* work area. or *All workers* cleaned *their* work areas.
Wrong:	*Everyone* has to do *their* duty.
Correct:	*Everyone* has to do *her* or *his* duty. or *All employees* have to do *their* duty.

In order to avoid sexist language and the awkward *his or her,* some writers use the pronoun *their* with a singular noun. Often, the problem is overcome by substituting the plural noun, as in the preceding examples. Although *they* is sometimes used as a singular in spoken English, its use is not acceptable in written English.

DANGLING MODIFIERS

A dangling modifier does not logically modify a word or words and is therefore unclear. In the following example, *walking through the factory* seems to modify *changes.* This connection does not make sense. In the corrected version a logical subject has been added to the sentence:

Wrong: *Walking through the factory, all the*
changes were clearly visible.

Correct: *Walking through the factory, the*
manager could observe all the changes.

Literally, the following sentence means that the wind read the report:

Wrong: *While reading the weekly sales report, the wind*
slammed the door shut.

The sentence can be corrected in this way:

Correct: *As John was reading the report, the wind slammed*
the door shut.

In these examples the reader may understand what the writer means even though the dangling modifier is confusing. In some cases the reader may have to reread the sentence in order to grasp the intended meaning.

SHIFT IN CONSTRUCTION

The writer must be consistent in the use of person, number, pronoun, voice, and tense. Shifts in construction are confusing because they change perspective in the middle of the sentence. To avoid a shift in construction, the writer should use pronouns that clearly refer to a logical antecedent.

Wrong:	*He discussed one's report.*
Correct:	*He discussed his (her, their, our) report.*
Wrong:	*One should proofread his report carefully.*
Correct:	*He should proofread his report carefully.*
Correct but Awkward:	*One should proofread one's report carefully.*
Better:	*Writers should proofread their reports carefully.*

USE OF PUNCTUATION

Punctuation aids clarity. Proper punctuation tells the reader which parts of a sentence are related and how they are related. Because it is beyond the scope of this text to discuss and illustrate all of the rules for punctuation, only the most important ones follow.

APOSTROPHE

Use the apostrophe to indicate possession.

The manager's office
The student's report

The company's retirement plan
The companies' retirement plans
A year's experience
Two years' experience
The employees' lunch breaks
The employee's lunch break

Use an apostrophe in contractions.

It's	It is
There's	There is
Don't	Do not
Mustn't	Must not
Couldn't	Could not
Shouldn't	Should not
You're	You are

In formal writing you should avoid contractions.

COMMAS

Coordinating Conjunctions. Use a comma to separate two independent sentences connected by a coordinating conjunction. *And, but, or, nor, for* are coordinating conjunctions.

> He finished his report, and then he went to the meeting.

> Susan wanted to move to Chicago, but she could not find a job there.

Introductory Subordinate Clauses. Use a comma to set off an introductory subordinate clause at the beginning of a sentence from the independent clause that follows. *If, when, before, because, since, although,* or *unless* often introduces the subordinate clause.

> If he can borrow the money, he will start his own business.
> Although he was very tired, he had to stay to finish the job.

Appositive. Set an appositive off with commas. An appositive is a noun or noun phrase that describes another noun.

> Mr. Baker, the president of Compact Disk Company, will be the speaker at the conference.

> Arthur Andersen, one of the Big Eight accounting firms, is looking for a manager for the London office.

Nonrestrictive and Restrictive Modifiers. Set nonrestrictive modifiers off with commas. A nonrestrictive modifier can be omitted without changing the meaning of the sentence. Restrictive modifiers are not set off by commas.

Nonrestrictive

John Smith, who was the best production worker, received a special bonus. (If the modifier is left out, the meaning of the sentence remains the same.)

Restrictive

The worker who has the best production record will get a special bonus. (If the modifier is left out, the meaning of the sentence changes.)

Introductory Phrases. Use a comma after introductory phrases.

To get the material for class, go to the reserve room in the library.

To analyze the data, review the necessary statistical techniques.

Excited over her success in sales, she began to think about her career options.

Thinking that everyone knew about the company takeover offer, he openly talked about it in the office.

Items in a Series. Use a comma to set off items in a series. Business writers prefer to use a serial comma preceding the word *and*.

During the afternoon she called clients, discussed the next meeting with her boss, ordered the new equipment, and finished the evaluation of her employees.

Sam Irwin demanded a higher salary, better hours, and a larger office.

Adjectives of Equal Rank. Use a comma to separate adjectives of equal rank.

She was an efficient, conscientious worker.

The beautiful, modern office arrangement was chosen to improve productivity.

Parenthetical Phrases. Use commas to set off parenthetical words or phrases such as *however, therefore, in fact, of course, for example, consequently, nevertheless, moreover, on the other hand*. They interrupt the normal sentence pattern by providing supplementary information.

The company will, however, start a new training program next month.

We will, therefore, add Roberson to the list of suppliers.

For example, most of the employees participate in the company's wellness program.

SEMICOLON

Independent Clauses. Use a semicolon to separate two independent clauses that are not connected by a coordinating conjunction. To join two independent clauses by comma is called a *comma splice*; it is a serious punctuation error.

> Prairie State University has a distinct mission; it wants to attract the nontraditional student.

Independent Clauses Joined by a Parenthetical Word. When a parenthetical word or phrase joins two independent sentences, it is preceded by a semicolon and followed by a comma.

> Our regular supplier has had difficulty meeting our growing needs; therefore, we will add Roberson to our list of suppliers.

> Porter Plumbing submitted the lowest construction bid; however, management decided to postpone the project.

Items in a Complex Series. Use a semicolon to separate items in a series with internal punctuation.

> For his report he interviewed Dr. Hallam, his accounting professor; Dr. Locker, his report writing professor; and Ms. Reed, the personnel director for a local company.

COLON

Use a colon to introduce a series.

> The professor considered four criteria in the evaluation of the report: correct use of the English language, reader adaptation, content, and organization.

Use a colon or a comma to introduce a direct quotation.

> At the end of the interview the recruiter said: "Mr. Jones, I am impressed with your resume. I will talk things over with personnel, and you will hear from me within a week."

QUOTATION MARKS

Use quotation marks to enclose direct quotations.

> The recruiter said, "Our company is dedicated to the welfare of the employees."

Use quotation marks to enclose the title of an article or a chapter in a book.

> He found the article by Keith Davis, "The Care and Cultivation of the Corporate Grapevine," helpful in planning his communication strategy.

Always place commas and periods inside quotation marks, colons and semicolons outside. Place question marks and exclamation marks inside quotation marks if they punctuate the quoted material, outside if they punctuate the entire sentence.

CONCISENESS

A writer who writes a report with the reader in mind, a writer who wants to assure that his report will be read, will strive for conciseness. Conciseness does not necessarily mean brevity. In a concise report every word counts in conveying the intended meaning. Sentences and paragraphs move forward, and the ideas are logically organized.

Concise writing requires practice and careful proofreading. The writer weighs every word carefully.

When proofreading for conciseness, you should follow these guidelines:

1. Look for words that restate what is already clearly written and eliminate them.

Weak: *The new uniforms are red in color.*

Better: *The new uniforms are red. (The word* red *implies color.)*

2. Find ways to eliminate "there is/are."

Weak: *There are 30 people interested in attending the conference on speed writing.*

Better: *Thirty people want to attend the conference on speed writing.*

3. Avoid camouflaged verbs.

Weak: *He came to the conclusion that the training program was too expensive.*

Better: *He concluded that the training program was too expensive.*

4. Omit *who, whom,* and *that* when possible.

Weak: *The customer was told that the goods had been ordered.*

Better: *The customer was told the goods had been ordered.*

Weak: *The factory workers whom the company had laid off in March were called back to work.*

Better: *The factory workers the company had laid off in March were called back to work.*

Weak: *Tom's broker, who is an expert in the computer field, makes a lot of money.*

Better: *Tom's broker, an expert in the computer field, makes a lot of money.*

Weak: *The cars that were sold in February had to be recalled.*

Better: *The cars sold in February had to be recalled.*

5. Replace wordy expressions with less wordy ones.

Wordy	Concise
In the month of June	In June
In the county of McLean	In McLean County
In the near future	Soon, next month
In the distant past	Three hundred years ago
For the reason that	Because
In view of the fact	Since, because
For the purpose of	For
At this point in time	Now
Due to the fact that	Because
In spite of the fact that	Although

ORGANIZATION AND LOGICAL DEVELOPMENT

Logical and Organized Presentation
Logical and organized presentation is systematic and orderly.

A report organized so that the development of ideas and arguments is clear and logical is easier for the reader to follow than a report that jumps from one idea to another. A **logical and organized presentation** can help to make even difficult material seem easier. On the other hand, fairly simple material can become confusing if points are not presented in logical progression. Let us compare the following two examples:

Organized Presentation

The good report writer plans his report before he begins writing. He asks a number of questions to bring the report into focus.

1. What is the purpose of the report?
2. What is the problem to be solved?

3. Who is the reader?

4. How much does the reader know?

5. How much does the reader *need* to know?

6. How will the reader use the report?

The answer to these questions will help the writer to choose the format, tone, level of formality, and depth of background information. The extent of planning will depend on the length of the report and the complexity of the problem. For long reports the writer will probably make a written plan; for reports of medium length he may simply jot down a few ideas; and for a short memo he may plan in his head. In any case, he will plan.

Unorganized Presentation

The extent of planning depends on the length of the report and the complexity of the problem, but the good report writer plans before he writes. For short reports less planning is necessary. He has to ask who the reader is and what the reader knows already about the problem. The answer to the question will help the writer to determine format, formality, tone, and depth of background information necessary. Medium-long reports and long reports require more detailed planning. Other questions the writer has to ask before he can start writing are: Who is the reader? How will the report be used? What is the problem to be solved? and What is the purpose of the report?

In the first example the arrangement of ideas makes sense, and the presentation flows naturally. The format also aids in making this sequence of ideas clear.

Importance of Planning

Elements of Planning—A Set of Questions

Results of the Questioning Process—Determination of Type of Report to be Written

Types of Planning—Types of Reports

In the second example the logical progression is interrupted as the writer jumps from one idea to another. An outline of the paragraph illustrates the lack of unity:

Types of Planning—Types of Report

Importance of Planning

Short Reports

Elements of Planning—A Set of Questions

Results of the Questioning

Medium Reports

Long Reports

More Questions for Planning

Even short reports benefit from a plan for presenting the information logically. Chapter 6 discusses planning in detail.

VISUAL IMPRESSION

Page layout has nothing to do with the content of the message; nevertheless, the design of the page influences the perception of difficulty. For example, a single-spaced page with no margins and no headings is perceived as being more difficult than a page with wide margins, ample white space, headings to break up the text, clearly identifiable paragraphs, and illustrations where appropriate. The content may be exactly the same as in Exhibit 3.1, but the perception of difficulty is not.

Perception of Difficulty
Appearance influences the perception of difficulty.

The page layout shown on the left side of Exhibit 3.1 is appealing and inviting. It does not threaten the reader. Paragraphing and headings allow the reader to rest while reading. The example on the right side, however, is without rest spots and looks unmanageable and frightening.

Clearly, the report writer must pay attention to the design and appearance of the page. Visual impression is an important element in effective reader adaptation.

SUMMARY OF LEARNING OBJECTIVES

To Write with Clarity and Precision.
Good writing is precise. The writer adapts his language to the level of the reader and chooses words that the reader understands. To ensure that the text is clear, the writer checks to see that words are used correctly.

To Understand the Use of Business Jargon.
The overuse of jargon distracts from the content of the message. The business writer should avoid jargon and buzzwords.

To Use Action Verbs to Make Writing Interesting and Lively.
Action verbs make reports more interesting and concise. The report writer puts action into the verb and does not camouflage it in a noun. While the passive voice is preferable in some cases, active voice is generally better writing.

To Master Correct Sentence Structure.
Shorter sentences are generally easier to read than longer sentences, but the level of difficulty is influenced by the complexity of the sentence and the

Exhibit 3.1 **Effective and Weak Page Layouts**

SUMMARY OF LEARNING OBJECTIVES

To Understand the Role of Reports in Modern Business Organizations. *How does the size of the company relate to the number of business reports written?*

Reports help in planning and decision making. They also provide records of transactions and agreements. The number of reports increases as the business expands or diversifies. As layers of organization are added in a company, the personal contact between upper and lower management decreases. Reports are needed for communication between the various levels in an organization.

How does career advancement affect report writing?

The types of reports will change as the writer advances in the company. At the beginning, reports will provide mostly information for upper managers; later, as a middle manager the writer will synthesize information and analyze it; finally, as an executive the writer will become mostly a user of reports.

Who requests reports? Who writes reports?

Report requests tend to travel down in the organization, while most reports travel up. All business persons write reports.

To Examine and Define the Basic Characteristics of Business Reports.

A business report should be clear, precise, concise, well organized, factual, objective, attractive in appearance, and business oriented

To Become Aware of the Differences between Business Reports and Term Papers.

In a term paper the writer's goal is to show the reader that he has mastered the material of the course. In the business report the emphasis is on the content and usefulness of the report rather than on the achievements of the writer.

To Recognize the Importance of Good Report Writing Skills in Career Development.

Business reports benefit the business for which they are written. Recommendations made by the writer can influence the advancement of fellow employees. Good business reports work "silently" for the writer, bringing direct personal benefits.

QUESTIONS AND PROBLEMS

1. Discuss how the growth of business has influenced business reports.
2. Discuss some of the possible reasons why improvements in technology have led to an increase rather than a decrease in the number of reports businesses produce.
3. What types of reports can you expect to write at various levels in your career?

SUMMARY OF LEARNING OBJECTIVES

To Understand the Role of Reports in Modern Business Organizations. How does the size of the company relate to the number of business reports written? Reports help in planning and decision making. They also provide records of transactions and agreements. The number of reports increases as the business expands or diversifies. As layers of organization are added in a company, the personal contact between upper and lower management decreases. Reports are needed for communication between the various levels in an organization. How does career advancement affect report writing? The types of reports will change as the writer advances in the company. At the beginning, reports will provide mostly information for upper managers; later, as a middle manager the writer will synthesize information and analyze it; finally, as an executive the writer will become mostly a user of reports. Who requests reports? Who writes reports? Report requests tend to travel down in the organization, while most reports travel up. All business persons write reports. To Examine and Define the Basic Characteristics of Business Reports. A business report should be clear, precise, concise, well organized, factual, objective, attractive in appearance, and business oriented. To Become Aware of the Differences between Business Reports and Term Papers. In a term paper the writer's goal is to show the reader that he has mastered the material of the course. In the business report the emphasis is on the content and usefulness of the report rather than on the achievements of the writer. To Recognize the Importance of Good Report Writing Skills in Career Development. Business reports benefit the business for which they are written. Recommendations made by the writer can influence the advancement of fellow employees. Good business reports work "silently" for the writer, bringing direct personal benefits.

QUESTIONS AND PROBLEMS

1. Discuss how the growth of business has influenced business reports. 2. Discuss some of the possible reasons why improvements in technology have led to an increase rather than a decrease in the number of reports businesses produce. 3. What types of reports can you expect to write at various levels in your career?

relationship of ideas. A longer sentence which coordinates or subordinates ideas may be easier to read than a series of unrelated short sentences. Items in a series must be grammatically and logically parallel.

To Review Punctuation.
The effective writer knows the rules for punctuation and correct grammatical usage and takes care to follow them.

To Write Concisely.
Good writing is concise. The concise writer does not waste the reader's time.

To Organize Material Logically.
The organization and the logical development of the material are major determinants in the level of difficulty. Page layout, headings, and illustrations also influence the perception of difficulty.

QUESTIONS AND PROBLEMS

1. What are elements of effective writing?
2. Discuss the importance of clarity and preciseness.
3. Discuss the use of simple and difficult words.
4. What makes a sentence simple or difficult?
5. Why should you use active rather than passive voice?
6. What is a camouflaged verb?
7. Discuss the rules for parallel structure in writing.
8. How do organization, page layout, and typeface help in making a text more readable?
9. How do you present numbers in reports?
10. Correct the following sentences:

    The economy effects the performance of the firm.

    Like he said, the meeting did not last very long.

    The building site was easily accessible.

    He decided to call the manager rather than writing to him.

    The company looked for someone who was experienced, had knowledge of computers, and an MBA.

    —He passed the managers office.

    —The instructor evaluated the students' report.

    —He rewarded his employee's very well.

    —The job was difficult but he did complete it on time.

    —Mrs. Semar the company's training director carefully read the participants evaluations.

    —If he can get the job he will move to New York.

To get the test results he went to the lab manager.

He had told the manager "that he wanted to go to school."

The supervisor said, "I have very good workers in my group."

The company celebrates their 25th anniversary this month.

A series of problems are contributing to the loss of sales.

Everyone knows their duty.

Reading the report, the fire alarm went off.

He should evaluate one's report carefully.

11. Identify whether the following sentences use active or passive voice. Change the passive voice to active voice.

The decision was made by a special committee.

The assembly line was slowed down by the supervisor for adjustment to the new product line.

A The office manager ordered new office equipment to accommodate the growing needs of the company.

P After much discussion it was decided that the training program should be adopted by the company.

12. Change the camouflaged verbs to action verbs.

Suggested .

The boss made the suggestion that the employees get back to work.

The department's recommendation is to buy three microcomputers with the necessary software packages.

The supervisor gave her permission for the line to be shut down.

CHAPTER FOUR

THE CLASSIFICATION OF BUSINESS REPORTS

LEARNING OBJECTIVES

- To understand the role of report classification systems.
- To use the classification systems as a tool in report writing.
- To examine the most commonly used formats for short reports.

THE PURPOSE OF CLASSIFICATION

Classifies
In classifying the writer describes the characteristics of the report.

A business person preparing a report must determine whether it should be informational or analytical, long or short, formal or informal. The writer has to decide whether the report is a special or a periodic report and whether the report is best transmitted in a memo or a letter. In deciding what kind of report to write, the writer **classifies** it but keeps in mind that any classification system is a tool and not an end in itself.

Even though specific report classifications may vary from company to company, the basic classification systems are the same. For example, a manager who wants information on sales for the past month may simply ask for an informational report on sales. The writer who understands classification systems will know what an informational report is. A logical classification system saves time and improves communication. Classification systems also aid in filing and, therefore, in retrieving reports.

CLASSIFICATION BY FUNCTION

Based on function, we can distinguish two major types of reports—informational reports and analytical reports. The classification by function is illustrated in Exhibit 4.1.

INFORMATIONAL REPORTS

Informational Reports
Informational reports present facts.

As we discussed in Chapter One, during the beginning of your career you may write many **informational reports**, which present facts without interpretation. You will research the facts, organize them, and present them as shown in Exhibit 4.2. If the report is detailed, you should include a summary.

Exhibit 4.1   **Classification by Function**

Informational Report
Introduction
Presentation of Facts
Summary

Analytical Report
Examination Report
Introduction
Presentation of Facts
Examination of Facts
Summary
Recommendation Report

	or	
Introduction		Introduction
Presentation of Facts		Conclusions
Examination of Facts		Recommendations
Summary*		Presentation of Facts
Conclusions		Examination of Facts
Recommendations		

*Some report writers omit the summary in the recommendation report. They believe the summary material is included in the conclusions and recommendations.

ANALYTICAL REPORTS

Analytical Reports
Analytical reports analyze facts.

The **analytical report** may be either an examination report or a recommendation report. The examination report examines or analyzes the data presented. Exhibit 4.3 is an examination report that analyzes the data on the use of the microcomputer lab.

The recommendation report is the most complete report. As illustrated in Exhibits 4.4 and 4.5, it expands on the informational and examination reports. It presents the data, examines it, draws conclusions, and makes recommendations. The information presented in Exhibits 4.4 and 4.5 is the same; the difference lies in the arrangement of the material. Many managers prefer to have the conclusions and recommendations early in the report, as is illustrated in Exhibit 4.5. Exhibit 4.4 uses an inductive order of presentation, whereas Exhibit 4.5 uses a deductive order.

Inductive
Inductive reports present conclusions and recommendations after the analysis of facts.

Inductive Presentation. The **inductive** presentation closely matches the sequence in which you do your work. You lead the reader through the same steps in the same sequence in which you went through them. You present the facts, analyze the facts, draw conclusions, and make recommendations.

Let us assume you are the supervisor of an assembly line. The workers in your department assemble handbrakes for cars. For the brakes to function properly, all the steps in the assembly must be done correctly. Lately an increasing number of brakes have not met the standards. The brakes must be taken apart and reassembled, a time-consuming and costly procedure. Your boss wants a report on how to solve the problem. You investigate and

Exhibit 4.2   **Informational Report**

```
TO:       Cheryl Black
FROM:     Todd Lozano  JL
SUBJECT:  Use of Computer Lab
DATE:     October 15, 19XX
```

The computer lab has been open for two months. Here is a summary of observations
concerning the use of the lab during the second month. The first month is not
included because all of the equipment had not arrived.

Equipment

The lab has 24 IBM Personal Computers and 6 printers. Software available at this
point includes word processing, spreadsheets, and data-base management. Manuals
on how to use the software are available.

Policy for Using the Lab

Students who are enrolled in a class that uses microcomputers have priority in
using the lab. Instructors and graduate assistants may work in the lab if computers are available.

Seven classes with an enrollment of 30 students each have incorporated the microcomputer into the curriculum; therefore, the lab must serve 210 students.

During lab hours, students may work in the lab as long as they wish. Some
students stay for four or five hours.

Lab Supervision

Shelly White organized the lab and set the schedules. She trained the ten
students who are employed in the lab, and she coordinates their work schedules.
She meets with the students once a week to discuss problems in procedure and
policy.

Procedure

Students submit their IDs when they check out equipment. They are assigned a
computer by the student worker. IDs are returned when students turn in the
software.

A number of students ask the student worker for help, but in many cases the
student worker does not have an answer. The student then often asks other
students in the lab for help. This raises the noise level and interrupts the work
of the other students.

Patterns for Lab Use

The lab is open from 8:00 a.m. until 9:00 p.m. Based on observations during the
last month, the following pattern for use of the lab emerged.

Time	Number of Students
8- 9 a.m.	3
9-10	15
10-11	18
11-12	5
12- 1 p.m.	15
```
```

Exhibit 4.2   **Informational Report** (*continued*)

| | Number |
Time	of Students
1- 2 p.m.	20
2- 3	30
3- 4	35
4- 5	25
5- 6	20
6- 7	37
7- 8	48
8- 9	45

The number of students includes those in the lab and those trying to use it. Some students wait almost an hour before they can get in. Some come back several times before they find a place.

Exhibit 4.3   **Examination Report**

TO: Cheryl Black
FROM: Todd Lozano ꓘ
SUBJECT: Use of Computer Lab
DATE: October 15, 19XX

The computer lab has been open for two months. Here is a summary of observations concerning the use of the lab during the second month. The first month is not included because all of the equipment had not arrived.

Equipment

Policy for Using the Lab

Lab Supervision

Procedure

Patterns for Lab Use

Discussion

The use during morning hours is very light. In contrast, use after 2:00 p.m. is above capacity of the lab, with the exception of the dinner hour in the dorms. Many students have classes in the morning and in the early afternoon. This could account for the low user level during those times. One has to ask whether it makes sense to close the lab at 9:00 p.m. That is the time when many undergraduates begin to study.

Students are concerned about the policy for lab usage. It is difficult to justify the policy that a student may stay in the lab for as long as he wishes while others wait for hours to get in.

Students are frustrated about the level of computer knowledge of the student workers. They complain that it is difficult to get help and that there is general confusion in the lab.

Exhibit 4.4   **Recommendation Report (Inductive)**

TO: Cheryl Black
FROM: Todd Lozano ᒍᐯ
SUBJECT: Use of Computer Lab
DATE: October 15, 19XX

The computer lab has been open for two months. Here is a summary of observations
concerning the use of the lab during the second month. The first month is not
included because all of the equipment had not arrived.

Equipment

Policy for Using the Lab

Lab Supervision

Procedure

Patterns for Lab Use

Discussion

Conclusions

Based on the observations, one can draw the following conclusions:

        Current lab hours are not efficiently used by students.
        Current lab hours are not well coordinated with students' study habits.
        The policy concerning length of usage causes problems.
        The computer background of the student workers needs to be expanded.

Recommendations

The implementation of the following recommendations should help to solve some of
the problems:

1. Sign-up sheets should be prepared for lab use. The maximum time for anybody
   using the lab should be two hours unless there are empty computers.

2. Lab hours should be publicized and students should be encouraged to use the
   lab in the morning.

3. The lab should be kept open until 10:00 p.m. on a trial basis.

4. The weekly meetings between supervisor and student workers should include
   additional training of the students on the equipment so they will be able to
   answer more questions.

Exhibit 4.5   **Recommendation Report (Deductive)**

TO: Cheryl Black
FROM: Todd Lozano *JL*
SUBJECT: Use of Computer Lab
DATE: October 15, 19XX

The computer lab has been open for two months. Here is a summary of observations concerning the use of the lab during the second month. The first month is not included because all of the equipment had not arrived.

Conclusions

Recommendations

Equipment

Policy for Using the Lab

Lab Supervision

Procedure

Patterns for Lab Use

Discussion

present your findings in an inductive report. The elements of your report might include the following:

Problem: *An increasing number of brakes fail to meet production standards.*

Facts: *Carl Retton is absent very often. John Crotts, who is taking over for him, is not familiar with the process. In addition, several workers do not get along. They argue and disrupt the workflow.*

Conclusion: *The problem is caused by personnel difficulties and violations of company policies.*

Recommendation: *The workers should be reprimanded. If there is no improvement, they should be fired.*

The advantage of the inductive approach is that the reader becomes familiar with all the facts before being confronted with the conclusions and recommendations. The inductive approach is persuasive and guides the reader. On the other hand, it is time consuming for the readers who may be interested only or mostly in the conclusions but are forced to read all of the details.

If the writer knows that the reader is likely to agree with the facts, the inductive presentation may not be effective. Such a reader may become impatient and not finish the report. If the reader has to be persuaded, then the inductive approach can help in accomplishing the task.

Deductive

Deductive reports present conclusions and recommendations before the analysis of facts.

Deductive Presentation. The **deductive** report presents the problem, the conclusions and recommendations, and finally the supporting facts and analysis. A deductive report on the assembly-line problem would be organized as follows:

Problem: *An increasing number of brakes fail to meet production standards.*

Conclusion: *The problem is caused by personnel difficulties and violations of company policies.*

Recommendation: *The workers should be reprimanded. If there is no improvement, they should be fired.*

Facts: *Carl Retton is absent very often. John Crotts, who is taking his place, is not familiar with the process. A number of workers do not get along. They argue and disrupt the workflow.*

Many businesses like this approach because of its directness. Its disadvantage is that readers who do not like the recommendations may simply quit reading the report before they reach the supporting data.

The following points should help you in choosing between the deductive and inductive presentations:

1. The deductive presentation saves time because it gives the important information first.

2. For a report intended to persuade the reader to a certain viewpoint, the inductive approach is advantageous because it presents all of the information before drawing any conclusions and making any recommendations. The presentation of the findings and the analysis of the data should lead the reader to the same conclusions as the ones presented by the writer.

3. If the writer knows that the reader will react negatively toward the conclusions and recommendations, they are best presented at the end. This order allows time to build arguments to convince the reader. Ideally, the reader will then accept conclusions he would not have accepted before the presentation of the data.

The organizational patterns discussed in the remainder of this chapter can be applied to either the inductive or deductive organization of the report. These patterns refer to the order of the presentation and discussion of facts within the report and not to the overall organization of the report.

DETERMINATION OF THE REPORT FUNCTION

The writer must determine the kind of report the reader wants. The decision is not up to the writer. Sometimes the reader will specify whether she wants only information or also examination and recommendations. Sometimes the writer may have to ask the requestor what she wants. In some cases the writer may know the potential reader well enough to know what the reader prefers.

Some managers prefer to just get the information; they do not want others to influence their decision. They prefer to analyze the information themselves, draw their own conclusions, and make their own recommendations. Some managers want the analysis input from others because they want to know how others interpret the data. Some managers may want to know the writer well before requesting a complete analytical report, which requires insight and analytical ability.

CLASSIFICATION BY TIME

PERIODIC REPORTS

Some reports are written at regular intervals. For example, a sales representative may have to write weekly sales reports. An accountant may have to write monthly statements for clients. An affirmative-action officer may have

Periodic Reports
Periodic reports are written at regular intervals.

to send reports to the government on a regular basis. Because these reports are written at regular intervals, they are also called **periodic reports**. In many cases they are part of the standard assignment of a particular job and included in the job description. For example, no one sends a request each Friday for a sales report on Monday. The sales representative is expected to have the report ready without any special request.

SPECIAL REPORTS

Special Reports
Special reports help in solving special problems.

In contrast to periodic reports, **special reports** are written only on special request. For example, upper management may want a study of the feasibility of a new layout of the production line. Clearly such a report would not be written on a regular basis but only when a particular problem exists. The solution may involve a team approach. For example, the manager of the production division may appoint a team to study the feasibility of a change in assembly-line layout. The team may include people from production, personnel, finance, and engineering. After the report is finished, the team will be dissolved.

PROGRESS REPORTS

Progress Reports
Progress reports provide an update on a project.

To ensure that management knows whether long-term projects are on schedule, **progress reports** are written. They are usually written in connection with special projects; functions generating periodic reports rarely require progress reports. You will find more information on progress reports in Chapter 5.

CLASSIFICATION BY SUBJECT

The classification by subject clarifies the major emphasis or subject of the report. The writer may emphasize different data depending on whether the report is an accounting, production, sales, or personnel report. Once the writer has determined the subject of the report, the preparation of the report will be easier because the focus is clear.

CLASSIFICATION BY FORMALITY

Level of Formality
A formal report is less personal than an informal report.

To determine the appropriate **level of formality**, the writer must find out who the reader is and what the topic of the report is. A short memorandum to a coworker may be quite informal. However, a report outlining the recommendations to upper management for a million-dollar project ·may be much more formal.

In an informal report, the writer may say: "These are my recommendations. What do you think, Tony? I would like to discuss the results with you during the coming week." In a formal report the writer uses a less personal style. The writer does not use the name of the recipient.

Personalization would be restricted to the cover letter that transmits the report. The letter might read: "I suggest a meeting to discuss the recommendations." In the report itself the writer might say: "Management should examine the results carefully before implementing any changes."

Some people insist that a formal business report should never use the personal pronouns *I*, *we*, and *you*. Although this may still be true for very formal reports, the avoidance of personal pronouns easily leads to an overuse of the passive voice. A report that uses personal pronouns is not necessarily less objective than a report that omits them. In most business reports the use of personal pronouns is acceptable and even preferable.

No absolute guidelines exist for determining when a report must be formal and when it can be less formal, but some general rules will help you in deciding on the level of formality:

1. Longer reports are more formal than shorter ones.

2. Special reports are more formal than periodic ones. The corporate annual report is an exception to this rule. The corporate annual report is very formal even though it is a periodic report.

3. Reports sent to a group of people rather than to only one person are more formal.

4. Reports that go up in the organization are usually more formal than reports to people at the same level in the organization.

5. Reports that go outside the work area or department are more formal than reports that stay inside the work area.

CLASSIFICATION BY READERSHIP

Readership classification often determines the format of the report. Internal reports, sent to people within an organization, are often written in memo format. External reports, sent to people outside the organization, are usually written in letter form. Both internal and external reports are presented as formal reports when they address complex and special problems.

CLASSIFICATION BY FORMAT

Format
The format of the report depends on its intended use.

The formality, the subject, the function, and the time interval influence the **format** of the report. A formal, in-depth examination of production costs will not be presented in a memo but on quality paper with a special cover and a title page. It may have a cover letter, a bibliography, a table of contents, and an executive summary. The periodic sales report, on the other hand, may be presented on a preprinted form or in a memo report.

After the writer knows what kind of report she has to write, after she has determined the type of project the report has to address, after she knows whether the report is periodic or special, she can determine the format. The format of the report is a function of the other classification areas.

The report forms illustrated in this chapter are representative of the ones used in many businesses. In some cases you may be allowed to develop your own format, but some companies insist on uniform formats. Your company may insist on a special size, color, and weight of paper for internal reports and a different paper and format for external reports. You will have to check to determine what your particular company expects you to do.

MEMORANDUM REPORTS

Memorandum Reports
Memorandum reports are used internally.

The report writing principles of **memorandum reports** and letter reports are the same. The difference lies in the format of the presentation. Most companies have preprinted memorandum forms because memos are the most frequently written business reports. It would be a waste of time if the memo headings had to be typed each time. Preprinted memos are either full sheets ($8\frac{1}{2}$ by 11 inches) or half sheets.

The length of memorandum reports ranges from one or two hand-written sentences to several typed pages. They can be quite personal or rather formal. The report on the Fall Kick-off Day in Exhibit 4.6 illustrates a typical memo format.

Format of Memo Heading. The memo heading identifies the sender, the receiver, the subject matter, and the date of writing. Three typical setups for this information are shown below:

```
TO:        Virginia Morris
FROM:      William Eick
SUBJECT:   Workflow in Word Processing Department
DATE:      December 15, 19XX
```

or

```
TO:        Virginia Morris         FROM:   William Eick
SUBJECT:   Workflow in Word        DATE:   December 15, 19XX
           Processing Department
```

or

```
December 15, 19XX
TO:        Virginia Morris
FROM:      William Eick
SUBJECT:   Workflow in Word Processing Department
```

All three formats are acceptable and widely used.

Exhibit 4.6 **Memo Report**

TO: Sharon Malone
FROM: Sandra Reese *SR*
SUBJECT: Chamber of Commerce Women's Division 19XX Kickoff Day
DATE: June 23, 19XX

Here is a status report on the preparation for 19XX Kickoff Day.

Place and Time

Kickoff Day is scheduled for September 20, 19XX. The Rolling Meadows Country Club
will again be the site. The schedule for the day is as follows:

12 noon - 4:00 p.m.	Sports Activities
4:00 p.m. - 5:00 p.m.	Relaxing Time
5:00 p.m. - 6:00 p.m.	Cocktail Hour
6:00 p.m. - 7:30 p.m.	Dinner
7:30 p.m. - 8:30 p.m.	Dinner Speaker
8:30 p.m. - 8:45 p.m.	Business Meeting

Sports Activities

I have tentatively arranged for golf, tennis, and badminton. Participants will
have to provide their own equipment, but they may use the club facilities free of
charge. In case of rain, outdoor activities will have to be cancelled.

Members may play bridge and other games in the clubhouse.

Cocktail Hour

Members and their guests can meet during the cocktail hour. Participants will pay
for their own drinks. The cocktail hour has been a huge success in the past, and
I expect many people to attend this year.

Dinner

The club has three choices for dinner:

$9.00: Tossed salad, pork steak, french fries, mixed vegetables, vanilla
pudding

$10.00: Tossed salad, stuffed chicken breast on rice, mixed vegetables,
chocolate cake

$12.00: Jello salad, roast beef, potatoes, peas, ice cream

The menu decision has to be submitted by September 15.

After-Dinner Speaker

Because the theme for the coming year is professional self-development, I
recommend we tie the after-dinner speech to the theme. Two possible speakers are:

Susan Levine, Professor of Psychology at Midwest University
Topic: How to Deal with Stress

Exhibit 4.6   **Memo Report** (*continued*)

Malone   p. 2   June 23, 19XX

        Catherine Sullivan, President of Blooming Grove National Bank
        Topic: Women and Financial Investments

Both women are well-known speakers.

<u>Publicity and Registration</u>

Information should be sent out around September 1. Reservations for dinner and
activities must be made by September 15, either by mail or phone.

Use of Titles in Memo Heading. In the memo heading, a complimentary title such as Mrs., Miss, Mr., or Ms. is not used with the writer's name. A complimentary title may precede the name of the receiver, but in most cases complimentary titles are omitted altogether. The receiver may be a group of people and might be identified as "all employees" or "sales managers."

If the writer does not know the name of the person she writes to, she can use the position title of the receiver instead.

TO: Sales Agent

or

TO: Affirmative Action Officer

In more formal memos the writer may add position titles following the names of the sender and the receiver.

TO: Vivian Fernandez, Vice President Finance
FROM: Mine Veral, Special Project Manager

Information in Subject Line. The information in the subject line must be descriptive. Its purpose is to tell the reader what the memo is about.

A vague subject line:

SUBJECT: Sales

can be improved by adding specific information:

SUBJECT: Sales Data of District 5 for June 19XX

Subject lines should be constructed with care. They should answer when, where, why, what, and how whenever appropriate. The improved subject line above, for example, provides information on what (sales data), where (district 5), and when (June 19XX). The reader of that subject line knows what the memo will be about.

Spacing and Paragraphing. Memos are usually single-spaced with double spacing between paragraphs. Paragraphs are blocked rather than indented because the blocked style looks more modern, is easier to use, and saves time.

Headings within the Memo. Headings help the reader to locate the main points of the memo report. Headings may be either centered or positioned at the left margin. In long memos, where both headings and subheadings are appropriate, the major heading may be centered and the subheading placed on the left margin. Alternatively, both headings may be placed on the left margin. The major heading is often typed in all capital letters.

FISHER-PRICE TOYS

U.S. Division

or

FISHER-PRICE TOYS

U.S. Division

or

FISHER-PRICE TOYS

U.S. Division

Page Identification. One-page memos do not carry a page number; however, memos longer than one page require page numbers. Headings for second pages always give the page number and the date; some also provide the subject or the name of the receiver. The following examples illustrate acceptable second-page headings:

Workflow in Word Processing Department   Page 2   December 15, 19XX

or

Virginia Morris   Page 2   December 15, 19XX

or

Virginia Morris
Page 2
December 15, 19XX

Signature of Sender. Memos are not signed at the end. Writers should initial them after their typed names in the memo heading.

LETTER REPORTS

Letter Reports
Letter reports are external reports in letter format.

Letter reports are used for external communication. They follow the same format as normal business letters, but they tend to be less personal and are usually longer.

The letter report has the following parts: letterhead, date line, inside address, salutation, body, complimentary close, signature block, information on attachments, carbon copies, and initials of the typist.

The letter report can be typed in blocked form or in modified blocked style. In blocked form all major parts of the letter begin on the left margin. In the modified blocked style the date, complimentary close, and signature block begin at the center of the page; paragraphs may be blocked or indented.

Letterhead. The company letterhead is professionally designed. Traditionally it is centered at the top of the page although the letterhead of some companies is on the left margin. The letterhead includes the company name, mailing address, telephone number, and telex number.

Date Line. In the blocked style the date appears on the left margin. The name of the month should be spelled out to avoid misunderstanding. The clear identification of the month is particularly important in reports that go to foreign branches or businesses because in other countries the order of the date is day, month, year, rather than month, day, year as in the United States.

Inside Address. The inside address, also called the letter or envelope address, identifies the name and title of the recipient, the name of the recipient's company, and the mailing address. A complimentary title should always precede the recipient's name (*Mr.*, *Mrs.*, *Miss*, or *Ms.*). As in the memorandum, a position title may follow the name.

Salutation. In most letter reports you will use the traditional salutation *Dear Mr.*, *Dear Mrs.*, *Dear Miss*, or *Dear Ms.* If you do not have the name of the recipient, you have several options, but none of them is completely satisfying.

1. Use of job title
    Dear Sales Agent:
    This salutation sounds impersonal and would not be appropriate for a warm and personal style.

2. Dear Sir:
    This salutation is not only old-fashioned but also objectionable because the receiver may be a woman. Unless you are certain that the receiver is a man, you should stay away from this salutation.
    The salutation for men, regardless of age or marital status, is *Dear Mr.* When the recipient is a woman, you must choose from among *Mrs.*, *Miss*, and *Ms.*, no easy task. Women who prefer a particular form of address should let people know. They can identify their preference in the signature block. In Europe, professional women are always addressed with the complimentary title *Mrs.*, regardless of whether they are married or not.

3. Subject line
    Some businesses are beginning to use a subject line when the name of the receiver is unknown. The subject line makes the letter

report less personal, but it does identify the topic of the letter very clearly.

Body of the Letter Report. The body of the letter report is single-spaced with double spacing between paragraphs. A letter report can employ headings to identify the material more effectively for the reader. For example, the headings in the letter report in Exhibit 4.7 clearly identify the problems, the possible solutions, and the costs. The rules for headings in letter reports are the same as in memo reports. As in the memo report, the writer may also use illustrations and itemization.

Complimentary Close and Signature Block. The complimentary close, followed by a comma, is normally used at the end of the letter report. The typed name of the writer appears four lines below. Professional titles are added either after the name or underneath it. Some common complimentary closings in business correspondence are

Sincerely,

Sincerely yours,

Yours sincerely,

Respectfully,

Respectfully yours,

Cordially yours.

Secretary's Initials and Copies. The secretary normally types her initials at the left margin. If the writer's initials appear also, they precede the secretary's initials.

If you want to send copies of a letter to additional people, you place their names below the secretary's initials, preceded by the notation *cc* for carbon copy or *xc* for Xerox copy. If you do not want the recipient to know that you are sending copies to other people, you may send blind copies. Use the notation *bcc* for blind carbon copy and the names of the additional recipients on the carbon copy only.

Sincerely yours,

William Shevrin

WS/jp

cc: Fred Brown
    Rose Bittner

Exhibit 4.7   **Letter Report**

SCHOLZ HOME IMPROVEMENT CO.
Hoopsten, WI 31761
312 Main Street

[handwritten: Your return adress]
[handwritten: phone # Date]

[handwritten: 3]

September 20, 19XX *[handwritten: 3]*

Mr. John Whalen
541 Porter Avenue
Hoopsten, WI 31761

Dear Mr. Whalen:

After inspection of your basement, I have decided that water-proofing is possible.

Problem

The water problem in your basement seems to result from several factors:

1. Rainwater on the paved driveway next to the house runs off against the foundation. Before the driveway was paved, the water could seep into the gravel.

2. Tests next to the foundation walls indicate that the tiling is either broken or was incorrectly laid. In any case, the tiling does not do its job. The problem is compounded by the paved driveway.

3. As you know, the sewers in many houses in your area back up after heavy rains. During the last 20 years we have averaged about two heavy storms every season. The storm sewers are inadequate for the size of the housing development.

Suggestions *[handwritten: Solutions]*

My firm has been able to solve water problems similar to yours for many home owners. I recommend the following:

1. Create space between the house and the driveway. Because the rainwater runs directly from the driveway to the foundation, it is important that the driveway not touch the walls. I recommend taking out a two-foot-wide section of the driveway along the house. The area should be filled in with gravel. In addition, the outside of the foundation has to be waterproofed.

2. Replace the tiling. The changes in the driveway and the replacement of the tiling should be done at the same time. At this point the entire outside of the foundation can be waterproofed.

3. Install a valve in the drain in the basement. To solve the sewer problem, I can install a valve in your basement, so that the water cannot back up. I have installed several valves of this type, and they are working extremely well.

Exhibit 4.7   **Letter Report** (*continued*)

Whalen   p. 2   September 20, 19XX

Cost and Time Frame

I could start with the work any time this month. It will take about one week from start to finish.

The entire job--digging out around the foundation, replacing the old tile, and installing the valve for the sewer--will cost $3,400.

Guarantee

The tiling work is guaranteed for ten years. After the job has been done, your basement will be dry, and you can finish the area without having to worry about water.

Sincerely,

Robert Scholz

Robert Scholz

(RS/em) *up to us — yes or no*

FORM REPORTS

Form Reports
The information on form reports is recorded on a preprinted form.

Form reports are used more and more frequently. The report writer fills in blanks on a preprinted form. Accident reports, sales reports, and sometimes job applications are examples of form reports. The lawn service company whose report is presented in Exhibit 4.8 chose a form report for communicating with customers. The form report is easily filled out by the employee inspecting the lawn. It is easily read by the customer who immediately knows the condition of his lawn.

Form reports are useful when companies receive many reports on similar topics. For example, an insurance company uses forms for the reporting of accidents. When all accident reports are organized the same way, insurance clerks spend less time looking for location, time, and other details of the accident. The form also ensures that all important information is provided.

BULLETINS

Bulletins
Bulletins are announcements to large audiences.

Bulletins are announcements. Because they go to a large audience, a memorandum report or letter report would not be as appropriate. The bulletin report tends to be about a page long. It has a title to identify the subject of the report. The date is also given, but neither writer nor receiver is identified. The announcement on the Deferred Pay Account in Exhibit 4.9 was placed on bulletin boards in all departments of the company.

SUMMARY OF LEARNING OBJECTIVES

To Understand the Role of Report Classification Systems.
With the help of the classification system, the writer determines whether the report is informational or analytical, formal or informal, internal or external, in memo or letter format. The classification system provides direction for the writer.

To Use the Classification Systems as a Tool in Report Writing.
Classification by Function. Reports can be divided into two major groups, informational and analytical. The analytical report can be further subdivided into examination and recommendation reports. The writer must consider the request for the report, the preference of the reader, and the topic to determine the report function.

Information can be presented either inductively or deductively. In inductive reports the conclusions and recommendations follow the analysis of data; in deductive reports the conclusions and recommendations precede the analysis of facts.

Exhibit 4.8   **Form Reports**

PERFECT LAWN
212 Garden Road
Deercreek, IL 61531
(309) 438-5796

Lawn Analysis

Customer:
Address:
Date:

Name of Inspector:

Cost per Treatment:

Number of Applications per Season:

```
-------------------------------------------
                      No      Slight   Severe
                    Problem  Problem  Problem
-------------------------------------------
Watering   ---------|--------|--------|
                    |        |        |
Mowing     ---------|--------|--------|
                    |        |        |
Thatching  ---------|--------|--------|
                    |        |        |
Density    ---------|--------|--------|
                    |        |        |
Crabgrass  ---------|--------|--------|
                    |        |        |
Dandelions ---------|--------|--------|
                    |        |        |
Weeds      ---------|--------|--------|
                    |        |        |
Grubs      ---------|--------|--------|
                    |        |        |
Other      |        |        |
Insects    -------------------------------
```

We will call you during the next few days to answer any questions you may have
about our services.

Exhibit 4.9   **Bulletin Report**

October 26, 19XX

TAX BREAK SOON AVAILABLE TO ALL EMPLOYEES AT APPLIANCE INC.

If you have always wanted a legal way to reduce the bite of federal taxes, you can soon have it.

Starting in January, every employee at Appliance Inc. can sign up for the **DEFERRED PAY ACCOUNT.**

Here is how it will work:

1. You tell the company how much money you want placed in a new savings account in your name. The initial limit is 7 percent of your salary or wages.

2. The company deposits the amount you have specified into your account.

3. The company gives you a matching 50 percent contribution.

4. The company does not withhold any federal income tax on the earnings that go into the Deferred Pay Account.

5. Your deferred pay accumulates and grows over the years in your account.

6. You receive all your deferred pay plus its earnings when you retire or leave the company.

7. When you receive the payout, you will be eligible for special tax advantages.

You will be hearing more about this plan in the weeks ahead.

Classification by Time. Reports that are written at regular intervals are periodic reports. Reports that are written to help solve special problems are special reports.

Classification by Subject. The classification by subject helps the writer to determine the focus of the report.

Classification by Formality. Short reports tend to be less formal than long reports.

Classification by Readership. Reports for people inside the company are internal reports; reports for people outside the company are external reports.

To Examine the Most Commonly Used Formats for Short Reports.

Memorandum Report. Memorandum reports are the most frequently written reports in business. They are mostly used for communication within companies. Memo headings identify the receiver, sender, subject, and date. Memos are single-spaced and blocked.

Letter Reports. Letter reports are mostly used for communication outside the company. The letter report has the same parts as the regular business letter. It differs from the typical letter in that it uses headings and illustrations. It also tends to be longer and more formal.

Form Reports. Companies that process quantities of similar information often use form reports. Form reports guarantee uniformity of arrangement. They help the reader find and evaluate information.

Bulletins. Bulletins address a large audience. They are less personal than letter and memorandum reports. Company announcements are typically presented in bulletin format.

QUESTIONS AND PROBLEMS

1. What is the purpose of classification systems in report writing?
2. Discuss the classification by function.
3. Discuss inductive and deductive arrangements of data.
4. What is the difference between periodic and special reports?
5. Discuss the difference between examination and recommendation reports.
6. When do you use a memorandum and when a letter report?
7. What is the purpose of form reports?
8. What is the purpose of bulletins?
9. Why do more and more businesses use blocked form for letters and memos?
10. What are the parts of the memorandum headings?
11. Obtain a report from a local business and classify it according to the classification systems discussed in this chapter.

CHAPTER FIVE

SHORT AND

SPECIAL

REPORTS

LEARNING OBJECTIVES

- To study the content and organization of the most frequently written business reports:

  Minutes   Justification Reports
  Press Releases   Staff Reports
  Progress Reports   Job Descriptions
  Proposals   Policies and Procedures
  Feasibility Studies   Annual and Quarterly Reports

Everyday business affairs require many more short reports than long reports. This chapter discusses the short reports most frequently written.

MINUTES

PURPOSE OF MINUTES

Minutes
Minutes are a record of a meeting.

The **minutes** of a meeting serve as a summary and a reminder for those who attended it. For those who were unable to attend, the minutes provide information of what went on. With the information from the minutes even people who did not attend the meeting can go into the next meeting well informed. Minutes are often distributed outside the group that was asked to attend the meeting because they contain information needed to coordinate efforts. They may also be sent to upper management.

Minutes are customarily approved at the following meeting after any necessary changes have been made.

Sometime during your career you will have to write minutes. A secretary is not always available to do the job. You may also be elected secretary for professional and civic organizations and be expected to take minutes in that position. Regardless of whether you write the minutes or simply approve them, you must know the elements of effective minutes.

One of the most important skills necessary for writing minutes is the ability to listen carefully. Although you might think that shorthand would help, shorthand alone does not guarantee the correctness or the accuracy of the minutes. In writing minutes you will need to summarize and selectively present information. Grasping key ideas and arguments is therefore much more important than the ability to record proceedings verbatim.

To record meetings on tape and write the minutes afterward is a waste of time. No company will want to pay you to listen to the same meeting twice. A recording can occasionally be helpful if you want to check or keep a complete record of some controversial points. In that case you must consider the legal ramifications of taping meetings. Unless you have permission to tape, you may be violating the law.

Ideally, the notes you take at a meeting will serve as a rough draft. To expedite the writing, minutes are normally written in chronological order. You may give the rough draft to the secretary or dictate the minutes so the secretary can type them. Minutes should be distributed as soon as possible after a meeting.

FORMAT OF MINUTES

The two basic formats for minutes are the memo and the titled report. In either format the heading must give the subject, date, and place of the meeting. The following is an example of the heading for minutes in memo form:

TO: Patti Gahr
                   Doris Gonzales
                   Vivian Fernandes
                   Bruce Milliard
                   Frank Westphal

FROM: Cathy Bourke

RE: Minutes of Meeting of Training Supervisors, March 15, 19XX

DATE: March 16, 19XX

Present: Bourke, Gahr, Gonzales, Fernandes, Milliard
Absent: Westphal

Minutes for the same meeting, if written as a titled report, would be headed as follows:

Minutes of Meeting of Training Supervisors
March 15, 19XX

Present: Bourke, Gahr, Gonzales, Fernandes, Milliard
Absent: Westphal

The minutes must indicate who was present and who was absent. If the group is small, a list of people absent and present is usually included in the heading. If the list is long, it can be presented on a separate sheet at the end of the minutes.

People who make important contributions or who bring up an important argument should be identified by name. The writer can exercise some discretion in deciding whether to name and quote an individual. If there are any votes, the writer must identify the person who made the motion and the person who seconded it, the precise wording of the motion, and the precise outcome of the vote. A typical motion and vote might be reported in the minutes as follows:

> Tanton moved to study the possible effects on workflow and turnaround time from centralizing word processing before any decision be made. (Chang seconded.) The motion passed: 5 yes, 1 no, 1 abstention.

Minutes are kept on file. Management may want to refer to them later to see, for example, who was present when a new policy was established. Members of the committee that established the policy may want to review the major arguments for or against it.

Minutes may have the following parts:

1. **Heading.** The writer can identify the subject of the report either with a title or subject line of a memo heading. The name of the group that met and the date of the meeting must be identified.

2. **Attendance.** In the minutes, usually at the beginning, the writer lists the names of people present and absent. The names of guests, people who normally do not attend the meeting but who for a particular reason were present, are given too.

3. **Opening and Closing.** Minutes may start out by stating the beginning time of the meeting and close by providing the exact ending time. It is customary to approve the minutes of the last meeting at the beginning of the new session. The approval of the minutes guarantees that committee members agree to the content of the minutes.

4. **Record of the Meeting.** Minutes are arranged in chronological order. Topics discussed can be presented in itemized or paragraph form. Minutes must provide enough detail so that people who did not attend the meeting will know what took place.

5. **Votes.** If any voting takes place, the minutes have to state who made a motion, who seconded the motion. The minutes also have to provide the precise outcome of any vote.

The precise content of minutes depends on the nature of the meeting, the task of the group, and the formality of the meeting. Exhibit 5.1 illustrates one possible pattern for minutes.

Exhibit 5.1   **Minutes**

SPECIAL MEETING OF JOINT-APPRENTICESHIP COMMITTEE

January 16, 19XX, 2:00 p.m.

Members Present: Remmers, Ranney, Gonzales, DuBois, Gahr, Fox

This meeting was called for the purpose of evaluating David Swain, Maintenance
Apprentice, because he is approaching the 6,999-hour mark.

The committee members were given Mr. Swain's evaluation sheets, which had been
filled out by Selecting Shift Supervisors John Remmers, Mark Utendorf, and Vivian
Grever. The Selecting Shift Supervisors evaluated Mr. Swain because they supervise him when he is working on shift rather than during the day. Miss Gahr informed the committee about the amount of time supervisors have spent with Mr.
Swain for training on certain projects.

The evaluations were discussed. All of them showed a lack of improvement. The
committee discussed the fact that at the previous meeting Mr. Swain was given up
to 6,999 hours to show improvement. It had also been decided that the advancement
to the 7,000-hour level would be withheld if Mr. Swain did not improve.

Mr. Swain was informed of the decision after the previous meeting. At that time
he was offered the opportunity to move to the day shift in order to improve his
performance. During the day he would be able to work with Journeymen Maintenance
Mechanics. Mr. Swain turned the opportunity down.

Because of the most recent evaluations, the committee decided that Mr. Swain would
be held at 6,999 hours and would not be allowed to advance to the 7,000-hour
level. At the end of 1,000 hours (approximately six months) he will be evaluated
again. If at this time he still does not show sufficient improvement, the Joint-
Apprenticeship Committee will decide whether to keep Mr. Swain or remove him from
the apprenticeship program.

The committee will once more offer Mr. Swain the opportunity to move to the day
shift. Mr. Swain will have two weeks to consider this move.

The committee decision and recommendation will be discussed with Mr. Swain on
January 17.

The meeting was adjourned at 3:00 p.m.

NEWS RELEASES

News Release
A news release an-
nounces corporate news
to the public. It may
also be called a *press
release*.

The **news release** is public-relations material. News releases often announce perfomance records, management decisions, awards to individual employees, the reasons for layoffs, or other information of interest to the public. They must be objective. Management, of course, wants to represent its actions in as positive a light as possible, but accuracy and ethical conduct are required when reporting information.

If you write a news release, you will usually write as a spokesperson for the company. Therefore you refer to the writer as Company X rather than as *I*. You may say: "The company has decided," or "management has determined."

To increase the probability that the release will be used, the message should be newsworthy, timely, and in proper form. The most important facts should be stated first. Because many people will read only the headline and the first paragraph, additional information should follow in descending order of importance.

If at all possible, you should limit the news release to one page. Longer releases are stapled so that the pages do not become separated. All news releases should be double-spaced and typed on company letterhead or on plain paper with the company name and address typed near the top. The end of the release should be marked clearly.

The name and telephone number of a person who can be contacted for more information should be included. Users occasionally want more detailed information than is given in the release.

Sometimes press releases are presented orally to the public or to employees before they are submitted to the media. You will need to check with particular newspapers for submission policies and deadlines. Large companies sometimes also send copies of news releases to stockholders, as the example in Exhibit 5.2 illustrates.

News releases should have the following information:

1. **Identification**. You must identify the report as a news release, and write the words FOR RELEASE or FOR IMMEDIATE RELEASE at the top. You also have to list the name of the company, address, and contact person.

2. **Message**. The message has to be timely and newsworthy and answer *who*, *what*, *why*, *where*, *when*, and *how*. You should present the most important facts first. Additional facts should be given in descending order of importance.

3. **Ending**. You should mark the end of the release clearly, so that the newspaper editor or the radio or television announcer knows that the release is complete.

Exhibit 5.2   **Press Release**

1900 Avenue of the Stars
Los Angeles California 90067
(213) 553-3900
For Additional Information, Call:

REPUBLIC CORPORATION
NEWS RELEASE

Contact: Ralph O. Briscoe
           Republic Corporation

           Melvyn S. Rifkind
           Rifkind Pondel & Parsons
           (213) 478-3523

FOR IMMEDIATE RELEASE

Los Angeles, California -- November 20, 1984 -- Republic Corporation (NYSE) and Triton Group Ltd. (OTC) today jointly announced that they have signed a definitive merger agreement providing for the acquisition of Republic by Triton. The merger agreement provides for the merger of Republic with a wholly-owned subsidiary of Triton. In the proposed merger, holders of Republic common stock will receive $33 in cash and one share of Triton convertible preferred stock for each share of Republic.

Republic is a diversified company with operations in graphics, film and video processing, aviation and metals. Triton, which is the successor to the Chase Manhattan Mortgage and Realty Trust, has entered into an agreement to acquire Simplicity Pattern Company. The acquisition of Simplicity is scheduled to be consummated promptly after approval by the Triton stockholders at their annual meeting scheduled for December 19, 1984. Completion of the Simplicity acquisition is a condition to the Republic merger. Simplicity is the largest producer of patterns for the home sewing market.

--00--

Source: Reprinted with permission of Rifkind Pondel & Parsons, Santa Monica, California.

PROGRESS REPORTS

Progress Report
A progress report is an update on a project.

If you are working on a long project, you may be asked to write **progress reports**. Progress reports usually summarize what has been accomplished to date. The emphasis is on the interim between the last and the current progress report. The writer has to provide information on the tasks completed on time, tasks which are behind schedule, and tasks which are ahead of schedule. If there are discrepancies between the schedule and the actual accomplishments, then the reasons for the differences must be explained.

The writer of a progress report should identify what remains to be done, describe any foreseeable problems in detail, and analyze their impact on the schedule. If the project is off schedule, the report must include suggestions for making up time.

Severe financial penalties are often incurred if a project is not completed as scheduled. For example, a construction firm may have to pay thousands of dollars in damages for every day a job goes beyond the scheduled completion date.

Progress reports are organized deductively. The length depends on the complexity of the project. In some cases a chart summarizing the tasks that have been completed may be enough; in other cases a lengthy report with statistical information may be necessary. The example in Exhibit 5.3 falls between these extremes.

Progress reports have the following parts:

1. **Identification**. The project has to be identified precisely.

2. **Summary of Completed Tasks**. The report summarizes all the jobs which have been completed to date. The emphasis is on the jobs which were completed since the last progress report.

3. **Identification of Problems**. Any difficulties have to be reported in detail. The writer also has to analyze the implications of any problems for the completion of the task.

4. **Remaining Work**. The report has to identify what remains to be done and if there are any foreseeable problems.

5. **Ending**. The writer states whether the overall job is on target, ahead of schedule, or behind schedule. He also makes suggestions on how to get a job back on schedule.

PROPOSALS

Proposal Report
In a proposal report the writer proposes to do a project.

A construction bid is a **proposal report**, as are proposals for grants from businesses, private foundations, and the government.

Most organizations that solicit proposals require a specific format that the writer must follow exactly. Not following the format, not providing all

Exhibit 5.3 **Progress Report**

TO: John Lorenzen
FROM: Joe Barrett *JB*
RE: Progress on K-Supermarket Construction
DATE: September 30, 19XX

The construction of K-Supermarket is on schedule.

By the beginning of September the construction of the building had been completed. During September the following jobs were finished:

1. Construction of interior walls.
2. Installation of electricity, gas, and water.
3. Application of insulation to outside walls.

The jobs left for October are:

1. Painting. The paint has not arrived yet; however, I called the dealer today and was promised it would be delivered within the next 3 days. No schedule problems are anticipated as a result of the delay.
2. Installation of light fixtures.
3. Installation of counters, shelves, and freezers.

At this point I see no difficulty in completing the project by October 31, as scheduled.

background and supplementary information requested, or even double-spacing the proposal when single-spacing is requested may result in elimination of the proposal from consideration. The writer must follow all of the requirements for submitting a proposal even though they may seem unnecessarily rigid and arbitrary.

Some proposals are solicited. For example, management may want to remodel the offices and may request bids for the job. The firms submitting proposals know that the job will be awarded to one of them.

Some proposals are unsolicited. The College of Business at Pacific University, for example, may submit a proposal to a multinational corporation for funding research in international business communication. In this case the proposal must show both that the research will be beneficial to the company and that the writer is capable of doing it. The writer must be convincing and persuasive.

Items that must be addressed in both solicited and unsolicited proposals are the following:

1. **Qualifications of People Doing the Project**. Proposals ask for money or other support and must show that the people who will be involved have the necessary experience.

2. **Purpose of the Proposal**. The reader must understand the objectives of the project. A clear and precise purpose statement is required.

3. **Significance**. The writer must show that the project is both viable and worthwhile by demonstrating that it will have a positive impact and will solve a problem.

4. **A Detailed Plan of Execution**. The proposal must provide a detailed methodology. If the proposal is for a survey, for example, it must be specific about plans to use a questionnaire, interview people, or observe people, and it must show plans for data analysis.

5. **A Detailed Time Schedule**. The reader must know how long it will take to complete the project. If the writer's company faces a crisis in production quality, for example, and the proposal suggests ways to solve the problem within the next two months, management must be able to judge whether the proposal is realistic. It may be too optimistic. With a few changes, however, it might be implemented in the proposed two-month period.

6. **An Itemized Budget**. The writer must show in detail how much the project will cost. The solution proposed may be more expensive but offer a higher quality result than other proposals. It is also possible that the problem could be solved with less money. In the proposal stage the budget is obviously based on estimates; therefore, in times of high inflation, the writer may want to include a clause that the budget will be increased if costs rise beyond a certain level. Budgets should be realistic. Construction bids have to include information on quality and cost of material to be used.

Proposals must be geared to the specific reader and to specific situations. The format and content of a proposal depend on the nature of the problem and the proposal guidelines. In Exhibit 5.4 the company wants to protect its computer room against fire; the proposal addresses the method and the cost of accomplishing that goal.

FEASIBILITY STUDIES

Feasibility Report
A feasibility report examines whether a project can be done.

A **feasibility report** investigates the chances of success of a project. Let us assume your boss asks you to do a feasibility study of whether production schedules in the plant could be tightened. In this case you would concentrate on the possibilities of tightening the schedules. You would also examine ramifications of any changes in the schedules. While the feasibility study might outline the method for tightening the schedules, the method would not be the focus of the report.

Feasibility reports concentrate on this question: Is the undertaking possible and, if so, under what circumstances? Once the basic feasibility has been determined, the details of implementation must be examined. These include how long it would take and perhaps how it would affect the morale of employees. In many ways the feasibility report is a preliminary report on basic possibilities. The object is to find out the chances of success before making a more detailed investigation of solutions to a problem.

Let us assume your business has been expanding, and you need more space. Rather than move to another location or build an addition onto the present building, you may want to make increased use of the basement. Parts of it are already being used for storage. Before you plan the reorganization necessary to move offices into the basement, however, you need to know the feasibility of installing restrooms there. The building is 20 years old, you are the fifth owner, and you are not familiar with the construction and the plumbing layout. You contact a contractor and present your plan. After an examination of the basement, the contractor sends you the feasibility report presented in Exhibit 5.5.

Feasibility reports must give information on the following points:

1. **Feasibility.** The report must clearly indicate whether or not the project can be accomplished. This information is usually presented at the beginning of the report because it is the most important point.

2. **Problems.** The reader wants to know how easy or complicated the project will be. If the problems are staggering, the reader may determine that the project is not feasible financially even though it may be feasible technically.

3. **Time Frame.** The complexity of the problem will largely determine the amount of time required to complete a project. The reader must know how long it will take from beginning to end. A project requir-

Exhibit 5.4   **Proposal**

HERRMANN FIRE EQUIPMENT CO.
1615 S.W. Adams Street Scottsdale, CA 90123

January 7, 19XX

Mr. David Woodbury
Senior Programmer, Analyst
American Appliance Co.
1201 E. Bell Street
Oceanside, CA 93786

Dear Mr. Woodbury:

Here is our proposal for installing a fire-suppression system for your computer room. The proposal covers a Fenwal Total Flooding Suppression System designed for 5 percent concentration at 74°F and a fire detection system designed for early warning fire protection.

Scope of Work

The fire-suppression system will be provided in accordance with NFPA Pamphlet 12-a, "Halogenated Extinguishing Agent Systems, Halon 1301," and NFPA 72-E, "Standard on Automatic Fire Detectors."

All Fenwal equipment is designed to meet applicable requirements of Underwriters Laboratory Inc., and all items will bear the UL markings.

Equipment for this system will be supplied by Herrmann Fire Equipment Company. The system will be specifically designed to suppress fires in your computer room.

Automatic Operation

The system is designed to provide automatic protection. Any fire will be detected by cross-zoned ionization detectors in fire-suppression areas. These detectors will be located to conform to a standard spacing recommended by Underwriters Laboratory, Fenwal Inc., and all applicable codes and standards.

Manual Operation

The system can also be operated manually.

Services

Herrmann Fire Equipment Company will provide schematic drawings and calculations for the system and check the system after installation.

Price

The Fenwal Fire Suppression System will be supplied and installed for $15,806.00.

This price is based on a shipping date on or before March 1. The order must be received at least 30 days prior to the shipping date. The price does include freight charges.

Exhibit 5.4   **Proposal** (*continued*)

Woodbury   p. 2   January 7, 19XX

The price does not include:

1. Mechanical or electric fire dampers.
2. AC connection to the fire control panel.
3. Sealing of the rooms to be covered by the fire-suppression system.

Terms

One-third of the price has to be paid with the placement of the order. The
remainder is due upon completion of the work.

This proposal shall become a contract agreement only when accepted by American
Appliance Co. and approved in writing by an executive officer of Herrmann Fire
Equipment Company.

Sincerely,

Robert Kuller

Robert Kuller
Herrmann Fire Equipment Company
Sales Engineer

P.S. Also see the attached "General Section," which is part of this proposal.

Exhibit 5.5   **Feasibility Report**

HOLLAND PLUMBING SERVICES

Pine Grove, WI 53705

August 20, 19XX

Mr. Robert Reiner
20 Main Street
Pine Grove, WI 53705

Dear Mr. Reiner:

It is possible to install restrooms in the southeast corner of the basement of
your business, but the installation would be complicated and rather costly.

Water supply is no problem because there are water pipes within ten feet of the
area of the planned restroom. The sewer lines are more complicated. The waste-
water stack that is close to the planned restroom has a 2" pipe that is sufficient for sinks and water fountains, but not for toilets. Toilets have to drain
into a 4" pipe. Unfortunately, the closest 4" pipe is at the other end of the
building, roughly 50' away.

The pipe is deep enough so that the slope of the new pipe would not be a problem.
The installation would, however, involve considerable work. The concrete floor
would have to be cut open. The pipes could then be laid, and new concrete would
have to be poured. The entire sub-floor work would take about a week.

You may want to reconsider the planned layout of the office area in the basement
and consider putting the restrooms closer to the existing 4" sewer pipe.

I will be glad to give you estimates on both options.

Sincerely,

John Holland

John Holland

ing only a day might be done any time; one that will take two weeks requires careful planning so that ongoing business activities will not be unduly interrupted. The feasibility study gives an estimate of the time necessary to solve the problem or complete the task. It usually does not provide a detailed time study.

JUSTIFICATION REPORTS

Justification Report
The justification report is a suggestion report.

A **justification report** is an unsolicited recommendation report. A manager, supervisor, or employee has observed a problem and writes a report to suggest ways of solving it. The reader, who did not ask for the report, may not be very interested in reading it. A justification report must, therefore, clearly and quickly identify the problem and offer a solution.

The typical justification report has the following parts:

1. **Purpose.** Here the writer identifies the problem and outlines the recommendation for solving it. Conciseness and clarity are necessary. Otherwise, the intended reader may simply put the report in the wastebasket.

2. **Benefits of the Recommendation.** The writer shows how implementation of the recommendation can save time and money, improve quality, or increase motivation. So that the points will be clear, they may be itemized. Giving the most important benefit first will capture the attention of the reader.

3. **Method of Implementation.** The report must demonstrate the feasibility of the recommendations and outline methods of implementation. Cost and time estimates must be realistic and supportable.

4. **Conclusion.** This section sums up the main reasons why the writer believes that the recommendations will work.

5. **Discussion.** This section may be very short. If the problem is complex, however, the writer may analyze it in more detail.

A justification report that describes in detail the benefits of a recommended purchase is illustrated in Exhibit 5.6.

STAFF REPORTS

Staff Report
Staff reports are written by a manager's staff.

A **staff report** is a managerial recommendation report. It is usually written in memo form, often following a standardized format used throughout a company. The staff report can be arranged inductively or deductively. The term was first used in the military. In many businesses it now refers to reports written by a manager's staff. Business people write many different kinds of reports, however, and to group all of them under the label staff reports

Exhibit 5.6   **Justification Report**

TO: Michelle Clyne
FROM: Kent Waltz
RE: MAPPER 1100 Report Processing System
DATE: June 30, 19XX

I recommend the installation of the MAPPER system to increase efficiency and accuracy of work in Department 61.

What Is MAPPER?

MAPPER 1100 is a real-time, display-oriented report-processing system utilizing a report structured database.

MAPPER provides a unique user-oriented reporting capability. Reporting applications can be quickly implemented. An extensive set of report-processing functions is provided for searching, sorting, computing, and printing. A run language is available that provides functional sequencing with logical, computational, and formatted report generation.

What Can MAPPER Do?

MAPPER can help the company to save time and money in the following areas:

1. Analysis of Expenses
    The Sales Department would be able to compare expenses of each branch, region, and area. The sales manager has indicated that he would like to have comparisons every month. With MAPPER this task would take about 6 hours, whereas manually it would take at least 60 hours and even then the calculations would be in rough form.

2. Budget Preparation
    MAPPER could save the company up to 40 hours a year by making budget preparation easier and more routine. In addition, MAPPER would allow the company to make changes easily.

3. Partial Entries for Large Journal Vouchers
    Up to 32 hours of accounting time could be saved monthly. The greatest savings might be in computing the commission voucher, which would take run capability.

4. Burden Distribution
    The job now takes 15 to 20 hours monthly. MAPPER could save up to 15 hours.

5. Material at Vendor Inventory
    A major part of the time of one cost accountant is spent keeping track of material at vendor. MAPPER would save between 15 and 20 hours a month by selecting information directly from Accounts Payable and posting automatically. Returns from vendors could also be handled automatically.

6. Inventory Transfer
    MAPPER would save about 5 hours monthly in the calculation of figures to be used for the transfer of monthly production from In Process to Finished Goods inventory.

7. Fringe-Benefit Accrual
    The automatic computation and recording of fringe-benefit accrual should save approximately 5 hours monthly.

Exhibit 5.6   **Justification Report** (*continued*)

Michelle Clyne   p. 2   June 30, 1985

Conclusion

MAPPER would save the company up to 180 hours every month. Precise figures are
difficult to calculate because they will depend on the complexity of the jobs to
be performed. The company would also benefit in the area of quality. Reports
would be more complete, timely, and accurate.

does not provide any information on the content of a particular report. It merely indicates which person or persons in the organization prepared the report. A personnel report for improving the hiring process or a report analyzing equipment, as in Exhibit 5.7, could be labeled a staff report.

JOB DESCRIPTIONS

Job Description
Job descriptions detail the requirements for a job.

If you are in a supervisory position, you may need to write **job descriptions** for the people you supervise. In case of vacancies you will have to evaluate existing job descriptions and update them. A job description lists the qualifications necessary for a job and the duties to be performed.

The job description is a very common American report; it is found less frequently in other countries. Americans describe the position and look for the best qualified person to fill it. In the Middle East, on the other hand, management tends to think in terms of whether a person would fit into the company rather than what the specific qualifications are. A manager in the Middle East often determines how and where to use a new employee only after the person is hired.

Job descriptions in the United States provide the following information:

1. **Job Title**.
2. **Responsibilities**. This section may be divided into routine and special tasks or main and secondary tasks.
3. **Job Classification**. The job description has to identify the level of the job. For example, it is necessary to identify whether the job opening is for a class I or class II typist. Salary ranges may also be specified.
4. **Lines of Authority**. The employees have to know who reports to them and to whom they report.
5. **Education and Experience**. Is a university degree necessary? What licenses or certificates are required? The requirements have to be necessary to perform the job. If they are not necessary, the company may be accused of discrimination.
6. **Personal Information**. Information on age, height, weight, and vision should be specified only if the information is necessary for performing the job. If this information is not essential to the job, the company may be accused of discrimination.

The job description illustrated in Exhibit 5.8 emphasizes experience, knowledge, and ability rather than formal education. One can assume, however, that any serious candidate in today's banking environment would need a college background to function in that job. The job description specifically mentions effective communication, including the ability to make presentations and write business reports.

Exhibit 5.7   **Staff Report**

TO: Bob Morris
FROM: Dictionary Software Evaluation Committee
RE: Results of Software Trial
DATE: October 16, 19XX

We have completed our evaluation of two software packages:

1. Development Documentation Tool (DDT), DATAMANAGER, and First Structured
    Graphics

2. Excelerator

Recommendations

Based on the experience and reactions of the analysts and support personnel who
tested these products, we make the following recommendations:

1. We should not buy Development Documentation Tool, DATAMANAGER, or First
    Structured Graphics. These products should be returned to the vendor.

2. We should continue to explore the dictionary and text-documentation support
    capabilities of Excelerator.

3. A standard workstation for support of structured analysis should be developed.

4. A fully integrated data dictionary with the processes it is intended to sup-
    port should be a long-range goal.

Rationale

While DDT and DATAMANAGER together form a dictionary that is easy to use, the
data-flow diagrams produced by First Structured Graphics are unacceptable.
Excelerator, on the other hand, is an outstanding graphic tool that includes a
very limited dictionary. The committee decided that the need was greater for a
drawing tool. Although time did not permit an in-depth evaluation of the
dictionary and documentation features of the Excelerator, they appear to be
adequate in the short term.

The committee concluded that the Excelerator would save time over manual methods
of preparing data-flow diagrams.

The librarian identified an additional use of Excelerator that would justify a
workstation. The presentation graphics feature of Excelerator can be used to
produce detail system flows, module call maps, and user view charts. Other
departments that have a need to document flows and hierarchical relationships may
also benefit from this feature of Excelerator.

Exhibit 5.8   **Job Description**

Position

Vice President of Pacific National Bank, Retail Division

The Retail Division Vice President reports to the President.

Functions of the Job

1. The Retail Division Vice President assumes the responsibility for planning,
    organizing, directing, and monitoring all retail banking activities; adminis-
    tering the sales management function; directing the Electronic Funds Transfer
    activities; and developing marketing concepts for retail banking products.

2. As Division Head, the Vice President ensures that all activities of the Retail
    Banking Division support the bank's overall business goals and objectives.

Major Duties and Responsibilities

1. The Vice President is in charge of the Retail Division. In this position he
    or she:
    a. Is in charge of personnel decisions including employment decisions,
       salary reviews, performance reviews, disciplinary actions.
    b. Administers the sales function, which includes selling bank products,
       developing incentive programs, providing sales training.
    c. Plans and directs all retail product development.
    d. Develops and coordinates media plans and marketing concepts for retail
       products.
    e. Serves as President's Circle Officer for selected customers.
    f. Attends the following meetings:
       (1) President's Circle Officers Meeting.
       (2) Bank Retail Division Committee Meeting.
    g. Prepares and monitors the Retail Division budget.

2. The Retail Division Vice President has additional responsibilities in the
    bank. He or she:
    a. Participates in the bank-wide planning process.
    b. Participates in Bank Marketing Committee meetings.
    c. Assists in bank-wide training programs.

Necessary Knowledge and Skills

The Retail Division Vice President has to be able to:
1. Relate to people.
2. Make effective oral presentations to internal and external groups.
3. Define problems precisely and clearly.
4. Prioritize multiple job responsibilities.
5. Work under pressure.
6. Handle confidential information.
7. Manage employees.
8. Write effective business letters.
9. Research, summarize, and write effective business reports.

POLICIES AND PROCEDURES

Policies and Procedures
Policies and procedures inform employees of company rules.

Most companies have manuals that inform employees of **policies and procedures**. Employees can refer to a manual when questions arise about vacations, sick leave, and health insurance. The supervisor does not have to explain every policy to every employee. Manuals therefore save time, but only if they are clear, precise, detailed, and complete.

Let us assume a company has a new policy on absences. The new policy has to be stated clearly. It must describe, as in Exhibit 5.9, what will happen to people who violate the policy. It has to detail what will happen to one-time offenders and to repeat offenders. Terms must be defined so that no misunderstandings will occur. Employee policy manuals are often regarded by the courts as the equivalent to employment contracts, making precise language critical. Courts tend to interpret ambiguities against the employer.

Procedures manuals give a step-by-step description of processes. For example, a supervisor must know what to do in case of an accident. He has to know whom to inform, and what forms to fill out. The correct sequence of steps is important so that the process runs smoothly. The supervisor must fill out an accident report before notifying the insurance company of a claim. Not following procedures wastes time. Exhibit 5.10 illustrates typical procedures for processing an accident claim.

ANNUAL AND QUARTERLY REPORTS

Most organizations prepare regular reports on business activities to inform stockholders, employees, the government, and possible investors. The systematic review and summary of events also help management in the decision-making process.

Annual Reports
Annual reports are accounts of organizations' activities and performances during the previous year.

Annual reports are written by many organizations, government offices, and universities. They provide an update on activities, accomplishments, use of resources, and future plans. Annual reports are group efforts, compiled from information in departmental reports.

Department reports contain more detail than composite annual reports. A production department, for example, may include production quotas, level and quality of productivity, price and quality of resources used. It may comment on quality standards in the department. The report may list the names of the people in the department, recognize outstanding performances, and record turnover in personnel. It documents financial performance relating to cost of labor, cost of raw materials, overhead, and profit. Information from the departmental reports is then used for the company's annual report.

Exhibit 5.9   **Policies**

PERSONNEL POLICY
ATTENDANCE IMPROVEMENT PROGRAM

Purpose

It is the purpose of this policy to ensure the satisfactory attendance of all employees.

Policy

Punctuality and regular attendance are expected of all employees. This is important not only in maintaining high productivity but also in promoting morale among all employees.

General Rules

1. All employees must be in their assigned places and ready for work at the designated starting time.

2. All employees shall remain in their respective places of work during working hours. Employees shall not visit other employees or other departments except in the line of duty.

Reporting of Absences

1. If an employee cannot report to work, the supervisor should be informed a day in advance if possible or, in the case of an emergency, as soon as possible.

2. Reasons for absences or tardiness must be stated in writing.

3. If an absence of more than one day is likely, the employee has to inform the supervisor how many days he or she expects to be absent.

4. Absences exceeding three days will require a physician's statement before the employee may return to work.

Definition of Absences

1. Excused Absence - Any absence that is excused in writing by management prior to the occurrence and all absences covered by the current contract (jury duty, funeral leave, work-related injuries, vacations).

2. Unexcused Absence - Any absence that is not excused unless the employee calls the plant and reports off prior to the scheduled work time.

3. Absence Due to Sickness - Any unexcused absence during which the employee is under care of a physician. To qualify for this classification, the employee must present a doctor's certificate stating that the employee was under the doctor's care during the absence.

4. Occasion - Each day of an unexcused absence will be counted as one (1) occasion. Each occurrence of an absence due to sickness will be counted as one (1) occasion. If a doctor's certificate is not presented, each day of an absence will be counted as an unexcused absence.

Exhibit 5.9   **Policies (*continued*)**

Personnel Policy   p. 2

Timetable

Each employee's attendance record will be measured on the basis of 12 consecutive
months. After the first 12 months have elapsed, the first month will be dropped
from the measurement period upon the completion of each consecutive month. For
example, at the conclusion of month 13, month 1 will be dropped.

Enforcement

The following disciplinary actions will be taken:

3 occasions -- verbal warning
6 occasions -- written warning
9 occasions -- 3-day suspension
12 occasions -- suspension with intent to terminate

Exhibit 5.10   **Procedures**

Procedures for Processing Workers' Compensation Claims

1. When an accident occurs, the supervisor is responsible for filing an accident report with the Personnel Office.

2. The Personnel Office files Form 45 (state form).
    a. If the accident is recordable, the form is sent to the State Industrial Commission and to the insurance company.

    b. If the accident is not recordable, the form is only sent to the insurance company.

3. Medical bills are sent to the Personnel Office by the employee, the hospital, or the doctor. The amounts are recorded and then sent to the insurance company.

4. The insurance company sends payment to the Personnel Office, the hospital, or the doctor.

5. If lost time is involved, the insurance company sends the compensation check to the Personnel Office, which forwards the amount to the employee.

6. The insurance company is informed by telephone when the employee returns to work.

7. If a claim is questionable, the insurance company will be notified by the Personnel Office via telephone or letter. If necessary, the insurance company will conduct further inquiries. The insurance company will determine whether the claim is justified. The insurance company will send a justification to the Personnel Office if the claim is denied.

8. If an employee seeks a settlement for an injury, the employee has two options.
    a. The employee can obtain a lawyer who will file an adjustment with the State Industrial Commission. The Personnel Office will be notified and will forward the information to the insurance company. The insurance company will turn the case over to its lawyers. The insurance company's lawyers and the employee's lawyer will meet to settle the case. If they cannot agree, then the case will go before the arbitrator of the State Industrial Commission. Present at the hearing will be the employee, his or her lawyer, the insurance company's lawyer, the Personnel Office manager, and any necessary witnesses.
    b. The employee may contact the Personnel Office directly about a settlement. The Personnel Office will then contact the insurance company. The insurance company will make an initial settlement offer by phone based on the facts and the information provided by the Personnel Office. If the employee is not satisfied with the settlement, the insurance company will discuss the matter with the employee directly. If they reach an agreement, the arbitrator of the State Industrial Commission has to approve it. If the employee and the insurance company do not reach an agreement, the employee may go to a lawyer.

9. Settlement checks are usually sent to the Personnel Office. They are then recorded and forwarded to the employee.

Corporate annual reports are required by law to contain comparative financial statements and an auditors' report. Almost all go beyond these legal requirements. Most companies use their annual reports to give a history of their performance through pictures, graphs, and stories about products, employees, and customers. Most annual reports begin with a letter to the stockholders. Typically written by the chairman of the board, it gives an overview of the company's performance.

Quarterly Reports
Quarterly reports summarize an organization's performance for the last three months.

Most organizations also prepare **quarterly reports** which are less detailed than annual reports. Corporate quarterly reports, for example, present a summary of the financial performance and a brief letter written by the president. The quarterly report seldom includes pictures, graphs, or detailed descriptions and reviews of management, marketing, or production activities. Exhibit 5.11 illustrates a quarterly report.

SUMMARY OF LEARNING OBJECTIVES

To Study the Content and Organization of the Most Frequently Written Business Reports.

Minutes are summaries of meetings. They are arranged chronologically.

News Releases inform the public of important company events and decisions. Accuracy is essential.

Progress Reports inform the reader whether or not a project is on schedule. They are organized deductively.

Proposals may be solicited or unsolicited. They identify the qualifications of the person who will do the project. The reader needs a detailed plan for execution and a budget, particularly when comparing several proposals.

Feasibility Studies examine whether or not a project can be done. The report should be arranged deductively.

Justification Reports are unsolicited recommendation reports. They are presented in deductive order to hold the interest of the reader.

Staff Reports are written for management by management staff.

Job Descriptions must clearly identify tasks to be performed and the qualifications considered necessary to perform them.

Policies and Procedures inform employees of rights, obligations, and company rules. They must be clear and unambiguous.

Annual and Quarterly Reports are periodic and systematic summaries of an organization's activities and performance. They are used both internally and externally.

Exhibit 5.11   **Corporate Quarterly Report**

May 9, 1985

**To the Shareholders of
Masco Industries, Inc.:**

Masco Industries net income for the three-month period ended March 31, 1985, increased 17 percent from the comparable period in 1984 to $7.5 million or $1.10 per share. Net sales, aided by recent acquisitions, were $148 million, an increase of 6 percent from the previous year.

Sales of custom engineered components for the first quarter increased 10 percent, sales of oil-field and related products increased 8 percent while other specialty industrial products sales decreased 5 percent, primarily as a result of decreased steel production, which impacts demand for certain of our products.

Net income for a portion of the quarter was favorably impacted by our equity in the earnings of Nimas Corporation, a newly formed corporation, comprised of the industrial and defense operations of NI Industries and owned 50 percent by Masco Industries and 50 percent by Masco Corporation. This equity income, combined with income from the investment of our excess cash in marketable securities, resulted in a lower tax rate for the quarter.

Although the softening experienced in some of our markets during the last half of 1984 has continued, resulting in a modest decline in operating profit for the first quarter of 1985, when compared with the strong first quarter of 1984, recent acquisitions and our business outlook for the remainder of the year lead us to believe 1985 will be a year of significant growth for Masco Industries.

The Company also announced the election of Mr. Peter R. Fink as a new Director. Mr. Fink is President and Chief Executive of R. P. Scherer Corporation, manufacturers of specialty pharmaceutical products. His election expands the Board of Directors to six members.

Richard Manoogian
President

Consolidated Condensed Statements of Income

	Three Months Ended March 31		Twelve Months Ended March 31	
	1985	1984	**1985**	1984
Net sales	**$148,240,000**	$140,220,000	**$553,010,000**	$467,310,000
Cost of sales	**103,830,000**	96,760,000	**384,280,000**	328,250,000
Selling, general and administrative expenses	**21,390,000**	17,470,000	**78,650,000**	65,830,000
	125,220,000	114,230,000	**462,930,000**	394,080,000
Operating profit	**23,020,000**	25,990,000	**90,080,000**	73,230,000
Other expense, net	**10,340,000**	13,650,000	**43,070,000**	7,740,000
Income before income taxes	**12,680,000**	12,340,000	**47,010,000**	65,490,000
Income taxes	**5,200,000**	5,930,000	**22,140,000**	31,150,000
Net income	**$ 7,480,000**	$ 6,410,000	**$ 24,870,000**	$ 34,340,000
Earnings per share (1)	**$1.10**	$ .94	**$3.66**	—
Average shares outstanding	**6,800,000**	6,800,000	**6,800,000**	—

(1) Assumes 6,800,000 shares outstanding at January 1, 1984, which shares were issued May 1, 1984.

Net income for the twelve months ended March 31, 1984, is not comparable to 1985 due to interest expense on the $320 million of 16 percent Subordinated Debentures and the elimination of interest income on the receivable previously due from Masco Corporation, both of which resulted from the 1984 restructuring of the Company.

Source: Masco Industries, Inc. 1985 Annual Report.

QUESTIONS AND PROBLEMS

1. Locate and examine at least two short reports that are typical for your major field of study.
2. What is a staff report?
3. What are the major parts in a progress report, justification report?
4. Familiarize yourself with *The Wall Street Journal Index* or any other index. Write instructions (procedures) for its use.
5. Write a progress report on a project you are doing for one of your classes.
6. Write a report on the feasibility of your going to Europe next summer.
7. Discuss the main parts of a job description.
8. Write a job description for the officers of a student organization of which you are a member.
9. Your university is in the process of establishing quiet dorm floors where students can study without the typical dorm noise. Write policies for those quiet floors.
10. Take minutes of the next club meeting you attend. Review your minutes several days after the meeting to check how much they help you in reconstructing what went on during the meeting.

CHAPTER SIX

REPORT

PLANNING

LEARNING OBJECTIVES

- To study the planning process for reports.
- To examine the parts of a report plan.
- To examine three types of report plans.

In order to communicate successfully, the report writer must carefully study the biases, the needs, and the background of the reader. The writer furthermore must look at the report's intended use. In short, the writer must plan before beginning to write.

Planning is essential to successful communication, but a plan is exactly that, a plan. It provides a working basis, but it can never anticipate all eventualities. The plan, therefore, should be not only as complete as possible but also flexible. After all, the plan is a tool, not an end in itself. It will always need revisions and improvements before it is implemented. If the writer clings to the first draft because she has decided it is THE PLAN, the problem may remain unsolved. An architect makes many preliminary drawings before the final blueprints. Similarly, a report writer usually revises a plan several times before it is workable.

Planning is an essential element in good report writing, but the extent of planning in any given situation will depend on the complexity of the problem. In this chapter we will discuss three types of plans:

1. Informal plan—a simple outline, usually just a few notes for the writer's own use.

Intermediate Plan
The intermediate plan is usually written in memo form.

2. Intermediate plan—usually no longer than one page.

Formal Proposal
The formal proposal is a written and formal report plan.

3. Formal proposal—a statement of several pages that becomes the organizational plan for a large project.

The writer can send an **intermediate plan** as a memo or a **formal proposal** as a formal planning document to the person who requested the report and ask for verification of the plan.

THE PLANNING PROCESS

If you have ever conducted an experiment in biology, planned a research report for marketing, or outlined a term paper for an English class, you have already used many of the tools necessary for successful planning.

You may ask yourself why a plan is necessary. You may argue that you are familiar with the problems you face on the job and are reluctant to waste time on planning when you could already work at solving the problem and write the report.

An article in *The Wall Street Journal* reported the following about planning:

> In a work environment, where day-to-day pressures are extremely demanding, formal planning systems *require* managers to devote time to thinking about the future of their businesses. As a supplement to "gut feel," formal systems constitute an analytical, rigorous, and methodical approach to organization.[1]

Planning helps to approach a problem rationally rather than emotionally. Planning helps to organize an approach to collecting the data, organizing the facts, analyzing alternatives, and communicating findings in a written report. Planning helps to arrive at conclusions that are based on facts rather than on feelings. Planning helps to arrive at a good decision based on a logical examination of all the facts. A plan provides guidance.

Let us assume your company has decided to take advantage of the latest technology and automate the office. You are asked to evaluate word processing systems and present your findings and recommendations in a formal report to upper management. From the beginning of the investigation, you are excited about the available equipment, which you think can boost productivity and save money. After looking at all the cost factors, you recommend a centralized word processing system because it is most cost effective.

The system is installed, but the predicted boost in productivity and savings just does not materialize. You are asked to determine where the problem lies. When you talk to people and observe how they work, you find that most of them are used to working independently. The new system does not take this work style into consideration. Workers feel threatened and uncomfortable with the new arrangement. You come to the conclusion that a decentralized system would have been much better for your company.

This problem could have been avoided if you had talked to people at the beginning, observed their work styles, and made a recommendation that took those factors into consideration. You should have planned your investigation better.

THE SCIENTIFIC METHOD

Scientific Approach to Problem Solving
The scientific approach is an orderly and organized process for solving problems.

When you write a business report or when you carry out a business project, you apply the **scientific approach to problem solving**. In order to plan the report or the project well, you must be familiar with the steps of the scientific process as outlined below:

1. Identify the problem—To identify the problem correctly, you must distinguish between problem and symptom. Let us assume your business is losing money. At first thought you may say that the loss of money is the problem. It is, however, more likely that the loss of money is the symptom of other problems. Perhaps the declining profits are caused by poor marketing, lack of quality control, poor training of employees, or a combination of some or all of these factors.

2. Determine the methodology—How are you going to collect the necessary information? Will you talk to department supervisors? Will you call them? Will you look at past records? Will you send questionnaires to departments? Are you going to contact all departments, or will you select just a few?

3. Collect information and identify possible sources of the problem— Which departments lose money? How long has this been going on? What are possible reasons? What are possible solutions? What do the experts suggest?

4. Organize the information and the approach to solving the problem— What is the best or most appropriate order of investigation?

5. Evaluate the information—What do the facts mean? How are the facts related?

6. Draw conclusions and make recommendations—Based on the findings and the analysis, what is the best course of action to solve the problem?

7. Write the report and distribute it to the people who need the information.

These steps do not necessarily occur sequentially. It is more likely that you will evaluate the information at every step and then redefine the previous steps based on the new information. The process is similar to a continuous loop, as presented in Exhibit 6.1, rather than one circle.

The actual plan will depend on the type of report you are writing. So that your report will meet the needs of the reader and will be ready on the requested date, a detailed report plan should include the following:

Orientation to the Problem
Definition of the Problem

Exhibit 6.1   **The Planning Process**

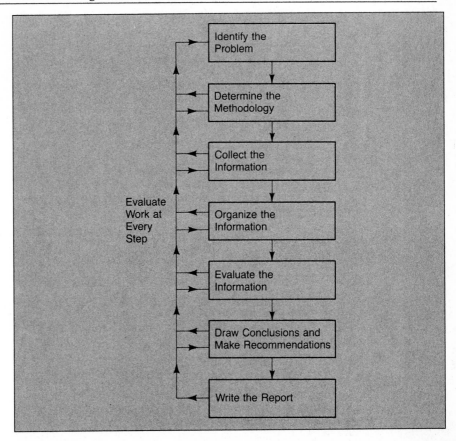

Problem Statement

Purpose Statement

Scope Statement

Limitations

Resources Required

Time Schedule

Method of Collecting Data

Tentative Outline

The terminology may vary from organization to organization, but the content of the plan will be the same.

ORIENTATION TO THE PROBLEM

The orientation may give the history or chronology of earlier attempts to deal with the problem. This background information may be included to save time when considering options that were discussed at earlier times. The writer may help the organization avoid repeating mistakes by pointing out what has and what has not worked or why the company is looking at alternatives to present systems and practices.

For example, management may consider introducing word processing because of changes in the workflow, changes in space requirements and space availability, and cost and quality of clerical help. You may think this information superfluous because everyone in the company knows about the problems. That is not necessarily true. It is possible that management is not familiar with all the changes. Also, the readers of the report may need to be *reminded* of the reasons for the investigation. The orientation to the problem saves the readers' time, because they will not need to find background information themselves.

DEFINITION OF THE PROBLEM

The clear identification of the problem is possibly the most difficult task. Yet, it is the most important step in the planning process. A problem that is not clearly understood cannot be solved. Defining the problem can mean a search through a labyrinth of parts and processes, departments, rules, organizational setups, and personalities.

You may know that your company's sales are down, but nobody will explain why. The cause could be in many areas. Should you examine advertising, personnel, marketing budget, product quality, production schedules, or customer relations? Should you look at the whole or at a combination of several factors, or is the problem in only one of the areas? If you concentrate on the marketing department and write a report on how to improve advertising, when in reality the problem is caused by a decline in product quality, you have written the wrong report.

Some preliminary research may help you put the problem into focus. Many business people say that at this point they physically tour the company, talk to many people, observe, ask questions, compare notes, and listen. No one way works best. Experience helps, but it alone is not enough.

Problem definition is time consuming and requires reflection. When you believe you have the problem clearly in mind, write it down, think about it further, and discuss it with others. But keep in mind that a committee agreement on what the problem is provides no guarantee that it has been correctly identified. Adjustments and changes may still be necessary as you collect more data.

When you are planning a report to solve complex problems, group discussions can help define the problem. Because major problems are seldom caused by one factor, the experience of people with different backgrounds may be needed for the task. Some companies form special committees or task forces to pinpoint problems.

If people from several departments are involved in planning, the departments will be more likely to accept the recommendations in the final report. If, for example, the marketing manager after much research defines the problem of declining sales as a production problem, production will be hesitant to accept the problem definition. If both the marketing and the production departments define the problem as a production problem, the report on how to solve the problem will be more readily accepted.

Brainstorming
In brainstorming either a group or an individual collects and organizes ideas to define the problem.

When group members first try to focus on the problem, they may engage in **brainstorming**. Usually brainstorming is thought of as a group effort, but the process also applies if you are working alone. In brainstorming the following guidelines are useful:

1. Write down whatever comes to mind as quickly as possible without stopping to analyze the ideas.

2. Continue brainstorming until you have exhausted all possible answers to the basic questions: what, where, when, how, why.

3. Examine basic assumptions, especially those you intend to use for value judgments.

4. Consider as many alternative solutions as possible.

5. Consider the implications to your organization of the problem and its potential solutions. What are the implications for cost, profit, procedures, people, materials, equipment, and legalities?

PROBLEM STATEMENT

When you believe that you have the problem clearly in mind, write it down again. You can use one of three formats: a question, a declarative sentence, or a fragment. If your assignment is to analyze a new training program, for example, you might state the problem in one of these ways:

Question form:	*How does the new program affect the departments in the company?*
	or
	What are the results of the new training program?
Declarative sentence:	*This report examines the results of the new training program.*
	or
	This report analyzes the effect of the new training program on the departments in the company.
Fragment:	*To examine the results of the new training program.*

All three types of problem statements are acceptable. If the writer asks a question such as "How can we measure the success of the new training program?" or "What elements have contributed to the success of the new training program?" then this question must be answered in the report. The writer can check the progress against the question and easily determine whether the focus is still on the problem. The question form tends to be more lively and interesting than the other two; it is concise and provides focus.

Questions that call for a *yes* or *no* answer do not get to the bottom of the problem, and they usually do not give much guidance in organizing and planning the report. For example, a better question than "Is the new training program successful?" would be "How successful is the new training program?" This problem statement forces the writer to examine the reasons for success or failure of the new training program and then conclude whether it is actually working or not. Ultimately, the reader wants to know not only *yes* or *no* but also *how, why, when,* and *where*.

The declarative form is best when the problem is stated as a hypothesis, as in the following examples:

The new advertising campaign has resulted in a 20 percent increase in sales.

No relationship exists between training and job satisfaction.

The first hypothesis is a positive hypothesis—there is a relationship. The second hypothesis is a null hypothesis—there is no relationship. (A later chapter on primary research will discuss hypothesis formation in detail.)

The fragment form, "to examine the results of the new training program," is a combination of purpose and problem statement. It works well for shorter and less complex reports. For difficult problems, which require more detailed planning, the writer may want to keep purpose and problem separate.

To continue the example, assume that you have decided the problem statement is "How does the new training program affect the departments in the company?" In the report you must examine the impact of training on each of the company's departments. In a list of all possible areas of impact, you might include the following:

Salaries	Selection for programs
Mobility	Time spent in training
Job satisfaction	Productivity
Quality	Trends
Cost	

When brainstorming to produce a tentative list, you should not be concerned about repetition and overlap. You can organize and refine the list later. The final list might look something like this:

Aspects of Inquiry	Possible Impact	Departments
Cost	Direct cost of training	Marketing Personnel Production Finance
	Indirect costs, time spent in training	Marketing Personnel Production Finance
Productivity	Impact on quality	Marketing Personnel Production Finance
	Impact on quantity	Marketing Personnel Production Finance
Selection process	Employees select	Marketing Personnel Production Finance
	Management selects	Marketing Personnel Production Finance
Mobility	Upward mobility	Marketing Personnel Production Finance
	Outward mobility	Marketing Personnel Production Finance
Salaries	People with training	Marketing Personnel Production Finance
	People without training	Marketing Personnel Production Finance

continued

Aspects of Inquiry	Possible Impact	Departments
Satisfaction	Absenteeism	Marketing Personnel Production Finance
	Accidents	Marketing Personnel Production Finance
	Attitudes	Marketing Personnel Production Finance
Trends	National economy Competition Product line	

The breakdown of the problem statement into key components provides a tentative list for the investigation and report organization. A careful review of the list can show crucial omissions and signal the need for reorganization and grouping of aspects.

PURPOSE STATEMENT

In a good request for a report, the purpose for the report will be clear. Often, however, the person requesting information may not know exactly how it will be used. The information requested may seem necessary, but the ultimate use may still be unclear. In this case it is the writer's task to formulate the purpose and show the purpose statement to the requester for verification. Without a clear purpose statement the writer may easily write the wrong report for the situation. Questions that may help in formulating the purpose are the following:

1. What is the purpose of this report? Is the report to inform, persuade, analyze data, compare options?

2. What is the problem?

3. Who will read the report?

Although the purpose statement needs to answer only the first question directly, the writer must know the answers to the other two. An example of a purpose statement would be "The purpose of this report is to examine available word processing systems and to recommend the system most appropriate for Grawe and Fine, Inc."

Some researchers use the words *problem* and *purpose* interchangeably. If the terms are used precisely, however, the purpose of the report is to do something: to solve the problem, to provide information, to evaluate data. The problem, on the other hand, is something that requires investigation. It may be a question that requires an answer. It may be a situation that as yet lacks focus but that clearly needs looking into. Conceptually, the problem and the purpose statements have different functions. The following examples may help to distinguish between the two:

Problem: *What is the best word processing system for the corporation?*

Purpose: *To recommend a system to upper management for implementation.*

Problem: *What are the major activities of the sales representatives in any given week?*

Purpose: *To summarize the major activities and present the report to the sales manager for training new sales representatives.*
or
To summarize the activities and present the report to upper management to show that the activities warrant a higher salary.

SCOPE STATEMENT

Scope
Scope focuses on selected aspects of a problem.

Scope is the narrowing of the problem to the most important elements in order to reach the stated purpose. For example, there may not be a need to examine the impact of a proposed solution on all departments. The recipient of the report may only need to know the impact on the production and advertising departments. Or headquarters may want a study of the impact of a training program in the eastern division only. Or the personnel manager may want to know the impact on job satisfaction and attitudes. In the scope statement the writer clearly states the aspects of the problem to be examined in detail. The scope statement can be part of the problem statement, or it can be a separate statement. The choice will depend on the amount of detail requested and considered necessary.

Limitations
Limitations have a negative influence on the writing and planning process.

LIMITATIONS

In the scope statement the writer consciously sets the boundaries for the report. **Limitations**, on the other hand, are beyond the control of the writer. Limitations affect the applicability and usefulness of the report. For example, the inability to collect information on the advertising budget of Company X is a limitation if the purpose of the report is to compare advertising of Company Y and Company X. An important aspect of the investigation is missing. The data on Company X may be based on press reports and hearsay, but the writer cannot verify the data by looking at the records of Company X. Conclusions concerning advertising expenditures by the two companies must therefore be considered with caution.

As another example, assume you are working under extreme time pressure. If you had three weeks, you could prepare an in-depth report. Because the report must be ready in three days, you can at best provide an overview and give an analysis of selected aspects of the problem. Still another type of limitation involves conflicting and inaccurate information. You might, for example, have to examine the possibility of establishing a subsidiary in a developing country where population and income statistics are often not available or conflicting and inaccurate.

Because limitations affect the reliability of a report, they should be clearly stated. The writer must be aware of them in the planning process. Some projects may have to be terminated until major limitations can be overcome.

A statement of limitations might read: "Because of production deadlines this report has to be prepared in three weeks. For the investigation a budget of $XX is available."

RESOURCES REQUIRED

A report must include information about the need for any special equipment, staff, time, or money. If a project will need two additional people for two months and you do not mention this fact, someone reviewing the proposal surely will ask, "How will the research be done and by whom?" If collecting your data on site selection for a new plant requires travel and on-site inspection, you must state the cost involved in collecting the information. Management may want to postpone a project if the cost exceeds a certain limit. Therefore, you must determine what resources are available, what resources you would need to do an exceptional job, and what the minimum would be to do an acceptable job. You have to set priorities, rank the options available to solve the problem, and decide which aspects are most important. The budget should reflect the priorities established.

TIME SCHEDULE

In the time schedule you spell out steps in the project along with corresponding dates. Be realistic and allow for a few more days than the minimum. The schedule will become a working schedule for the project and will also help your management to measure your progress. A typical timetable for a survey might be:

September 1	Finalize questionnaire
September 6	Mail questionnaire
September 30	Key responses into computer
October 1	Perform computer analysis
October 2–6	Analyze computer output
October 8–10	Write report
October 15	Complete report

METHOD OF COLLECTING DATA

Your written plan must describe how you will collect the information for the report. This description will usually be more detailed if you plan to use primary research or a combination of primary and secondary research than if you will rely on secondary research alone. For primary research you may need a detailed description of sample size, sample selection, and type of investigation (that is, telephone, mail questionnaire, personal interview, type of statistical analysis). This information will help the reader decide if the methods you plan to use are valid and appropriate for the stated problem. For a detailed discussion of samples and data collection see Chapter 9.

TENTATIVE OUTLINE

The tentative outline will provide guidance in the research process and help with organizing the final report. It is a working outline; it will probably change as you progress.

THREE TYPES OF PLANS

THE INFORMAL PLAN

To plan a one-page memo you may simply want to make a few notes for yourself. No official plan is necessary. In organizing your thoughts you should answer three questions:

What is the problem to be solved?

Who is going to read the report?

What use will the reader make of the information provided?

For short and simple reports you may just plan in your head, but you do have to organize your thoughts.

THE INTERMEDIATE PLAN

An intermediate plan consisting of a statement of purpose, problem, and method may be all that is necessary for reports between two and eight pages long. This intermediate planning approach is illustrated in the following example.

Tim Richards, the new personnel vice president, wants a report on how the Women in Management program is doing. Terry Morris, his assistant, has two weeks to write a report. In view of the time frame and the wording of the request, Terry decides that she must write a short plan in order to clarify the purpose, state the problem, and outline her approach (method). She does not need special resources, there are no limitations, and the report is not so complex that she has to make a detailed time schedule.

The plan could look like this:

Purpose: *To inform management of the current status of the project.*

Problem: *What is the status of the Equal Employment Opportunity (EEO) policy in the company?*
1. *To describe the EEO policy of the company.*
2. *To compare current figures concerning women in management with those of the past three years.*
3. *To describe the current program:*
    a. Selection of participants.
    b. Level of commitment.
    c. Curriculum.
4. *To discuss appropriate methods for improving the effectiveness of the Women in Management program.*

Method: *The report will be based on the company's current EEO report and on a report of the materials covered in the Women in Management program.*

The plan tells Tim Richards what Terry intends to do, and it has enough detail to help her collect the information and organize the report.

THE FORMAL PROPOSAL

Formal proposals are written when major projects are involved. They can serve several functions: they can become a guide for writing a report, they can be used to inform management or other interested persons of an intended project, or they may serve as a request to start a project. A formal proposal may include the following sections:

Title Page
Purpose or Objective
Description of the Problem

Orientation to the Problem
※ Scope Statement
※ Limitations
※ Budget *(optional)*
※ Timetable *What kind of*
※ Methods *↓of PRIMARY & Secondary Research*
Significance or Impact of the Study *optional*

Not all proposals have identical formats. Format, organization, and headings depend on the nature of the study and the guidelines established by those requesting a proposal or research plan. Most of the information provided in the proposal becomes part of the final report. Because the proposal is a plan for action, it is written in future tense; that is, "This report will examine. . . ." In the final report, after the research has been completed, this statement is changed to "The report examines the effects. . . ."

The formal proposal in Exhibit 6.2 is a report plan for examining insurance policies.

SUMMARY OF LEARNING OBJECTIVES

To Study the Planning Process for Reports.
The planning process follows the scientific approach to problem solving. Planning helps the writer understand the problem and organize the material. As a memo to management, the plan helps the requester decide if the report will provide the necessary information.

To Examine the Parts of a Report Plan.
In the report plan the writer defines the problem and the scope of the report. He clearly states any limitations, required resources, time schedules, and the method for collecting data.

To Examine Three Types of Report Plans.
The complexity of the plan depends on the complexity of the problem. Three types of plans are the formal proposal, the intermediate plan, and the informal plan. Planning is a tool, not an end in itself.

QUESTIONS AND PROBLEMS

1. Why is planning for report writing important?
2. Discuss the steps in the planning process. What are the functions of each step?
3. Discuss the difference between scope and limitations.

4. What is the purpose of stating the methodology in the report plan?
5. What is the difference between the report problem and the report purpose?
6. Contrast the planning process for the short, medium-length, and long reports.
7. Describe three situations that would require a business report and determine whether each situation demands an informal, intermediate, or formal plan.
8. Identify a problem of an organization to which you belong. Write a problem statement and scope statement to help you solve the problem.

NOTES

[1] John M. Stengrevics, "Corporate Planning Needn't Be an Executive Straitjacket," *The Wall Street Journal,* 26 September 1983.

Exhibit 6.2   **A Formal Proposal**

AN EXAMINATION OF INSURANCE POLICIES

A PROPOSAL

Submitted to

Committee for Graduating Seniors

Prepared by

Steve Buckingham

October 6, 19XX

Exhibit 6.2   **A Formal Proposal** (*continued*)

Audience for the Information

The report will be submitted to the Committee for Graduating Seniors. The information will be made available to all graduating seniors.

Orientation to the Problem

Most students are insured by their parents and are therefore not familiar with insurance policies. Yet, as soon as they graduate, most students will have to buy car insurance, health insurance, and life insurance. In order to receive full benefits and to purchase the most suitable policy, an understanding of various policies is necessary.

Problem Statement

This report will examine and analyze several automobile and life insurance policies from the standpoint of the new graduate's needs.

Scope Statement

This report will compare the automobile insurance policies and life insurance policies of State Farm, Allstate, and Prudential. Automobile insurance will be compared in the areas of liability coverage, physical-damage coverage, uninsured-motorist coverage, medical coverage, and cost. Life insurance will be compared in the areas of term insurance, endowment insurance, annuities, and cost.

Limitations

Because this report must be ready in two weeks, I may not have time to interview salespeople from all three companies.

Method

I will conduct mostly secondary research. I will attempt to interview insurance salespeople and study insurance literature. I also plan to interview recent graduates to collect more information on their insurance experience.

Tentative Outline

I. Introduction

II. Auto Insurance

    A. Liability Coverage
        1. State Farm
        2. Allstate
        3. Prudential

    B. Physical-Damage Coverage
        1. State Farm
        2. Allstate
        3. Prudential

    C. Uninsured-Motorist Coverage
        1. State Farm
        2. Allstate
        3. Prudential

Exhibit 6.2 **A Formal Proposal** (*continued*)

A Formal Proposal   p. 2

    D. Medical Coverage
        1. State Farm
        2. Allstate
        3. Prudential

    E. Cost
        1. State Farm
        2. Allstate
        3. Prudential

III. Life Insurance

    A. Term Insurance
        1. State Farm
        2. Allstate
        3. Prudential

    B. Endowment Insurance
        1. State Farm
        2. Allstate
        3. Prudential

    C. Annuities
        1. State Farm
        2. Allstate
        3. Prudential

    D. Cost
        1. State Farm
        2. Allstate
        3. Prudential

IV. Summary and Conclusions

Tentative Bibliography

CHAPTER SEVEN

SECONDARY

RESEARCH

LEARNING OBJECTIVES

- To understand the role of secondary research in report writing.
- To recognize different types of libraries.
- To understand the organization of libraries.
- To become familiar with computer searches.
- To evaluate sources and compile bibliography and note cards.
- To become familiar with secondary sources useful to the business writer.

THE ROLE OF
SECONDARY RESEARCH IN REPORT WRITING

Secondary research is a study of printed sources. It involves going to the library to find out what may already have been written about solutions to problems similar to the one you are researching. There is no point in sending out questionnaires, going through interviews and conducting surveys to find out what type of insurance new graduates need if the results of a similar study are available in the latest issue of *The Journal of Risk Management* or another insurance journal. You would be wasting time reinventing the wheel.

Studying the published results of the insurance investigation would provide you with basic information. After determining how the published study is similar to or different from your company's problem, you could concentrate your research on how your company could best attract recent graduates and what types of policies you would have to develop to fill their needs. The study of published materials allows you to spend most of your time on those aspects that are unique to your problem.

Secondary research sources are not limited to materials in libraries. Your company has numerous reports on operations, personnel matters, marketing strategies, and other topics. These reports have not been published in the sense that they have appeared in journals, but they are readily available to you. Government reports, tax reports, pamphlets, employee manuals, and customer-relation materials are all source materials for secondary research.

TYPES OF LIBRARIES

To the person who has never been to a library, it is a confusing place—rows upon rows of books and bound periodicals, maps, and cabinets with microfilm, all bearing numbers that make no sense; in short, a maze with a stuffy atmosphere. To the regular user, however, a library is a superb example of excellent organization. Detailed information from around the world is available within minutes. Rather than a source of frustration, the library is a source of knowledge.

To share in the excitement and challenge, the user must understand how a library works. Some things are organized the same in all libraries, and some things are different.

GENERAL LIBRARIES

Only the Library of Congress carries all of the books, magazines, and journals published in the United States. Other libraries carry only the materials that best meet the needs and wants of their users. Public libraries, which have clients with many different interests, are rather diversified. They have materials on many topics, but most of the books and periodicals are geared to the general user rather than the expert in a particular area. Public libraries are *general libraries*.

RESEARCH LIBRARIES

Most universities have extensive libraries. The materials are selected to complement the work in the classroom and facilitate research by students and faculty. These libraries are more academically oriented than public libraries. They have collections of journals in such specialized areas as science, business, and history. They carry materials that serious scholars would need in their research; therefore, these libraries are sometimes referred to as *research libraries*. They have different clients than public libraries.

SPECIAL PURPOSE LIBRARIES

More and more companies are establishing their own libraries. This development shows that secondary research does play an important role in business. Managers have found that a library saves them time. Between 1978 and 1982, the number of company libraries rose from 5,000 to 5,600. Some experts believe that the number will exceed 7,200 by 1990. In addition, many companies are enlarging their libraries. For example, Wang Laboratories, Inc., increased the size of its library from 2,000 square feet to 3,000 square feet and increased the library budget to $300,000.

Of course, company libraries are specialized. They carry only those materials that are essential for the company's business. State Farm Insurance, for example, concentrates on materials that are related to insurance, such as insurance journals, government regulations relating to insurance, data processing materials, and legal documents. Most accounting firms and law firms have libraries for their special needs. Company librarians would not spend money on fiction, philosophy, or ancient history because they are building *special purpose libraries*.

LIBRARY SYSTEMS

Fortunately, most libraries belong to a library system. Libraries within the system have an agreement that they will share their materials. In central Illinois, for example, a resident of Peoria can visit the public library and request materials from Illinois State University. In addition to the regional systems there is the interlibrary loan system. Students at Illinois State University may request a book from any library in the country through interlibrary loan. The fast, reliable service increases the available sources tremendously.

THE ORGANIZATION OF LIBRARIES

Libraries either use the Dewey Decimal System or the Library of Congress system for cataloging their holdings. In recent years more and more libraries have switched from the Dewey Decimal System to the Library of Congress cataloging system because it provides a more detailed breakdown of areas of knowledge.

Under the Dewey Decimal System, knowledge is broken down into 10 categories using numbers 000 through 900. The Library of Congress system uses letters of the alphabet and thus allows for the creation of more areas of knowledge, as shown in Exhibit 7.1. Business is grouped with social sciences under the letter H. Business publications can be found under the subcategories HD and HF. The **call numbers** consist of letters followed by numbers to identify a particular book or periodical:

Call Number
The call number is the identification number for each book in the library.

HD 30.28 .A24 1983 Amara, Roy, and Andrew J. Lipinski. *Business Planning for an Uncertain Future, Scenarios & Strategies*. New York: Pergamon Press, 1983.

HF5718.J6 *The Journal of Business Communication*. The journal is published by the Association for Business Communication.

THE CARD CATALOG

The card catalog is most useful for finding books. The two types of card catalogs are the author–title catalog and the subject catalog. If you have either the title of the book you need or the author's name, you can locate the

Exhibit 7.1   **Classification Systems**

The classifications under the Dewey Decimal System:

000	General Works	500	Pure Science
100	Philosophy	600	Useful Arts
200	Religion	700	Fine Arts
300	Social Sciences	800	Literature
400	Philology	900	History

The classifications under the Library of Congress System:

A	General Works	O	not used yet
B	Philosophy and Religion	P	Language and Literature
C	History	Q	Science
D	Universal and Old World History	R	Medicine
E,F	America	S	Agriculture
G	Geography, Anthropology, Sports	T	Technology
H	Social Sciences	U	Military Science
I	not used yet	V	Naval Science
J	Political Science	W	not used yet
K	Law	X	not used yet
L	Education	Y	not used yet
M	Music	Z	Bibliography and Library Science
N	Fine Arts		

Author–Title Catalog
The author–title catalog lists books by author or title.

Subject Catalog
Books are listed according to subject matter.

book by using the **author–title catalog**. Cards for authors and titles are in alphabetical order. If there is no card, the book is not available in the library, but the librarian may be able to obtain it for you through interlibrary loan.

In many cases you may know the topic you want to investigate but not the titles or authors of any books on the topic. In that case your options are to refer either to the two-volume *Library of Congress Subject Headings* or to the **subject catalog**. The *Library of Congress Subject Headings,* usually located near the reference desk, will provide you with a list of subject headings and subheadings that are used in cataloging books. Knowing the terms may save you time when you use the subject catalog.

Subject catalog cards are in alphabetical order. Under every subject you find the titles of books relating to the particular subject. Working with the subject catalog requires imagination. You must be able to think of possible subject headings under which information on your topic could be listed. Where would you look if you wanted information on training programs, on the ethics of advertising to children, on factors to be considered in site selection for a new subsidiary, or on the effect of aerosol cans on the environment? Fortunately, cards direct you to several subject headings with the notations *see also* or *listed under.*

Let us assume you are preparing a report on improving your report writing skills. You are looking for research on precise and concise writing and on effective use of the English language. If you know neither authors who have written on the subject nor the titles of any books, you must start with the subject catalog. Under what subject could you find material? Because you are working on the improvement of writing, you might start with the word *writing* and find these subheadings:

Writing addresses

Writing as a profession

Writing—copying process

Writing—history.

These headings do not appear useful. As you thumbed through the subject cards, however, you came across the word *rhetoric*. Looking up *rhetoric,* you find among the subheadings:

Rhetoric—ancient

Rhetoric, dictionaries

Again, nothing appears useful. As you think of other possibilities, the subject *composition* comes up. Under that subject you find a card with this notation:

See letter writing, rhetoric, also subdivision composition and exercises under names of languages, e.g. English language—composition and exercises.

You try *English language,* and this time you are lucky. Depending on the books your library carries, you may find the following titles:

PE	Brinegar, Bonnie Carter.
1475	Technical writing: a guide with models.
B74	Glenview, Ill.: Scott, Foresman Co., 1983.
1983	

PE	Flesch, Rudolf Franz. 1911-
1497	How to write plain English: a book for
l3	lawyers and consumers/Rudolf Flesch;
F57	foreword by Michael Pertschuk. New
1979	York: Harper & Row, 1979.

PE	Gunning, Robert. 1908-
1408	The technique of clear writing, rev. ed.
g93	New York: McGraw-Hill, 1968.
1968	

Finding these books took quite some time. If you had known the title of one of the books or the name of one author, the search would have been much easier. For example, assume you had known that Rudolf Flesch wrote several books on your topic. You could have gone directly to the author–title catalog. Under Flesch you would have found several entries, including *How to Write Plain English: A Book for Lawyers and Consumers.*

The catalog card may give additional valuable information. The card in Exhibit 7.2, for example, lists other subject headings pertinent to the topic. The author–title catalog, if used as a guide to the subject catalog, can save the researcher much time.

The catalog card may also indicate whether the book has a bibliography. If it does, the researcher can again save time by checking the sources listed in the bibliography against the author–title index, thus bypassing the subject index.

Many people argue that books are too outdated to be useful in business research. In many cases this is true. If you want the latest information on advertising, for example, you will hardly find it in books. Although the lag-time between collecting the material for a book, the writing, and the printing has become shorter, it can still be about two years. For up-to-date information you should look at the periodical literature.

Yet, books do have their place in business research. If you look for the foundations of a theory in marketing, for a discussion of the principles of advertising, for research on the similarities and differences between various management theories, or for information on standard accounting practices, books will be helpful. Books provide background information; they can give detailed discussion of timeless principles. In an article an issue can be discussed in detail, but seldom will an article put the issue in context.

Exhibit 7.2   **Copy of Catalog Card**

```
PE
1497    Flesch, Rudolf Franz, 1911-
  13        How to write plain English:  a book for
          lawyers and consumers/Rudolf
F57     Flesch; foreword by Michael Pertschuk.
1979    --1st ed.--New York:  Harper & Row,
          © 1979
          xiii, 126p.; 21cm.
          Includes index.


          1. English language--rhetoric
          2. English language--terms and phrases
          3. Law--Lanugage.  I.  Title
INS    in 11 Ap 80 c1    IAIAca    76-26225
```

PERIODICALS INDEX SYSTEM

Where do you start to look for articles? Even if you know the title and author of an article, you will not find them in the catalog. Neither, obviously, can you search through all the journals to find information. For your search of periodical literature you must be familiar with the **periodicals index system,** which catalogs periodical articles by particular fields of interest. The index you will probably use most is the *Business Periodicals Index.*

Periodicals Index System
The periodicals index system organizes and lists periodical articles.

Most periodicals indexes provide, in every volume, detailed instructions on their organization and use. Exhibit 7.3 gives information on how to use the *Business Periodicals Index.*

Some indexes, such as the *Accountants' Index,* are organized by both subject and author. The *Business Periodicals Index* and others are organized by subject, as illustrated in Exhibit 7.4. To use the *Business Periodicals Index* effectively you should follow these steps:

1. Starting with the most recent volume, look up your subject in the index. You may have to try several subject headings and cross references.

2. Pick out all promising articles under your subject and copy all the information listed. If the title of the periodical is abbreviated, check the abbreviations in the front of the index for the complete title.

3. Repeat the process using the next most recent volumes, and work backward through as many volumes as necessary. This system will assure you of finding the most up-to-date material.

4. Use the *Periodical Directory* at the library to find the location for the periodicals you need. Copy the location for each. Some libraries assign call numbers to periodicals. If your library does, you need to check the call number only once. The *Harvard Business Review,* for example, has the same call number regardless of whether you are looking for an article published in June 1967 or July 1986.

NEWSPAPER INDEXES

When you think about newspapers with material relevant to business interests, you probably think immediately of *The Wall Street Journal,* but several other newspapers carry extensive business information. *The New York Times, The Christian Science Monitor, The Los Angeles Times,* and other major newspapers in cities all over the country can be helpful to the business researcher. The easiest to use, however, are *The Wall Street Journal, The New York Times,* and *The Christian Science Monitor* because they are indexed.

The Wall Street Journal Index is organized by subject and corporations. If you want to read about changes in car manufacturing at Chrysler, for example, you can look under either auto or Chrysler. The first half of the index lists corporate news alphabetically by company (Exhibit 7.5). The sec-

Exhibit 7.3 *Business Periodicals Index* Instructions

Explanatory Notes

ARRANGEMENT. *Business Periodicals Index* is a subject index and all entries are arranged in one alphabet. Subject headings beginning with numerals appear before those beginning with the letter A.

SUBJECT HEADINGS. This Index uses specific headings and subheadings. Biographical articles are indexed under biographees. An article describing a company is indexed under the name of the company.

REFERENCES. *See* references guide the user from a term not used as a heading to a term that is used. *See also* references guide the user from a term used as a heading to related headings under which additional material may be found. *See also* references have been made for most companies from their primary industry.

Sample entries:

Building industry *See* Construction industry
Construction industry
    See also
    Red Seal Development Corp.
Builders feel used by user fees proposals [for FHA and VA
    mortgage loans] B. Thompson. *Prof Build Apartm Bus*
    50:32+ My '85
                Accidents
Trench deaths spur crackdown. *Eng News-Rec* 214:56 Je
    13 '85
                Statistics
Housing and construction. See Financial and business
statistics section in issues of Federal Reserve Bulletin

EXPLANATION. The first line in the sample entry directs the user from a term not used as a heading to the established heading Construction industry. On the second line is the subject heading **Construction industry**. Under this heading the user is referred by a *see also* reference to an article which is about a particular company in the industry, Red Seal Development Corp. After the *see also* is an article about the construction industry entitled "Builders feel used by user fees proposals," by Boyce Thompson. This article will be found in the periodical *Professional Builder/Apartment Business*, volume 50, page 32 and continuing on later pages of the May 1985 issue. A title enhancement, "for FHA and VA mortgage loans," has been added by the indexer to clarify the meaning of the title. Square brackets are used to indicate these editorial interpolations. On the next line the user will find the subheading **Accidents.** This is a subdivision of the heading **Construction industry**. Under this subheading appears an entry about accidents in the industry. The last entry—**Statistics**—is another subheading for this industry and the reader will find the entry entitled "Housing and construction" which is a regular feature in the *Federal Reserve Bulletin.*

Exhibit 7.4   **Arrangement of *Business Periodicals Index***

---

94   BUSINESS PERIODICALS INDEX

Coal industry—*cont.*
Data processing
The Colliery Planning System—a microcomputer-based
  aid to colliery (production) planning. K. P. Beaumont.
  flowchart tabs *J Oper Res Soc* 36:175-81 Mr '85
Programs
Representing discrete events in system dynamics models:
  a theoretical application to modelling coal production
  [computer simulation packages] R. G. Coyle. flowcharts
  graphs *J Oper Res Soc* 36:307-18 Ap '85
Export-import trade
Coal mining: the pits. *Economist* 295:75-6 My 4 '85
Taxation
Strategy and market structure in western coal taxation.
  C. D. Kolstad and F. A. Wolak, Jr. bibl graphs tabs
  Rev Econ Stat 67:239-49 My '85
Great Britain
See also
  National Coal Board (Great Britain)
The British coal stalemate. N. Madlin. *Manage Rev*
  74:10-12 Mr '85
Western states
Strategy and market structure in western coal taxation.
  C. D. Kolstad and F. A. Wolak, Jr. bibl graphs tabs
  Rev Econ Stat 67:239-49 My '85
Coal miners
See also
  Strikes—Coal miners

Coated fabrics
High-performance coatings and finishes expand uses. R.
  G. Mansfield. *Text World* 135:58-60 My '85
Coated paper *See* Paper coatings
Coatings
See also
  Coated fabrics
  Paper coatings
  Release agents (Coatings)
  Zinc coating
Coating a mighty laser's lens [Nova Laser] J. Donohue
  and S. R. Jones. il *Chem Week* 136:14 Ap 17 '85
A hot idea for icy windshields [electrically heated coatings]
  J. Schwartz. il *Chem Week* 136:17-18 Ap 24 '85
Mobay executive counts gains for two-component
  urethanes. *Chem Mark Rep* 227:21 Ap 22 '85
Tripod for growth: Material Sciences counts on joint
  venture, acquisitions to propel coil business. T. N.
  Troxell, Jr. graph tab *Barrons* 65:33 Jl 1 '85
Coaxial cables
See also
  Local area networks—Cables
Cobalt
Cobalt and manganese from low-grade ores. *Chem Eng
  News* 63:8 Ap 1 '85
Cutting dependence on strategic metals [processes that
  use less cobalt and chromium] J. Fierman. il *Fortune*
  112:69 Jl 22 '85

Source: *Business Periodicals Index*, September 1985, Vol. 28, No. 1, p. 94. *Business Periodicals Index* Copyright © 1985 by The H. W. Wilson Company. Material reproduced by permission of the publisher.

ond half lists general news alphabetically by subject (Exhibit 7.6). The index provides a short abstract of every article so you can determine at once whether the article will be useful.

BUSINESS DIRECTORIES

For a detailed list of Business Directories look under "Useful Secondary Sources for the Business Researcher" at the end of this chapter.

Business directories are especially helpful if you need information on a particular company. You can find the address, the names of major officers, location of subsidiaries, lists of products manufactured, sales, and profit. Some directories, such as the *Dun and Bradstreet Handbook of Credits and Collections*, provide credit ratings of corporations. Most directories are published yearly and are updated regularly throughout the year. Exhibits 7.7 and 7.8 illustrate listings in *Standard and Poor's Register*.

If, for example, you want information on American Software, Inc., you will look first in the *Standard and Poor's Index* to find the page numbers for

Exhibit 7.5   *The Wall Street Journal Index:* Corporate News

---

CHICAGO PNEUMATIC TOOL CO.
Net loss July 1 -13 wks $1,987,000; net loss July 1 -26 wks $5,933,000. 8/11-12;2

CHICAGO RIVET & MACHINE CO.
Quar div $.30, 9/20; 9/2. 8/16-47;2

CHICAGO SUN-TIMES
Publishers of the Boston Globe and the Toronto Sun surfaced as potential buyers of the Chicago Sun-Times, but their interest so far is exploratory. 8/12-6;5

CHIEF CONSOLIDATED MINING CO.
Net loss June 30 quar $39,331; net loss June 30 -6 mos $72,224. 8/12-11;1

CHIEFTAIN DEVELOPMENT CO. LTD.
Directors have recommended a 3-for-2 stock split, and have called a special shareholders' meeting Sept. 29 to vote on the proposal. 8/10-36;4
Three-for-two stock split subject to shareholder approval September 29, 1983, 10/14. 8/11-26;4
Chieftain Developments Co.'s Pacific Coast Energy Corp. unit will head a group to study the feasibility of a $1.2 billion (Canadian) liquefied natural-gas project on the west coast of Vancouver Island, British Columbia. 8/18-11;2

CHIGNIK CANNING
Canned-salmon sales appear unhurt by the latest recall. (Business Bulletin) 8/18-1;5

CHRYSLER CORP.
The Reagan administration intends to sell to the public the 14.4 million Chrysler Corp. stock warrants that the government holds; profit may top $262.8 million. 8/1-2;2
GM is betting that rebates and discount financing offers are still needed to spur the current new-car sales recovery; Ford is gambling just the opposite; Chrysler is hedging. 8/1-2;3
An executive vice president, sales and marketing, announced his retirement. 8/1-11;2
Produced 65,776 cars and trucks in July; produced 569,474 cars and trucks in 1983 to date. 8/2-12;2
1.8 million Chrysler Corp. common shares will be offered at $27.625 each, a total of $50.5 million, Aug. 1. 8/4-4;2
Officials are informally talking with bankers about setting up a $300 million line of credit. 8/4-4;4
Firm sold 30,132 units in July 21-31 period; sold 74,785 units for all of July. 8/4-4;5
Major tire makers cut prices about 1% in supply agreements for '84 model cars. 8/4-8;4
Produced 8,680 units in week ended July 30; produced 494,160 units in 1983 to date. 8/5-2;4
Firm's chairman, Lee Iacocca, asked the government to hold off on the planned sale of its 14.4 million warrants to buy Chrysler stock. 8/8-7;3
Auto makers scheduling overtime instead of recalling idled workers. 8/9-35;1

Source: *The Wall Street Journal Index.* Corporate News, August, 1983, p. 18. Reprinted by permission of *The Wall Street Journal Index,* © Dow Jones & Company, Inc. 1983. All Rights Reserved.

various entries, as shown in Exhibit 7.7. The information on American Software is given in Exhibit 7.8.

COMPUTER SEARCH SYSTEMS

Most libraries have computer systems that can help you in your secondary research. Basically, the systems are programmed to search material either by author–title or by subject. You should become familiar with the system available at your library.

Author–Title Searches. OCLC is a widely used computer program in special, corporate, university, and public libraries throughout the United States. OCLC allows you to search for books by name of author, title, or a combination of author and title. You can also search for books that are published in a series and for periodicals by title. The system does not have the capability to search for articles in periodicals or to do a subject search.

Exhibit 7.6   *The Wall Street Journal Index:* General News

AUTOS

(*see also* **Recreational Vehicles**)

The Reagan administration intends to sell to the public the 14.4 million Chrysler Corp. stock warrants that the government holds. 8/1-2;2

Chrysler Corp. officials are informally talking with bankers about setting up a $300 million line of credit. 8/4-4;4

Tough Road Ahead: U.S. auto makers face severe challenge of holding down costs as sales, production and profits grow. 8/5-42;1

Rebounding Profits: Spurred by a booming economy, firms' earnings rose 10% in the second period, in first gain since 1981; further increases expected; many retailers did well; auto makers' net surged to $1.89 billion; but some groups had losses; survey table shows, by industries, earnings reported for second quarter. 8/8-1;6

Chrysler Corp. Chairman Lee Iacocca asked the government to hold off on the planned sale of its 14.4 million warrants to buy Chrysler stock. 8/8-7;3

New Jersey's high insurance rates on autos hurt drivers and insurers; increases in premiums mean that the cost of the basic coverage will soar. 8/11-23;4

The government will proceed with its plan for a public offering of 14.4 million government-owned Chrysler Corp. warrants. 8/12-4;2

William B. Tanner Co., the Media General broadcast-services unit that federal agents raided last week, supplied women, new cars and cash-filled envelopes to clients and prospects, according to a government affidavit by an FBI agent. 8/15-5;1

AUTOS—Prices

High new-car prices keep many lookers looking, not buying; through long sales slump, U.S. tags rose steadily as firms stressed profits; domestic auto makers get a boost from import curbs. 8/3-1;6

Major tire manufacturers agreed to supply tires for 1984-model cars at prices about 1% below those for 1983 models; makers also agreed to accept a 2% limit on price increases for 1985- and 1986-model cars. 8/4-8;5

Daimler-Benz AG raised car prices in West Germany an average 2.8%. 8/16-44;3

American Motors Corp. set the suggested retail price for the least costly of its new 1984-model line of Jeep Cherokees at $9,995. 8/18-3;4

AUTOS—Production

U.S. auto and truck output rose in July to 611,147 units but under 1% from 1982; for the first seven months of 1983, auto and truck output was 5,003,539 units. 8/2-12;2

Auto shortages among dealers won't end soon; retooling for 1984 models prevents boosting output from levels set in June. 8/3-2;2

Auto makers plan to build about 1,671,416 cars in the current quarter, including about 550,740 units in August. 8/3-2;2

U.S. auto makers plan to build 88,554 cars Aug 6. week; up 17% from 75,778 units a year earlier. 8/5-2;4

Vokswagenwerk AG signed an agreement to begin assembling vehicles in Tunisia. 8/5-24;4

U.S. auto makers are scheduled to build 96,145 cars Aug.

Source: *The Wall Street Journal Index.* General News, August, 1983, p. 101. Reprinted by permission of *The Wall Street Journal Index,* © Dow Jones & Company, Inc. 1983. All Rights Reserved.

Database
A database is a collection of files integrated into a file system.

OCLC is useful for interlibrary loans. Its **database** contains the titles of all holdings of OCLC libraries. If your library does not have a particular book, OCLC can locate it at another library.

Subject Searches.
DIALOG, BRS, and ORBIT are subject-search systems used by many libraries. Each system consists of a number of databases in a variety of fields. The user pays a fee for any material received through the privately owned systems. Some of the DIALOG databases in the business area are:

ABI/INFORM, August 1971–present.
Covers all phases of business management and administration.
Scans about 550 publications for articles.

ADTRACK, 1980–present.
Indexes advertisements in 148 major U.S. consumer magazines.

ECONOMIC LITERATURE INDEX, 1969–present.
Indexes 260 economic journals.

ECONOMICS ABSTRACTS INTERNATIONAL, 1974–present.
Abstracts approximately 1,800 journals in addition to books, directories, and reports.

Exhibit 7.7   *Standard and Poor's Corporation Records:* Index Section

Interim Consol. Earns.: Sept. '84	2196	**AMERICAN SHIP BUILDING CO.**	**1725**
AMER. PREPAID PROFESSIONAL SERVICES INC.		Executive Changes	9137
Initial Offering of Class A Common	9135	Interim Consol. Earns.: June '85	9478
Address	9135	Interim Consol. Earns.: Mar. '85	9935
AMER. PRESIDENT COS. LTD.	**9883**	Estimates Fiscal 1985 Second-Quarter Net Gain from	
Interim Consol. Earns.: Sept. '85	9135	Sale of Ohio Shipyard	9935
Interim Consol. Earns.: June '85	9477	Interim Consol. Earns.: Dec. '84	1918
Common Listed on Midwest SE	9477	**AMER. SIGN & INDICATOR CORP.**	
1985 Capital Spending Plans	9477	Debentures described under BRAE Corp.	
Executive Changes	9477	**AMER. SMELTING & REFINING CO.**	
Interim Consol. Earns.: Apr. '85	9934	Debs. Described under Asarco, Inc.	
Forecasts 1985 Net Income	9934	**AMERICAN SOFTWARE INC.**	**8987**
Interim Consol. Earns.: Sept. '84	2196	Interim Consol. Earns.: July '85	9137
AMER PYRAMID RESOURCES INC.		Interim Consol. Earns.: Jan. '85	9935
Common Deleted from NASDAQ System	9934	Interim Consol. Earns.: Oct. '84	1918
AMER. QUASAR PETROLEUM CO.	**9897**	Interim Consol. Earns.: July '84	2197
Annual Letter to Stockholders-1984	9136	**AMER. SOFTWARE TECHNOLOGY INC.♦**	**8962**
Once More Reschedules Date for 1985 Annual		**AMER. SOLAR KING CORP.●**	**1848**
Meeting of Stockholders	9136	Interim Consol. Earns.: Apr. '85	9478
Deleted from NASDAQ System	9136	Forecasts Fiscal 1985 Results	1918
New Loan Agreement	9136	**AMERICAN SPECTRUM MARKETING CORP.★**	**1890**
Sells Certain Properties in British Columbia; Status of		**AMER. SPORTS ADVISORS INC.●**	**9208**
Debt Reduction	9136	Interim Consol. Earns.: Apr. '85	9478
Completes Exchange Offers for 14% Debentures,			
1993, and 12.5% Convertible Notes, 1995	9477		

Source: *Standard and Poor's Corporation Records.* New York: Standard and Poor's, January 9, 1986. Reprinted by permission.

FIND/SVP REPORTS AND STUDIES INDEX, 1977–present.

Indexes and describes industry, market, and research reports from more than 300 U.S. and international publishers.

HARFAX INDUSTRY DATA SOURCES, 1979–present.

Contains financial and marketing information for 65 major industries.

HARVARD BUSINESS REVIEW, 1971–present.

Contains complete articles of Harvard Business Review from 1979 on. Abstracts earlier articles.

MANAGEMENT CONTENTS, 1974–present.

Indexes and abstracts articles from more than 400 U.S. and international journals in the area of management.

PTS ANNUAL REPORTS ABSTRACTS.

Provides abstracts of more than 3,000 annual reports issued by publicly held U.S. corporations and selected international companies.

PTS PROMT, 1972–present.

Abstracts information from thousands of newspapers, business magazines, government reports, trade journals, and bank letters.

STANDARD & POOR'S NEWS, 1979–present.

Provides information on more than 10,000 companies, covering interim earnings, management changes, contract awards, mergers, acquisitions, and corporate background.

Exhibit 7.8   *Standard and Poor's Corporation Records:* Standard Corporation
Descriptions

American Software, Inc.

CAPITALIZATION
(July 31 '85, after sale of 500,000 Cl. A Com. shs.
Sept. 19 '85)

LONG TERM DEBT- None.

STOCK-

	Auth. Shs.	Outstg. Shs.
Common $0.10 par:		
Cl. A	*10,000,000	4,249,970
Cl. B	5,000,000	†2,625,000

*Incl. 270,000 optioned to employees, with
123,750 for future grants; 2,700 optioned to others;
and 2,625,000 conversion of Cl. B.
†Closely held.

CORPORATE BACKGROUND
Company develops, markets and supports integrated computer applications software systems for
use in mainframe IBM and IBM plug-compatible computers. Systems perform various business tasks,
mainly in the areas of forecasting and inventory
management, and purchasing, materials control, and
financial management.

SUBSIDIARIES- wholly owned- American Software Research & Development Corp.; American Software International, Inc.; American Software FSC.

EMPLOYEES- Aug. 30, 1985, 322.

INCORPORATED in Ga. in 1970 under the name
American Computer Systems, Inc. In 1978, merged
American Software & Computer Co. and adopted
present title.

CHAIRMAN, CO-CHIEF EXEC OFFICER & SECY,
T.L. Newberry; PRES, CO-CHIEF EXEC OFFICER &
TREAS, J.C. Edenfield; V-Ps, J.L. Altman, C.D.
Bhame, C.E. Crouch, Paul CiBono, Jr., J.J. Ferguson,
J.C. Gable, J.M. Keese; CONTR, M.R. Noyd.

DIRECTORS- T.L. Newberry, J.C. Edenfield, D.H.
Gambrell.

OFFICE- 443 E. Paces Ferry Rd., N.E., Atlanta,
GA 30305 (Tel.: 404-261-4381). ANNUAL MEETING-
As set by directors.

STOCK DATA
CL. A COM. has preference over Cl. B Com. in
any fiscal year to non-cumulative cash dividends of
$0.05 a sh. before any cash dividends are paid on Cl.
B in such year. Cash dividends may be paid on Cl. A
without any dividends being paid on Cl. B, and cash
dividends paid per sh. on Cl. B in any year may not
exceed dividends per sh. paid on Cl. A in such year.
Stock dividends are payable on each class in each
respective class. In LIQUIDATION, Cl. A has preference to $0.10 a sh. before any distribution is made
on Cl. B. CONVERTIBLE- Cl. B is convertible into Cl.
A, share-for-share. VOTING POWER- Cl. A and Cl. B
have 0.1 and 1.0 vote per share, respectively,

except that Cl. B elects a majority of directors.
PRE-EMPTIVE RIGHTS- Cl. A, none. Cl. B shareholders have pre-emptive rights to any Cl. B stock
sold, and Cl. B may not be issued without the
approval of Cl. B stockholders.

CLASS A COM. OFFERED-

Date	Shares	Price	Comm.
2-24-83	*1,750,000	$24.00	*$1.60
9-19-85	†1,000,000	10.00	†0.68

*Prudential-Bache Securities Inc., NYC, Dean
Witter Reynolds Inc., San Francisco, et al; incl.
1,000,000 for stockholders. An additional 175,000
Cl. A shs. were available for over-allotments- none
were taken.
†Prudential-Bache Securities, Inc., NYC, Johnson, Lane, Space, Smith & Co., Inc., Swergold,
Chefitz & Sinsabaugh, Inc.; incl. 500,000 for stockholders. An additional 150,000 shs. were sold by
stockholders to cover over-allotments.

STOCKHOLDERS- July 6, 1985 (of record): Cl. A
Com. 580; Cl. B Com. 2. Sept. 20, 1985, T.L.
Newberry owned 5.6% of the Cl. A Com. and 50% of
the Cl. B Com.; J.C. Edenfield owned 5.3% of the Cl.
A Com. and 50% of the Cl. B Com.; and Tower Capital
Management, Inc. owned 8.0% of the Cl. A Com.
(341,250 shs.).

TRANSFER AGENT & REGISTRAR- First Natl.
Bank, Atlanta.

PRICE RANGE- Cl. A Com. OTC bid (NASDAQ:
AMSWA):

1984	19½	11	1983	30¾	17¼

DIVIDENDS- Cl. A Com. $0.10 par: Apr. 1, 1985,
3-for-2 split.

EARNINGS AND FINANCES
AUDITORS- Peat, Marwick, Mitchell & Co.,
Atlanta, Ga.

EARNINGS, Y-E Apr. 30: Thou. $

	Revs.	Oper. Inc.	Depr. & Amort.
1985	29,575	8,007	1,009
1984	21,078	6,242	596
1983	16,090	5,168	82
1982	8,754	797	72
1981	6,400	1,137	55
1980	4,050	444	45
a1979	2,663	†178	N.R.
a1978	1,498	†189	N.R.

	Inc. Taxes	Net Inc.	*Sh. Earns.
1985	4,200	5,470	0.86
1984	3,474	4,233	1.00
1983	2,419	3,319	0.92
1982	315	644	0.18
1981	549	648	0.19
1980	207	253	0.07

| a1979 | 67 | 131 | 0.04 |
| a1978 | 96 | 95 | 0.03 |

*As reported by Co.
†Aft. dedctg. depr. & amort.
aUnaudited.

ADJTD. EARNS. for Apr. '85 3-for-2 stk. split: $

1984	1983	1982	1981	1980	1979	1978
0.66	0.61	0.12	0.13	0.05	0.03	0.02

Annual Report- Consol. Inc. Acct. Yrs. End. Apr.
30: Thou. $

	1985	1984	1983
Revenues	29,575	21,078	16,090
Cost & exps	21,568	14,836	10,922
Oper. income	8,007	6,242	5,168
Other inc., net	2,672	2,067	663
Total income	10,679	8,309	5,831
Depr. & amort.	1,009	596	82
Income taxes	4,200	3,474	2,419
Interest	---	6	11
Net income	5,470	4,233	3,319
*Sh. Earns.	$0.86	$0.66	$0.61

*Avge. shs.: 1985—6,374,970; 1984—
6,375,000; 1983—5,431,850, adjtd. for Apr. '85
3-for-2 split.

Consol. Bal. Sheet Apr. 30: Thou. $

Assets—	1985	b1984
Cash	312	370
Mktble. secs	18,628	22,911
Receivables, net	7,581	7,536
Inc. tax refund. rec	---	174
Prepayments, etc	1,057	638
Tot. curr. assets	27,578	31,629
*Net property	10,999	3,243
Other assets	296	197
Total assets	38,873	5,069
Liabilities—		
Curr. debt mat	---	5
Accts. pay	688	479
Accruals	1,284	795
Income taxes	101	---
Defr. inc. tax	2,841	3,215
Defr. rev	2,745	4,831
Tot. curr. liabs	7,659	9,325
†Cl. A com. stk. p.		
$0.10	375	375
aCl. B com. stk. p.		
$0.10	263	263
Paid-in cap	16,097	16,098
Retain. earns	14,479	9,009
Total liabs	38,873	35,069
Net wkg. cap	19,919	22,304
Equity per comb. sh.	$4.90	$4.04
*Depr. & am. res	1,721	754
†Shs.:	3,749,970	3,750,000

aShs.: 2,625,000.
bReflects Apr. '85 3-for-2 stk. split.

Source: *Standard and Poor's Corporation Records.* New York: Standard and Poor's, January 9,
1986. Reprinted by permission.

TRADE AND INDUSTRY INDEX, 1981–present.
*Provides indexing and selective abstracting of 275 trade and industry journals and
selective coverage of 1,200 business publications.*

DIALOG allows you to search for periodical articles. Depending on the
database, you may receive an abstract or brief description of the article, but
most databases simply provide the **citation**. Unless you specify a particular
year or years, each search starts with the most recent publication and automatically searches back in time.

In order to use computer searches effectively, you must be familiar
with the basic principles underlying catalogs and periodical indexes. Before

Citation
The listing of a publica-
tion in a catalog is
called a citation.

starting a subject search, you must know what subject titles and subtitles a database uses. Computerized searches can save you time that you can use more productively for reading and evaluating sources.

EVALUATION OF SOURCES

Once you have identified useful sources, you must decide which ones to read. This section of the chapter will give you a general overview of the evaluation of material. A detailed discussion of how to analyze secondary research sources is found in the chapter on analysis.

The answers to these three questions will help you to decide:

1. How old is the source? Was it published several months ago, one year ago, five years ago?

2. Who is the author? Is the author a recognized expert in the field? Is the author a member of, or prominent spokesperson for, a special-interest group?

3. Is the article published in a scholarly journal, a popular magazine, or a special-interest group publication?

Finding the answer to the first question is easy, because the periodical or book carries the date of publication. That will not tell when the material was actually researched and written, but you can assume that at the time of publication the material was not outdated.

Questions about the author may be more difficult to answer. Sometimes periodicals provide a profile of the writer, including company or university affiliation and research interests. You might also check various *Who's Who* directories to find more information.

The third question is the most difficult. Scholarly journals by their very nature should be unbiased. They tend to be published by or affiliated with universities. The editing board of a scholarly journal checks the quality of the articles submitted and tries to assure objectivity. With magazines you must be more careful. You might query the editor of a magazine from a commercial publisher about the selection process for articles. Some publications are produced by special-interest groups such as political parties, labor unions, and churches. The articles might be useful, but you must evaluate the materials and the source carefully for bias.

No strict rules exist for determining whether a periodical is classified as a journal or as a magazine, but the information in Exhibit 7.9 should help you to make a decision.

After deciding which sources will be useful and appropriate, you must go through three steps before you can use them in a report:

1. List all the sources you are going to use. Compile a preliminary bibliography based on useful information in the card catalog and index systems.

Exhibit 7.9   **Distinction between Journals and Magazines**

	Journal	Magazine
Publisher	University Professional organization	Commercial enterprise
Editor	Professor	Full-time paid
Review	Peer-review, review-panel names often listed	Different from magazine to magazine
Frequency	Usually quarterly	Often biweekly or monthly
Advertising	Few paid ads	Many paid ads
Authorship	Authors almost always listed	Many anonymous or staff written articles, some authors identified

2. Determine whether the information will be useful.

3. Carefully read and evaluate the content of the material and critically analyze it. This process will be described in Chapter 12.

BIBLIOGRAPHY CARDS

Library research requires paper, index cards, pen or pencil, and coins for the copying machine.

If you compile your **bibliography** on index cards, sources are easily added, deleted, and alphabetized. For every source you should write down the following information:

Bibliography
A bibliography is an alphabetized list of sources on a given topic.

Books	Articles
Name(s) of author(s)	Name(s) of author(s)
Title of book	Title of article
Name of publisher	Title of periodical
Place of publication	Volume number
Year of publication	Month and year of publication
Edition number	Page numbers
Call number	Call number of periodical

So you can directly type your bibliography for the report from the bibliography cards, you should use the format of the stylebook which you intend to use for the entire report. For a detailed discussion of documentation look at Chapter 8.

You should assign letters to your bibliography cards so you can key them to your note cards. The two sample index cards in Exhibit 7.10 show how to enter your bibliography information on the card. You may put the

Exhibit 7.10   **Annotations on Bibliography Cards**

HF 5718.J6

Ober, Scot, and Alan P. Wunsch.

"The Status of Business Communication Instruction
in Postsecondary Institutions in the United
States." The Journal of Business
Communication
Spring (1983):5-16.

Examines what courses are offered, who takes
courses, how many assignments are given, which
textbooks are used, in which departments courses
are offered.
Provides helpful tables. Sample is probably more
weighted toward schools that offer bus. comm. in
schools of business. Junior colleges are included.

HD 30.28 .42 1983

Amara, Roy, and Andrew J. Lipinski.

Business Planning for an Uncertain Future,
Scenarios & Strategies.
New York: Pergamon Press, 1983.

Gives step-by-step strategies for planning in
corporate settings; develops a model for planning
and provides guidelines for using the model; gives
case examples and political framework of planning.
The political aspects of planning and
communicating in the planning process are
particularly helpful.

Annotation
An annotation provides
a very short summary
or comment of a
source.

call number in any corner of the card as long as you are consistent. You may want to put a brief **annotation** of the source on the index card. The annotation will help you determine whether you have information on all areas of your topic. It can also serve as a starting point in future research projects. In the annotation you may also want to identify the major topics in the source book or article, compare the positions taken with other sources, and list particularly helpful features.

NOTE CARDS

As soon as you take some source materials from the shelf, you may be able to tell that they will not be useful. Before you discard the index card, however, you might want to consider whether the material could be useful for another project. If the material looks promising after first inspection, you can begin reading and note taking.

Preliminary Skimming.

Before you take extensive notes or copy an entire article, get an idea of what the article is about. Determine the background, problem, purpose, scope, major findings, conclusions, and recommendations. If the article is well organized, you should find the background, purpose, and scope in the first few paragraphs. Sometimes the title may look promising but, after you have read the opening paragraphs, you may find that the article does not address your problem at all or that it is only tangentially related. In that case you can eliminate the article without further reading.

Next examine the conclusions and recommendations found either at the end or at the beginning of the article. Next you can use headings and topic sentences to get a rough idea of the major points. If the article has no headings, you can still pick out topic sentences to get an idea of the content.

Note Taking.

You may write notes on either index cards or notepaper. The cardinal rule common to both is that *you should only write on one side of the paper, never on front and back*. Regardless of the system you use, you need to include the following information:

1. The corresponding letter from the bibliography card or the name of the author.

2. The note itself.

3. The page number of the article or book to which the note corresponds.

Many researchers recommend the use of index cards as the only efficient way to take notes. The system does work well; however, if you use notepaper properly, you get the same results. The advantage to index cards is that you have every note on a separate card. On the other hand, if notes are on paper, you can cut them up and assemble a rough draft of the report. This will work, of course, only if you have not written on the back of the sheet.

Note Content.

When recording information, you must decide whether to quote or **paraphrase**. Paraphrasing is the summarizing of material in *your own words*. Paraphrasing is more than a rearrangement of words in a sentence or the leaving out of several words. Most of your notes will be summaries of the materials you read.

Paraphrase
A paraphrase is a summary or comment of a source in the writer's own words.

To do a good job of note taking, you must understand the arguments, the facts, and the context of the source material. You use your *own* words. Effective paraphrasing requires constant checking of the material against your problem statement. Note taking is an active and creative effort.

In addition to summarizing the material, you may want to make special comments on how the material relates to your problem. You may want to write down why you agree or disagree, why the argument is good or weak. If you put your own ideas down, make sure that you label them as your own on the note card, so you will not confuse them later with source material.

If you made a detailed plan for your report, with a precise problem statement and a carefully formulated scope statement, you can decide, while taking notes, where the material will fit in the final report. You might even enter the appropriate heading from the plan outline on the card. If you use this approach, however, you should be careful not to stick to the plan outline simply to avoid rekeying the cards. The outline of the plan is tentative. Research findings may prompt you to change the outline and the planned organization of the report.

Direct quotations should be reserved for special situations. Let us assume you are researching how corporations report negative information in their annual reports. In this particular case you want to repeat the exact words used by the chairman of the board in the letter to the stockholders:

> Fiscal 1982 was a pivotal year for our company. Although earnings declined substantially because of write-offs related to divestment actions on unprofitable businesses, we believe we are now positioned for improved profitability. The strength of our four core businesses—Grocery Products, Formula Feeds, Restaurants, and Protein Technologies—in a difficult economic year underscores our positive outlook.[1]

Not using the chairman's own words could lessen the impact of the message.

If you want to define a technical term and show that you have used either a widely accepted definition or the standard dictionary definition, you should use a direct quotation. Amara and Lipinski used quotations to give several key definitions of planning in their book, *Business Planning*:

> One of the best overall definitions of planning is the following from Donald Conover of Western Electric (Committee on Science and Technology 1976, p.126): "The real planners are the managers who make the final decisions, and what we call planning is the support service intended to help make decisions better." The key message is the essential unity of thought *and* action, or planning *and* decision making. Even though thought precedes action, the interweaving should be so close that they become almost indistinguishable.[2]

If you find that the author made a precise, clear point that would be very difficult to improve on, you may also use a direct quotation. If you were trying to explain what the goals of a business school should be, for example, you might decide to use the following quotation:

> A business school should provide for young men [The material is obviously dated. Today you would say men and women or people.] special means of training and correct instruction in the knowledge and in the arts of modern finance and economy, both public and private, in order that. . .they may prudently manage their affairs and aid in

maintaining sound financial morality; in short, to establish means for imparting a liberal education in all matters concerning finance and economy.[3]

Do not become lazy and begin to copy everything. *Quotations should be used sparingly.* The purpose of your report is to solve a problem, not to repeat how another writer solved a similar problem. The adaptation of the source material to your situation clearly requires more than quoting secondary sources. When recording direct quotations on your note cards, check immediately that they are exact, that no words are missing, and that the original punctuation is copied correctly. The checking now will save you much time later.

USEFUL SECONDARY SOURCES FOR BUSINESS

GUIDES TO BOOKS

Business Books and Serials in Print. New York: Bowker, 1977.
> *This publication lists books on economics, agriculture, industry, finance, investment, insurance, and taxation.*

Business Information Sources. Lorna M. Daniells, ed. Berkeley, CA: University of California Press, 1976.
> *This guide is arranged by subject area and by type of material: handbook, periodical.*

Cumulative Book Index: A World List of Books in the English Language. New York: Wilson, 1928–present.
> *This index, which is arranged by title, author, and subject, lists English-language publications from all over the world. It was formerly titled* United States Catalog.

Publishers' Weekly. New York: Bowker.
> *This publication lists new books published during the week.*

Subject Guide to Books in Print. New York: Bowker, 1957–present.
> *This guide lists books currently in print in the United States.*

GUIDES TO PERIODICALS

Accountants' Index. American Institute of Certified Public Accountants. New York: American Institute of Certified Public Accountants, 1921–present.
> *This index covers books, government documents, and periodical articles dealing with accounting published in English. The materials are arranged by author, title, and subject in one alphabet. The index does not provide any annotations.*

The Applied Science and Technology Index. New York: Wilson, 1958–present.
> *This publication indexes periodicals in the fields of chemistry, engineering, physics, geology, automation, electronics, petroleum, and transportation. Before 1958 the index was part of the* Industrial Arts Index.

Business Periodicals Index. New York: Wilson, 1958–present. Prior to 1958 the index was part of the *Industrial Arts Index*.

> *This publication indexes periodicals in the areas of business, finance, labor relations, insurance, advertising, and office management.*

Index of Supermarket Articles. Chicago: Supermarket Institute, 1936–present.

> *This index is arranged by subject and category. It indexes articles on supermarkets and the food industry.*

Index to Labor Union Periodicals. Ann Arbor: University of Michigan, School of Business Administration, 1960–present.

> *This index lists union periodicals and gives very brief annotations.*

Personnel Management Abstracts. Ann Arbor: University of Michigan, 1955–present.

> *This publication gives short abstracts of articles in the areas of manpower, personnel management, and industrial relations.*

Readers' Guide to Periodical Literature. New York: Wilson, 1900–present.

> *This guide indexes popular current periodicals. For the serious researcher this index tends to be too limited.*

Small Business Index. Metuchen, NJ: Scarecrow, 1978.

> *This is a listing of books, pamphlets, periodical articles, and government documents related to starting a small business.*

INDEXES TO NEWSPAPERS

Index of the Christian Science Monitor. Corvallis, OR: H. M. Cropsey, 1960–present.

> *This index is published monthly.*

New York Times Index. New York: New York Times Co., 1913–present.

> *Material is indexed by subject, person, and name of organization.*

The Wall Street Journal Index. Princeton, NJ: Dow Jones Books, 1958–present.

> *The index is arranged in two parts: corporate news and general news. Each listing is followed by a short abstract.*

GUIDES TO GOVERNMENT PUBLICATIONS

American Statistics Index: A Comprehensive Guide and Index to the Statistical Publications of the United States Government. New York: Congressional Information Service, 1973–present.

> *This publication indexes all statistical publications in print.*

Guide to U.S. Government Serials and Periodicals. McLean, VA: Documents Index, 1962–present.

> *This guide gives a brief description of publications and audience for which materials are intended.*

Monthly Catalog of United States Government Publications. Washington D.C.: Government Printing Office, 1895–present.

> *This publication is the most comprehensive guide to government publications.*

U.S. Department of Commerce Publications. Washington D.C.: U.S. Department of Commerce, 1952–present.

> *The guide is updated annually.*

GUIDES TO DIRECTORIES

Dun and Bradstreet Reference Book. New York: Dun and Bradstreet, 1859–present.
> *This book gives the financial rating of nearly three million companies in the United States and Canada.*

Dun and Bradstreet Reference Book of Corporate Management. New York: Dun and Bradstreet, 1967–present.
> *This book lists corporations with annual sales over $20 million and/or over 100 employees. It also provides information on corporate officers.*

Moody's Investors Service: Moody's Manuals. New York: Moody's Investors Service, 1955–present.
> *Moody's provides information on officers, dividends, loans, and debts. It is a valuable source for investors.*

Standard and Poor's Register of Corporations, Directors, and Executives, United States and Canada. New York: Standard and Poor's, 1928–present.
> *This is a comprehensive guide to over 37,000 U.S. corporations.*

This list is by no means complete. It gives just a few of all the guides and directories you may find useful in your research. Very few libraries will have all of them, however. You may also want to check the *City and County Data Book,* handbooks for business, corporate publications such as annual reports, and pamphlets and leaflets published by the federal and state governments.

SUMMARY OF LEARNING OBJECTIVES

To Understand the Role of Secondary Research in Report Writing.
Secondary research tells the writer what research has been done to solve similar problems; therefore, secondary research saves time.

To Recognize Different Types of Libraries.
There are general purpose libraries, research libraries, and special-purpose libraries.

To Understand the Organization of Libraries.
Libraries have author–title catalogs and subject catalogs that help in finding books. Index systems help in the search for periodical articles. For the business writer the *Business Periodicals Index* is probably the most useful.

To Become Familiar with Computer Searches.
Computer searches can save time and allow an in-depth search for information. OCLC is an author–title search. DIALOG is a database system for subject searches. It allows searches for articles in periodicals.

To Evaluate Sources and Compile Bibliography and Note Cards.
The researcher must determine whether an article or a book is useful for the project at hand. The name of the author, name and reputation of the peri-

odical, date of publication, and the reviewing system can help to evaluate the credibility of an article.

On the bibliography card are written the name of author, title of article, title of book or periodical, place of publication, name of publisher, date of publication, and page numbers. An annotation of the source may be added.

On the note cards are written quotations, summaries of major ideas, and the researcher's own comments. Direct quotations should be flagged so that they can be distinguished from paraphrased material.

To Become Familiar with Secondary Sources Useful to the Business Writer. The sources listed at the end of the text of this chapter will help the researcher find secondary information more efficiently.

QUESTIONS AND PROBLEMS

1. Prepare an annotated bibliography of at least ten sources for a topic in your area of study.
2. Why have many libraries switched to the Library of Congress cataloging system?
3. What is the organization of the *Business Periodicals Index?*
4. Look at your research plan to determine subject headings under which you may find material for your report. Check those subjects in the library.
5. Compile a list of journals in your major. Give a brief description of the focus of each journal.
6. Examine several journals in your field for currently popular topics.
7. You have an employment interview with a corporation two weeks from now. Find out about the financial position of the company, major products, and location of subsidiaries. List the sources you consult and record the findings.
8. Compile an annotated bibliography of books and articles on business communication published during the last year.
9. Discuss the use of computers in secondary research.

NOTES

1 Ralston Purina Company, *Annual Report* (St. Louis: Ralston Purina, 1982) 2.
2 Roy Amara and Andrew J. Lipinski, *Business Planning for an Uncertain Future, Scenarios & Strategies* (New York: Pergamon, 1983) 19.
3 Joseph Wharton, "Project for a School of Finance and Economy to Form a New Department of the University" in *Liberal Education and Business,* ed. William M. Kephart et al. (New York: Columbia UP, 1963) 25.

CHAPTER EIGHT

DOCUMENTATION

OF SOURCES

LEARNING OBJECTIVES

- To understand the reasons for documentation and the problems of plagiarism.
- To become familiar with the format for quotations.
- To document sources correctly.
- To compile bibliographies.

REASONS FOR DOCUMENTATION

All secondary sources that you use in your report must be documented regardless of whether you quote or paraphrase. Documentation is important for these reasons:

1. Documentation allows the reader to check the sources you have used in your report. The reader may want to see the material in context or know who wrote the article or report. The reader may even want to read the entire article from which you quoted.

2. Documentation indicates that you researched what others have written about the same topic. It shows that you are up-to-date, and, therefore, documentation lends credibility to your work.

3. Documentation is necessary for legal reasons. Not giving credit where credit is due can cause legal problems. To use material without giving the source is unethical.

PLAGIARISM

Plagiarism
Plagiarism is the unauthorized or unacknowledged use of secondary material.

Using material without documentation is called **plagiarism** and is punishable by law. If you refer in your report to interviews, lectures, unpublished papers, television or radio broadcasts, books, magazines, or journals, you must credit the source.

Information that is considered general knowledge, however, need not be documented. For example, you do not have to document the fact that the United States has 50 states. You would not need to document the statement that Saudi Arabia is a principal producer of crude oil, but you would have to document the source for specific production statistics. The reader must

154

know whether the source is the Saudi government, the U.S. government, a private research firm, or the Soviet Union. Each of these entities would look at the statistics from its own frame of reference and have a different definition for production of crude oil. If you are not certain whether an item is general knowledge, you should document it.

COPYRIGHT LAWS

Copyright Laws
Copyright laws are intended to prevent the illegal use of secondary sources.

Copyright laws provide protection for published material. If you write a book, for example, you copyright the book. Anybody who wants to duplicate or photocopy material from your book must obtain your permission. You may legally charge the user of the material.

Under copyright laws material is protected for the author's life plus 50 years. After that time the material is in the public domain. Once the copyright has expired, you need not pay for material used, but you still must document the source.

Copyright laws allow for the educational use of material. For example, if you quote material from a copyrighted book in a term paper report, you do not have to ask for permission. If you photocopy an article for your own use, you do not have to ask permission or pay the author. If, however, you use the material in a book that will be published and sold, you must obtain permission. In most cases you will be allowed the use of a limited amount of material, usually a paragraph, free of charge, but you may have to pay for longer quotations.

STYLE MANUALS

Style Manuals
Style manuals provide guidelines for documentation.

If your company has specified a particular documentation format, you must follow it precisely. If you are allowed to make format decisions, you may choose one of a number of **style manuals** on the market. A style manual provides guidance in preparing manuscripts and documentation. Most style manuals discuss margins, indentations, headings, capitalization, and formats for footnotes and bibliographies. The style manuals most frequently used are:

Gibaldi, Joseph, and Walter Achtert. *MLA Handbook for Writers of Research Papers.* 2nd ed. New York: The Modern Language Association of America, 1984.

Turabian, Kate L. *A Manual for Writers of Term Papers, Theses, and Dissertations.* 4th ed. Chicago: U of Chicago P, 1973.

APA (American Psychological Association) Publication Manual. 3rd ed. Washington, DC: American Psychological Association, 1983.

A book that gives detailed instructions on how to document government sources is:

Garner, Diane L., and Diane H. Smith. *The Complete Guide to Citing Government Documents*. Bethesda, MD: Congressional Information Services, 1984.

Professional journals may have their own format, or they may use a modified version of the *MLA Handbook* or the *Manual for Writers of Term Papers, Theses, and Dissertations*. The discussion in this chapter is based on the *MLA Handbook*.

FORMAT FOR QUOTATIONS

SHORT QUOTATIONS

You should use quotations sparingly, but when you quote, you must check that the quotation is precise and clearly marked. Quoted words or phrases can be part of a sentence, as in the following example:

> The writer has to know that "all quotations—whether a word, phrase, sentence, paragraph, or more—should correspond exactly to the original source in spelling, capitalization, and interior punctuation. . . ."[1]

LONG QUOTATIONS

Quotations longer than four lines or longer than one sentence are set off from the text by triple spacing. The quoted material is indented ten spaces from the left margin. Quotations set off in this way are not enclosed in quotation marks.

> *Internal memory* is one of the more glamorized parts of the modern computer. In some respects the use of the word *memory* is misleading since the average person tends to think of it in terms of human memory and the associated reasoning abilities of the brain.[2]

ELLIPSES

The ellipsis, a series of three periods with spaces between them, indicates that something was omitted from the original text. Because omissions from the original can change the intended meaning, the writer must make it clear that material has been omitted. Omissions in the middle of a sentence are indicated by three periods.

> "In performing their jobs, managers may rely. . .on the authority that is. . .attached to the position they occupy."[3]

If the omission occurs at the end of a sentence, it is indicated by three periods plus a fourth period to mark the end of the sentence.

"Words used in questionnaires should be readily understandable. . . ."[4]

ADDITIONS

Sometimes the writer may want to add a comment or clarify a term in the quotation. The writer's own comments or additions within a quotation are set off by square brackets. If the typewriter does not have a key for square brackets, they must be added by hand.

"These laws [called Green River Ordinances] reflect both the fear of local merchants and the suspicion of householders toward house-to-house selling."[5]

EMPHASIS

Emphasized or italicized words in the original must be emphasized and italicized in the quote. If the writer wants to add emphasis, he has to indicate that the emphasis was added and was not present in the original.

"The programmer uses the *flowchart* [emphasis added] to design programs that contain instructions to the computer on how to handle each step in a process."[6]

PLACEMENT OF DOCUMENTATION

There are two components to documentation: reference notes and the bibliography.

REFERENCE NOTES

Reference notes are traditionally called footnotes because they originally were placed at the bottom or foot of the page. Today, footnotes can be at the bottom of the page, in the text, or at the end of the report or chapter.

Footnotes. Placement of the footnote at the bottom of the page requires a note number in the text following the quoted or paraphrased material. The writer places the number half a line above the typed text. The number follows all punctuation except a dash. When all cited information in a paragraph is from a single source, a single footnote can be used. Its number follows the last sentence in the paragraph containing information from that source. In practice, this sentence is often the last one in the paragraph. Footnoted material is numbered sequentially throughout a report. In books the numbering is often by chapter. Exhibit 8.1 illustrates the proper placement of note numbers.

Exhibit 8.1   **Footnotes at Bottom of Page**

> German law prohibits any defaming reference to a competitor or his goods and
> services in ad campaigns. For example, it would be totally unacceptable to make
> remarks about a competitor's status in the market, history, or nationality. The
> competitor's name need not be included in the advertisement to cause such state-
> ments to be considered unfair. The mere mention of the competitor's business
> category is considered a violation of the law.[1]
>
> American advertising law, on the other hand, does not forbid the use of a
> competitor's trademark or trade name in an ad.[2] It was because of this difference
> in advertising law that Burger King ran into legal problems when it promoted its
> international advertising campaign, the "Battle of the Burgers," in Germany. The
> ad's headline read: "Let the others stew in their own fat." Underneath were the
> captions: "Burger King grills" and "It tastes better from the fire." Burger King
> knew the ad campaign was illegal, but it was considered necessary to educate
> German customers who "don't yet know there's any difference between hamburgers."[3]
> This indirect reference to other hamburger restaurants that fry their hamburgers
> violated German law and had to be discontinued.
>
> _____
>
> [1]Rudolf Mueller, Doing Business in Germany: A Legal Manual (Frankfurt/Main:
> Fritz Knapp Verlag, 1971) 66.
>
> [2]Louis W. Stern and Thomas L. Eovaldi, Legal Aspects of Marketing Strategy
> (Englewood Cliffs, N.J.: Prentice Hall, 1984) 57.
>
> [3]Wellington Long, "Burger Battle Goes Overseas," Advertising Age 20 August
> 1984: 44.

The footnote is separated from the last line of the text by a solid line
usually about 1½ inches long. The line is a single space below the last line
of text. The footnote entry is indented the same amount as paragraphs in the
text. The number of the footnote is typed half a line above the entry. Based
on the second edition of the *MLA Handbook*, footnotes are double-spaced.
However, because many business reports are single-spaced, it is more appropriate for footnotes to be single-spaced as well. Footnotes in double-spaced
reports can be either single- or double-spaced. If the footnote entry is longer
than one line, the following lines start on the left margin. Two footnotes on
the same page are separated by a line of space.

Footnotes are not used as much today as they were used in the past because they are difficult to type. Unless you are an experienced typist, you may misjudge the space left at the bottom of the sheet for footnotes. You can overcome the problem with the use of a master sheet on which the lines are numbered, starting at the bottom margin (Exhibit 8.2). If you place the master sheet behind the sheet you are typing on, you will always be able to see how many lines are left.

Let us assume a page needs two footnotes that take two lines each. The footnotes will occupy a total of four lines, plus a line of space between them and another one between the first footnote and the text. Total space needed is six lines. At the number 6 on the master sheet, the footnotes begin.

The placement of footnotes at the bottom of the page is the most logical placement because it allows the reader to check the source without having to turn back and forth in the report. The reader is less likely to check references if they are at the end of the report.

With computers and word processing, the placement of footnotes at the bottom may become more popular again. A number of word-processing packages allow for the placement of footnotes at the bottom. The writer must identify the footnote and give the proper command. The computer will then automatically place the footnote or footnotes on the appropriate pages. Specific instructions depend on the particular software package and hardware.

A complete footnote entry is necessary only if a work is cited the first time. Later an abbreviated form, giving the name of the author and the page number, is sufficient. If the article does not list the name of the author, the second reference cites the title of the article and the page number. If the

Exhibit 8.2 **Mastersheet for Typing Footnotes at Bottom of Page**

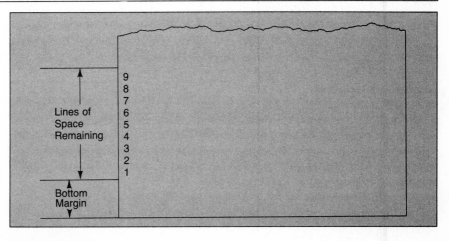

Lines of
Space
Remaining

9
8
7
6
5
4
3
2
1

Bottom
Margin

second entry immediately follows the first entry, then the writer may use *Ibid.* in the second entry:

[1]Wilson T. Price, Computers and Application Software: An Introduction (New York: Holt, 1985) 27.

[2]William A. Simcox, "A Design Method for Graphic Communication," ABCA Bulletin 47.1 (1984): 5.

[3]Ibid. 3.

[4]Price 60.

When footnotes are used, a bibliography is required at the end of the report or book to list in one place all the sources cited.

Endnotes. Endnote references are at the end of the report or chapter. Most journals use endnotes because they are easier to type and print. The disadvantage is that the reader must turn back and forth between the endnotes and the text. As a result, most readers do not check references.

The format for endnotes is the same as the format for footnotes. Published articles that use endnotes do not include a bibliography. Some instructors may require them for reports written as class assignments.

In-Text References. The placement of the reference in the text is the most convenient for the writer. It is the easiest to type. Depending on the format, the in-text placement can also benefit the reader. The writer has three options when placing the reference in the text.

Complete Citation in the Text. If the report has only one or two references, the writer may choose to place the complete citation within the text. The following example illustrates this option:[7]

> Business communicators (Murphy, Hertha, and Herbert Hildebrandt. *Effective Business Communication.* 4th ed. New York: McGraw-Hill, 1984, p. 27) point out that "the effective communicator should be considerate of the receivers and whenever possible emphasize—honestly—points they will regard as favorable or beneficial."

The reader has the complete source information, but the full citation in the sentence interrupts the flow of the sentence. Full documentation in the text should be used sparingly.

Identification by Name of Author. The same sentence, rewritten to identify the reference by name of author, would read as follows:

Business communicators point out that "the effective communicator should be considerate of the receivers and whenever possible emphasize—honestly—points they will regard as favorable or beneficial" (Murphy and Hildebrandt 27).

The writer may also use the author's name in the text and place the page number in parentheses. Referring to the author by name in the text may give more credibility to the information. In this case the above footnote would read as follows:

Murphy and Hildebrandt point out that the "effective communicator should be considerate of the receivers and whenever possible emphasize—honestly—points they will regard as favorable or beneficial" (27).

This reference system is easy to type and provides the name of the author; it does, however, not give any information on the publication. This type of entry requires a bibliography.

If the report refers to more than one publication by the same author, the writer must identify which publication the note refers to. If the report uses two articles by Palmer, for example, then the writer adds the title of the publication (Palmer, *Consumer Economics* 3).

Abbreviated notations may appear in the middle of the sentence or at the end of the sentence.

The article (Palmer 2) discusses the importance of consumer economics in public schools.

The article discusses the importance of consumer economics in public schools (Palmer 2).

Identification of the Reference by Number. If the reference is identified by number, it is written as follows:

Business communicators point out that "the effective communicator should be considerate of the receivers and whenever possible emphasize—honestly—points they will regard as favorable or beneficial" (2:27).

With this notation the reader has no idea that the quotation is from the book by Murphy and Hildebrandt. The number 2 refers to the bibliography. The item is taken from the second entry in the bibliography, page 27. With this type of reference the bibliography entries must be numbered. This system is easy to type, but the reader is given no useful reference information in the text.

BIBLIOGRAPHIES

Bibliographies list all of the works used in the report alphabetically by the last name of the author. Bibliography entries are numbered if the references in the text refer to works by number. The bibliography is also called *works cited*. Bibliographies use hanging indentation; that is, the first line of an entry is on the left margin and the remaining lines are indented. When the report is written in blocked style, the bibliography may be blocked also. The name of the author appears in reverse order: last name, first name. Although the second edition of the *MLA Handbook* says that bibliography entries are to be double-spaced, it may be more appropriate to single-space bibliography entries in a single-spaced business report. Bibliography entries in a double-spaced report can be either double- or single-spaced. In all cases, entries should be separated by a line of space.

Sometimes bibliographies are annotated. Annotations are brief summaries or descriptions of works used in the preparation of the report. The annotation starts on a new line. Exhibits 8.3 and 8.4 illustrate the various types of bibliographies.

FORMAT FOR FOOTNOTES AND BIBLIOGRAPHY

In the paired examples that follow, the first entry is the footnote or endnote; the second entry is the bibliography.

BOOK WITH ONE AUTHOR

[1]William G. Zikmund, <u>Business Research Methods</u> (Hinsdale, IL: Dryden, 1984) 81.

Zikmund, William G. <u>Business Research Methods</u>. Hinsdale, IL: Dryden, 1984.

BOOK WITH TWO AUTHORS

[2]Thomas J. Peters and Robert H. Waterman, Jr., <u>In Search of Excellence</u> (New York: Harper, 1982) 55.

Peters, Thomas J., and Robert H. Waterman, Jr. <u>In Search of Excellence</u>. New York: Harper, 1982.

BOOK WITH THREE AUTHORS

[3]William H. Cunningham, Ramond J. Aldag, and Christopher M. Swift, <u>Introduction to Business</u> (West Chicago: South-Western, 1984) 142.

Exhibit 8.3   **Sample List of Works Cited**

WORKS CITED *final Report*

Coyle, J.S. "Scanning Lights Up a Dark World of Grocers." <u>Fortune</u> 97 (March 1978): 76-78.

McAusland, Randolph M.N. "Scanning 1981: The Momentum Builds." <u>Supermarket Business</u> 36 (February 1981): 10-12.

Oneill, Robert E. "Life in the Fast Checkout Lane." <u>Progressive Grocer</u> 63 (February 1984): 87-94.

Shulman, Richard E. "Price Removal Forces Discipline; Benefits Shopper As Well As Retailer." <u>Supermarket</u> 35 (July 1980): 25-30.

Surveys – don't appear on works Cited – Appendix for Copy of Survey

Exhibit 8.4   **Annotated Bibliography**

Tentative **BIBLIOGRAPHY** *for Proposal*

Coyle, J.S. "Scanning Lights Up a Dark World of Grocers." <u>Fortune</u> 97 (March 1978): 76-78.
Supermarkets cannot ignore the badly needed cost management benefits that scanning offers.

McAusland, Randolph M.N. "Scanning 1981: The Momentum Builds." <u>Supermarket Business</u> 36 (February 1981): 10-12.
The use of computer scanning devices is growing rapidly because operators begin to see their potential in the areas of production and management.

Oneill, Robert E. "Life in the Fast Checkout Lane." <u>Progressive Grocer</u> 63 (February 1984): 87-94.
This article discusses how grocers can profit from selling their scanning data to market researchers.

Schulman, Richard E. "Price Removal Forces Discipline; Benefits Shopper as Well as Retailer." <u>Supermarket</u> 35 (July 1980): 25-30.
The grocery retailer and the consumer can make a successful transition to scanning.

Cunningham, William H., Ramond J. Aldag, and Christopher M. Swift. <u>Introduction to Business</u>. West Chicago: South-Western, 1984.

BOOK WITH MORE THAN THREE AUTHORS

[4]Richard C. Huseman, et al., <u>Business Communication</u> (Hinsdale, IL: Dryden, 1981) 1.

Huseman, Richard C., et al. <u>Business Communication</u>. Hinsdale, IL: Dryden, 1981.

MORE THAN ONE BOOK BY THE SAME AUTHOR

[5]Edward T. Hall, Beyond Culture (Garden City, NY: Anchor Books, 1977) 31.

[6]———, The Silent Language, 7th ed. (Garden City, NY: Doubleday, 1976) 15.

Hall, Edward T. Beyond Culture. Garden City, NY: Anchor Books, 1977.
———. The Silent Language. 7th ed. Garden City, NY: Doubleday, 1977.

AN ANONYMOUS BOOK

[7]The World Almanac & Book of Facts 1985 (New York: Newspaper Enterprise Association, 1984) 25.

The World Almanac & Book of Facts 1985. New York: Newspaper Enterprise Association, 1984.

AN EDITED BOOK

[8]Richard C. Huseman, James M. Lahiff, and John D. Hatfield, eds., Readings in Business Communication (Hinsdale, IL: Dryden, 1981) 1.

Huseman, Richard C., James M. Lahiff, and John D. Hatfield, eds. Readings in Business Communication. Hinsdale, IL: Dryden, 1981.

A BOOK WITH MISSING PUBLICATION DATA

For missing data you should substitute the following abbreviations:

n.p.	no place of publication given
n.p.	no publisher given
n.d.	no date given
n. pag.	no pagination given

If *n.p.* refers to place, the abbreviation should be placed before the colon; if it refers to publisher, it should be placed after the colon. The abbreviations are to appear in the place of the data they represent.

AN ARTICLE IN A PERIODICAL

[9]Scot Ober, "The Influence of Selected Variables on the Grading of Student-Written Letters," ABCA Bulletin, 47.1 (1984): 8.

Ober, Scot. "The Influence of Selected Variables on the Grading of Student-Written Letters." ABCA Bulletin 47.1 (1984): 7–10.

AN ARTICLE IN A MAGAZINE

[10]Stephen Koepp, "The Year of Big Splashes," Time 6 January 1986: 78.

Koepp, Stephen. "The Year of Big Splashes." Time 6 January 1986: 78–79.

AN ARTICLE IN A NEWSPAPER

[11]Arthur S. Harris, "Sorry, No Number: The Corporate Dropouts," Wall Street Journal 16 April 1985: 30.

Harris, Arthur S. "Sorry, No Number: The Corporate Dropouts." Wall Street Journal 16 April 1985: 30.

AN EDITORIAL ARTICLE

[12]"Expedite the Bhopal Case," editorial, Wall Street Journal 16 April 1985: 30.

"Expedite the Bhopal Case." Editorial. Wall Street Journal 16 April 1985: 30.

AN ANONYMOUS ARTICLE

[13]"Brazil: Still Ailing," Time 8 April 1985: 47.

"Brazil: Still Ailing." Time 8 April 1985: 47.

The documentation for publication dates of weekly magazines is different from journal articles. When documenting weekly magazines, the complete date is given but no volume number.

GOVERNMENT PUBLICATIONS

References and bibliography entries for government publications use the following sequence: name of government agency, title of publication, place of publication, publisher, date, page numbers. If all data are not available, the information provided on the document is given. The many different types of government publications make it impossible to show all of them here. The following examples illustrate the principles of government documentation:

[14]United States, Department of Commerce, National Technical Information Service, Directory of Federally Supported Information Analysis Centers, 3rd ed. (Washington: GPO, February 1974) 3.

United States Department of Commerce. National Technical Information Service. Directory of Federally Supported Information Analysis Centers. 3rd ed. Washington: GPO, 1974.

[15]United States House, Committee on the Budget, President Reagan's Fiscal Year 1986 Budget: A Summary and Analysis Prepared by the Staff of the House Budget Committee. 99th Cong., 1st sess. (Washington: GPO, 1985).

United States. House. Committee on the Budget. President Reagan's Fiscal Year 1986 Budget: A Summary and Analysis Prepared by the Staff of the House Budget Committee. 99th Cong., 1st sess. Washington: GPO, 1985.

[16]United States House, Committee on Interior and Insular Affairs, Entitled the "California Wilderness Act of 1983", H. Rpt. 98–40, (Washington: GPO, 1983) 35.

United States. House. Committee on Interior and Insular Affairs. Entitled the "California Wilderness Act of 1983. H. Rpt. 98–40. Washington: GPO, 1983.

[17]"Federal Communication Commission Authorization Act of 1983" (PL98-214, 8 December 1983) 1470.

"Federal Communication Commission Authorization Act of 1983." PL98-214, 8 December 1983.

References and bibliography entries for state and local documents begin with the geographic area or political affiliation. Most local or state governments do not have their own printing offices. Unless the name of the printing office is specifically mentioned, it can be omitted in the documentation.[8]

[18]New York, Department of Transportation, Bureau of Highway Operations, 1985 Annual Condition Report on Bridges and Tunnels, 1986.

New York. Department of Transportation, Bureau of Highway Operations. 1985 Annual Condition Report on Bridges and Tunnels 1986.

PERSONAL LETTERS

[19]Judy Geigner, Director of Personnel, Communications, Inc., letter to John McCurdy, Professor of Consumer Economics, 25 December 1985.

Geigner, Judy, Director of Personnel, Communications, Inc. Letter to John McCurdy, Professor of Consumer Economics. 18 April 1986.

PERSONAL INTERVIEWS

[20]Sharon Sullivan, Vice President, Computer Services, Inc., Bloomington, IL, personal interview, 21 November 1985.

Sullivan, Sharon, Vice President, Computer Services, Inc., Bloomington, IL. Personal interview. 21 November 1985.

COMPUTER SOFTWARE

[21]ThinkTank Version 2.00, computer software, Living Videotext, 1985.

ThinkTank Version 2.00. Computer software. Living Videotext, 1985.

RADIO AND TELEVISION PROGRAMS

[22]<u>This Week with David Brinkley</u>, ABC, WHOI, Peoria, IL, 12 May 1985.

<u>This Week with David Brinkley</u>. ABC, WHOI, Peoria, IL. 12 May 1985.

SPEECHES AND LECTURES

[23]Sarah Getz, "Code of Conduct for Secretaries," Monthly Meeting of Professional Secretaries, Bloomington, IL, 8 March 1986.

Getz, Sarah. "Code of Conduct for Professional Secretaries." Monthly meeting of Professional Secretaries. Bloomington, IL. 8 March 1986.

SUMMARY OF LEARNING OBJECTIVES

To Understand the Reasons for Documentation and the Problems of Plagiarism.
The report writer must document the sources he uses for both ethical and legal reasons. If the writer uses a large amount of copyrighted material, he may need permission from the author.

To Become Familiar with the Format for Quotations.
Quotations must be precise. The writer must indicate whether he has added to, deleted from, or changed emphasis of the material quoted. Short quotations can be incorporated in the text; long quotations, which are set off as indented blocks, are not enclosed in quotation marks.

To Document Sources Correctly.
References can be at the bottom of the page, at the end of the report, or in the text. The in-text citation giving name of author and page number is used more and more frequently. All reports using material from secondary sources must have a bibliography unless the writer is permitted to use endnotes and, therefore, to omit the bibliography.

To Compile Bibliographies.
Bibliographies traditionally use hanging indentations. They are alphabetized by last name of author. An annotated bibliography provides a brief description or summary of the work used for the report.

QUESTIONS AND PROBLEMS

1. Discuss the term *plagiarism*.
2. What are some of the reasons for documenting sources used in writing reports?

3. Discuss the use of style manuals.
4. How do you handle omissions, additions, and emphasis in quotations?
5. What is the format for long quotations?
6. Where in the report can you put reference notes?
7. Discuss the advantages and disadvantages of footnotes at the bottom of the page and endnotes at the end of the report.
8. What are the options for referencing material in the text?
9. Under what circumstances do you number the entries in the bibliography?
10. What is a hanging indentation? When do you use it?

NOTES

[1] Joseph Gibaldi and Walter S. Achtert, *MLA Handbook for Writers of Research Papers,* 2nd ed. (New York: The Modern Language Association of America, 1984) 48.
[2] Wilson T. Price, *Computers and Application Software: An Introduction* (New York: Holt, 1985) 68.
[3] Richard D. Steade, James R. Lowrey, and Raymond E. Glos, *Business: Its Nature and Environment,* 10th ed. (West Chicago: South-Western, 1984) 101, 307.
[4] William G. Zikmund, *Business Research Methods* (Hinsdale, IL: Dryden, 1984) 287.
[5] Steade 307.
[6] Louis E. Boone and David L. Kurtz, *Contemporary Business,* 4th ed. (Hinsdale, IL: Dryden, 1985) 358.
[7] Hertha A. Murphy and Herbert W. Hildebrandt, *Effective Business Communication,* 4th ed. (New York: McGraw-Hill, 1984) 27.
[8] Diane L. Garner and Diane H. Smith, *The Complete Guide to Citing Government Documents* (Bethesda, MD: Congressional Information Service, Inc., 1984) 10.

CHAPTER NINE

PRIMARY

RESEARCH

LEARNING OBJECTIVES

- To become familiar with the characteristics of and the research designs for primary research, such as search through company records, observation, surveys, and experiments.
- To understand the steps involved in conducting primary research.
- To understand the advantages and disadvantages of the different types of primary research.

In many cases the research studies you find through secondary research in the library are related to your problem, but they do not fit exactly. Your product may be different, and thus pricing strategies may be different. Your labor force may be larger, hold different values, and live in a different environment from that in the studies you have read; therefore, your labor force may react differently to training programs, job sharing, and job enrichment.

Secondary research is a starting point and will save you time, but it will seldom completely solve a particular problem. Primary research furnishes the rest of the information needed.

Descriptive or Ex Post Facto Research
The researcher describes the characteristics of a population.

This chapter will discuss the search through company records, observation research, survey research, and experimental research. The first three of these are also called **descriptive** or **ex post facto research** because they describe findings. The researcher, collecting material, does not interfere or change any conditions to influence the outcome. In **experimental research**, on the other hand, the researcher changes the environment and then tests the influence of the interference.

Experimental Research
The researcher interferes to test a hypothesis.

SEARCH THROUGH COMPANY RECORDS

When searching through company records, the researcher checks company documents to solve a problem. What were hiring practices in the past? How does the company deal with late accounts? What were the sales for each one

Exhibit 9.1   **Steps in Conducting the Search through Company Records**

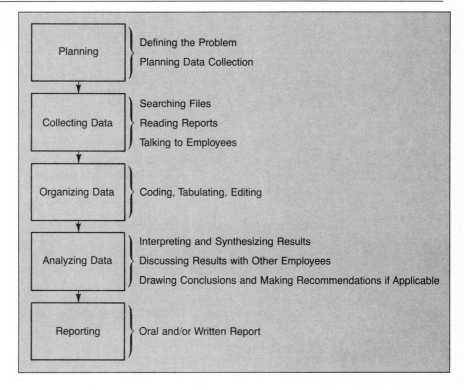

of the last five years, and how do they compare with the current year? When was the policy manual revised the last time? All of that information should be available in the company records. Exhibit 9.1 details the steps involved in this type of research.

PLANNING

Before examining any company files, the researcher must define the problem and determine exactly what is needed. At each stage it may be helpful to talk to people who are knowledgeable about the history of the company. If Pat Long is examining the hiring and promotion practices at Illington Glass Company, for example, she should not only look at the personnel records but also talk to people in personnel. They can tell her where old personnel records are stored and how they were kept. If she is examining the reasons for declining sales, however, she will have to examine past sales records and talk to people in sales in order to be efficient in her search.

COLLECTING DATA

Some pieces of information will be easy to find; others may take longer. For example, 25 years ago few companies kept records on the hiring and promoting of minorities and women. A search through the records for that type of information would be time consuming and not very productive. The search might have to be supplemented by personal interviews with people who were involved in that process at that time. Filing systems, too, have changed. Different keywords may be used for the same subject, and older files may be stored in a warehouse. Even so, company records provide helpful information on past practices and can also serve as a guideline in determining what is acceptable and unacceptable in a company. By showing what has worked in the past and what has not, they help management to avoid repeating past mistakes.

ORGANIZING AND ANALYZING DATA

Based on past records, Pat Long can determine whether sales follow a cyclical pattern or whether there is a long-term or short-term pattern of decline. Once she has established a pattern, she can look for the reasons. At this point she may go through additional records. She might also decide to search the literature at the library for information on how to combat declining sales.

REPORTING

Depending on the nature of the problem and the use of the material, the search through company records may result in a written report, an oral report, or both. The report could be informational or analytical.

ADVANTAGES OF THE SEARCH THROUGH COMPANY RECORDS

- The search is conducted at the company; therefore, it is inexpensive.
- The search can be tailored to the specific problem. For example, the company's own past sales figures can be used in analyzing a decline in sales. If the researcher studies problems of declining sales through secondary research, on the other hand, the data and the conditions described may not be valid for the company.

DISADVANTAGES OF THE SEARCH THROUGH COMPANY RECORDS

- Company records, especially older ones, are often not well organized.
- Needed data may not have been kept.
- People who might help may not be with the company any longer.

GUIDELINES

The following guidelines will help you to make an efficient search through company records:

1. Define the problem clearly.
2. Plan the approach. Decide which records might be most helpful.
3. Identify people in the company who might know about similar problems and who might know where and how records have been kept in the past.
4. Concentrate on relevant information.
5. If necessary, discuss findings with knowledgeable employees.

OBSERVATION RESEARCH

Observation research is used frequently in business. You may have driven through an intersection and noticed a person recording on a pad of paper each time a car passed. Usually, traffic counts are now done automatically. However, if it is important to know the traffic pattern in the intersection and not just the raw count, manual observation is still used in many cases. The data might be needed to decide whether the intersection should have a traffic light, a stop sign, or nothing. In a shopping mall you may see people observing shoppers and recording their observations. They may observe what fashions are popular in the area, how many men carry purses, or what shoes women wear.

At first glance observation might appear to be casual and almost haphazard, but it is highly structured. Exhibit 9.2 presents an overview of the steps in observation research.

PLANNING

Research requires planning. The researcher must clearly understand the problem and purpose of the study. Let us assume the problem is increasing traffic on the west side of town resulting from a new subdivision. The purpose of the study is to determine whether a traffic light is needed between Center and Main Street to help improve traffic flow. To fulfill that purpose, someone must observe the traffic flow and record the findings.

DEVELOPING THE OBSERVATION SCHEDULE

Research Design
The design is the plan for collecting and analyzing data.

Observation Instrument
The observation instrument is the form on which the data are recorded.

Once you have decided an observation is the best way to collect the data, you must choose a **research design**, and you must design an observation instrument. The sample **observation instrument** presented in Exhibit 9.3 continues the example of the traffic study. The pattern of the intersection, as

Exhibit 9.2   **Steps in Conducting Observation Research**

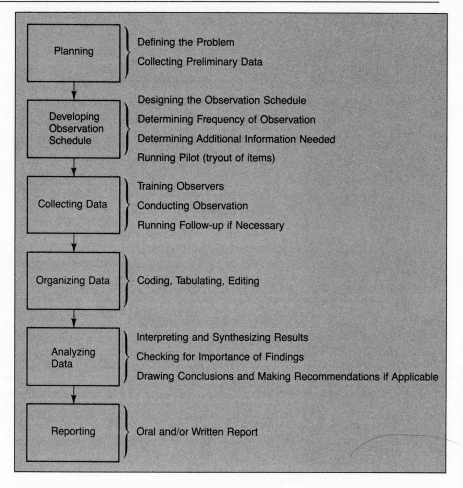

illustrated in Exhibit 9.4, might also be on the sheet together with a code for the various route possibilities. The instrument asks for information in addition to the actual count of cars. The time of observation is necessary because it obviously makes a difference whether the count is taken during rush hour or during midmorning. The date is also important. The traffic flow may vary during the week, and Saturdays and Sundays may have a different traffic pattern from weekdays.

The observation instrument must provide space for recording special occurrences during the observation. If a traffic accident blocked the intersection for half an hour, for example, the traffic count will be lower than under normal circumstances. The weather may have an influence on traffic flow.

Exhibit 9.3   **Observation Instrument**

Traffic Count

Observer _____ Date _____

Location _____ Time _____

Weather _____

Special Occurrences _____

NM SM	NM WC	NM EC	SM NM	SM WC	SM EC	EC WC	EC NM	EC SM	WC EC	WC NM	WC SM

Exhibit 9.4   **Key to Observation Schedule**

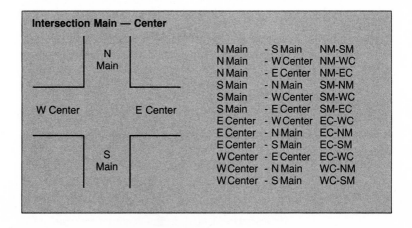

Intersection Main — Center

N Main	- S Main	NM-SM
N Main	- W Center	NM-WC
N Main	- E Center	NM-EC
S Main	- N Main	SM-NM
S Main	- W Center	SM-WC
S Main	- E Center	SM-EC
E Center	- W Center	EC-WC
E Center	- N Main	EC-NM
E Center	- S Main	EC-SM
W Center	- E Center	EC-WC
W Center	- N Main	WC-NM
W Center	- S Main	WC-SM

Rain, sunshine, heat, and cold may affect the number of people driving. The person who will evaluate the data must know about the special conditions.

The name of the person who records the observation should be on the instrument so that the evaluator can ask questions, if necessary. The name is also useful in comparing instruments. Let us assume the city has three observers for the same intersection observing at different times and on different days. When examining the instruments, the evaluator may notice that the recordings of observers A and B show similar patterns, whereas the ones for observer C are different. It is possible that during C's time something special was going on, but it is also possible that C simply did not record accurately. The name of the observer on the instrument serves as a check for accuracy.

COLLECTING DATA

Observation research is observing with a particular purpose. The observer records *exactly* what happens, leaving out nothing, adding nothing, and changing nothing.

If the phenomenon occurs too frequently to be recorded each time, the researcher can either ask the observer to record every *n*th item or to record in predetermined intervals. The fashion observer in a shopping mall, for example, may record the shoe fashions of every fifth woman passing by. The person observing consumer behavior at the checkout counter may observe for two minutes, record for one minute, observe for two minutes. That decision is *not* made by the observer but by the researcher in charge of the project. The observer must follow all procedural instructions carefully.

ORGANIZING AND ANALYZING DATA

The evaluator tabulates the data and determines any patterns in the observation. In the traffic count example, the evaluator would summarize the number of cars that went in each possible direction through the intersection and, based on the pattern for various times of the day, recommend whether to install a traffic light, a stop sign, or nothing.

REPORTING

The results of observation research are reported in written or oral form or both.

ADVANTAGES OF OBSERVATION RESEARCH

- Observations are comparatively inexpensive and fast.
- The data is well organized on the instrument and easy to tabulate in most cases.
- Observation of traffic or fashion patterns does not require extensive training.

DISADVANTAGES OF OBSERVATION RESEARCH

- The observation is limited in its use. Many things simply cannot be observed. To count the traffic or to record styles or coat colors is easy; however, to observe the reasons for certain behaviors is absolutely impossible. You can observe students going into a certain store, for example, but you cannot tell why they go there. Is it the atmosphere, the prices, the selection of goods, or the proximity to dorms? Other forms of primary research would have to be used to answer these questions.

- Physical phenomena such as fashions are easy to record. More difficult to observe and record are various types of behavior, such as the interaction between an instructor and students. You can record how many people participate and how many women versus men enter into discussions. If you want to observe how the instructor motivates students to participate, however, you must define what you mean by motivation and determine what constitutes motivating behavior on the part of the instructor. The observation of behavior is not impossible, but it takes more preparation than a traffic count.

- In observing behavior, two observers may record the same situation differently. Observers of behavior must therefore be carefully trained.

GUIDELINES

These guidelines should help you in conducting observation research:

1. Define the problem clearly.
2. Plan the observation form carefully to make certain that all necessary information will be recorded.
3. Select reliable observers who will observe and record accurately. If you observe yourself, be accurate.
4. Repeat observations to check reliability and accuracy.

SURVEY RESEARCH

Like all research, survey research must be planned carefully. Exhibit 9.5 outlines the steps involved.

PLANNING

Many problems do not lend themselves to conducting an experiment or observation. For example, reasons for certain behavior cannot be observed. The best way to find out why people watch certain TV programs or buy certain products is to ask them. A candidate wanting to know how people will vote

Exhibit 9.5   **Steps in Conducting Survey Research**

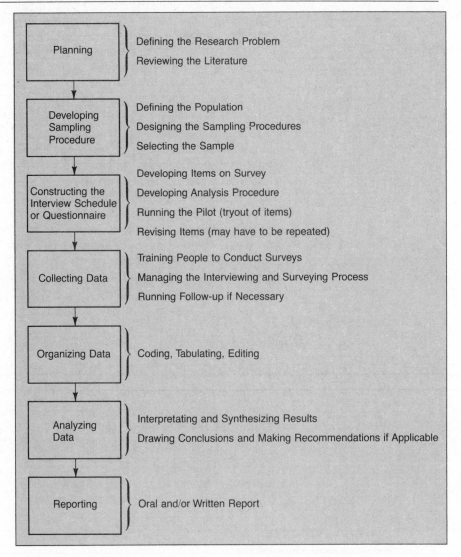

Planning	Defining the Research Problem
	Reviewing the Literature
Developing Sampling Procedure	Defining the Population
	Designing the Sampling Procedures
	Selecting the Sample
Constructing the Interview Schedule or Questionnaire	Developing Items on Survey
	Developing Analysis Procedure
	Running the Pilot (tryout of items)
	Revising Items (may have to be repeated)
Collecting Data	Training People to Conduct Surveys
	Managing the Interviewing and Surveying Process
	Running Follow-up if Necessary
Organizing Data	Coding, Tabulating, Editing
Analyzing Data	Interpretating and Synthesizing Results
	Drawing Conclusions and Making Recommendations if Applicable
Reporting	Oral and/or Written Report

in the next election must ask them how they would vote if the election were today. City officials must ask people how they would react to an increase in taxes or to a bond issue to build a new park or hospital.

In all of these situations the researcher would conduct a survey. Surveys focus on people. They concentrate on people's attitudes and opinions about their environment, their experiences, their communities. With the help of a survey, the researcher tries to assess the characteristics of large groups.

SAMPLING PROCEDURES
AND QUESTIONNAIRE DESIGN

Sample
A sample is a subset of a larger population.

The researcher will seldom survey the entire population of a city, state, or country. Surveying a **sample** of the population is less costly and more efficient. Sampling procedures and the construction of questionnaires are discussed in detail in Chapter 10.

ORGANIZING AND ANALYZING DATA

The researcher, in interpreting the data, tries to generalize from the sample to the population as a whole. That is possible only if the sample is representative of the population from which it was drawn. A survey of workers about the relationship between the workers and management, for example, cannot be generalized to all companies. It can only be generalized to the one plant. If the survey is conducted in a random sample of auto manufacturing plants, then the results can be generalized to all auto manufacturing plants. Care still must be taken, however, because other variables such as geographic location could influence the results. In any case, the researcher could not generalize from auto plants to the steel industry or the computer industry.

REPORTING

The researcher will report the results in an informational or analytical report to be used by management in the decision-making process.

TYPES OF SURVEYS

The three ways to collect data with a survey are by telephone interview, mail survey, and personal interview.

Telephone Interviews. Many researchers seem to think only of the advantages of the telephone interview, for it is used extensively. You and your friends have probably been interviewed by telephone at least once. The topics of telephone interviews range from consumer surveys to political opinion polls and sales pitches for new products.

The Advantages. The advantages of the telephone interview are that:

- The telephone interview is fast. The surveyor can reach many people in a short period of time and obtain immediate answers. No danger exists that information might not be returned, as is the case with the mail survey.
- The telephone interview is inexpensive.
- The telephone interview is convenient for the interviewer, who can simply call again later if people are not home.

The Disadvantages. The disadvantages of the telephone interview by far outweigh its advantages:

- The call may come at an inconvenient time, and the person may refuse to answer questions or, even worse, give careless answers. Obviously the results of such an interview are not very useable.

- Most people refuse to give personal information over the telephone. They may be reluctant to talk about their income, political or religious affiliation, educational background, or products they buy.

- The telephone interview forces an immediate response, even though the interviewee might need to think about the answer for a while. Maybe the interviewee does not immediately remember data the interviewer asks for, but, feeling pressured, the interviewee gives an answer. Few people, for example, can give the exact number of dollars they spend on groceries or clothing every month.

- Telephone samples are not representative of the population because only people with telephones can be reached.

- People may be impatient because they are tired of being interviewed by telephone. They argue that they have the telephone for their private use and not for the convenience of researchers.

- Much nonverbal communication is lost over the telephone. The interviewer cannot observe facial expressions and hand movements, yet nonverbal signs can give distinct meanings to the verbal responses. Posture and body movements could indicate whether the person is telling the truth or simply wants to finish the interview.

Guidelines. These guidelines will help you in conducting successful telephone interviews:

1. Plan the telephone interview carefully. Have the list of questions ready.

2. Time how long the telephone interview will take and then adjust the timeframe. The interview should not be longer than five to ten minutes.

3. Call at a time that might be convenient for the person you want to interview. Dinnertime and lunchtime are not convenient.

4. Avoid very personal questions. Only ask questions to which the respondent can be reasonably expected to know the answer.

5. Introduce yourself at the beginning of the survey and clearly state the purpose of your call. Name the organization you are working for.

6. It may be helpful to call a day before the interview to introduce yourself and the organization and to ask for an interview. At that point you can set a time when you will call. People may appreciate your thoughtfulness and be more willing to cooperate.

7. State your questions clearly and pleasantly. If your voice indicates that you are serious about the interview, the respondent may be more serious too.

8. At the end of the interview thank the person for the time and cooperation given to you.

Mail Surveys. Many researchers send out questionnaires in order to collect data. Because bulk mailings are inexpensive, mail surveys are used extensively. A growing concern exists, however, about the effectiveness of mail surveys.

The Advantages. The advantages of mail surveys are that:

- Mail surveys are comparatively inexpensive. Many people can be reached with the same mailing.
- People can answer at their own convenience. They are not pressured to answer immediately.
- People can think about the question and the answer. This can increase accuracy and objectivity.
- With a good sample the results can be generalized to large groups of the population.

The Disadvantages. The disadvantages of mail surveys are that:

- It may be difficult to reach the target group. People resent being inundated with junk mail, and the overuse of mailing lists has added to the problem. Many companies buy mailing lists from mailing-list companies, competitors, or banks. Often they are outdated or addressees do not have the characteristics that the researcher is seeking. Many people, like the college student who receives a questionnaire about retirement communities, are on mailing lists by mistake.
- Even people who are willing to answer a questionnaire often put it at the bottom of a pile of mail and forget it.
- The response rate to questionnaires can be as low as 10 percent and is seldom higher than 60 percent. Even if the researcher starts with a representative sample, the sample may not be representative after all the responses are in. Whole groups with certain characteristics might not answer and would not be represented in the final data. Furthermore, to determine which groups did not respond might be very difficult.
- People who answer may have characteristics that are not common in the population as a whole.
- People may exaggerate in their answers. For example, successful people tend to overstate their earnings. They may give answers that reflect

their feelings and desire for prestige. They may say they go to the theater, donate money to charities, travel, and buy new cars every two years, simply because they think they should be doing these things. The results are therefore not reliable.

Guidelines. These guidelines will be helpful in working with mail surveys:

1. Plan the questionnaire very carefully. Organize the questions logically.

2. State the purpose of the questionnaire.

3. Carefully select the sample. The target group for a seminar to improve secretaries' business communication skills, for example, would be the secretaries themselves if the seminar were scheduled after work hours and the secretaries were to pay the fee. The target group might be the office managers if the seminar were scheduled during work hours and the company were to pay.

4. Provide a stamped envelope for the return of the questionnaire.

5. Send the questionnaires via first class mail, and make sure that they do not look like advertisements.

6. You may want to give a token of your appreciation; some companies enclose a quarter or a pencil.

7. If the sample is not too large, you might want to call the people in the sample ahead of time and ask for their cooperation.

Structured and Unstructured Interviews
The structured interview asks questions in predetermined form and sequence. The unstructured interview resembles a conversation.

Personal Interviews. If conducted well, the personal interview is a powerful tool for collecting data. There are two types of personal interviews, the **structured interview** and the **unstructured interview**. In the structured interview, such as a census, the interviewer follows a set of questions written on an interview schedule. The interviewer does not rephrase questions or change the order of the questions because even the slightest change in wording can distort the meaning of the question and influence the results of the study. The interviewer must also be careful not to allow his intonation to suggest a certain answer or preference.

Sometimes the interviewee may fail to understand a term or even the entire question. When this happens, the interviewer should repeat the question. He should not, however, provide his own definition or clarification of the question.

In the unstructured interview the interviewer creates the atmosphere of a conversation. He is not bound to follow a certain pattern for the questions. The interviewer may repeat the question, repeat the answer, ask additional neutral questions, make comments to clarify answers, or get the interviewee to explain a response in more detail. A neutral question, for example, might be, "Anything else?"

The unstructured interview (the name is actually misleading) might seem to be much easier to conduct than the structured interview, but the opposite is true. The temptation in the unstructured interview is to have a friendly chat. Lacking a preset list of questions, the interviewer must remember what has been discussed in the interview and what is still to be covered. To conduct an unstructured interview properly requires training.

During a job interview you are in an unstructured interview situation. The interviewer asks personalized questions that relate to you and your background. A good job interview, however, has an invisible structure. The first few minutes are devoted to making you feel at ease. Next the interviewer may ask you questions, but they usually are worded to create the feeling of a relaxed conversation. Then you are given an opportunity to ask questions. The interviewer closes the interview and, after you have gone, writes down his observations, impressions, and perhaps a decision. The unstructured interview is really highly structured.

The interview is often used as a follow-up to other types of investigation, but it can also be used at the beginning of the research project. At the beginning, it serves the purpose of setting the scope of the study, clarifying the problem, and formulating the hypothesis. At the end, it helps interpret unusual findings, examine some aspects of the problem in more depth, and put into perspective some major groups in the sample.

The interview can also be used as the major research plan, especially if the target group is small.

The Advantages. The advantages of the personal interview are that:

- The interview is flexible and adaptable to individual situations.
- The interview permits probing into the reasons and the context for attitudes. The interviewer finds out not only the attitudes people have but why they have them.
- The interviewer can observe the nonverbal behavior of the respondent in addition to the verbal responses.
- Ambiguous words can be clarified.

The Disadvantages. The disadvantages of the personal interview are that:

- The personal interview is expensive and takes much time.
- Interviewer bias can creep into the questions and the answers. The intonation, dress, and nonverbal behavior of the interviewer may elicit a certain response.
- Clarifying statements may influence the respondent.
- Noise in the office or incoming telephone calls can interrupt the interview and interfere with the interview process.

Guidelines. These guidelines will help in conducting successful personal interviews:

1. Prepare for the interview by going over the questions beforehand.
2. If the interview is lengthy—half an hour or more—always make an appointment. Unstructured interviews should always be scheduled.
3. When you make the appointment, say how long the interview will take.
4. Arrive on time.
5. If you have not done so before, ask at the beginning of the interview whether you may take notes or record the interview.
6. If you want to quote the person afterward, obtain permission first.
7. Be courteous.
8. Stick to the topic of the interview, and do not waste the interviewee's time.
9. At the end thank the person for the time and cooperation given to you.

EXPERIMENTAL RESEARCH

The two basic types of experiments are the lab experiment and the field experiment. The research principles are the same for both, but in the lab environment the researcher has more control over the experiment than in the field environment, that is, the real world. The basic steps for conducting experimental research are illustrated in Exhibit 9.6.

PLANNING

Hypothesis
A hypothesis is an unproven supposition that is testable.

At the beginning of every experiment is a problem. For example, Peggy Rehm may notice that the secretaries in her office who write on the new microcomputers seem to be more productive and have a more positive attitude toward their work than those who do not use a microcomputer. She may also notice an improvement in the quality of the work. Based on her observations, she believes a relationship between the microcomputers and the work performance may indeed exist. Of course, at this point she cannot be certain. Perhaps the secretaries writing on microcomputers received a pay raise or have a new supervisor. To determine the impact of the microcomputer, Peggy can formulate a **hypothesis**.

Exhibit 9.6   **Steps in Conducting Experimental Research**

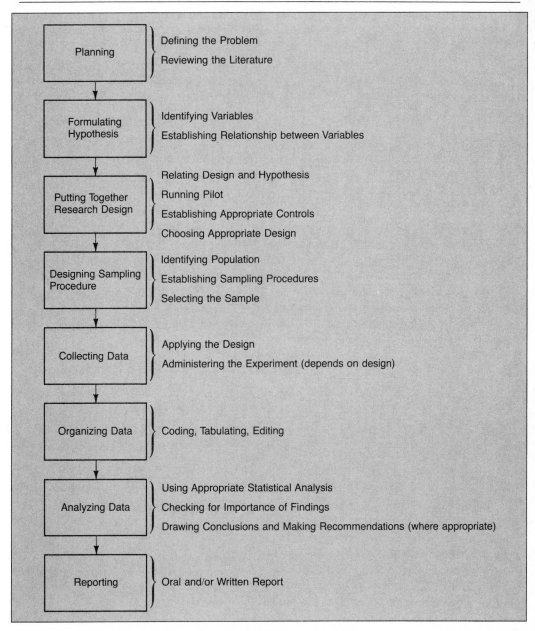

Planning	Defining the Problem Reviewing the Literature
Formulating Hypothesis	Identifying Variables Establishing Relationship between Variables
Putting Together Research Design	Relating Design and Hypothesis Running Pilot Establishing Appropriate Controls Choosing Appropriate Design
Designing Sampling Procedure	Identifying Population Establishing Sampling Procedures Selecting the Sample
Collecting Data	Applying the Design Administering the Experiment (depends on design)
Organizing Data	Coding, Tabulating, Editing
Analyzing Data	Using Appropriate Statistical Analysis Checking for Importance of Findings Drawing Conclusions and Making Recommendations (where appropriate)
Reporting	Oral and/or Written Report

FORMULATING THE HYPOTHESIS

Unlike the problem statement, which is usually stated as a question, the hypothesis is always stated in declarative form. These are examples of hypotheses:

Secretaries who write on microcomputers are more productive than those who do not.

Secretaries who write on microcomputers have a positive attitude toward their work.

Secretaries who write on microcomputers produce higher quality work than those who use typewriters.

Advertising has a positive impact on sales.

Advertising increases sales.

A hypothesis is never based simply on guessing and is never randomly picked. The researcher formulates a hypothesis only when reasonably certain that the results of the experiment will support it. A hypothesis is based on theory, observation, past research, and practical problems. The researcher or other people may have observed, for example, that customers tend to select items on the shelf that are in front and at eye level. Of course, there may be other reasons than location to explain why the products are selected. Perhaps the color is more attractive or perhaps the customer's preferred brand simply happens to be in that location. Because there may be a relationship that is worth testing, the researcher may formulate the hypothesis: shelf location influences sales. A good hypothesis gives guidance in the experiment by stating precisely what is to be tested.

The three hypotheses stating that a positive relationship exists between the use of microcomputers and work performance can be labeled hypothesis 1 (H_1), hypothesis 2 (H_2), hypothesis 3 (H_3) so that they are not confused. A hypothesis can also be formulated that no relationship exists between the use of microcomputers and work performance and attitude. This is called a **null hypothesis** (H_0). The positive hypotheses and the null hypotheses for the example would be:

Null Hypothesis
Any change in the relationship between variables in a null hypothesis is not due to the experiment.

H_1: *Secretaries who write on microcomputers are more productive than those who do not.*

H_0: *Microcomputers have no influence on productivity of secretaries.*

H_2: *Secretaries who write on microcomputers have a positive attitude toward work.*

H_0: *There is no relationship between the use of microcomputers and attitude toward work.*

H_3: *Secretaries who write on the microcomputer produce higher quality work than those who use typewriters.*

H$_0$:   *There is no relationship between the use of microcomputers and the quality of work.*

The null hypothesis is the opposite of the positive hypothesis. It is not always explicitly stated, but it is always implied. The outcome of hypothesis testing confirms or disconfirms a hypothesis. A hypothesis must therefore be testable. If the problem statement does not lend itself to a hypothesis that can be tested, then the problem is not amenable to scientific investigation. The value statement that American companies should adopt the Japanese practice of making decisions by consensus, for example, cannot be tested scientifically. The statement does not establish a relationship between **variables** or point toward a way to test them. Value words such as *should, ought, better,* or *best* should not be used in a hypothesis because they cannot be measured.

Variables
A variable is a characteristic that can be measured.

Hypothesis testing involves the testing of the relationship between variables. In the example, the hypotheses clearly state the relationship between the use of a microcomputer (a variable), quantity (a variable), quality of work (a variable), and attitude toward work (a variable).

IDENTIFYING VARIABLES

Each hypothesis in the example establishes a specific relationship between two of the variables: *microcomputer, quantity of work, quality of work,* and *attitude toward work.* So that they can be measured and related to each other, variables must be specific. They must be *operationalized;* that is, they must be stated in quantifiable terms.

The researcher in the example must define *higher quality* exactly. It may be the number of errors in a business letter or report or the number of retypes required because of errors. *Quantity* is easier to measure because output can be counted in numbers of pages or letters. *Attitude toward work* is difficult to measure. It might be measured in the number of sick days that secretaries take, the length of coffee breaks, the number of arguments in the office, or the number of complaints to supervisors about coworkers or work environment. The researcher can list a number of attributes of attitude but will probably never be able to list them all. To resolve the problem, the researcher could use a validated attitude survey that has been tested for accurately measuring attitudes.

ESTABLISHING RELATIONSHIPS BETWEEN VARIABLES

Dependent and Independent Variables
The dependent variable is expected to change as a result of change in the independent variable.

The two types of variables in an experiment are: **dependent** and **independent variables**. In the example, the *use of the microcomputer* is the independent variable, whereas *quantity, quality,* and *attitude* are the dependent variables. The independent variable is presumed to be the cause of the dependent variable. The dependent variable is supposed to occur as a result of the independent variable; it is influenced by the independent variable.

In an experiment the independent variable is manipulated by the researcher, who might introduce microcomputers into one office but not in the other or increase or reduce advertising outlays. The dependent variable, on the other hand, is *not* manipulated. It is observed for changes. The researcher manipulates the use of microcomputers and then observes work performance and attitudes.

While the independent variable is manipulated, all other variables must be held constant. If the researcher introduces microcomputers and at the same time changes the furniture in the office and introduces flextime, he cannot test whether changes in work performance and attitude are the result of the use of the microcomputer, of flextime, or of the new furniture. If the researcher changes advertising outlay for a product and at the same time changes the packaging of the product, he will not know whether sales change as a result of advertising or changes in packaging.

One of the basic requirements is to manipulate only one variable and to keep all of the others constant. This is, of course, possible in a lab environment. There the researcher can change the light, for example, while keeping the temperature constant and the amount and quality of food the same. In the field, control is much more difficult. The researcher may not be able to keep everything constant. The supervisor may resign in the middle of the experiment and a new one may be hired. Furthermore, business activity does not stand still until an experiment is completed.

PUTTING TOGETHER THE RESEARCH DESIGN

In order to test the hypothesis, the researcher must have an experimental design. The design is the plan, the structure, or the strategy for testing the hypothesis and defines the method of collecting and analyzing the data. We will discuss two basic designs: the controlled before–after design and the time design. The design is dependent on the problem statement and the hypothesis. Once you understand the principles of research design, you can consult books on research to familiarize yourself with more details.

The Controlled Before–After Design. In the controlled before–after design there are a **control group** and an **experimental group**. After both groups take a pretest, the independent variable is manipulated in the experimental group only. Then both groups take a posttest as illustrated in the following example:

Control Group
No treatment is given to the control group in an experiment.

Experimental Group
The treatment is administered to the experimental group.

Experimental Group	Control Group
Pretest	Pretest
Manipulation of Independent Variable	
Posttest	Posttest

Let us assume a report-writing instructor would like to test what impact the use of a microcomputer has on writing anxiety. The hypothesis is that the use of a microcomputer decreases writing anxiety. In this case both groups take the writing anxiety test as a pretest at the beginning of the semester. Then the experimental group writes all assignments for the semester on the microcomputer, whereas the control group writes all assignments as before—with paper and pencil and typewriter. At the end of the semester, both groups take another writing anxiety test. The scores for the tests are as follows:

	Experimental Group	Control Group
Pretest	90 average	95 average
Manipulation	yes	no
Posttest	45 average	65 average

The lowest possible score on the writing anxiety test is 26 points; the highest is 130. The higher score means higher writing anxiety.

There is a difference of 5 points in the pretest and a difference of 20 points in the posttest. The difference in the pretest is due to factors that are beyond the researcher's control. They may be due to natural differences between students. The difference in the posttest is due to differences beyond the control of the researcher *and* due to the impact of the experiment, namely, the microcomputer used in writing. Both groups have less anxiety at the end of the semester than at the beginning.

The researcher must ask whether the decrease in writing anxiety resulting from the manipulation is significant. If the control group improves by 30 points, and the experimental group by 31 points, the one point is assumed to be due to the manipulation. The researcher could argue, however, that a one-point difference is not significant enough to count. That one point could be the result of error or it could be the result of the manipulation. However, one point may not be enough to justify the spending of thousands of dollars for microcomputers in order to decrease writing anxiety.

Researchers set guidelines for expected results, and the changes must be significant enough to ensure that the additional cost of equipment will be balanced by higher output. For example, cost factors will play a role in the acceptance criteria of a new package design. Even if a new design increases sales significantly, management still must determine whether the sales increases are high enough to pay for the new design and also increase profits.

The validity of the controlled before–after design depends on an important assumption: that the control group and the experimental group have the same characteristics. This is a big assumption indeed. The people must be randomly assigned to the groups to assure that they have the same characteristics, and even then the researcher cannot be absolutely certain. There is always a degree of error because people are always different.

The maturity factor also influences the results. The instructor would expect that during the semester both groups would change their attitude toward writing. The instructor is interested in whether the difference between the groups narrows or widens.

Another problem is that the pretest–posttest system may sensitize people to the experiment, both those in the control group and those in the experimental group. They become aware of what the researcher is looking for. At the very minimum they know that they are part of some project, and that in itself may change their behavior.

The design can be extended to a controlled before–after design with one experimental group and two control groups or even with one experimental and three control groups.

Time Design. The time design has the same setup as the controlled before–after design, except that the dependent variable is again measured at a later date. Both groups in the example would take another writing anxiety test, perhaps two months after the posttest:

Measure ──────→Manipulate ──────→Measure ──────→Measure

In a variation of the time design, the dependent variable is measured twice before the manipulation of the independent variable and twice after the manipulation:

Measure ──────→Measure ──────→Manipulate ──────→Measure ──────→Measure

This design allows for a closer monitoring for changes over time. Between the first and the second measurements both groups should change at the same rate. The third measurement, after the manipulation, should show different results. The fourth measurement, then, will show whether the manipulation has long-lasting results. If the manipulation has a lasting influence, the two groups will change at different rates. If the manipulation produces short-term results, the two groups will change at approximately the same rate again.

The remaining steps in experimental research will be discussed in greater detail in the following chapters: sampling and data collection in Chapter 10 and the organization and analysis of data in Chapters 11 and 12.

ADVANTAGES OF EXPERIMENTAL RESEARCH

Lab Experiment. The advantages of the lab experiment are that:

- There is a high level of control of variables.
- Subjects or items can be randomly chosen and assigned to control and experimental groups.

- The manipulation of the independent variable can be closely monitored.
- The lab experiment is precise and lends itself to duplication.

Field Experiment. The advantages of the field experiment are that:

- There is the possibility of some random selection and assignment into groups.
- Strong manipulation of the independent variable is possible.
- The experimental situation reflects the complex situation of real life and business environment.
- Broad hypotheses can be tested.
- The field experiment is flexible and applicable to actual business situations.

DISADVANTAGES OF EXPERIMENTAL RESEARCH

Lab Experiment. The disadvantages of the lab experiment are that:

- The lab situation is artificial.
- Because the lab situation is artificial, the results cannot easily be generalized. For example, do the results of tests of drugs with animals really apply to humans? Most business problems simply cannot be tested in a lab environment.

Field Experiment. The disadvantages of the field experiment are that:

- There is a problem with random selection and assignment.
- Variables are difficult to isolate and manipulate.
- Any experiments with people raise ethical questions. Is it ethical to put people into a control group if the hypothesis states that the new training program accelerates the upward mobility of participants? Because a hypothesis is formulated only after some reason exists to believe that an experiment will support it, the people who are randomly assigned to the control group are automatically at a disadvantage.

Because the experiment is limited in its use, it is often replaced by or supplemented with field studies, which permit no randomization and very little control. The examination comes *ex post facto*. This means that the researcher not only has no influence on the variables but also cannot study how the relationship of dependent and independent variables has changed. Yet often a field study is all that is possible. After examining the possible advantages of a new training program, for example, hardly any company would continue the old program and at the same time start the new program in order to set up an experimental design. It is even less likely that people would be assigned randomly into the two programs. In most cases the company will adopt the new program. It is impossible to determine the effectiveness of the training program with an experiment.

GUIDELINES

These guidelines will help in conducting experimental research:

1. Carefully define the problem.
2. Formulate the hypothesis you want to test. You may have one or several hypotheses.
3. Identify the independent and dependent variables clearly. Put the variables in testable form, and establish the relationship between the variables.
4. Formulate a testable hypothesis.
5. Choose an appropriate research design. The design will depend on the problem and the hypothesis.
6. Choose your sample according to the rules of sampling. Assign subjects to the control and experimental group to ensure reliability.
7. Be aware of the ethical implications of using people in experimental research.
8. Be aware of the problems of generalizing from a sample to the population in general.
9. Conduct your research with honesty and integrity.

SUMMARY OF LEARNING OBJECTIVES

To Become Familiar with the Characteristics of and the Research Designs for Primary Research, such as Search through Company Records, Observation, Surveys and Experiments.

The search through company records often is the starting point of the data collection.

In observation research data is recorded on an observation instrument. The observer records phenomena as he sees them. There is no manipulation of variables.

Survey research can be done by telephone, mail, or interview. The interview is the most expensive of the three. For surveys to be valid, researchers need training in data gathering. The questionnaire is used extensively in survey research.

In the experiment the researcher manipulates variables. The development of an appropriate research design is crucial in experimental research. A widely used design is the controlled before–after design. In this design a pretest is administered to a control and an experimental group. Then the variable is manipulated in the experimental group. A posttest is administered to both groups. The difference between the changes in the two groups is assumed to be caused by the experiment. A basic assumption in experimental research is that the experimental and control groups have the same characteristics.

To Understand the Steps Involved in Conducting Primary Research.
All primary research starts with planning and the definition of the problem. The research design and the method for data collection depend on the type of research to be conducted. The data must be organized and analyzed before it can be reported.

To Understand the Advantages and Disadvantages of the Different Types of Primary Research.
The researcher must know the advantages and disadvantages of the research approach he selects so that he can choose the most appropriate method for solving the problem. The telephone survey, for example, is fast and inexpensive but not very accurate. The experiment is more accurate but raises ethical questions concerning the random selection and manipulation of people.

QUESTIONS AND PROBLEMS

1. Discuss the major differences between primary and secondary research.
2. Define the terms *ex post facto* research and experimental research.
3. What are some of the shortcomings of experimental research in business?
4. What are some of the advantages and disadvantages of the telephone interview, the mail survey, and the personal interview?
5. When would you use a telephone interview, a mail questionnaire, or a personal interview?
6. What is the role of the research design?
7. What are major differences between the field and the lab experiments?
8. Discuss some of the ethical considerations in experimental research.
9. How would you test the following hypotheses? Explain and justify your choice.
   a. Pub II is a bar with patrons who are more working class than white collar.
   b. Saturday is the biggest shopping day in Campus Town.
   c. Of the students who spend an evening at the university library, fewer than 50 percent appear to be studying.

d. Food service in the cafeteria would be smoother with an additional food line.

e. The college male prefers to date women who are four inches shorter than he.

f. The average shopping time before making a purchase in the university book store is ten minutes.

g. Most shoppers go to the university book store because of its proximity to classrooms and dorms.

h. Men and women exhibit different classroom behaviors in accounting classes.

CHAPTER TEN

TOOLS FOR

PRIMARY

RESEARCH:

SAMPLING AND

QUESTIONNAIRE

LEARNING OBJECTIVES

- To examine various types of samples and become familiar with the sampling procedure.
- To apply the principles of questionnaire design.
- To write effective questions for a questionnaire.
- To tabulate results.

This chapter and the previous one complement each other. Good primary research requires mastering the tools presented in this chapter: sampling techniques, questionnaire design, and editing and tabulating questionnaire results.

SAMPLING

Theoretically, a marketer could interview all customers or test his product in every city with every consumer group, but, of course, time and cost constraints make such a procedure undesirable and impossible. The researcher may therefore decide to select only a small group out of the population. This small group is the sample. Any research results apply to this sample only. If the researcher wants to draw conclusions and generalize the conclusions to the entire population, the sample must be comparable to the population or representative of it.

Representative
The sample must have the characteristics of the population.

The larger the sample, the greater is the likelihood that it is **representative** of the population. If a population of 100 people has a sample of 2 people, then it is unlikely that the sample is representative of the 100. A sample of 60, on the other hand, makes representativeness likely but is more expensive, of course. A researcher must weigh accuracy against cost and decide on the best balance, that is, how much accuracy to sacrifice to keep the cost down.

Let us assume a marketer has to draw a sample in a city with more than 500,000 people. In order to be 95 percent certain that the sample does not have an error larger than 3 percent, the researcher needs a sample of 544 people. This assumes that the population is rather homogeneous in the characteristics relevant to the research. In a town of 10,000 people, the researcher would need a sample of 516. Exhibit 10.1 illustrates the sample size for

Exhibit 10.1   Sample Size for Various Population Sizes and Percentages of Error

| | Error | | | |
Population Size	±1%	±2%	±3%	±5%
1,000	a	a	353	235
2,000	a	760	428	266
3,000	a	890	461	278
4,000	a	938	479	284
5,000	a	984	491	289
10,000	3288	1091	516	297
20,000	3935	1154	530	302
50,000	4461	1195	538	304
100,000	4669	1210	541	305
500,000 to ∞	4850	1222	544	306

[a]In these cases more that 50% of the population is required in the sample. Since the normal approximation of the hypergeometric distribution is a poor approximation in such instances, no sample value is given.
Source: Adapted from Nan Lin, *Foundations of Social Research* (New York: McGraw-Hill, Inc., 1976), p. 477. Reprinted with permission.

various population sizes and percentages of error. The table applies to fairly homogeneous groups. If the populations are heterogeneous, the samples would need to be larger.

RANDOM SAMPLE

Random Sample
Each item in the population has an even chance to be selected.

Random sampling is defined as every member of the population having an equal chance of being selected for the sample.

Let us assume you work in quality control. At the end of the assembly line, a worker puts electric switches into a box, 50 in each box. You examine five switches in every box; that is, you draw a sample of five switches out of each box. Each switch in the box has an equal chance of being selected. If your samples of five are truly random, you should have the same percentage of faulty switches from each box.

The researcher, no matter how careful, can never be certain that the random sample is representative of the population. If the sample is random, then the chances that the sample is representative are greater than if the sample is not randomly drawn.

The researcher wants the sample to be reliable as well as random. **Reliability** means that successive samples from the population will have the same characteristics. If the researcher draws several samples of ten screws out of a box of screws, the first few samples may be quite different. As more samples are drawn, this difference decreases. In the context of a questionnaire, reliability means that samples from the same population will answer the questionnaire with the same results.

Reliability
Successive tests will bring the same results.

Validity
The valid test measures what the researcher wants it to measure.

Validity, on the other hand, means that the test actually measures what the researcher wants to measure. For example, the assumption is that a test to measure writing anxiety actually measures writing anxiety and not writing ability or vocabulary level. On first thought, validity might not seem to be a problem because the researcher will design an experiment or a questionnaire that measures what he wants to measure. In reality this can be quite difficult. Think of the controversy surrounding intelligence tests.

Many people argue that intelligence tests do not actually test intelligence but rather measure adaptation to the particular culture of a person. If you decide to go to graduate school for an MBA, you must take the Graduate Management Aptitude Test. Presumably the GMAT measures how well you will do later in management, but critics argue the test measures how well you will do in graduate school. Although many highly educated people work on designing these costly tests, serious doubts exist about their validity.

SYSTEMATIC RANDOM SAMPLE

On first thought, the term *systematic random sample* does not seem to make much sense. You may think that a sample is either random or systematic. Actually, the two can be combined.

Let us assume you want to draw a sample of the members of the Association of Business Communication (ABC). You want to study the educational background of business communication instructors and the courses they teach. You could cut up a printed list of the names, put them all in a bowl, and draw your sample. However, you can obtain a random sample with less work than that. You can randomly choose a starting point on the list of names and then select every *n*th name on the list after that. You can obtain a membership list from the ABC office at the University of Illinois. It contains 1,200 names in alphabetical order, and you want a sample of 250 names for your research.

The systematic random sample in this case is based on the assumption that people whose last names start with *M* do not have different characteristics from people whose last names start with *R*, *E*, or any other letter in the alphabet. Last names are assumed to have no bearing on the variables important to the study.

One important limitation has to do with the outcome of the study. You may generalize your findings only to members of ABC. You cannot generalize to all business communication instructors because the people who are members may have different characteristics from the instructors who are not members.

STRATIFIED RANDOM SAMPLE

The population is divided into strata, or layers. Each stratum has its own characteristics: income, education, values, and lifestyles. The researcher determines which characteristics are important for the study and then draws a random sample from each stratum. In stratified random sampling the final sample should have the same proportion of men, women, college graduates, blacks—if those are the important characteristics in the study—as in the population.

CLUSTER SAMPLE

Cluster sampling, used frequently in surveys, is a successive random sampling of groups in the population. For example, a researcher may draw a random sample of Chambers of Commerce in the country, then draw a sample of small businesses from the sample of Chambers of Commerce, and finally draw a sample of individual employees in those businesses.

QUOTA SAMPLE

Quota sampling is nonrandom. It is based on knowledge of various strata or characteristics in the population that are suitable for the research. The purpose of quota sampling is to ensure that various subgroups in a population, such as young people, old people, or middle-aged people, are represented to the extent the researcher desires. The researcher will decide how to select the sample and how to meet the quota. Thus the process may introduce bias, as the following example shows.

A research firm hired students to conduct a quota sample based on age. When the researchers began to analyze the sample, they found that most of the people under 25 were students. The student workers had included other students in the sample to fill the quota. Quota samples tend to include people who are easy to find and willing to be interviewed.

SUMMARY OF SAMPLING TECHNIQUES

Random sampling is assumed to result in a sample that is representative of the population from which the sample is drawn. Once the sample has been selected, people or items should be randomly assigned to experimental or control groups if an experiment is conducted.

Research findings, based on samples, can be generalized only to the population from which the sample was drawn. A sample based on names in the telephone book, for example, is representative of the people listed in the book and *not* of all people living in the city, not even of all people owning telephones, because the book does not give the names of people with unlisted numbers.

THE QUESTIONNAIRE

The purpose of the questionnaire is to help answer the research question or solve the research problem. The questionnaire is the instrument used to collect the necessary data for testing a hypothesis through surveys. It is the tool to gather data on opinions, attitudes, and facts.

Questionnaire design takes time and care. Because good questionnaires are difficult to write for a number of reasons, many questionnaires are weak. The data they collect is biased and often unreliable. The questions may be ambiguous, may be leading, or may play on the emotions and prejudices of the respondent. An understanding of the steps in conducting survey research, discussed in Chapter 9, is important to good questionnaire design.

THE OVERALL PLANNING OF THE QUESTIONNAIRE

Before writing specific questions, the researcher must determine the precise goal of the questionnaire. Does the researcher, for example, need facts on what automobile-care products, over-the-counter drugs, cleaning products, or processed foods consumers use? Does she want to collect information about people's attitudes toward drugs, processed food, or pollution? Does she want both facts and attitudes? In any case, the purpose and the goal of the questionnaire, which are determined by the problem, must be clarified before the researcher writes any questions.

To save time and to help in writing the questions, the researcher must also determine the key areas to be investigated, a process similar to breaking a problem down into subfactors.

THE SEQUENCE OF QUESTIONS

When collecting data, the researcher is usually interested not simply in what people think in general, but also whether patterns exist in the attitudes of people. For example, the researcher may want to distinguish between what young and old people think about ways to solve pollution problems. A problem may require finding out whether men and women have different attitudes toward advertising. A solution may depend on knowing whether political affiliation, religious affiliation, or educational level makes a difference in attitudes toward collective bargaining or affirmative action.

Profile of Respondent
The profile establishes the personal data of the respondent.

Where does the researcher put those questions? On many questionnaires the **profile of the respondent** is established at the beginning. Some people resent giving this kind of information, however, and may discard a questionnaire that begins with personal questions. If profile questions are put at the end of the questionnaire, the respondent may have become interested in the topic, and the profile questions may appear to be a natural extension of the other questions. The profile questions may also make more sense after the respondent has read the entire questionnaire. The researcher should include only those personal questions that relate directly to the hypothesis and problem.

The designer of the questionnaire also must consider the sequence of the main questions. Questions should follow each other in a logical order. If question 8 asks about the use of personal-hygiene products and question 9 asks about attitudes toward company profits, the respondent will have a difficult time seeing a logical connection between them and may become frustrated.

Finally, a questionnaire must concentrate on a central issue that relates to the problem. A title at the top of the questionnaire is helpful in identifying this central issue.

THE WORDING OF QUESTIONS

The wording of questions is probably the most difficult aspect of designing a questionnaire. The overriding consideration is clarity. Questions must be absolutely clear and unambiguous. The question "How much did you make last year?" is so personal, that many people might resent it. The question is also unclear. Most people would assume that they are supposed to give information on their income. They might wonder, however, whether the quesiton asked for before-tax income or after-tax income and whether they were to include income from wages, from investments, or both.

The question "How much did you make last year?" creates another problem. How many people actually remember their exact income? They probably would need to refer to their tax return records, and most will not go through that much trouble for a questionnaire. Therefore, they will either leave the question blank or give a *ballpark* figure that may be a poor guess. The researcher might increase the response rate by asking for income ranges, such as $10,000 to $14,999, $15,000 to $20,000, and higher.

The following example illustrates the difference between ambiguous and clear questions:

Poor: *How do you bank?*

Better: *What banking conveniences do you use?*
Mark all that apply.

_____ *Drive-up window*
_____ *Lobby*
_____ *Automatic teller*
_____ *Other, please specify* _____

It is possible that the researcher actually wanted to find out what kinds of accounts people have. In that case the question might be:

Better: *What types of bank accounts do you have?*
Mark all that apply.

_____ *Checking Account*
_____ *Now Account*
_____ *Savings Account*
_____ *Other, please specify* _____

The first question of the next pair is ambiguous:

Poor: *Which organizations do you support?*

Better: *Which of the following organizations did you financially support last year?*
Mark all that apply.

_____ *Heart Fund*
_____ *Easter Seal*
_____ *March of Dimes*
_____ *Other, please specify*_____

The improved questions make it easier for the researcher to tabulate the answers.

The researcher must consider whether the respondent can be reasonably expected to have the necessary background information to be able to answer. If a question asks "Do you support the U.S. decision to leave UNESCO?" then the respondent must be familiar with UNESCO and the problems that led up to the decision to leave UNESCO in order to give an intelligent opinion. To ask people "How do LIFO and FIFO affect the income statement and balance sheet in inflationary times?" is pointless if they do not know what the terms LIFO and FIFO mean.

Leading Questions
Leading questions suggest the desired answer.

A researcher must be alert for **leading questions** that suggest the answer. Leading questions come in many forms and disguises. Some researchers may not be aware that they are suggesting an answer, yet they may be so personally involved in the issue that their own beliefs influence the wording of the question. In other cases the answer may be suggested more openly.

The question "You are concerned about inflation, aren't you?" has the answer built in. The respondent is not given a chance to answer anything but "yes" whether or not inflation is a major worry.

"Do you watch educational TV?" will draw many "yes" answers. Even if people do not watch educational television, they may say "yes" because they think they should watch it. Moreover, this question is ambiguous. What is educational television? Is PBS educational television by definition? What types of programs are educational? Educational television would need to be defined or, even better, the term should not be used at all.

Poor: *Do your children watch educational television?*

_____ *Yes*
_____ *No*
_____ *Don't know*

Better: *Which of the following television programs do your children watch?*

_____ *Sesame Street*
_____ *Electric Company*
_____ *Real People*
_____ *Fame*
_____ *Other, please specify*_____

The question "Do you watch educational television?" also appeals to what is called social desirability. Many people will give the answer they think is socially acceptable rather than describe what they actually do or believe. A question that asks whether people support local charities will not receive many valid responses because most people, regardless of what they actually do, will say they support local charities. They feel they are expected to support them; admitting they did not would reflect poorly on them.

Poor: *Do you support charities to help the poor?*

    _____ *Yes*
    _____ *No*
    _____ *Don't know*

Better: *Which of the following charities did you support last year, either with money or volunteer help? Mark all that apply.*

    _____ *United Way*
    _____ *Salvation Army*
    _____ *Goodwill Industries*
    _____ *Other, please specify_____*

Each question should address only one topic. The question "What do you like best about herb tea?" assumes that you like herb tea. It also asks what you like best about it. This is two questions in one. The respondent does not know which of the two questions he is expected to answer.

Poor: *What do you like about herb tea?_____*

Better: *Do you like herb tea?*

    _____ *Yes*
    _____ *No*
    _____ *Don't know*

If your answer was yes, then complete this question. Otherwise go to #X.
What do you like about herb tea? Mark all responses that apply.

    _____ *Flavor*
    _____ *Lack of caffeine*
    _____ *Price*
    _____ *Other, please specify _____*

THE FORM OF QUESTIONS

The information sought will partially dictate the form of the question.

Fixed-Alternative Items. The most popular forms of the fixed-alternative type are either–or and multiple-choice questions. The respondent is given a choice of several alternatives from which to choose one.

Either–Or Questions. The either–or question is the simplest of the fixed-alternative types:

> *Does your city have a public transportation system?*
> _____ *Yes*
> _____ *No*
> _____ *Don't know*

This type of question polarizes the responses. The true–false, agree–disagree, and approve–disapprove questions also fall into this category.

The either–or question has two distinctive advantages. It helps in achieving uniformity and reliability. The respondent's answer is based on previously established response categories. Fixed-alternative questions are easy to code and tabulate.

The major disadvantage is that the questions tend to be superficial. Many problems are too complex to lend themselves to a yes–no type of question. The respondent may become discouraged by being forced to choose one of the options without being able to give an explanation.

Multiple-Choice Questions. A respondent given multiple choices must choose one, as the following examples illustrate.

> Which of the following best describes your occupation?
>
> | | |
> |---|---|
> | _____ Secretary | _____ Sales |
> | _____ Professional/Technical | _____ Manager/Owner |
> | _____ Farmer | _____ Retired/Unemployed |
> | _____ Housewife | _____ Skilled/Unskilled Laborer |
> | _____ Other, please specify_____ | |

Check the category that best approximates your *total* pretax household income.

> | | |
> |---|---|
> | _____ under $9,999 | _____ $30,000 to $34,999 |
> | _____ $10,000 to $14,999 | _____ $35,000 to $39,999 |
> | _____ $15,000 to $19,999 | _____ $40,000 to $49,999 |
> | _____ $20,000 to $24,999 | _____ $50,000 or over |
> | _____ $25,000 to $29,999 | |

Multiple-choice questions, like either–or questions, do not probe for reasons behind the responses. A respondent may simply check an alternative to conceal ignorance. None of the options may fit the attitudes or the facts relating to that particular respondent.

Open-Ended Questions. Open-ended questions overcome some of the disadvantages of the first two question forms. Here the respondent can be asked for his reasons for certain attitudes, and he can also express his opinions. This advantage has a built-in disadvantage. Because open-ended questions take time and great care to answer, many people may simply skip them. If they answer them in great detail, on the other hand, the researcher is confronted with the time-consuming task of tabulating the responses. The examples below illustrate that open-ended questions are broad:

> In your opinion, what can the cultural organizations do to better serve *your* particular needs?
>
> What types of activities do you enjoy most during your leisure time?

Both questions might be easier to answer if they were asked in the form of a checklist.

Checklist. In a checklist the respondent is given a number of alternatives. He marks as many as apply to him.

> I use a terminal to keyboard (check all that apply):
>
> _____ Business letters sent outside the company
> _____ Interoffice memos
> _____ In-house reports
> _____ Reports sent outside the company
> _____ Other, please explain _____

A checklist should include an *other* category because rarely will all possibilities be given. Many respondents like this form because they are not forced to decide what they like best or least. They simply check all responses that pertain. Checklists are easy to tabulate.

Fill-in Questions. The fill-in question is a variation of the open-ended question; however, the respondent is not asked to write a lengthy comment. Usually the fill-in question asks for specific numbers, as the examples illustrate.

> How many people live in your household?_____
>
> How many years of schooling have you completed?_____

The tabulation of this form takes longer than if the question provided categories from which to choose. Moreover, this form lends itself only to short and factual answers.

Scales. Scales help in measuring the intensity of feelings, agreements, and disagreements. The goal of the scale is to put the answers of an individual on some continuum of the attitude in question. The scores of a respondent on a particular topic can be added and averaged. In this way the researcher can obtain a profile of the attitude toward a certain topic. A manager who wants to find out secretaries' attitudes toward word processors, for example, can use a questionnaire with scale-type questions. The attitude for each individual is determined by adding up the scores for every individual and then averaging them. The manager can also average the scores of the group to get a feel for the attitudes. Let us examine the following statement in this context:

The use of a microcomputer in writing helps to overcome writer's block.

Strongly Agree	Agree	Don't Know	Disagree	Strongly Disagree
1	2	3	4	5

For the tabulation assume that:

Respondent A marked   2

Respondent B marked   2

Respondent C marked   3

Respondent D marked   4

Respondent E marked   2

The average in this case is 2.6, but researchers must be careful with using averages. Perhaps 10 employees mark 2, and 10 employees mark 4. The average, 3, is misleading. The score is polarized, and the result would have to be reported as polarized rather than as an average.

Some researchers prefer a scale of seven items. They think that a more detailed scale, as in the example below, is more accurate and differentiates the answers better.

The instructions for the word-processing package are

Excellent	Very Good	Good	Average	Fair	Bad	Very Bad
1	2	3	4	5	6	7

Some researchers think that even a scale of seven items is not discriminating enough. They believe a scale should have 10 items, but providing appropriate labels for ten options may be a problem. When a scale has more than seven categories, researchers usually do not label each one. They may simply write as follows:

The instructions for the word processing package are

Excellent									Poor
1	2	3	4	5	6	7	8	9	10

An advantage of scales is that the response labels can be geared toward the question. Appropriate labels can help the respondent in answering the questions. Scales can emphasize level of interest, frequency, importance, quality, and satisfaction. Several possibilities are illustrated below.

How do you rate the quality of the new Bluebell Cereal?

Excellent	Good	Fair	Poor
1	2	3	4

or

Very Good	Fairly Good	Neither Good nor Bad	Not Very Good
1	2	3	4

How satisfied are you with the new office arrangement?

Very Satisfied	Quite Satisfied	Somewhat Satisfied	Not at All Satisfied
1	2	3	4

How important is it to verbally explain the safety procedures to new employees?

Very Important	Fairly Important	Neutral	Not So Important	Not at All Important
1	2	3	4	5

How often do you have contact with customers?

All of the Time	Very Often	Often	Sometimes	Hardly Ever
1	2	3	4	5

or

Very Often	Often	Some-times	Rarely	Never
1	2	3	4	5

or

All of the Time	Most of the Time	Some of the Time	Just Now and Then
1	2	3	4

Ranking. In scaling, a respondent could give every item on the questionnaire the same number. In ranking, on the other hand, the respondent is forced to put items in a certain order. No ties are allowed.

Rank the following cities in order of preference (one is highest) for living:

_____ New York	_____ Chicago
_____ Atlanta	_____ Boston
_____ San Francisco	_____ Los Angeles
_____ Dallas	_____ Denver
_____ Houston	_____ Phoenix

Rank the universities according to your preference for obtaining an MBA.

_____ University of Illinois
_____ University of Michigan
_____ University of California/Berkeley
_____ University of Texas
_____ University of Colorado

To establish whether certain population groups share certain preferences is fairly easy. Women students and men students, for example, may have different preferences for a university.

Two assumptions concerning ranking can cause difficulty. First, the preference of a respondent is assumed to decrease or increase in equal intervals. Second, the preference is assumed to decline or increase in equal segments for all respondents. In reality, one respondent may possibly, and in fact may likely, rank the University of Illinois and the University of Michigan about the same. The same respondent may not have much of an opinion about the University of California Berkeley but may be totally uninterested in the University of Texas and the University of Colorado. The ranking does not indicate all the attitudes.

THE APPEARANCE OF THE QUESTIONNAIRE

The questionnaire should have visual appeal to the person who is asked to answer it. If the questionnaire looks disorganized and confusing, the response rate will probably be affected negatively. A questionnaire should not be unnecessarily long, but at the same time the questions should not be crowded together. Enough white space is needed on the page and between the questions to distinguish various items.

The design should be consistent. If the answer boxes for one yes–no question are at the right of the question, they should be on that side for all other yes–no type questions. If they are at the left, they should always be there. Consistency in the placing of response space is most important. It helps not only the person who answers the questions but also the person who will tabulate the answers later.

THE COVER LETTER

The cover letter presents the questionnaire to the person who is asked to answer the questions. It should explain the purpose of the questionnaire and motivate the recipient to answer and return it. A cover letter that stresses the benefit of the research to the recipient may encourage a high response rate. A cover letter accompanying a service department survey might begin, "So that we can serve you better, we would like to ask you to take a few minutes to answer the attached questionnaire." The implication is that if customers give their opinions of the service, the service can be improved. The researcher should supply an addressed and stamped envelope for use in returning the questionnaire.

The cover letter in Exhibit 10.2 encourages the reader to respond in several ways:

1. It shows a reader benefit.
2. It gives the purpose of the study.
3. It tells the reader how the results will be used.
4. It identifies the groups being surveyed.
5. It promises confidentiality.
6. It encourages the reader to respond by a specific date.
7. It directs the reader to use the enclosed envelope.

THE PILOT QUESTIONNAIRE

Before the questionnaire is sent to the printer, it is a good idea to test the questions. You may first want to show it to some friends and colleagues to eliminate obvious ambiguities and awkward wordings. You should also try to tabulate a few questionnaires to see whether there are any difficulties with the questions. After you have made revisions based on the feedback from friends, you may want to run a full pilot study with a small sample to further revise and refine the questionnaire. Only after you have com-

Exhibit 10.2   **Cover Letter for Questionnaire**

September 15, 19XX

Dear Educator:

Does your school have computers that are not used?

Many schools have started the school year with additional electronic equipment for their business classes. Yet, research indicates that many teachers will not use the available technology because they do not feel comfortable with it.

This survey attempts to do three things:

1. Determine the current status of the use of technology in business courses in secondary and post-secondary schools.

2. Determine the level of computer literacy and technological skills of teachers.

3. Identify what methods state departments of education, schools, and departments use to aid teachers in developing technological skills.

The following groups are being surveyed: state departments of education, National Association of Business Teacher Education schools, and secondary schools.

Please take a few moments to complete the enclosed questionnaire. This study will help in the development of training seminars and training packages for teachers who are interested in using the new technology effectively.

Your comments will be held in strictest confidence. Coding is used for group identification only.

You may make additional comments in the margins of the survey form. So that we can complete the study and use the results to effectively train teachers in the use of technology, please return the questionnaire by October 10 in the enclosed envelope.

Sincerely,

Marcy Hayes

Marcy Hayes, Ph.D.
Professor of Business Education

pleted this process should you send the questionnaire to the complete sample.

Set a date when you will close the collection and begin the tabulation. Actually, you may find that most of the returned questionnaires come back fairly fast. You may receive some more after a follow-up letter or a reminder; however, usually the response rate to those is fairly low.

THE TABULATION AND EDITING OF RESULTS

Tabulating the responses by computer is advantageous because computerized data can be easily reused. As you code the responses, or even before, check for obviously wrong or invalid answers. The answers of people who are careless in filling in the blanks, for example, may not reflect their true attitudes. You would like to eliminate those questionnaires or, at least, the carelessly answered questions. In some questionnaires the researchers include *test* questions to test the honesty of the respondent. They may include items that are wrong:

Which one of the following television shows do you watch at least once a month?

_____ All in the Family
_____ M*A*S*H
_____ Dallas
_____ Dynasty
_____ The Streets of Dallas

Because the program listed last does not exist, the questionnaires of those people who mark the last option should be checked carefully for inconsistencies. Editing is time consuming and yet is a necessary process.

A questionnaire response on attitudes toward the use of terminals in writing is illustrated in Exhibit 10.3. The questionnaire is a copy from respondent #1. Exhibit 10.4 shows the tabulation for respondent #1 on an op-scan sheet. Columns 1 to 23 are the recordings of the answers. Each answer has one column. Because this respondent has a terminal at her desk, she left column 13, question 10, blank. Columns 24 and 25 identify the respondent; 01 stands for respondent #1.

Exhibit 10.5 illustrates the frequency count of the last question. It shows that 37 people believe writing takes less time with the help of a terminal. Fourteen people believe it takes about the same amount of time, and four people think it takes more time. The statistical analysis of the data will be described in a separate chapter.

The questionnaire in Exhibit 10.6 was designed by a marketing research class. You may want to analyze the questions and see where some improvements could be made.

Exhibit 10.3   **Questionnaire Response**

USE OF VIDEO DISPLAY TERMINAL FOR COMMUNICATING
IN BUSINESS

The results of this questionnaire will be used to study the use of terminals in communication. We would very much appreciate your help in providing information by answering the following questions. Please complete the questionnaire by using a check mark to indicate the most appropriate answer(s).

1. What is your sex?
   ✓ Male   ___ Female

2. What is your age?
   ___ under 21   ___ 36-40   ___ 51-55
   ___ 21-25   ___ 41-45   ___ 56-60
   ___ 26-30   ✓ 46-50   ___ 61 plus
   ___ 31-35

3. In what type of business firm do you work?
   ___ Food   ___ Paper, fiber, and wood products
   ✓ Publishing, printing   ___ Metal products
   ___ Petroleum refining   ___ Motor vehicles
   ___ Electronics, appliances   ___ Office equipment (includes computers)
   ___ Aerospace   ___ Soaps, cosmetics
   ___ Pharmaceuticals   ___ Other (Please identify)_____
   ___ Tobacco   _____

4. What is your job title? (Check the title which describes your job best.)
   ___ Supervisor   ✓ Manager   ___ Systems Analyst/Designer
   ___ President   ___ Programmer   ___ Instructor/Trainer
   ___ Admin. Ass't.   ___ Project Leader   ___ Other_____

5. On the average, I use the terminal to type letters, reports, and/or other types of information approximately
   ___ 1-3 times daily.   ___ 7-9 times daily.
   ✓ 4-6 times daily.   ___ 10 or more times daily. (Give approximate number)_____

6. I have used a terminal for
   ___ 1-6 months.   ___ 25 months to 3 years.
   ___ 7-12 months.   ___ Over 3 years (Specify number of years.)____
   ✓ 13 months to 2 years.

7. My keyboarding (typing) skills are
   ✓ Excellent (know proper fingering for the keyboard, type rapidly, seldom make typing errors).
   ___ Good (know proper fingering, have fairly good speed, make minimal number of typing errors).
   ___ Fair (know proper fingering, type slowly, make more than average number of errors).
   ___ Poor (use "hunt and peck" system, type slowly, make too many errors).

8. Which of the following applies to you?
   ✓ I have a terminal at my desk to use whenever I need to use it.
   ___ I share the use of a terminal with 1-3 people.
   ___ I share the use of a terminal with more than 3 people.

Exhibit 10.3   **Questionnaire Response** (*continued*)

2

9. How is the information typed by you printed?
    - ✓ I have a printer at the desk.
    - ____ The unit shares three or four terminals.
    - ____ The printer is in a central location shared by many.
    - ____ Other (Please explain)

10. I prefer to
    - ____ Work in longhand and have secretary type my work.
    - ____ Dictate using a recorder/have typing done by word processing.
    - ____ Dictate to a secretary.
    - ✓ Keyboard myself.

11. I am more creative
    - ____ Using paper and pencil.
    - ✓ Using the terminal.
    - ____ Dictating to a secretary.
    - ____ Dictating to a recording device.

12. Which best expresses your feelings about the use of terminals? (Check all that apply.)
    - ____ I am apprehensive about terminals.
    - ____ Terminals are cold and impersonal.
    - ____ Terminals help in personalizing my communications.
    - ____ Terminals help me in communicating faster and more efficiently.
    - ✓ I don't have any special opinion on the use of terminals.

13. (Answer this question only if you share a terminal.) How would your attitude towards the use of a terminal differ if you had one at your desk and did not share it?
    - ____ I would feel more positive about using a terminal.
    - ____ I don't mind sharing the use of a terminal with others.
    - ____ It would not change my feeling; I dislike using terminals.

14. The use of a terminal
    - ✓ Has increased the number of my written communications.
    - ____ Has decreased the number of my written communications.
    - ____ Has held constant the number of my written communications.

15. Use of the video display terminal to produce written communications has
    - ✓ Increased the sharing of ideas with colleagues.
    - ____ Discourages the sharing of ideas with colleagues.
    - ____ Does not change the frequency of sharing ideas.

16. When using the terminal for communicating, I believe I am
    - ✓ More concise
    - ____ Less concise
    - ____ No difference

17. When using the terminal for communicating, I believe I am
    - ____ Inhibited in the flow of ideas
    - ✓ Relaxed
    - ____ Unaffected (unchanged)

Exhibit 10.3   **Questionnaire Response** (*continued*)

3

18. I use the terminal to keyboard (check all that apply)
       ✓ Business letters sent outside of the company.
       ___ Inter-office memos, letters, and reports.
       ___ Memos, letters, and reports sent outside of the company.
       ___ Other (Please explain)_____

19. Before I input information, I
       ✓ Put key points on a piece of paper.
       ___ Make a detailed outline.
       ___ Write key paragraphs out in longhand.
       ___ Write entire report out in longhand.
       ___ Compose directly on the keyboard and do not make any notes.

20. I find it easier to
       ✓ Plan with pencil and paper.
       ___ Put the plan on the video display terminal.

21. I find it easier to organize the flow of thought and presentation
       ___ On paper.
       ✓ On the terminal.

22. I revise material
       ✓ Always on a printout.
       ___ Always directly on the screen.
       ___ Sometimes on the printout.
       ___ Sometimes on the screen.

23. Using the terminal to prepare my communications
       ✓ Takes less time than the method I used previously.
       ___ Seems to take about the same time as I spent previously.
       ___ Takes more time than the method I used previously.

NOTE: Please attach or staple to this questionnaire a sample of a <u>recent</u> business letter or memo
       that was written by you. Please block out any confidential information. You may also
       block out your company name, if you desire.

RETURN THIS QUESTIONNAIRE AND THE ATTACHED SAMPLE OF YOUR COMMUNICATION TO:

       Dr. Jean Grever & Dr. Iris Varner
       Department of Business Education and
          Administrative Services
       Illinois State University
       Normal, IL 61761

Exhibit 10.4   **Op-scan for Exhibit 10.3**

Exhibit 10.5   **Frequency Count for One Question**

SPSS BATCH SYSTEM

FILE   NONAME   (CREATION DATE = 01/31/XX)

Q23

CATEGORY LABEL	CCDE	ABSOLUTE FREQ	RELATIVE FREQ (PCT)	ADJUSTED FREQ (PCT)	CUM FREQ (PCT)
	0.	37	67.3	67.3	67.3
	1.	14	25.5	25.5	92.7
	2.	4	7.3	7.3	100.0
	TOTAL	55	100.0	100.0	

VALID CASES   55   MISSING CASES   0

Exhibit 10.6   **Questionnaire**

Dear Recipient:

This questionnaire is being conducted to obtain information that will be utilized by various non-profit McLean County cultural organizations to design programming which better reflects the needs of this community. Your full cooperation is needed if this project is to be successfully completed.

The questionnaire must be completed by the husband, wife, or head of the household. Upon completion, please fold and mail it in the postage-paid and pre-addressed envelope provided. It is very important to the success of the project that you return the completed questionnaire as promptly as possible. You were selected through a random process, and your responses are completely anonymous.

Along with the questionnaire you will find enclosed a pre-addressed postage-paid postcard. Upon completion of the survey, please fill out the card and drop it in the mail so that we might send you a package of premiums and discounts for various community events as a token of our appreciation for your participation.

This study, a learning exercise for a marketing research class, is being conducted by Illinois State University with the anticipation that the results will be of value to the McLean County organizations which sponsor cultural programs and activities for the community.

Thank you for your time and your cooperation.

                                        Sincerely,

                                        Jon F. Bibb
                                        Jon F. Bibb, Professor of Marketing

                                        Gary R. Sudano
                                        Gary R. Sudano, Professor of Music

Source: Reprinted with permission of the College of Fine Arts, Illinois State University.

Exhibit 10.6   **Questionnaire** (*continued*)

Questionnaire   p. 2

ARTS COUNT: A McLEAN COUNTY SURVEY

INSTRUCTIONS: For this study, cultural activities and programs will include
Visual Arts (e.g. painting, sculpture, photo, crafts), Performing Arts (e.g.
dance, theater, music) and Museum and Gallery Exhibitions.

1. Within the past year, have you attended any cultural activity(s) (Visual Arts,
    Performing Arts, Museum and Gallery Exhibitions) in McLean County? (including
    those offered by high schools, colleges and local organizations)

              YES _____   NO _____   If NO, please proceed to question #4.

2. Please check which type(s) of cultural activities you have attended in McLean
    County:

    ____ Visual Art exhibits (e.g. painting, sculpture, photography, crafts)

    ____ Dance performances (e.g. folk, ballet, modern, jazz)

    ____ Theater productions (e.g. plays, musicals, poetry readings)

    ____ Musical performances (e.g. symphony, band, solo recitals, chamber music,
         chorus)

    ____ Museums (e.g. historical items, artifacts, exhibits)

    ____ Other (please specify) _____

3. Please indicate the number of times within the past year you have attended
    each of these activities in McLean County:

    Visual Arts exhibits   ____ times   Music performances   ____ times
    Dance performances   ____ times   Museums   ____ times
    Theater productions   ____ times   Others (please specify) ____ times

4. Please rank the following categories within each cultural activity in the
    order which you are most likely to attend, ranging from 1, most likely to
    attend to 4, least likely to attend.

    Art Exhibits   Dance Performances:
        ____ Paintings   ____ Folk (ethnic)
        ____ Sculpture   ____ Ballet
        ____ Photography   ____ Modern
        ____ Crafts   ____ Jazz
        ____ Other (please specify)   ____ Other (please specify)

    ____ Would not attend art exhibits   ____ Would not attend dance performances

Exhibit 10.6   **Questionnaire** (*continued*)

Questionnaire   p. 3

Theater Productions: Musical Performances:
____ Dramas   ____ Symphonic Music
____ Comedies   ____ Opera
____ Musicals   ____ Solo Recitals and Chamber Music
____ Poetry Readings   ____ Choral Music
____ Other (please specify)   ____ Other (please specify)
     _____   _____
____ Would not attend theater   ____ Would not attend musical
     productions   performances

9. Please check the cultural activity(s) in which you would like to see addi-
    tional programs. (Please check all that apply) (If additional programs are
    desired, please specify)

    ____ painting (specify) _____   ____ dance (specify) _____

    ____ sculpture (specify) _____   ____ theater (specify) _____

    ____ photography (specify) _____   ____ music (specify) _____

    ____ crafts (specify) _____   ____ other (please specify) _____

                                           _____

10. Are you interested in any additional classes in the arts areas?

              YES _____   NO _____

11. If YES, please elaborate. _____

                               _____

SUMMARY OF LEARNING OBJECTIVES

To Examine Types of Samples and Become Familiar with the Sampling Procedure.

Reliable samples have the characteristics of the population from which they are drawn. The larger the sample, the greater is the likelihood that it is representative of the population. In determining sample size, the researcher has to balance accuracy and cost of sampling.

To achieve representativeness, the sample should be drawn randomly. The systematic random sample, the stratified sample, and the cluster sample are types of random samples. The quota sample is a nonrandom sample.

To Apply the Principles of Questionnaire Design.

The questionnaire should ask only questions that are related to the research problem. Personal questions must be handled tactfully. A cover letter must explain the purpose of the questionnaire and the benefit to the respondent. The instructions must be clear and unambiguous.

To Write Effective Questions for a Questionnaire.

Questions must be clear and easy to answer. The questionnaire form must provide space for the answers. The questions can take a variety of forms, such as yes–no questions, open-ended questions, fill-in questions, scales, and rankings.

To Tabulate Results.

Before tabulating, the researcher has to edit the returned questionnaires. Results can be tabulated by computer or by hand.

QUESTIONS AND PROBLEMS

1. Give at least ten guidelines for preparing a questionnaire.
2. Define the terms *randomness*, *validity*, and *reliability*.
3. Discuss some of the difficulties in ranking questions.
4. What are some of the shortcomings of either–or questions?
5. How can you check whether the respondents answer accurately?
6. Discuss the role of the cover letter when sending out questionnaires.
7. Find a questionnaire in a magazine or newspaper and evaluate the design.
8. Design a questionnaire for solving a research problem you have defined. Try the questionnaire out on some friends. Tabulate the results.
9. What are some advantages and some disadvantages of using questionnaires in research?

CHAPTER ELEVEN

ANALYSIS WITH

STATISTICS

LEARNING OBJECTIVES

To understand the purpose of statistics.

- To be able to differentiate between qualitative and quantitative data.
- To use measures of central tendency and measures of dispersion effectively.
- To use measures of correlation correctly.
- To understand the meaning and purpose of simple and multiple regression.

When the secondary research results are on note cards and the primary questionnaire is tabulated, much still remains to be done. The remaining task, analysis, is not only a challenging but also an exciting part of the report writing process.

Some people believe that a report writer does not need to know statistical tools, because, after all, he writes reports. A statistician, they argue, does the statistical work, and the report writer uses the results. Even if this were true, report writers still have to understand statistics in order to know what certain statistical techniques can do and when they should be used. For example, they should understand when a simple correlation should be used, when a simple regression is appropriate, or when a multiple regression analysis is needed—even though someone else does the actual statistical work. To intelligently report statistical information obtained from secondary sources, report writers must understand what the statistics mean. They must also determine how to use the statistical results.

This chapter will present some of the most frequently used statistical tools which every report writer should be familiar with. We will examine the use and meaning of measures of central tendency, measures of dispersion, correlation measures, and basic inferential statistics. The emphasis is on the meaning of statistical results rather than on the actual computation of various statistical formulas. For a detailed treatment of statistics, you may consult one of the following books:

Bradley, Iver E., and John B. South. *Introductory Statistics for Business and Economics*. Hinsdale, IL: Dryden, 1981.

Huff, Darrell. *How to Lie with Statistics*. New York: Norton, 1954.

Lapin, Lawrence L. *Statistics for Modern Business Decisions*. New York: Harcourt, 1973.

Zikmund, William G. *Business Research Methods*. Hinsdale, IL: Dryden, 1984.

THE PURPOSE OF STATISTICS

Statistical analysis will help you in the interpretation of your research. The four major purposes of statistics are to help in:

1. Reducing large volumes of data to a manageable size.
2. Studying populations and samples.
3. Making decisions.
4. Making inferences.

With the help of statistics you can draw conclusions. Of course, the possibility of error always exists, but statistics help in determining the probability of error and the level of uncertainty in the results. You can determine that a certain inference is correct at a certain level of significance.

The two basic forms of research data are qualitative and quantitative data.

QUALITATIVE DATA

Qualitative Data
Qualitative data is non-numeric data.

As the term indicates, **qualitative data** is related to the "quality," or the attributes, of data. Let us assume you are working on a report determining the new site for a subsidiary. You have collected data from the library and visited the various sites under consideration. As the result of your work, you have information on cost of land, availability of workers, water supply, tax structure, transportation networks, cultural opportunities, schools, and recreational facilities. You can organize, present, and discuss your material according to those categories.

Some of the data you collected will be in the form of numbers, but some will not. For example, the caliber of the schools will be difficult to assess. You may look at graduation requirements, extracurricular activities, athletic programs, scores on national aptitude tests, and the percentage of students going on to college. Ultimately you will have to judge whether the schools are good, bad, or average on the basis of this qualitative information.

Many people argue that, in order to overcome pay discrimination between men and women, every job should be assigned a number of points. Jobs of equal value, that is, jobs with equal points, should pay the same salary. The difficulty lies in determining the points and agreeing on the criteria used to describe a job. Once there is agreement on those things, the rest is indeed easy. No matter how many criteria are used—education, social benefits, work hours, and work hazards, to name just a few—the decision is ultimately a qualitative one. It is qualitative, even though a job is given a specified number of points for each criterion, because someone must decide how many points to assign.

Your search for a lucrative and rewarding job after graduation will be an attempt to quantify qualitative data. You may spend many hours researching the companies you are interested in. You may also read a number of books on how best to sell your skills and prepare your resume. The authors of the job-hunting books you may consult often provide step-by-step procedures for choosing the right position. They may suggest drawing up a list of all the things to consider: pay, location, advancement possibilities, fringe benefits, and size of company.

Because these factors are not likely to be equally important to you, you will assign weights (a number) to each factor. All factors together represent the job characteristics you consider important. The factors, therefore, must add up to one, and their weights are always the same. Regardless of where the job is, for example, location carries the same weight each time you examine a job opportunity.

For each job you analyze, you evaluate the factors and assign points to each factor. You decide beforehand the highest number of points you want to give. In the example that follows, the highest number of points for the pay factor is 50. In comparing two jobs, one with high pay and one with lower pay, you may assign 50 points to one and only 30 points to the other. You then assign points to the other job factors for each job.

By multiplying the weights by the points, you get weighted values. When you add the weighted values, you will get weighted averages, which makes possible a clear ranking of the job offers. The weighted average is influenced by the two decisions you make: (1) the assigning of weights to the job factors and (2) the assigning of points to each job factor.

Let us assume you are evaluating two job offers, one in Chicago and one in Denver. Pay is about the same. You like to ski; in fact, that is your favorite winter pastime. Denver is the better location for skiing. Advancement within the Denver firm appears more promising, but the Chicago job offers much better fringe benefits. The company in Denver is fairly small, whereas the Chicago firm is large, and you have always wanted to work for a large corporation.

You have to rank your priorities and assign the points. You then multiply and add the scores (Exhibit 11.1). Based on your analysis, you should take the job in Denver.

In this example you worked with qualitative data. Because you worked with numbers, you may think the data was quantitative. The fact is that you converted qualities to numbers. This process allows you to apply statistical

Exhibit 11.1   **Quantifying Qualitative Data: The Calculation of Weighted Averages**

		Denver		Chicago	
	Weights	**Points**	**Average Value**	**Points**	**Average Value**
Pay	.5	40	20	40	20
Location	.2	50	10	30	6
Advancement	.2	40	8	30	6
Fringes	.05	30	1.5	50	2.5
Size	.05	30	1.5	50	2.5
			41		37

analysis to qualitative data. You have "clean" data; the outcome looks clear and convincing and has the illusion of scientific certainty. The process can be very helpful as long as you are aware of its shortcomings.

Because qualitative data is connected to subjective judgment, you have to be careful in its use. If you are not certain exactly what you are looking for in a job, for example, you cannot assign weights and points intelligently. If you have had a bad day and want to get far away, Denver may seem to provide that distance. The results of your analysis may therefore show a clear preference for Denver, but intuitively you are not convinced.

QUANTITATIVE DATA

Quantitative Data
Quantitative data is numeric data.

In contrast to qualitative data, **quantitative data** is completely objective. If you want to find the average height of the students in your class, you simply measure everyone and compute the average. Scores on an objective test in your report writing class are quantitative data. You either marked the correct answer or you did not. You either understood the point or you did not. Based on the scores, the instructor can figure the average for the class.

A score on a writing assignment may at first seem to be a quantitative measure too, but that score is actually based on qualitative judgment. The instructor may have a scale for certain mistakes: spelling, 2 points off; grammar, 3 points off; punctuation, 1 point off; lack of reader adaptation, up to 20 points off. The instructor decides whether a report loses, for example, 15 or 20 points on reader adaptation. Two instructors may be very close in their scoring and evaluating of a report, yet their scores may also differ. To overcome these differences, instructors can grade papers together so that they will use the same standards. We say they establish interrater reliability. After interrater reliability has been established, two instructors will give identical or close to identical scores.

In working with quantitative data you will have to examine carefully the sample and the variables you want to measure. You also have to check the data for accuracy, reliability, and validity. Those terms were discussed along with sampling; you may want to reread the material. If the sample is not representative of the population, your findings cannot be generalized to the population. If you do not control the independent variables carefully, then your results may be misleading.

DESCRIPTIVE STATISTICS

After you have collected and organized your data, you may have rows and columns of numbers. In this form the information is not particularly useful. To make it meaningful, you need a way to summarize the overall tendencies of particular sets of data and to establish relationships between sets of data.

MEASURES OF CENTRAL TENDENCY

Measures of Central Tendency
Measures of central tendency examine the clustering of data.

One way to summarize the general shape of raw data is to indicate where the midpoint occurs—the point statisticians call the *mean* or the *median*—or to indicate the most frequently occurring number, the *mode*. These devices are called **measures of central tendency**.

Newspapers and news broadcasts often carry reports about average income, average cost of living, average cost of housing, and average medical costs. In our everyday language we use the term *average* rather loosely. Average can have three meanings: arithmetic mean, median, or mode.

Mean
The mean is the arithmetic average.

Arithmetic Mean. The arithmetic **mean** is probably used most frequently and, of all the measures of central tendency, is probably the best understood. To determine the mean income of a sample, simply add all the income figures of the sample (X) and then divide the sum by the number of observations (N). The symbol used for the arithmetic mean is the lower case Greek letter *mu*, written as μ.

Let us assume you have collected the following data on incomes:

$$X = \$15,000$$
$$X = 17,000$$
$$X = 20,000$$
$$X = \underline{22,000}$$

Sum $\$74,000$

The mean income is:

$$\mu = \frac{\$74,000}{4} = \$18,500.$$

In this example the mean is a fair representation of the income of the surveyed group. The lowest and highest figures are not far apart, and the mean is the midpoint between the two middle figures.

In many cases, as in the following example, the mean by itself may be misleading and may not give a very realistic picture.

$$
\begin{array}{rr}
X = & \$\ 12,000 \\
X = & 12,000 \\
X = & 13,000 \\
X = & 15,000 \\
X = & 18,000 \\
X = & 19,000 \\
X = & 20,000 \\
X = & 20,000 \\
X = & 20,000 \\
X = & 55,000 \\
X = & \underline{60,000} \\
& \$264,000
\end{array}
$$

The mean value is:

$$\mu = \frac{\$264,000}{11} = \$24,000.$$

This mean value is misleading. The two high-income figures cause the mean to fall between the nine lowest and the two highest figures. Because the mean gives no indication of this fact, the median might be a more accurate representation of the data.

Median
The median is the midpoint—half the data is above, half the data is below.

Median. The **median**, which is depicted by the letter M, gives the central value when all values are arranged in increasing or decreasing sequence.

Of 11 income figures, the sixth one is the central value. In the example for calculating the mean, half of the sample was above $19,000 and half below. The median was therefore $19,000.

If you have an even number of observations in your sample, you average the two central values. Let us assume you have two incomes of $60,000 in the example. This raises the number of observations from 11 to 12. You have two central income figures: $19,000 and $20,000. You calculate the median by averaging these two figures to arrive at a median of $19,500.

The formula for finding the median can be expressed as:

$$M = \frac{n+1}{2}.$$

In the example the difference between the mean and the median is $5,000. The two high-income figures that raise the mean for the sample actually distort what the average person makes. In this case the report writer might provide both of the figures and thus show that the sample is half above and half below $19,000 and that the mean income is $24,000. The comparison puts both figures in perspective.

If income is important for marketing a particular product, management should know more than the mean income. Let us assume that the target market is an income range of $20,000 to $30,000. The mean in the example falls within this range. Based on this information only, management should market the product to this group. The median, however, indicates that half the families are under the specified threshold. Before making a decision, management may want to study the situation in more detail.

Mode
The mode is the most frequently occurring value.

Mode. The **mode**, another measure of central tendency, tells which value occurs most frequently. In the example, three families make $20,000. No other income level applies to as many families; therefore, the mode is $20,000. The mode may be helpful but must be used carefully. A researcher who presents only the mode may misrepresent the data because the mode may, and often does, represent a minority of the total population. The following example illustrates the point:

$X = \$14,000$	$X = 30,000$
$X = 15,000$	$X = 33,000$
$X = 17,000$	$X = 45,000$
$X = 17,000$	$X = 50,000$
$X = 17,000$	$X = 50,000$
$X = 17,000$	$X = 60,000$
$X = 20,000$	$X = 70,000$
$X = 22,000$	$X = 72,000$
$X = 25,000$	

The mode in this case is $17,000. The median, which is the ninth value on the list, is $25,000, and the mean income is $33,764.70.

No relationship exists between those numbers. They can all be helpful, but the report writer must understand the meaning and know when and how to use each one. So that the reader of a report can put measures of central tendency in perspective and judge whether the mean, median, and mode fairly represent the facts, the report writer should include the actual figures in a report table or appendix.

Bimodal Distribution
The bimodal distribution has more than one cluster.

The Bimodal Distribution. In a **bimodal distribution**, which has two or more clusters, a calculation of the mean may be senseless. The following example of test results illustrates the point. As the results in the example show, the highest score of a 100-point test was 93, the lowest 75.

$$
\begin{array}{rcr}
2 & 75 = & 150 \\
4 & 77 = & 308 \\
5 & 79 = & 395 \\
3 & 81 = & 243 \\
1 & 83 = & 83 \\
4 & 88 = & 352 \\
5 & 90 = & 450 \\
5 & 91 = & 455 \\
2 & 93 = & \underline{186} \\
& & 2,622
\end{array}
$$

Based on these scores, the mean is 84.58, or 85 points. The median is 88 points. There is no mode.

The mean value in this case does not help the instructor in analyzing the results of the test. Based on the popular interpretation of the mean, the instructor might assume that the scores are clustered around that value and that many test scores would be at or around 85. The data shows that this is not the case at all. There are two distinct groups in the class. One group performed in the upper 70s and the other in the upper 80s and lower 90s. Almost half of the class did not do well.

The graphic distribution of the test scores in Exhibit 11.2 clearly shows the two clusters.

Exhibit 11.2   **Bimodal Distribution**

Skewed Distribution
The values are clustered at one extreme.

The Skewed Distribution. The scores of a test may be **skewed** to a particular side. A test might result in the following scores:

$$
\begin{array}{rcr}
1 \times 62 & = & 62 \\
1 \times 67 & = & 67 \\
1 \times 71 & = & 71 \\
2 \times 75 & = & 150 \\
2 \times 77 & = & 154 \\
3 \times 83 & = & 249 \\
3 \times 84 & = & 252 \\
4 \times 87 & = & 348 \\
5 \times 88 & = & 440 \\
5 \times 90 & = & 450 \\
4 \times 93 & = & 372 \\
1 \times 94 & = & 94 \\
1 \times 96 & = & \underline{96} \\
& & 2,805
\end{array}
$$

These test results are skewed toward the upper scores, as the results and also the graphic illustration in Exhibit 11.3 show. If the scores are skewed, measures of central tendency are not particularly helpful in understanding the results. The mean of 85 and the median of 87 (there is no mode) do not indicate that the distribution is skewed.

The instructor must look at the actual scores to determine whether to calculate a measure of central tendency. With a class of 30 this may be fairly easy to do. If the instructor has 200 scores, the trends may not be that clear. In that case, calculating both a measure of central tendency and a measure of dispersion might be best.

Exhibit 11.3 **Skewed Distribution**

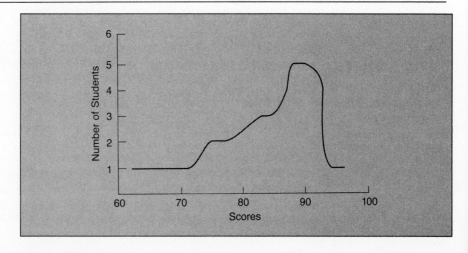

MEASURES OF DISPERSION

As indicated by the example of skewed data, measures of central tendency by themselves are usually not enough to describe the pattern of data. Management may want to know not only the average sales for the entire company and each district but also the differences between the various districts. An instructor may want to find out not only the average score but also the distance between the highest and the lowest scores. Measuring those differences can be as important as measuring the central points. To examine the differences, the researcher uses **measures of dispersion**.

Measures of Dispersion
Measures of dispersion examine the scattering of data.

Range
The range gives the extreme values.

Range. The most frequently used measure of dispersion is the **range**. If the highest score on the test is 90 and the lowest is 75, then the range is:

$$90 - 75 = 15$$

The range provides a concise summary of the variation of the values. It tells how far the highest and lowest values are apart, but it neglects all the values in between. It does not tell anything about the pattern of the distribution. To overcome this shortcoming, a researcher might also need to calculate the mean and the median.

Most scores on a test might be fairly close together except for one very high and one very low score. Perhaps the lowest score is 50 and the highest is 100, but the majority of scores are around 85. In that case the range is somewhat misleading. It tells the extremes, but only two scores are at those points. No other score is even close. To avoid an emphasis on the extremes, which happens if the absolute range is stated, researchers will often give a range within which 80 percent or 90 percent of all scores fall. In this way the reader or user of the data has more accurate information on the distribution of the data.

Variance. The variance is another measure of dispersion. The range shows the distance between highest and lowest scores, whereas the variance shows the average distance between the mean and the actual test scores. The variance is more useful because it tells more about the distribution of the data than the range.

In calculating the variance, all the individual variances between observations and mean are squared. The squared variances are added and then divided by the number of observations. The formula for calculating the variance is as follows:

$$\text{Variance} = \frac{\Sigma \, (\text{Observation} \; - \; \text{Mean})^2}{N \text{ of Observations} \; - \; 1} = \frac{\Sigma \, (x - \bar{x})^2}{n - 1}.$$

Note: To use population rather than sample data, the denominator is n rather than $n - 1$.

The following is a calculation of the variance for the same test results used in the bimodal-distribution example:

$$(x - \bar{x})^2$$
$$(75 - 83)^2 = -8^2 = 64$$
$$(75 - 83)^2 = -8^2 = 64$$
$$(76 - 83)^2 = -7^2 = 49$$
$$(77 - 83)^2 = -6^2 = 36$$
$$(78 - 83)^2 = -5^2 = 25$$
$$(78 - 83)^2 = -5^2 = 25$$
$$(79 - 83)^2 = -4^2 = 16$$
$$(81 - 83)^2 = -2^2 = 4$$
$$(88 - 83)^2 = 5^2 = 25$$
$$(88 - 83)^2 = 5^2 = 25$$
$$(89 - 83)^2 = 6^2 = 36$$
$$(89 - 83)^2 = 6^2 = 36$$
$$(90 - 83)^2 = 7^2 = 49$$
$$\Sigma(x - \bar{x})^2 = \text{454 square points}$$

$$S^2 = \frac{454 \text{ Square Points}}{13 - 1} = 37.83 \text{ Square Points.}$$

You can see the numbers are getting high. Imagine the calculation of the variance if you deal with millions of dollars. Another difficulty is that the variance is not expressed in the same units as the observations. In the above example, the observations, in this case the test results, are expressed in points. Because all deviations are squared when calculating the variance, the variance is expressed in square points, a rather meaningless designation.

To overcome the difficulty of high numbers and squared deviations, statisticians take the square root of the variance. The result is the standard deviation.

Standard Deviation
The standard deviation calculates the distance from the sample mean.

Standard Deviation. The **standard deviation** is a practical and descriptive measure of dispersion. Its major advantage over the variance is that it is expressed in the same units as the data. The standard deviation is, therefore, easier to use and easier to understand. The standard deviation for the example is computed as follows:

$$\text{Standard Deviation} = S = \sqrt{\frac{(x - \bar{x})^2}{n - 1}} = \sqrt{37.83} = 6.15.$$

Normal Curve
The normal curve is a theoretical probability distribution. It is bell-shaped.

The standard deviation is particularly helpful if the population has a special distribution called the **normal curve**. The normal curve is a theoretical distribution of sample means. It is bell-shaped. Under a normal curve, 99.7 percent of all observations fall within ± 3 standard deviations of the mean, 95.5 percent fall within ± 2 standard deviations of the mean, and 68 percent fall within ± 1 standard deviation of the mean (Exhibit 11.4). For the busi-

Exhibit 11.4   **Normal Curve**

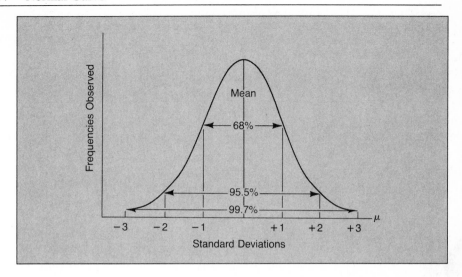

ness person the standard deviation together with the normal curve can be an important statistical tool.

A manufacturer for men's clothing, for example, has to make sure that the clothes produced actually fit the men in the population. He might take a sample of men and measure their height. If the average height of the men in the sample is 5 feet 10 inches with a standard deviation of ±2 inches, under the normal curve the manufacturer would calculate the following results:

> 68 percent of the men are within one standard deviation of the mean. They are between 5 feet 8 inches and 6 feet tall.

> 95.5 percent are within two standard deviations of the mean. They are between 5 feet 6 inches and 6 feet 2 inches tall.

> 99.7 percent are within three standard deviations of the mean. They are between 5 feet 4 inches and 6 feet 4 inches tall.

With this information the manufacturer can determine how much fabric he needs. He knows what percentage of slacks should have short or long legs. These calculations influence the manufacturing, budgeting, pricing, and marketing decisions.

Both the clustering and the variability of data are useful for the business person to know. A production manager who wants to improve quality control must know the numbers of acceptable and unacceptable products and by how many units of measurements the faulty products are outside the specified tolerance levels. If 95 percent of production is meeting the standard, the manager must determine by how much the 5 percent miss the standard. Based on the results of a measurement of dispersion, the production manager may learn how much improvement is needed. A low standard deviation indicates that the variability is fairly low. If the standard deviation in the quality check is high, production may need major attention and quality improvements.

MEASURES OF CORRELATION

Usually managers want to know not only the sales or advertising costs but also the relationship between sales and advertising. They want to find the relationship between the successful completion of training courses and productivity or between bonuses and job satisfaction.

In many cases researchers may know intuitively that certain phenomena are related. For example, it makes sense that relationships exist between the number of finished houses and the sale of appliances and carpeting, between the birth of new babies and the sale of baby food, and between hot weather and the consumption of soft drinks. They usually do not know, however, how strong or weak the relationships are. Most people do not care about the details of **correlation**, but in the business situation observation or intuition is not enough. Business people must know the nature and the strength of the relationship to gauge future product planning, marketing campaigns, expansion projects, and personnel forecasts.

Correlation
Correlation measures examine the strength of the relationship between variables.

A number of statistical techniques such as the simple correlation coefficient, the coefficient of determination, and the chi-square test can measure the relationship between variables. Because descriptions of all these measures exceed the scope of this chapter, the discussion will concentrate on the simple correlation coefficient and concentrate on its meaning.

The simple correlation coefficient measures the correlation between two variables. The value for the correlation can range from $+1$ to -1. A correlation of $+1$ indicates perfect correlation between two variables. If a company's sales go up along a straight line as advertising dollars go up, for example, the correlation is $+1$. A value of -1 indicates an inverse relationship. A company may find that sales go up as the price goes down. A value of zero means that no relationship exists between the variables.

Usually you hope for a high correlation between a new training program and job performance. If you find that the correlation coefficient between the training and job performance is very low or zero, your business would have to reevaluate the program. Perhaps the wrong people are participating in the program or it is not well designed. Perhaps the sessions are at the wrong time of the day.

Correlational research indicates only the strength and the direction of a relationship between two variables; it does *not* show whether there is a causal relationship, that is, whether one variable causes the other. A simple correlation may show a relationship between sales of soft drinks and hot weather, for example, but the report writer cannot say that hot weather causes the sales of soft drinks to go up. When looking at correlation research, the writer obviously has to keep the limitations of correlations in mind.

Correlations are nevertheless useful. They show the researcher which variables are related, and they help in exploring the nature of the relationship. If no relationship whatsoever exists, the researcher may dismiss further investigation. If, based on common sense, a relationship could be expected, the researcher should investigate why the statistical analysis does not show a correlation. If a relationship does exist, the researcher may want to formulate a hypothesis and conduct experimental research to test whether the relationship is causal. Correlation can help to eliminate irrelevant variables and focus on the important ones.

Variables may appear to be statistically related even though no actual relationship exists. Some things happen coincidentally. A correlation of the length of skirts and the movement of the stock market, for example, would be a chance correlation.

The correlation may be caused by a third factor. A correlation study may show that the sale of soft drinks is related to vacations, but more likely the correlation is based on hot weather. Most people take vacations during the summer, and in hot weather people drink more soft drinks.

Users of correlational research in the decision-making process should be aware of the shortcomings of this statistical tool. It can be helpful, but by itself it may not be enough. A wrong interpretation of the results may lead to poor planning and poor decisions. In many cases the report writer has to use more powerful statistical tools.

Some questions the report writer should ask when examining correlation research are as follows:

1. Was there a reason to assume that the variables were indeed related, or does it appear that the researcher blindly investigated any two variables? Did the researcher use a shotgun approach?

2. Did the researcher in any way imply a causal relationship between the variables?

3. Did the researcher repeat the study?

4. What other means did the researcher use to validate the results?

INFERENTIAL STATISTICS

Inferential Statistics
Inferential statistics are used to make predictions about a population based on a sample.

As we have seen, descriptive statistics describe and summarize data. For decision making and forecasting, businesses use descriptive statistics together with **inferential statistics**. In inferential statistics investigators make generalizations about the whole by examining a part. For example, the business person examines a sample and then projects the results to the entire population. Inferential statistics are subject to error, and the report writer must be aware of that possibility when reporting, analyzing, and presenting data. Because inferential statistics are based on probability, no certainty exists that the generalizations are true.

With the help of inferential statistics you can say that a forecast is true at a certain level of significance. Although you may assume that a hypothesis you tested is true, you must keep the possibility in mind that it is untrue. For example, you might find that the statistical results of your study support your hypothesis that—at a .05 **level of significance**—the use of microcomputers reduces writing anxiety. This finding really means that, given your sample size and the data derived from your testing program, you have found support for your hypothesis with this qualification: A 5 percent possibility exists that your sample is not typical of the entire population about which you are generalizing. Thus, conclusions drawn by using inferential statistics are, to a certain degree, always tentative.

Level of Significance
The level of significance indicates the probability level that the results are due to chance.

SIMPLE REGRESSION ANALYSIS

With a correlation you can measure the strength of the relationship between variables. With a **simple regression** you can measure whether this relationship is causal, that is, whether changes in the independent variable produce changes in the dependent variable. Regression, because it examines the causal relationship, is a more powerful tool than the correlation measures.

Simple Regression Analysis
Simple regression predicts the causal relationship between an independent and a dependent variable.

Let us assume a lumberyard wholesaler thinks that a relationship exists between sales and the number of building permits issued. He does a simple correlation that shows a strong correlation between sales and building permits but does not establish a causal relationship. He may decide to perform a simple regression analysis. The number of permits issued is the independent variable; sales are the dependent variable. Looking at past data, the wholesaler hopes to make inferences about future sales. He hopes to determine how well sales can be predicted from the number of building permits issued. If he can calculate future sales, he can make better decisions about inventory, number of employees, and size of buildings needed.

The wholesaler decides to collect data on building permits and sales from 13 wholesalers in the area. His findings are presented in Exhibit 11.5.

The figures can be plotted in a diagram (Exhibit 11.6). The values are not on a straight line, but the linear regression is based on the concept that there is a straight line. As Exhibit 11.6 shows, it is possible to draw several straight lines based on the data.

The problem is to determine which line is most accurate for forecasting sales. Line a suggests a higher increase of sales than does line b. Because the difference is rather great, the wholesaler would like to have a more accurate measure. He can use a simple regression analysis. The formula is as follows:

$$\hat{Y} = \hat{a} + \hat{\beta}_x$$
$$\hat{a} = \hat{Y} - \beta\bar{X}$$
$$\hat{\beta} = \frac{n\,(\Sigma XY) - (\Sigma X)\,(\Sigma Y)}{n\,(\Sigma X^2) - (\Sigma X)^2}$$

(continued)

Exhibit 11.5   **Data on Sales and Building Permits**

Wholesaler	Number of Permits	Sales in $000
1	$x = 86$	$y = 77$
2	$x = 92$	$y = 79$
3	$x = 93$	$y = 81$
4	$x = 102$	$y = 82$
5	$x = 140$	$y = 105$
6	$x = 120$	$y = 130$
7	$x = 130$	$y = 120$
8	$x = 145$	$y = 115$
9	$x = 120$	$y = 100$
10	$x = 105$	$y = 100$
11	$x = 103$	$y = 94$
12	$x = 160$	$y = 150$
13	$x = 158$	$y = 130$

Exhibit 11.6   **Relation of Sales Outlook and Building Permits**

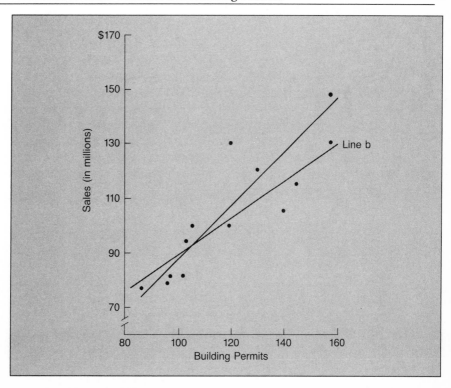

where:

$$\hat{\beta} = \text{the estimated slope of the line,}$$
$$\hat{a} = \text{estimated intercept of the y-axis,}$$
$$Y = \text{dependent variable (sales),}$$
$$\bar{Y} = \text{mean of dependent variable,}$$
$$X = \text{independent variable (permits),}$$
$$\bar{X} = \text{mean of independent variable, and}$$
$$n = \text{number of observations.}$$

The calculations are shown in Exhibit 11.7

$$\bar{Y} = 104.846$$
$$\bar{X} = 113.54$$

Calculate $\hat{a}$ and $\hat{\beta}$:

$$\hat{\beta} = \frac{13(169084) - 2118102}{13(193436) - 2414916} = \frac{7990}{99752} = .8$$
$$a = 104.846 - 95.63 = 9.216$$

Forecast sales with the regression formula:

$$\hat{Y} = \hat{a} + \hat{\beta} \times = 9.216 + .8X$$

Exhibit 11.7   **Calculation of Regression**

Y	Y²	X	X²	XY
77	5929	86	7396	6622
79	6241	92	8464	7268
81	6561	93	8649	7533
82	6724	102	10404	8364
105	11025	140	19600	14700
130	16900	120	14400	15600
120	14400	130	16900	15600
115	13225	145	21025	16675
100	10000	129	14400	12000
100	10000	105	11025	10500
94	8836	103	10609	9682
150	22500	160	25600	24000
130	16900	158	24964	20540
ΣY	$\Sigma(Y^2)$	ΣX	$\Sigma(X^2)$	ΣXY
1363	149241	1554	193436	169084

With the results shown in Exhibit 11.6, the wholesaler can forecast sales. If 80 permits are issued, he can expect sales of $73,216.

$$\hat{Y} = 9.216 + .8\ (80) = 73.216.$$

The report writer must be aware that linear regression or, for that matter, any statistical technique cannot promise that the forecast is correct in all details. Although no promise of certainty exists, statistical techniques do measure the likelihood of the relationship. Even with precise numbers, the business person has to make the final decision. The statistical techniques are merely an aid in the process.

The lumber wholesaler must examine more than the causal relationship between sales of building supplies and the issue of building permits. Before he begins to expand, he has to look at his current and long-range debts, examine space requirements, take into account the cost of a larger inventory, and determine whether the building boom in the area will last or will be short lived. The causal relationship between sales and building permits is only one factor in the decision-making process.

MULTIPLE REGRESSION ANALYSIS

Few business problems are two-dimensional, that is, have one dependent and one independent variable. Usually many variables influence sales; for example, a consumer deciding whether to buy a new car will consider not only price but also rate of interest, cost of keeping the old car, style, cost of maintaining the new car, and probably several other factors. With the help of multivariate analysis the consumer can examine all those variables at the same time. In contrast to the simple regression analysis that is two dimensional, the **multiple regression analysis** is multi-dimensional.

Multiple Regression Analysis
Multiple regression predicts the causal relationship between one dependent and two or more independent variables.

Before computers were in common use, an analysis of more than three variables was nearly impossible because the calculations became too complex. Computers, which have made multiple regression analysis possible, have given the business person a more accurate tool for forecasting.

A business person who tries to predict sales of cars solely on the basis of price leaves out important factors. With the help of multiple regression analysis the business person can determine how the various factors that make up the purchasing decision are related. The lumberyard wholesaler, for example, has to consider the income level in the area, prices, and general economic outlook in addition to the number of permits issued. Multiple regression analysis, because it takes more factors into account than the simple regression, is more realistic and has higher predictive powers.

The business person is guided not only by demands for accuracy but also by cost considerations. Both play an important role in collecting and analyzing data. The business person has to weigh the cost of additional accuracy. The sample may have to be larger; the study may have to be repeated for reliability and validity. Each attempt to raise accuracy also raises the cost. If an additional $10,000 is expected to increase revenue by $500,000, then the cost may be justified. If the $10,000 is expected to raise revenue by only $15,000, however, management may be hesitant to spend the additional money.

Time is a factor, too, particularly for a new product. More research and detailed analysis might add certainty but will also delay entering the market. Six months from now the competitive edge may have disappeared, and the added accuracy may have cost the company a share of the market. Statistics contribute to accuracy, but accuracy costs both time and money.

SUMMARY OF LEARNING OBJECTIVES

To Understand the Purpose of Statistics.
Statistics help in summarizing data, manipulating data, and making inferences from data.

To Be Able to Differentiate between Qualitative and Quantitative Data.
Quantitative data is numeric data. Qualitative data is nonnumeric data. Qualitative data can be converted into quantitative data, but an element of subjectivity is always involved.

To Be Able to Use Measures of Central Tendency and Measures of Dispersion Effectively.
The three measures of central tendency are the mean, the median, and the mode. The report writer may have to show all three to present data accurately. Measures of central tendency emphasize the clustering of data.

Measures of dispersion emphasize the distribution of data. The most important measure of dispersion is the standard deviation. The standard deviation is particularly useful in connection with the normal curve.

To Use Measures of Correlation Correctly.
Correlation studies measure the direction and the strength of the relationship between variables. They do not measure any causal links between variables.

To Understand the Meaning and Purpose of Simple and Multiple Regression.
Regression analysis establishes causal relationships between variables. It can be used in forecasting. The simple regression analysis makes predictions based on one independent variable; the multiple regression analysis makes predictions based on two or more independent variables. Multiple regression analysis is a more powerful forecasting tool.

QUESTIONS AND PROBLEMS

1. Define the meaning of *mean, median,* and *mode.* What are disadvantages and advantages of each measure?
2. Name several measures of dispersion. Explain why the researcher may want to calculate measures of central tendency and measures of dispersion.
3. What are the characteristics of correlation research? What can correlation research do and not do?
4. When would you use a correlation and when a linear regression?
5. When would you use a multiple regression analysis?
6. What are the differences between quantitative and qualitative data?
7. Discuss the role of statistics in writing good reports.
8. What is the purpose of statistics?
9. A report writer argues that, based on his study, sales will go up by 30 percent next year if the company increases its advertising budget by $50,000. Discuss this statement.
10. Someone has found that a high correlation exists between teachers' salaries and the consumption of liquor over a number of years. Discuss this correlation.

CHAPTER TWELVE

REASONING

WITH DATA:

ANALYSIS,

CONCLUSIONS,

RECOMMENDATIONS

LEARNING OBJECTIVES

- To be familiar with analysis aids.
- To become aware of problems in analyzing data.
- To analyze data.
- To draw conclusions.
- To make logical recommendations.

At this point in your work you have collected and statistically analyzed the data, but a mere presentation of the statistical results is usually not enough. The statistics do not speak for themselves; they must be seen in the context of the overall problem.

Analysis
The analysis examines the data and establishes patterns.

Analysis is never a completely objective process; subjective elements always come into play. Two people looking at the same set of data may analyze the figures differently, as when economists disagree on the effect of tax cuts. Some argue that tax cuts favor the rich more than the poor and, in addition, lower the revenue of the government. Other economists argue that tax cuts will raise the revenues and do not unduly favor or benefit rich people. Both have the same set of data, but they look at the figures differently.

Even if two people with the same background and the same goals agree on the major points of an analysis, they will seldom agree on everything. So that the problems of analysis can be minimized, every researcher has to be aware of the most common problems in analysis. A knowledge of the difficulties is a step toward eliminating them.

AIDS IN ANALYSIS

To avoid the problems of faulty analysis, you can take a number of steps. Experience, an open mind, and talking with others will help, although none is a cure-all. The struggle starts anew with every report you write, with every research project you undertake.

Awareness of History of the Problem.
You may find it helpful to examine other research studies that explored similar problems. What have other companies done, for example, to improve inventory control? You might also look at the history of the problem in your company. How long has the company had the present system? How many people work in the area? What kind of training do they have? You asked similar questions when you first defined the problem for the report and made your research plan or proposal.

The report-writing process is not totally linear. You will do a number of the steps simultaneously, and you may repeat a number of them. Going back over your notes to refamiliarize yourself with the precise problem statement is particularly important at the beginning of the analysis.

Consultation with Others.
Before you decide on a particular interpretation, you may want to find out how others interpret the findings. If you are good at interpreting, you are also aware of the difficulties and know that it is easy to overlook some aspects. Another person can also provide a fresh approach to the analysis. Perhaps in your analysis of a new training program you have overlooked the attitudes of the supervisors. Perhaps someone else can suggest how to make employees more open in their responses to questions about the program. Perhaps you should use a different statistical tool.

Understanding of Statistics.
Without a clear understanding of major statistical techniques discussed in Chapter 11, you will have difficulty understanding what the data mean and putting the results in context.

Critical Viewpoint.
Applying a critical viewpoint involves reevaluating your findings, your research design, your grouping of data, and your results. You must then reevaluate your interpretation of the data and the conclusions. You should constantly ask yourself whether you can justify your analysis. Are there any items you have overlooked? If you have strong feelings on a particular point and your interpretation conforms to your viewpoint, reevaluation is imperative.

Let us assume that you firmly believe training programs are a waste of money and do not benefit the company. Asked to research the effect of current training programs, you come to the conclusion that they are not worth the money the company spends on them. Upper management, however, believes they are an excellent tool for motivating and training employees, and several people have advanced successfully after undergoing special training. Given those circumstances, you should reexamine your results.

Knowledge of Logic.
The interpretation of data must be logical. Knowing the basic rules of logic will help you avoid some of the major flaws in interpreting data.

FLAWS IN INTERPRETING DATA

Some of the points in this discussion will overlap because one flaw in reasoning is often closely connected with another one. As in real life, it is difficult to separate all items neatly from one another.

Differing Views of Reality. The problem of people's differing views of reality relates to the discussion of the communication process in Chapter 2. Two people never perceive a phenomenon identically. Both bring their own backgrounds, feelings, and values to the interpretation. Travel brochures from Iceland describe summer temperatures as mild or even warm, for example, but a person from Singapore would probably disagree with that description. To the Singaporean, Iceland's summers are rather cold.

If differing viewpoints are considered wrong or unimportant, they may be neglected in an analysis. This neglect may not be done consciously. If it is a subconscious process, the problem is unlikely to be corrected, because, in order to correct a problem, the researcher must know that it exists.

The data may also be interpreted on the basis of emotions and feelings rather than a rational examination. Someone violently opposed to smoking has a different perception of nonsmokers' rights than a smoker. If the researcher has a particular perception of a situation, finding data to support that viewpoint is not difficult.

A Craving for the Sensational. Most people want to show that their work is important, and it is tempting to convey the message by implication. If a report sounds important, the writer may feel important.

Let us assume 53 percent of the sample studied in a market research project like a new product. In a spectacular interpretation the writer would not be satisfied with the presentation of the fact that a majority of the sample liked the product; he might report that an overwhelming majority liked it. The word *overwhelming* presents the problem, especially if the exact percentage is not given. Because most readers would not define 53 percent as an overwhelming majority, the writer longing for the spectacular might be tempted to omit the number. Similarly, in the late 1970s a number of people criticized business profits and labeled them *obscene*. The word certainly catches attention, but it conveys little meaning. It is emotional rather than factual. The report writer has to avoid language that overstates the situation and may influence management to make the *wrong* decision.

Preference for a Particular Viewpoint. A writer with a strong personal opinion about a situation may look only at data that will support that viewpoint or may simply neglect "unfriendly" data.

To guard against this possibility, the writer should look at all points of view and weigh all evidence carefully. Making a list of all advantages and disadvantages of a particular decision would be helpful. If the list contains mostly advantages, and the writer at the same time emotionally favors the decision, the signal should be clear: reevaluate.

For example, in an employee-performance review the supervisor concludes that the employee should receive a rating of outstanding. Ready to go on to the next case, the supervisor remembers receiving a number of complaints about that particular employee. The supervisor and the employee are personal friends, see each other socially, and their children play together. Despite the pressure to give this employee an outstanding rating, the supervisor must consider the complaints and reevaluate the entire file.

Value Judgments. Value judgments are usually based on emotions and insufficient data. The person making a value judgment is often unaware of making it.

Let us consider the following example. You are about to go to China on a business trip. To prepare for the trip, you read a number of books on cultural practices, including table manners, and eating habits. You learn that in China people eat dogs. Thinking of your pet dog you are absolutely horrified. You consider the eating of dogs to be outrageous and uncivilized. Obviously, the Chinese do not share your feelings.

In declaring the practice uncivilized and outrageous, you have made a value judgment based on your own cultural background and feeling of what is appropriate or acceptable. You may say that you would not want to eat this type of food. You might try it and decide you do not like it, but you may not condemn others for liking it. The Hindus are outraged that Americans eat beef. Try to explain that to a meat-loving American and the cattle industry.

Value judgments readily lead to generalizations. Basically there is nothing wrong with generalizations. In fact, unless you want to tailor every product to individual tastes, you have to generalize tastes. For example, you may find that college-educated single women in the 25 to 30 age group like a certain type of car. You will not please everyone in that group. If you have done your research well, however, enough women will like your company's car so that many will be sold.

When you make value judgments, be aware of what you are doing and learn to separate feelings from facts.

Inability to Distinguish the Important from the Unimportant. Some writers are afraid of omitting any data from their reports; they want to include every finding. All, they may argue, are related to the problem. Unfortunately the major points may get lost in the mass of minor details. The report may be useless because it is confused, disorganized, and difficult to read.

Insufficient Data. Often the report writer must generalize on the basis of a limited sample. In the 1970s many academic journals examined Japanese management practices, for example, and usually concluded that Japan's success was attributable in part to the lifetime-employment system. Scholars and journalists argued that this provided stability to the corporations. Often the writers had not been to Japan at all or had only visited major corporations.

A more critical examination showed that the lifetime-employment system affects only employees at large corporations; small corporations do not have the system at all. In addition, lifetime employment usually stops at age 55, the traditional retirement age in Japan. Women are never part of the system because they are expected to leave the workforce when they marry. Clearly the interpretation of the lifetime-employment system was based on insufficient data.

Comparison of Noncomparable Data.
Numerous studies on both sides of the Atlantic show that, based on tests given to high-school or college students, German students are superior to American students. This data is taken as proof that American students and the American system are not as good as the German. The difficulty lies in the sample selection for the tests. Although the sample may have been selected randomly and the research design may be good, the results are still misleading because the groups cannot be compared.

In the U.S., the young people who enroll in high school include students who will go to college, will have technical jobs, or will become unskilled workers. A number of students will drop out along the way. All attend the same school and are usually together in the same classrooms for many subjects.

In Germany, it is still common practice that after fourth grade students have to decide whether they will later attend a university, have a technical job, or become unskilled workers. Obviously one cannot compare test results of German university-bound high school students with American high school students. Those types of inaccurate studies continue to appear at regular intervals.

Statistical competency is not enough. To avoid comparing noncomparable data requires sensitivity and, as in the above example, cultural knowledge that few people have.

Inference of Faulty Cause–Effect Relationships.
Although a simple correlation does not prove a cause–effect relationship, people often infer a causal relationship when two things happen simultaneously or sequentially. The sun rises after the rooster crows, but the rooster does not make the sun rise. The rainfall in Ohio correlates with the number of letters in each month, but spelling does not cause the rainfall. Statistical relationships may be absolutely meaningless (rooster and sunrise). Intelligent observation and common sense are necessary in the study of cause–effect relationships.

Conviction that Conclusions are Essential.
Suppose that, after working hard on a report, you find out that you cannot draw any conclusions. You

believe that the study should be repeated on a wider scale and over a longer time period. To report that you cannot draw any conclusions or make any recommendations, however, seems like failure. After all, management is expecting a report to decide about inventory control, a new marketing plan, or new pricing strategies, for example.

Circumstances may have changed since you received the assignment. Perhaps new legislation was passed or there was an important court ruling on affirmative action. Unless you incorporate that information, your report is meaningless. If the report is due tomorrow, you obviously need an extension on the deadline. To turn your report in as if nothing had happened in the meantime would be dishonest and useless. As an extreme example, suppose you were about to finish a feasibility study for expanding your business into Iran when the Shah left the throne. No matter how good your analysis, you would have needed to reconsider your conclusions.

Skimpy Analyses. By the time you are ready to analyze the data, you are thoroughly familiar with the topic. The facts may appear clear and logical to you. However, the reader is not familiar with the details. To report that the reasons for the failure of a new product are obvious is not helpful to the person who asked you to do the study. You must present and explain the reasons and give the supporting evidence in an orderly manner. By insisting that the reasons are self-explanatory, you may lose the goodwill of the reader who is not familiar with the topic.

Unquestioned Reliance on Authorities. "If a reputable journal has printed it, it must be right" is an example of the belief that authorities are infallible. Even though journal articles are carefully selected, you should read them critically and with an open mind. Even noted economists cannot agree on how the deficit can be cured or what the economy will be like a year or even six months in the future. Read what they have to say, evaluate and interpret the data against your company's background and needs, and then decide. Think clearly and question authority. Had the Wright Brothers listened to authoritative opinion, they would not have learned to fly.

Oversimplification. Decision making would be easy if it were based on the simplistic statement that a decision is either right or wrong, that there is no in-between. Unfortunately, the either–or position does not allow for pulling the best from a number of positions and creating a new position. Interpreting data involves weighing factors and drawing conclusions. Statistical evidence that a new training program would be more successful at motivating employees than the old one, for example, must be weighed against other factors such as cost, mobility of employees, disruption at the workplace, and space requirements before a decision is made to implement the new program.

Guidelines. You must know the problems and fallacies of analysis in order to guard against them. The following guidelines may help you in this endeavor.

1. Keep the presentation and the interpretation of the data separate. Collect all your data before you begin a formal analysis. If you start the analysis after you have evaluated only half of your sample, you may fix certain conclusions in your mind and, as a result, leave out facts that will not agree with your first impression. On the other hand, the research process is not completely linear; you do many things at the same time. You may even reconsider your problem statement as you go through the report preparation.

2. Separate facts from opinion. A disciplined researcher is not emotional or prejudiced. Hearsay does not constitute a fact unless you verify it. You cannot rely on the company grapevine to decide on the performance of a new employee. On the other hand, the grapevine may provide the incentive to do some checking.

3. Approach your analysis in an orderly fashion. Just as you planned the methodology for collecting data, you should organize your findings according to breakdowns of your problem statement. This means you have to connect your interpretation to the problem statement. Keeping the problem in mind will help you to sort the relevant from the irrelevant information. It will help you to pick out the major points so that you will not become lost in trivia and meaningless detail.

4. Figure out your weaknesses, your gripes, and your emotional convictions. You may even want to put them on a sheet of paper and keep them handy so that you can check as you analyze your data.

PERFORMING ANALYSIS

Let us assume you are in charge of inspecting fast-food restaurants for a national chain. Looking over the inspection reports for recent months, you find that the restaurant in Prairie City has had poor marks several times. You decide to have a special inspection. Your company has three types of inspections: the spot check, two times in one day; the intermediate inspection, five times in two days; the in-depth inspection, twenty times over a four-day period.

Several people inspect the Prairie City restaurant, and you organize their observations as shown in Exhibit 12.1. Because previous reports indicated problems in quality, waiting time (company standard is five minutes), and service, the special inspection has concentrated on those areas.

After you have organized the data, you must analyze it. Some people, when confronted with a lot of information in text or table form, are over-

Exhibit 12.1   **Data on Restaurant Inspection**

Time	Service	Food	Waiting Time in Minutes
10:00 a.m.	Excellent	OK	1
10:30 a.m.	Excellent	OK	2
11:00 a.m.	OK	Poor	5
11:30 a.m.	OK	Poor	7
12:00 noon	Poor	Good	9
12:30 p.m.	Very poor	Excellent	10
1:00 p.m.	Poor	Excellent	7
1:30 p.m.	Good	OK	6
2:00 p.m.	Excellent	Poor	5
3:00 p.m.	Excellent	Poor	5½
4:30 p.m.	Excellent	Poor	4
5:00 p.m.	Good	OK	4
5:30 p.m.	Good	OK	4
6:00 p.m.	OK	Poor	6
6:30 p.m.	Poor	Excellent	7
7:00 p.m.	Poor	Excellent	8
7:30 p.m.	Poor	Good	6
8:00 p.m.	Excellent	Poor	4
9:00 p.m.	Excellent	Poor	3
10:00 p.m.	Poor	Poor	2

whelmed by the detail and start verbalizing the table. In the restaurant example, verbalizing could take the following form:

> At ten o'clock service was excellent, the food was OK, and waiting time was one minute. At 10:30 a.m. service was excellent, food was OK, waiting time was two minutes. . . .

This is not analysis of the data. Analysis should clarify information and not simply repeat it.

At the beginning of the analysis you have to determine categories for grouping the data. The way you group the data will depend partially on the problem you want to solve. The restaurant data falls into two patterns, off-hour and rush hour. The rush hour can be further divided into two time segments:

	Service	Food	Waiting Time
Off-Hours	Excellent	OK to poor	Within or slightly over standard
First Half of Rush Hour	Good to Excellent	OK	Over standard
Second Half of Rush Hour	Poor	Excellent	Far over standard

Your analysis based on this grouping of the data might be:

The data suggest three distinct patterns: (1) off-hours, (2) first half of busy hours, and (3) second half of busy hours.

During slow times the food is poor; service is excellent; waiting time exceeds the standard only slightly.

During the first segment of the rush hour service is good; food is acceptable; waiting time begins to increase.

During the second segment of the rush hour service deteriorates; the food is excellent; waiting time exceeds the standard by up to five minutes.

This sample analysis emphasizes the grouping of data into off-hours and two segments of rush hours. Service, food quality, and waiting time are discussed under each. An alternative would be to use service, food quality, and waiting time as the major groupings. The analysis might then read:

Service, food quality, and waiting time are influenced by customer traffic. Service is excellent during off-hours; it deteriorates throughout the busy times. Food quality is poor during off-hours but improves as busy time progresses. Waiting time is within the standard only during off-hours. During busy hours waiting time always exceeds the standard. It is longest during peak times.

After you have analyzed your data, you must summarize your findings. If you write a complete analytical report, you must also draw conclusions and make recommendations.

DRAWING CONCLUSIONS

Conclusion
The conclusion establishes the meaning of the data in terms of the problem.

Drawing **conclusions** is a logical step after interpreting the data. Relevant conclusions are based on objective data analysis. In the final report the conclusions may come at the beginning. The actual sequence of the presentation will depend on the purpose of the report, the reader–writer relationship, and the opinions of the reader. If the requestor of the report did not ask for conclusions and recommendations, the writer should not include them, of course.

Conclusions must come from the analysis, which seems obvious. Yet, reading some reports, you may wonder how the writer reached the conclusions. They do not seem to be supported by the data or the interpretation.

In the restaurant example, after you have analyzed the data and determined the patterns, you have to figure out what the patterns mean. You can draw conclusions related to the food, the service, and the length of waiting time during the three time periods. Because you are familiar with fast-food chains, you might draw the following conclusions based on the findings:

1. The food is poor or mediocre during off-hours and at the beginning of mealtimes because the cooks prepared too much. It has been waiting under warming lights.

2. The Prairie City restaurant does not follow company standards of quality. The cook keeps prepared food too long.

3. During the busy times, the food that has been prepared ahead is used up. The fresh food is excellent. The staff is capable of serving quality food.

4. The time standard set by the company is met only during off-hours. The Prairie City restaurant is incapable of meeting demand at peak periods because it has too few employees. The company standards are unrealistic.

5. Service at the beginning of rush hours and during off-times is excellent when workers are rested and friendly. During rush periods the problems include the small number of employees, the layout of the counters, and the need for training in customer relations.

Some conclusions would not make sense. Based on the data you have, you cannot conclude that the noise from the traffic outside affects the courtesy of the employees. You cannot conclude that the French fries would be better if the potatoes were fresh rather than frozen. Without further investigation you could not conclude that the employees are purposely rude.

In summary, the conclusions must relate to the data. A strong background in the business is helpful. If you have worked in a fast-food chain, for example, you may better understand the problems. On the other hand, your experience might prevent you from seeing things you did not experience while working as a cook or a cashier.

You should present your conclusions in an orderly fashion and support each one with data. If your analysis was orderly and concentrated on major points, this task will be relatively easy.

You must draw conclusions based on the importance of the data. One rude cashier does not justify the conclusion that employees at that restaurant are inconsiderate and rude. Isolated instances and observations must be seen in perspective. In drawing conclusions, these guidelines will be helpful.

1. Conclusions must follow logically from the analysis.

2. Conclusions cannot introduce new material.

3. Conclusions must relate to the problem.

4. Several analysis points may lead to the same conclusions; one analysis point may lead to several conclusions.

5. Conclusions must be objective.

MAKING RECOMMENDATIONS

Recommendations
Recommendations are specific suggestions for solving the problem.

Just as the conclusions logically follow the analysis, so the **recommendations** logically grow out of the conclusions. You cannot make recommendations unless you have drawn conclusions. If you do not draw conclusions about waiting time, you cannot make recommendations for solving the problem.

In the conclusions the report writer determines what the facts mean in view of the problem. In the recommendations the writer makes specific suggestions on how to solve the problem. The following examples illustrate the differences between conclusions and recommendations:

Conclusion: *The test results show that the students were not sufficiently prepared for the test.*

Recommendation: *Instructors should schedule a review session before each test.*

Conclusion: *Sales dropped because of poor quality control.*

Recommendation: *The company should hire a quality-control inspector.*

Conclusion: *The secretaries seem to be overworked.*

Recommendation: *The company should study workflow and workload to determine possible solutions.*

In these examples, additional recommendations might be made to solve the problem. When making recommendations, the report writer must determine whether they make sense in terms of the environment.

Recommendations must be specific. The simple statement that something has to be done is meaningless because it provides no specific guidance for action.

Sometimes writers are tempted to hedge. They do not want to commit themselves by saying, "Based on the conclusions, I recommend. . ." or "A careful consideration of the conclusions suggests that the problem can be solved if the following recommendations are implemented." They are afraid of being direct. Because they fear blame if the recommendations do not solve the problem, they hide behind conditional clauses such as:

1. Maybe the company might want to consider. . . .
2. Perhaps it would be helpful to. . . .
3. Under certain circumstances it might perhaps be advantageous. . . .

These are not recommendations. They do not direct the reader to take action. Furthermore, all of the vague words—*might, perhaps,* and *maybe*—utterly confuse the reader. If the writer concludes that no definite recommendations can be made based on the data, he should say so *clearly*.

Not every conclusion warrants a separate recommendation. Several conclusions might be combined. Sometimes several problems can be corrected with one recommendation. On the other hand, one conclusion may lead to several recommendations.

To return to the restaurant example, some logical recommendations can be based on the conclusions:

1. Survey how many hamburgers are served each day between 10:00 a.m. and 11.00 a.m., between 11:00 a.m. and noon, and between noon and 1:00 p.m. (The time span has to coincide with the busy hours and off-hours.)

2. Revise the volume of preparation based on the sales records.

3. Compare the waiting time with other restaurants in the chain. If the others have similar problems, the time standard needs to be reexamined and possibly be revised. If others have no problem, then examine reasons for the problem at Prairie City. (Of course, if you already know that the others meet the standard, you must change the recommendation.)

4. Train employees in courtesy.

5. Examine shift schedules with the goal of bringing in fresh employees at the middle of the busy hours in order to improve the service.

All of these recommendations come out of the conclusions. They are direct and in command form: *survey, revise, compare, train, examine.* The writer does not hedge. The reader knows exactly what is recommended and what is expected.

To make recommendations more effective, you should follow these guidelines:

1. Give the recommendation in a declarative statement.

2. Avoid words like *perhaps* and *maybe.*

3. Itemize your recommendations. This procedure is not absolutely necessary, but it will help the reader. It may also help you in reevaluating your recommendations.

4. Put each recommendation in a separate sentence. If you have several recommendations in one sentence, the reader may miss one.

Some writers combine conclusions and recommendations at the end of the report. Unless they are lengthy and detailed, this practice is acceptable; however, the novice writer may confuse the two. In short reports writers may draw conclusions as they go along, taking care to make a distinction between conclusions and recommendations in their minds. If conclusions are drawn at the end of every point in the analysis, only the recommendations would appear at the end of the report.

IMPROVING ANALYTICAL SKILLS

Many approaches are possible in learning how to analyze, draw conclusions, and make recommendations. One is to learn analysis by careful evaluation of other writers' reports. This involves examining how a good writer succeeds and how a poor writer fails.

As you look at a report, you can analyze the organization and ask whether it makes sense. You can examine the method, analysis, presentation, headings, summary, conclusions, and recommendations. You may have to read the report or article several times, and you may have to think about it. Then you will be able to determine whether you agree that it was the best way to present the data and the most effective analysis possible.

In effect, you will critically analyze the material by first abstracting the facts and then answering these questions:

1. Is the problem statement clear?
2. What are the strong and weak points of the methodology?
   a. How old is the data?
   b. Were the statistical tools appropriate?
   c. What sampling techniques were used?
3. Does the author accomplish in the report or article what was intended? For example, if the author at the beginning promises an answer to a certain question, you should check for the answer. If the author promises to examine four major points, you should check for the four points. You also must determine whether those four points are the most important ones.
4. Does the discussion relate to the problem, or does it go off on tangents?
5. Is the discussion objective? (Check the discussion against the interpretation guidelines.)
6. Do the conclusions logically follow the discussion?
7. Are the recommendations clear, and are they a logical outcome of the conclusions?

An evaluation of the analysis of another writer's work should help you to improve your own analytical skills. Analysis takes practice and experience yet in many ways is a natural process. When you read a newspaper article on a controversial topic, you probably evaluate the arguments as you go along. By the end of the article you either agree or disagree.

Often your conclusion is based on emotional approval or disapproval rather than on a rational analysis of the data, however. In many cases the supporting data in newspaper articles may be weak. The difference between this type of analysis and research analysis is scientific orientation. In research analysis you weigh the data carefully, disregarding personal feelings. You do not draw conclusions without support or proof. You have a definite methodology for objective analysis.

SUMMARY OF LEARNING OBJECTIVES

To Be Familiar with Analysis Aids.
An awareness of the history of the problem, an understanding of personal biases, consultation with others, a critical viewpoint, and a sound understanding of research tools can help the writer overcome common analysis problems.

To Become Aware of Problems in Analyzing Data.
Some of the more frequent problems in analyzing material are differing views of reality, a craving for the sensational, the temptation to make value judgments, the comparison of noncomparable data, an inability to distinguish the important from the unimportant, and confusion about cause–effect relationships.

To Analyze Data.
The writer groups the data and establishes patterns in order to examine the problem in detail. When analyzing, the writer must have the problem and the purpose of the report clearly in mind.

To Draw Conclusions.
Conclusions must be based on the analysis. They must be clear and concise. The conclusions cannot introduce new material.

To Make Recommendations.
Recommendations must be specific. Often they are itemized.
Although conclusions and recommendations can be combined, usually the best practice is to keep them separate. Conclusions are based on the facts and the analysis of the facts. Recommendations, on the other hand, are more subjective. They are based, to some extent at least, on the opinions of the writer.
To learn to analyze well takes time. Sometimes it helps to examine the analysis of material in reports and articles written by others.

QUESTIONS AND PROBLEMS

1. Discuss the differences between analysis, conclusions, and recommendations.
2. What are some of the basic fallacies in analyzing data?

3. How can you improve your analytical skills?
4. Read an article in your major field and write a critical analysis.
5. Analyze the organization and presentation of data in a newspaper article.
6. Select several tables in journals and newspapers. After you analyze them, compare your analysis with that of the author of the article.
7. What is the purpose of analysis?
8. Discuss the importance of grouping data before analysis.
9. Discuss the wording of recommendations.

CHAPTER THIRTEEN

_____

_____

_____

_____

_____

_____

_____

_____

_____

_____

_____

_____

_____

_____

_____

_____

_____

_____

_____

_____

_____

_____

VISUAL AIDS

VISUAL AIDS

LEARNING OBJECTIVES

- To understand the purpose of visual aids.
- To understand the underlying principles of tables and figures.
- To design effective and appropriate tables and figures.
- To understand the role of computer graphics in report writing.

Sometimes you may organize the results of statistical analysis into tables and graphs and then analyze the data further. At other times you may want to do an in-depth analysis of the information and then present the results in a table or graph. Or you may simultaneously analyze the findings and prepare visual aids.

A visual presentation of the material can help you analyze your material and, as a result, write a convincing and effective report. The visual presentation will also help the reader to understand the report.

THE PURPOSE OF VISUAL AIDS

When designing visual aids, you will follow many of the planning steps discussed in Chapter 6. Without a clear understanding of the problem, the purpose of the report, or the needs of the potential reader, you would find it difficult to create effective visual material.

For example, a line graph showing an upward sales trend might provide enough information if used in a public-relations report for customers. If your task is to forecast sales, however, you would find such a graph totally inadequate. You would need a detailed table that gives sales by product, month, and geographic area. In addition, you would need figures to compare this month's sales with those in the same month of the previous year. You might also include graphs to show, at a quick glance, the trends in sales.

As a first step, you will need to determine whether the visual aid is a supplement to the text or whether the visual presentation *is* the report. That decision will shape the composition and entire appearance of the report. Assume, for example, that you are in the business of repairing appliances and heating and cooling systems. Over the past few years an increasing number of customers have complained about the cost of having a repairman come to the house to fix the air conditioning, the refrigerator, or the furnace. They argue that the repairman charges too much for the time it takes him to repair the appliance. Many customers believe that the money they pay goes directly into the pocket of the repairman or the owner as income. How can you tell your customers what your costs are? You might talk to them or write a memo, but most customers would not read a report justifying your price. Writing such a report would probably be a waste of effort.

You need something that conveys your message quickly. A number of businesses use the back of the payment receipt for the purpose. As illustrated in Exhibit 13.1, this type of report is actually a sequence of pictures illustrating the factors that contribute to the price. Anyone who looks at it has instant information on fringe benefits, taxes, and overhead costs. The report

Exhibit 13.1 **Picture Report**

enables the customer to look at the price in perspective. Similar reports are frequently used in public-relations material because they make a complex point in a simplified way.

Used appropriately, the picture report can be effective, but it also has limitations. If you wanted to examine and, if necessary, redesign your firm's rate structure for repairs, you could not use a picture report. It simply would not give enough information to explain the new rates. In this case you would use an in-depth report to examine expenses such as taxes, materials, wages, fringe benefits, office cost, building maintenance, and heating and cooling. You would give precise figures and an analysis of the figures. You would need to decide *how* to spread the overhead cost over all the services your firm provides. You would also have to consider the competition. Finally, you would present a detailed analysis of some of the most frequently performed repair services. Because presentation and analysis are the main aspects of this type of report, the tables would *supplement* the text and clarify the figures and cost items, but they would not replace it.

Both the picture report and the in-depth report deal with the firm's expenses and the charge to the customer, but the purpose of the two reports is not the same. The first illustrates the business expenses so that the customer understands and accepts the price; the second helps management to set and evaluate the prices charged to the customer. The different purposes determine the character of the reports and the role of the visuals in them.

TABLES

Tables are a systematic arrangement of data in rows and columns. A company presenting information on its income could provide that information in text form. In its annual report, for example, Borg-Warner might have written:

> In 1983 Borg-Warner Corporation had net earnings of 182.6 million dollars. Of that sum depreciation amounted to 108.9 million dollars and amortization totalled 5.8 million dollars.

However, the company did not present the information in sentence form but in a table (Exhibit 13.2). The information is easier to grasp in a table than in a paragraph because the facts are categorized and arranged systematically.

In its simplest form a table can be part of the text. It may even be part of a sentence:

> We would like to order
> 1 bolt of linen #333/256 white at $10.00/yard,
> 1 bolt of Georgette #438/714 blue at $13.55/yard,
> 2 bolts of cotton #452/436 green at $5.35/yard.

Exhibit 13.2   **Tabular Organization of Income Information**

Borg-Warner Corporation and consolidated subsidiaries   19

Statement of changes in financial position
Year ended December 31

	(millions of dollars)	1983	1982	1981
Operations	Net earnings	**$182.6**	$167.4	$172.1
	Non-fund charges (credits) to earnings:			
	Depreciation	**108.9**	99.7	89.9
	Amortization of deferred charges	**5.8**	22.1	17.0
	Earnings of affiliates and services companies reinvested	**(45.5)**	(53.3)	(75.8)
	Provision for withdrawal from a product line, net of deferred taxes			42.5
	Other, net	**67.7**	41.7	42.5
	Total from earnings	**319.5**	277.6	288.2
	Funds provided by (used for) short-term assets and liabilities:			
	Receivables	**(8.1)**	(64.8)	22.0
	Inventories	**(8.5)**	76.3	(32.5)
	Other current assets	**4.6**	4.8	(16.6)
	Accounts payable and accrued expenses	**76.7**	10.8	58.4
	Income taxes	**32.9**	(12.9)	12.7
	Currency translation effect on working capital	**(12.4)**	(16.9)	(13.7)
		85.2	(2.7)	30.3
	Funds used for additions to deferred charges	**(32.7)**	(22.7)	(18.0)
	Funds used for other long-term assets and liabilities	**(52.0)**	(38.2)	(6.7)
	Net funds provided by operations	**320.0**	214.0	293.8
Dividends	**Dividends declared and paid**	**(65.9)**	(59.7)	(53.9)
Investments	Capital expenditures	**(152.8)**	(176.3)	(224.5)
	Disposal of property, plant and equipment	**10.6**	7.7	41.3
	Net long-term assets of businesses acquired or consolidated		(49.6)	(26.6)
	Net long-term assets of businesses divested	**5.6**	32.1	5.7
	Net other (increase) decrease in investments and advances	**8.2**	(23.5)	(52.4)
	Net funds used in investments	**(128.4)**	(209.6)	(256.5)
Financing	Increase (decrease) in notes payable	**(20.3)**	(57.0)	53.1
	Sale of adjustable rate convertible notes		100.0	
	Other increases in long-term debt	**15.0**	93.8	58.3
	Reductions in long-term debt	**(35.6)**	(88.5)	(38.3)
	Purchases of treasury common stock	**(7.3)**	(20.9)	(24.3)
	Sales of treasury common stock	**22.2**	19.2	16.0
	Net funds provided by (used for) financing	**(26.0)**	46.6	64.8
	Net increase (decrease) in cash and marketable securities	**$ 99.7**	$ (8.7)	$ 48.2

Source: Borg-Warner, *Annual Report,* 1983.

Ruled Table
Headings are set off
with horizontal lines.

In Exhibit 13.3 the writer believed it would be advantageous to use column heads, row heads, and rules. The result is a **ruled table**, which enables the reader to immediately separate the descriptors from the table data. The table might have a separate title and number, but this one is simple enough that it could also be incorporated in the text.

As a table becomes more complex, the need for setting it off from the text increases. The writer can add vertical lines to separate columns and create a **boxed table** as in Exhibit 13.4. The writer can also put a frame around the entire table including the title, source notes, and footnotes. This results in a **framed** or **fully boxed table**, as in Exhibit 13.5.

Boxed Table
The boxed table uses
horizontal and vertical
lines to separate data.

Labels added to Exhibit 13.4 identify the various parts of a table. The row titles are called stubs. The stub head identifies the stubs. In this particular table the stubs are years. Each column has a title or column head. The spanner further identifies the column heads. In this table the spanner head tells the reader that the column heads represent branches of Clover Department Stores.

Entries can also be separated by horizontal rules; however, rules should be used in tables only if they are functional. Look at the stock quotations in *The Wall Street Journal* and imagine that horizontal and vertical rules separated all the entries. They would create confusion rather than clarity.

Usually the column heads are at the top and the stubs are at the left margin of the table. In wide tables the writer may repeat the stubs on the right side of the table to facilitate reading. If columns are long, the column heads may be repeated at the bottom of the table. The decision will be influenced by the nature of the data.

In the stock quotations in *The Wall Street Journal* (Exhibit 13.6) the stubs are actually in the center of the entries. This placement facilitates reading. The stubs, in this case company names, separate the long-term price from the current price. Because the print is small and the rows are very close together, this arrangement makes it easier to read across the line.

Exhibit 13.3   **Ruled Table**

Table 4
Would you please send the following items:

Item	Order Number	Color	Quantity	Price/ Unit	Total Price
Cotton	103/254	white	1 Bolt	$ 50.00	$ 50.00
Linen	253/689	red	2 Bolts	200.00	400.00
Silk	587/052	blue	1 Bolt	600.00	600.00
Wool	932/853	green	3 Bolts	400.00	1,200.00
Total					$2,250.00

Exhibit 13.4   **Boxed Table**

Total Sales of Clover Department Stores, 1975–1985 (millions of U.S. dollars)							
→Year	Branches ← ———————————— Spanner Head						
	A	B	C	D	E	Total	
1975	12	8	10	20	10	60	
1976	12	10	9	20	14	65	
1977	15	13	13	24	15	80	
1978	18	14	16	25	17	90	
1979	21	17	16	26	20	100	
Stubs 1980	25	23	22	35	25	130	
1981	27	24	23	35	26	135	
1982	28	26	25	36	25	140	
1983	28	27	25	38	27	145	
1984	30	31	27	42	30	160	
1985	32	34	34	50	40	190	

Stub Head   **Column Heads**

The decision as to which information to put in the columns and which in the rows is not always obvious. If you want to design a table that shows the sales figures of Clover Department Stores by product line for each branch, for example, you can treat the branches either as stubs or as column heads. Exhibit 13.7 illustrates both possibilities.

Exhibit 13.5   **Fully Boxed Table**

Table 5 Breakdown of Sales by Product Line for Clover Department Stores, 1975–1985 (millions of U.S. dollars)				
Year	**Clothing**	**Appliances**	**Furniture**	**Total**
1975	30	20	10	60
1976	30	20	15	65
1977	35	25	20	80
1978	37	30	27	94
1979	42	33	25	100
1980	53	42	35	130
1981	55	43	37	135
1982	58	45	37	140
1983	60	46	39	145
1984	63	55	42	160
1985	75	64	51	190

Exhibit 13.6 Table Arrangement in *The Wall Street Journal* Stock Quotations

column heads

JANUARY 22, 1986

NEW YORK STOCK EXCHANGE COMPOSITE TRANSACTIONS

Tuesday, January 21, 1986

Quotations include trades on the Midwest, Pacific, Philadelphia, Boston and Cincinnati stock exchanges and reported by the National Association of Securities Dealers and Instinet

row heads

Source: New York Stock Exchange Composite Transactions, January 22, 1986, *The Wall Street Journal*. Reprinted by permission of *The Wall Street Journal*, © Dow Jones & Company, Inc. 1986. All Rights Reserved.

Exhibit 13.7   Stubs and Column Placement of Data

Table 8
Breakdown of Sales Figures by Product Line for Each Branch of Clover Department Stores, 1984 (millions of U.S. dollars)

Branch	Clothing	Appliances	Furniture	Total
A	15 (50%)	10 (33%)	5 (17%)	30 (100%)
B	12 (38%)	15 (48%)	4 (12%)	31 (100%)
C	12 (44%)	10 (37%)	5 (19%)	27 (100%)
D	20 (48%)	15 (36%)	7 (16%)	42 (100%)
E	16 (53%)	8 (27%)	6 (20%)	30 (100%)

Table 8
Breakdown of Sales Figures by Product Line for Each Branch of Clover Department Stores, 1984 (millions of U.S. dollars)

Product	Branch				
	A	B	C	D	E
Appliances	10 (33%)	15 (48%)	10 (37%)	15 (36%)	8 (27%)
Clothing	15 (50%)	12 (38%)	12 (44%)	20 (48%)	16 (53%)
Furniture	5 (17%)	4 (12%)	5 (19%)	7 (16%)	6 (20%)
Total	30 (100%)	31 (100%)	27 (100%)	42 (100%)	30 (100%)

Your decision on whether to use a descriptor as a stub head or a column head will often be based on mechanical considerations. Assume, for example, that you want to provide income statistics for ten different countries over the past five years. You could use the names of the countries either as the stub heads or column heads; however, they have different lengths, and some may be too long to fit on one line if used as column heads. Years, on the other hand, will easily fit in columns, and the columns will be the same width. Therefore, arranging the table with countries as stub heads and years as column heads makes more sense.

You must also decide the order in which to present the information. Countries, for example, are usually presented in alphabetical order. You could, however, arrange them from highest to lowest income, group them by geographical area or political orientation, or divide them into developed and developing countries. The arrangement will depend on what you want to emphasize in your report.

At times you may not have complete information. In the example, you might not have income information for all ten countries for all five years. You must indicate the missing data by entering *n.a.* for *not available* or a dash in place of the amount. You cannot use a zero, which would indicate that the country had no income in a particular year.

In many tables you may have numbers representing dollar amounts, acres, bushels, pounds, or gallons. Because the table would be crowded if you repeated the unit of measurement beside every number, you can omit it except with the first number in the column. The dollar columns in Exhibit 13.3 are an example. When all data in the table are in the same unit of measurement, you can indicate this in a table subtitle, as in Exhibits 13.4 and 13.5. Spanner heads may be used, as in Exhibit 13.4, to avoid repeating the same word or words in several column heads.

FIGURES

Figures provide overall information and impressions. In that sense, figures and tables complement each other. A report writer, for example, may present data in a table and also highlight the trends in a figure. Tables provide the reader with exact information, whereas figures concentrate on the visual impact of trends. At a glance the reader knows whether sales have increased or decreased, whether stock prices have gone up or down. The reader also gains some impression of the magnitude of the increase or decrease. Some of the most frequently used figures in business reports are line graphs, bar graphs, and pie charts.

LINE GRAPHS

In line graphs the dependent variable is *always* shown on the Y-axis (vertical), and the independent variable is *always* shown on the X-axis (horizontal). If you want to show sales over a ten-year period, sales are the dependent variable, and the years are the independent variable; therefore, sales are shown on the Y-axis and the years on the X-axis.

The Y-axis must start at 0; the X-axis need not. If the values you plot on the Y-axis are high numbers, starting at 0 can be cumbersome and detract from the effectiveness of the graph. In that case you can cut the Y-axis. Three ways of accomplishing this are shown in Exhibit 13.8. If you decide to cut the Y-axis, you must follow two basic rules:

Exhibit 13.8   **Cutting the Y-Axis**

1. All lines must be on the same side of the cut. You cannot have one line above and one line below the cut.

2. No line may cross the cut.

You must also pay attention to the scale you use for the axes. The difficulty is to determine what a *correct scale* is. Most people agree that an incorrect scale distorts the data but do not agree on what a correct scale is. The examples in Exhibit 13.9 show how the same data can give a different visual impression if the scale is changed.

A general guideline for a "correct" scale is that the space formed by drawing a vertical line from the first value on the *X*-axis and a horizontal line from the first value of the *Y*-axis should approximate a square. However, the marked intervals on the axes could be changed so that there is still visual manipulation of the data even though the first marked interval on the *X* and the *Y*-axis form a square (Exhibit 13.9). In a distorted graph the figures are correct. The writer does not manipulate the data. The distortion is visual.

The problem is that most people will remember the slope of the line rather than the numbers on the axes. If a line to show increases in union wages is almost vertical, people will remember the slope of the line rather than the exact numbers. If you design several graphs for comparison purposes, you have to use the same scale for each graph in order to avoid distortion. If you compare wage increases for various groups over the past ten years, for example, and you want to show the information in separate graphs, you must use the same scales for wages and for years in all of the graphs. You have an ethical duty to represent data fairly in visual aids.

Simple Line Graph. To show a change of sales figures over the past ten years for Clover Department Stores, you might use a simple line graph like the one in Exhibit 13.10. This and other graphs for Clover Department Stores are based on data presented in Exhibits 13.4, 13.5, and 13.7.

Exhibit 13.9   Scales of Coordinates and Visual Impact

Exhibit 13.10 **Simple Line Graph**

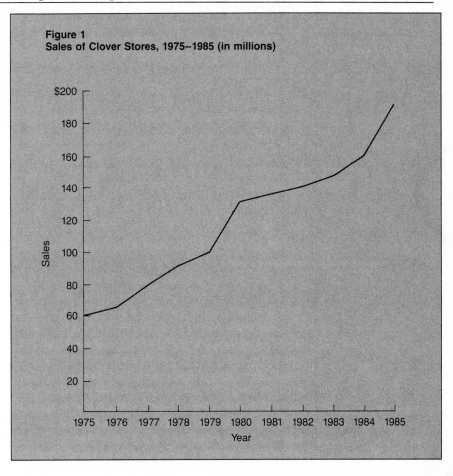

Figure 1
Sales of Clover Stores, 1975–1985 (in millions)

Multiple-Line Graph. Comparing data requires a graph with more than one line. If you want to compare the sales figures for Branches A, C, and D of Clover Department Stores for the past ten years, you can use a multiple-line graph, like the one in Exhibit 13.11. So that the lines are easy to distinguish, you can assign a different color or pattern to each one. You can use a **legend** to identify the various lines, or you can label the lines directly on the graph. Users of a multiple-line graph will read every value from a point on the line they want to examine to the *X*-axis. For example, the sales figures for 1983 were as follows: Branch A, $28 million; Branch C, $25 million; and Branch D, $38 million.

A multiple-line graph with three lines is easy to read, especially if the lines are not too close together. More than four or five lines can have a negative influence on readability because the graph may appear too crowded.

Legend
The legend provides the key to colors or patterns in the visual aid.

Exhibit 13.11 **Multiple Line Graph**

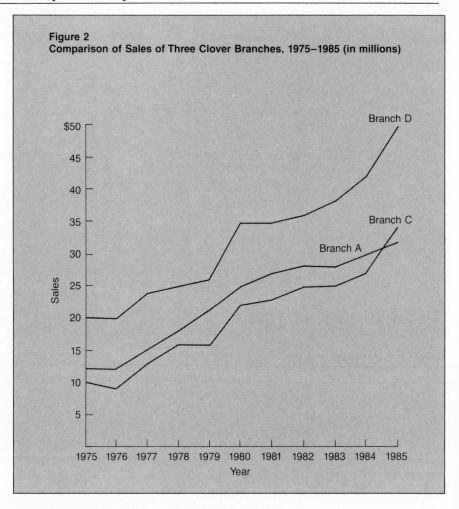

Figure 2
Comparison of Sales of Three Clover Branches, 1975–1985 (in millions)

The exact limit depends on the data. If the lines are spread out, a multiple-line graph with five lines may be easy to read. If the lines are close together, the graph may appear crowded with four lines.

Subdivided Line Graph. The subdivided line graph is also called a segmented or component line graph. It emphasizes the composition of data. For example, Clover Department Stores have three major product groups: appliances, furniture, and clothes. The sales in these three areas over the past ten years can be presented in a subdivided line graph like the one in Exhibit 13.12.

Exhibit 13.12 **Subdivided Line Graph**

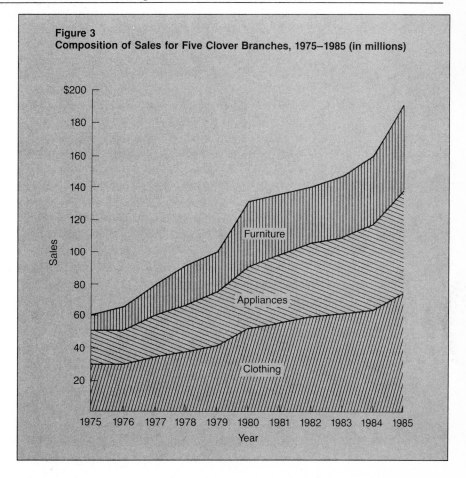

Figure 3
Composition of Sales for Five Clover Branches, 1975–1985 (in millions)

Total sales are represented by the top line. Each individual product group is represented by the area between the two lines framing the top and bottom of the area. These areas are also called *bands*. The reader gains an impression of the sales volume in each group, but, except for the band closest to the *X*-axis, the exact values are difficult to determine. For example, in order to get the value for 1983 for the second band, appliances, the reader would need to do some arithmetic. This would involve reading the figure for 1983 at the top of the appliance line and subtracting from it the value for 1983 clothing sales ($106 million less $60 million, or $46 million).

When trying to determine whether sales in a group have increased or decreased, looking at the shape of the curve is not enough. The curve on either side of the band may go up, and sales may still have declined. The important factor is the width of the band. If the band widens, then sales have increased; if the band narrows, sales have decreased. The subdivided line graph emphasizes the total and gives some impression of the magnitude of the individual components. You may decide to use both a multiple and a subdivided line graph to present data.

BAR GRAPHS

All of the bars in a bar graph have to be the same width; differences are expressed only in the length of the bar. Some of the principles for constructing line graphs also apply to bar graphs. The axes must be labeled, and the intervals on the axes must be even. The bar graph can also be cut, and the same rules apply as for line graphs. If the axis is cut, all bars must be cut. Exhibit 13.13 illustrates what happens if they are not. Unlike line graphs, the dependent variable in bar graphs can be shown on either the horizontal or the vertical axis.

As you look at the wage figures for workers of the three auto manufacturers in Exhibit 13.13, the first impression is that the workers at GM and

Exhibit 13.13 **Visual Manipulation of Data**

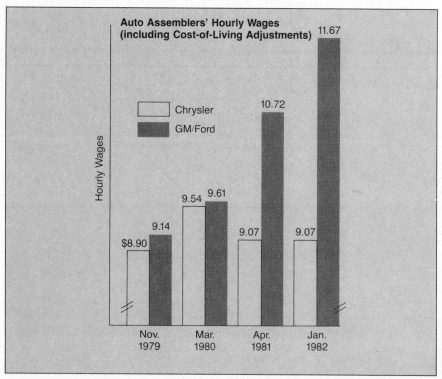

Source: "United Auto Workers and Auto Workers Hit Hard . . ." *The Wall Street Journal,* January 20, 1982.

Ford earn more than twice as much as the workers at Chrysler. This visual impression is what most readers will remember. Only after examining the bar graph more carefully do you notice that the Y-axis is cut. The bars are not cut, however, and this omission leads to a misrepresentation of the data even though the wage figures are written on every bar. The visual impact is clearly misleading.

Simple Bar Graph. If you want to show the sales figures for five branches of Clover Department Store for 1984, the best way to present this data visually is in a simple bar chart, as shown in Exhibit 13.14. Here the sales figures are indicated on the Y-axis, and the five stores are on the X-axis. The result is a **vertical bar graph**. In a vertical bar graph, the bars sit on the X-axis; that is, the dependent variable (sales) is on the Y-axis and the independent variable (branches) is on the X-axis. You could change the graph to a

Vertical Bar Graph
The bars sit on the X-axis.

Exhibit 13.14 **Simple Bar Chart**

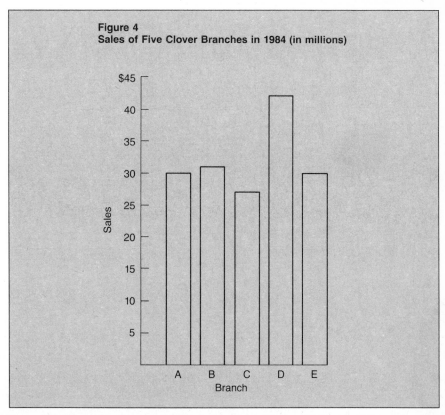

Figure 4
Sales of Five Clover Branches in 1984 (in millions)

Source: The United Auto Workers and Dale D. Buss, "Auto Workers Hit Hard by Giveups, Signaling Tough Times for Labor," January 20, 1982, *The Wall Street Journal.* Reprinted by permission of *The Wall Street Journal,* © Dow Jones & Company, Inc., 1982. All Rights Reserved.

Horizontal Bar Graph
The bars sit on the
Y-axis.

horizontal bar graph by putting sales figures on the X-axis and the branches on the Y-axis. In this case, as illustrated in Exhibit 13.15, the dependent variable is on the X-axis and the independent variable on the Y-axis.

Some experts suggest that quantities should always be presented in a vertical bar graph, whereas distances are best shown in a horizontal bar graph. If you examine bar graphs in annual reports, newspapers, and scholarly business journals, however, you will find that this distinction does not always hold true. While it is true that many people do use horizontal graphs for distances and vertical graphs for quantities, distances and quantity are not necessarily the deciding factors.

Often the decision is based instead on the mechanics of page layout and available space. If you must compare five stores, you can easily put that comparison in a vertical bar graph with sales figures on the Y-axis. If you compare 20 stores, the vertical bar graph is not practical because of the difficulty of fitting 20 names on one line. You could type the names of the stores at a slant or vertically, but they would be difficult to read. A horizontal bar graph with the names of the stores to the left of the Y-axis is the best arrangement.

Exhibit 13.15 **Horizontal Bar Graph**

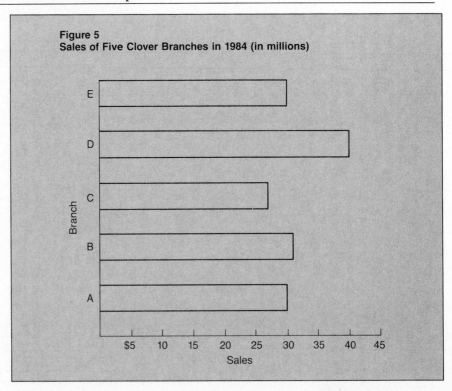

Figure 5
Sales of Five Clover Branches in 1984 (in millions)

Histogram. The histogram, illustrated in Exhibit 13.16, is a special type of simple bar graph. In a histogram the intervals between values are the same— in other words, a continuum, with no space between the bars. Age, weight, and income can be presented in a histogram.

You may wonder why the data, which is continuous, is not represented in a line graph. The age groups in the exhibit cover the same time intervals, and no age group is left out. The bars show how many people are in each bracket; however, the histogram does not show how many people are at each point in the bracket. If the brackets are small, the histogram approaches the continuum of a line graph. If the brackets are large, on the other hand, the data should be presented in a histogram.

Multiple-Bar Graph. To show a comparison of data, you can use a multiple-bar graph. For example, a comparison of the five branches of Clover Department Stores in the sales of clothes, appliances, and furniture is expressed in Exhibit 13.17. From the graph the reader can easily obtain figures for individual product sales but not the total sales figure. For that, the sales for

Exhibit 13.16 **Histogram**

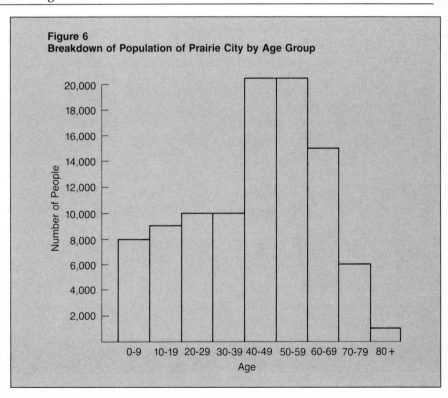

Figure 6
Breakdown of Population of Prairie City by Age Group

Exhibit 13.17 **Multiple Bar Graph**

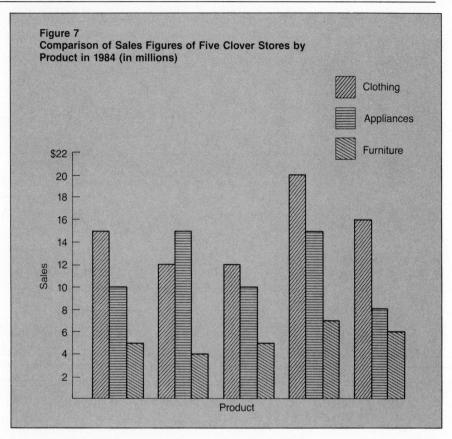

Figure 7
Comparison of Sales Figures of Five Clover Stores by Product in 1984 (in millions)

clothes, appliances, and furniture must be added. To make comparisons easier, you should either crosshatch (use a graphic pattern) or color the bars and provide a legend. At a glance the reader will then see which branch was highest in furniture sales, which in clothing sales, and which in appliance sales. No rules exist for determining how many parts each segment should have, but more than three variables for one branch would crowd the graph and make reading difficult.

Subdivided Bar Graph. The subdivided bar graph is also called a segmented or component bar graph. The data used in Exhibit 13.7 are presented as a subdivided bar graph in Exhibit 13.18. Each bar is the same size as in the simple bar graph, but this time the bar is subdivided into sales components: clothes, appliances, and furniture. The emphasis in the subdivided bar graph is on the total. The reader gets some idea of the magnitude of the components, but, for exact sales figures, must make some arithmetic calcu-

Exhibit 13.18 **Subdivided Bar Graph**

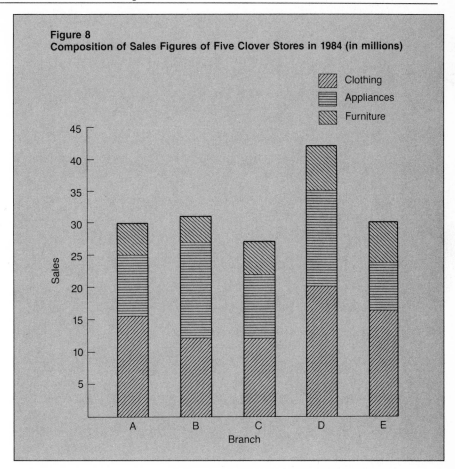

Figure 8
Composition of Sales Figures of Five Clover Stores in 1984 (in millions)

Clothing
Appliances
Furniture

lations. The writer can insert the numbers into the bar segments to help the reader only if the bars are large enough.

To decide between a multiple-bar graph and a subdivided bar graph, the writer must know whether to emphasize components or totals. In some cases the decision may be to present the data in both forms.

A special type of subdivided bar graph uses percentages rather than absolute figures. In Exhibit 13.19 all bars have the same length representing 100 percent. The various parts represent appliance sales in Store A as a percentage of total sales in Store A and appliance sales in Store B as a percentage of total sales in Store B. The reader must keep in mind that a larger percentage figure does not necessarily represent a larger absolute figure.

To illustrate, in 1984 Branch E sold $16 million and Branch D sold $20 million in clothing. In a multiple-bar graph, the bar for Branch E is

Exhibit 13.19 **Subdivided Bar Graph Based on Percentages**

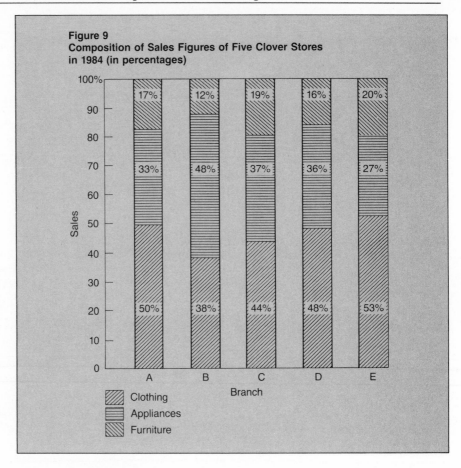

Figure 9
Composition of Sales Figures of Five Clover Stores in 1984 (in percentages)

shorter than for Branch D. In the subdivided bar graph showing absolute sales dollars, the clothing segment for Branch E is also shorter than for Branch D. In terms of percentages, however, $16 million represents 53 percent of the total sales of Branch E, whereas $20 million represents only 48 percent of total sales of Branch D. In the subdivided bar graph showing percentages, therefore, the clothing segment for Branch E is larger than for Branch D.

The writer must tell the reader whether the report is about percentages or absolute figures, and the reader must take care in order to understand it. When either figure by itself might be misleading, the report should include both percentages and absolute figures. For example, conservatives argue that military spending has plummeted, whereas liberals argue that military spending is skyrocketing. Who is right? Both are. As a percentage of total budget, military spending has decreased; the absolute budget for the military has increased. Advocates for either side usually do not point out the difference; they simply choose the argument that supports their point of view. The public, in the meantime, does not understand and may decide that both sides are lying. A business-report writer must ensure that the reader understands both the material and the context.

Bilateral Bar Graph. Bilateral bar graphs show both negative and positive values. The bars can be either vertical or horizontal. In the vertical bar graph the negative values are below the X-axis. In the horizontal bar graph the negative values are to the left of the Y-axis. Companies often show gains and losses in a bilateral bar graph, as in Exhibit 13.20. Clear labels are necessary for the positive and negative values.

PICTOGRAM

The pictogram is related most closely to the bar graph. Instead of a bar, the pictogram uses an illustration of the product or item. Barrels might be used to represent crude oil production, houses to represent housing starts, or people to represent population figures. Exhibit 13.21, for example, shows the immigration figures for the United States between 1950 and 1980.

Pictograms must be constructed carefully because they can easily mislead the reader. One basic rule is that all the pictures must be the same size. Quantity is represented by the number of pictures, not by the size of the pictures. If automobile production has doubled since last year, for example, there should be twice as many cars representing this year's production. It would be unacceptable to keep the same number of cars and double their size. Changes in size would be misleading, because the reader would have difficulty making precise visual distinctions between the sizes of items.

PIE CHARTS

Pie charts are frequently used to show how a typical family spends each dollar of income or how a company spends or uses one dollar of revenue. The reason for using the pie graph is that it represents 100 percent. Because the dollar contains 100 cents, each cent equals one percent. The reader can have some understanding of how money is spent without converting percentages into absolute figures. Absolute or raw figures can be used in a pie chart, but the best practice is to show the percentages also. Each segment in the pie should be labeled and the percentages should be placed next to the descriptor. Clover Department Stores could represent the breakdown by product in 1985 in a pie chart like the one in Exhibit 13.22.

A pie chart with four to seven or eight segments is most effective. Too many segments may make it difficult to read. Coloring or cross-hatching can set off the various segments.

Exhibit 13.20 **Bilateral Bar Graph**

Net Income (Loss)
Billions of Dollars

2.0

1.0

0

(1.0)

(2.0)

1972 1973 1974 1975 1976 1977 1978 1979 1980 1981

Earnings (Loss) per Share
Dollars

15.00

7.50

0

(7.50)

(15.00)

1972 1973 1974 1975 1976 1977 1978 1979 1980 1981

Source: *Annual Report*, Ford, 1981.

Exhibit 13.21 **Pictogram**

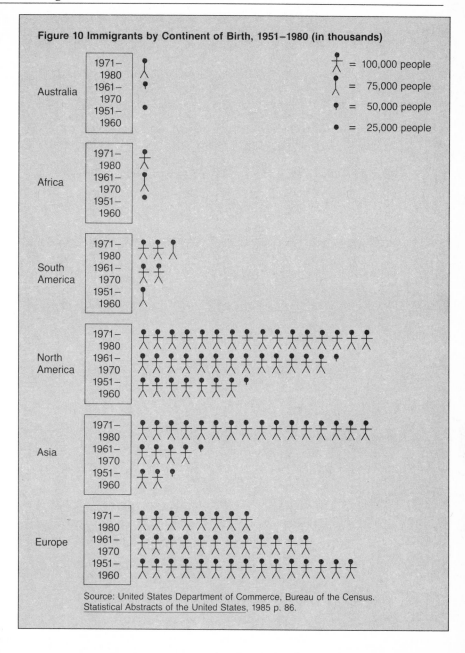

Figure 10 Immigrants by Continent of Birth, 1951–1980 (in thousands)

Source: United States Department of Commerce, Bureau of the Census. Statistical Abstracts of the United States, 1985 p. 86.

Exhibit 13.22 **Pie Chart**

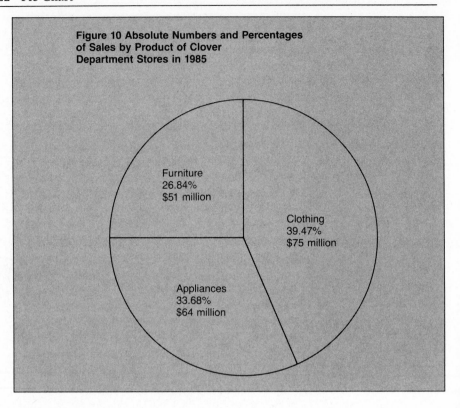

Figure 10 Absolute Numbers and Percentages
of Sales by Product of Clover
Department Stores in 1985

Furniture
26.84%
$51 million

Clothing
39.47%
$75 million

Appliances
33.68%
$64 million

STATISTICAL MAPS

Statistical maps are useful for illustrating sales territories, the location of branches in other countries, or production by geographic area. They are a combination of visual aids, as you can see from Exhibit 13.23. The most frequent combinations are:

> Geographic map and bar graph
>
> Geographic map and pictogram
>
> Geographic map and pie chart
>
> Geographic map and cross-hatching or color shading

The map in Exhibit 13.23 identifies temperature zones for one day in the United States. It also indicates weather fronts and precipitation.

Exhibit 13.23 **Statistical Map**

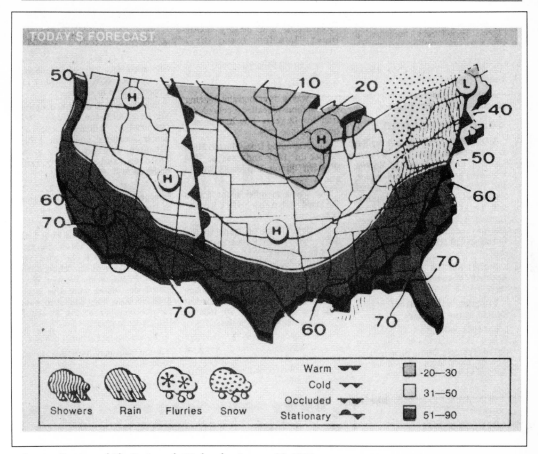

Source: Courtesy of *The Pantagraph,* Wednesday, January 22, 1986.

DIAGRAMS

Diagrams are used frequently in technical descriptions. Because descriptions of a product or process tend to be abstract, an illustration can help the reader to understand the text better. Diagrams can show how to put a bicycle together, how to assemble toys, or how to repair a vacuum cleaner, as in Exhibit 13.24. They are used to show the electric circuits in a building. The diagram is a simplified presentation of a complex system.

Exhibit 13.24 **Diagram for Vacuum Cleaner**

REPAIR PARTS FOR VACUUM CLEANER

The parts listed on these pages are only those parts which we feel the average person may want to replace himself.

If you need other parts or service, call your local store or catalog sales office. Give them the *Model Number:* 116_ _ _ _. The number is found on the bottom of each unit. They will have a complete listing of all replacement parts for your vacuum cleaner.

PARTS FOR POWER-MATE® ATTACHMENT
(THE POWER-MATE HAS ITS OWN MODEL NUMBER.)

ILLUS. NO.	PART NO.	DESCRIPTION
1	742509	End Brush
2	742030	Brush Beater (2)
3	742029	Bar Beater
4	742024	Belt (Cogged)
5	742763	Foot Pedal Pad
6	596181	Bulb, Light (15 Watt)
7	743063	Bulb Housing
8	742036	Bearing and Housing Assembly
9	742767	Bumper

CAUTION: Use the part number on all orders (not illustration number).

FLOWCHARTS

Flowcharts show processes. The workflow in an office or on an assembly line can be illustrated with the help of a flowchart. Because flowcharts show sequential steps, they can help to detect weak links in a process.

Flowcharts can be sophisticated and use specialized geometric symbols to classify the steps in a process. An oval usually stands for beginning and end, a diamond signifies a decision point, and the rectangle represents a major activity. Exhibit 13.25 illustrates the process for making investments. At the diamond, the investor must decide whether to go ahead with the investment. If the decision is to invest, the investor will initiate the steps necessary to purchase the stocks, bonds, or real estate. If the decision is *no,* the investor will go back to the start.

Exhibit 13.25 **Flowchart**

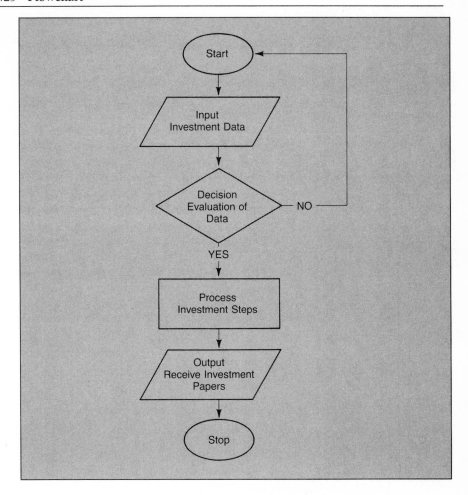

A flowchart can also identify how much time each step takes. One form of the flowchart is PERT, which is used in complicated planning processes. The planner determines how much time each step will take under the most favorable, the least favorable, and the most likely circumstances. Using this data the planner can determine how long a project will take from start to completion. The project depicted in Exhibit 13.26 takes nine and a half weeks.

A PERT chart identifies tasks that can be done simultaneously and tasks that must be done sequentially. Even though roofers can work while electricians install the wiring, for example, the wiring and the roof must be completed before plasterboard can be installed.

Exhibit 13.26 **PERT Chart**

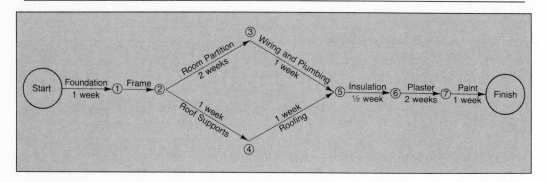

CONSTRUCTION OF VISUAL AIDS

PLACEMENT

If the material presented in the visual aid is necessary to the understanding of the report, it should be in the report proper. If the visual aid merely supplements the text, it can be placed in an appendix. The placement of a visual aid may also be influenced by the number of references made to it. Let us assume that a report contains a long, complex table important to an understanding of the text. Let us furthermore assume that the text refers to the table several times. The writer must decide whether the table should be placed closest to the first reference, somewhere in the middle of the text, or in an appendix. If the writer chooses to place it closest to the first reference, the reader will need to locate it again when later references occur. Because the search may be annoying, the reader might be best served if the table is in an appendix.

SIZE

In general, the size of visual aids should not exceed the margins of the written text. A visual aid that extends into the margins distracts readers by breaking the visual pattern. Specifically, the size of a graphic is determined by the amount of data presented. Although a single-line graph might fit easily onto a quarter of a page, a multiple-line graph might require more space. The reason is that, with several lines to show, a writer might need to use a larger scale and to include a legend to explain the meaning of the various lines and colors.

If a table has too many columns to fit within the margins, the writer can turn the paper horizontally in order to fit the table on it, as illustrated in Exhibit 13.27. The table will be more difficult to read, of course, and some readers may not even look at it. As an alternative, the writer can also extend

Exhibit 13.27 Side Placement of Visual Aid

Maintenance Costs for Subcompact Cars

Car (Engine)	PM Costs to 45,000 miles	Water Pump	Alternator	2 Front Brake Pads	Starter	Carburetor (Fuel Injectors)[1]	Fuel Pump (Fuel Injection Pump)[1]	Catalytic Converter	Lower Ball Joints	Transmission (FWD Cars)[2]	Relative Maintenance Costs[3]
Chevrolet Chevette (L4)	$366	$ 63	$156	$50	$157	$176	$39	$201	$ 68	$1044	Medium
Datsun 210 (L4)	358	47	241	24	160	235	36	333	73	784 •	Medium
Datsun 310 (L4T)	356	35	240	22	106	214	48	335	63	(808) •	Medium
Datsun 510 (L4)	350	99	287	23	202	229	42	334	73	715 •	Medium
Dodge Colt (L4T)	216	62	143	42	155	157	42	200	50	(1288) •	Medium
Fiat Strada (L4)*	315	72	283	42	126	(139)	(68)	243	170	(1016) •	Medium
Ford Escort (L4T)	115	98	145	82	95	204	39	308	153	(823) •	Medium
Honda Accord (L4T)	347	38	164	24	206	310	58	144	126	(623) •	Low
Honda Civic (L4T)	325	37	142	25	157	270	42	144	126	(586) •	Low
Honda Prelude (L4T)	385	41	170	38	206	310	56	144	138	(634) •	Low
Mazda GLC (L4)	236	73	204	40	174	272	36	645	44	(993) •	High
Mercury Lynx (L4T)	115	98	145	82	95	204	39	308	153	(823) •	Medium
Plymouth Champ (L4T)	216	62	143	42	155	157	42	200	50	(1288) •	Medium
Renault Le Car (L4)	412	137	224	43	170	315	51	269	86	(915) •	High
Subaru DL 1600 (HO4)	472	65	184	38	250	291	82	117	68	(884) •	Medium
Toyota Corolla (L4)	311	107	171	26	169	262	39	262	171	756 •	Medium
Toyota Tercel (L4)	374	83	181	27	171	242	36	124	137	414 •	Low
Volkswagen Jetta (L4T)	333	121	203	31	227	(94)	(137)	215	63	(1110) •	High
Volkswagen Rabbit (L4T)	333	121	203	31	227	(94)	(100)	215	63	(1110) •	Medium
VW Rabbit Diesel (L4T)	179	126	203	31	329	(123)	(371)	▲	63	(1110) •	High
Average Vehicle Maintenance Cost	306	79	187	38	167	241 (113)	45 (169)	250	97	743 (934)	

• Manual transmission, all others are automatic.

* At the time of printing, only 1980 data was available. While some cost difference for 1981 models can be expected, they should not be significant.

▲ Cars with diesel engines do not have catalytic converters.

[1] Because diesel and gas cars with fuel injectors do not have carburetors or fuel pumps, the cost of fuel injectors and fuel injection pumps is given. These are noted by parentheses in the carburetor and fuel pump column.

[2] For front wheel drive cars the entire transaxle assembly kit is usually replaced. This includes the transmission and the differential. FWD cars are noted by parentheses in the transmission column.

[3] This column gives you an idea of the relative cost of repairing each car based on the nine repairs listed in the chart, although many of the repairs are typical, there is currently no data available about exactly what will fail or how often. This column should only be used to compare the relative maintenance costs of the cars you are considering buying.

Due to stricter emissions requirements, cars sold in California may have different maintenance costs for some items.

Source: The Car Book. U.S Department of Transportation, 1981.

the page by pasting a sheet of paper to it and creating a foldout page. This is extra work, but the table will be easier to read if treated as a foldout.

NUMBERING

Visual aids are numbered. The numbers permit the writer to refer to them in the text by number rather than the more cumbersome description or title. Most report writers use separate numbering systems for tables and figures. A report can therefore have Table 1, Figure 1, Table 2, Figure 2, Table 3, Figure 3. Some writers label all visual aids as exhibits. This book is an example.

Traditionally, tables were given Roman numerals, and figures were given Arabic numbers. Today many report writers use Arabic numbers for all visual aids.

A report with several chapters identifies not only the number of the table and figure but also the chapter in which they are located. Table 1.2 refers to the second table in Chapter 1, for example, and Figure 5.3 is the third figure in Chapter 5.

TITLES

Every visual aid should have a descriptive title so that the reader immediately understands the focus. The title follows the number, either on the same line or the following line. You should strive for consistency in the placement of titles. The following list, and also Exhibit 13.28, illustrate the possibilities:

1. All table titles above the tables
2. All figure titles above the figures
3. All table titles below the tables
4. All figure titles below the figures
5. Titles for figures and tables sometimes alongside the table or figure

In older reports you may find that the table title is in all capital letters above the table, whereas the title for figures is in capital and lowercase letters below the figure. If you adopt this traditional practice, you must be consistent throughout the report.

Traditional: *(always above the table)*
TABLE I
1980–1985 SALES FOR BRANCHES OF CLOVER DEPART-MENT STORES IN CHICAGO

(always below the figure)
Figure 1
1980–1985 Sales for Branches of Clover Department Stores in Chicago

Exhibit 13.28 **Placement of Titles**

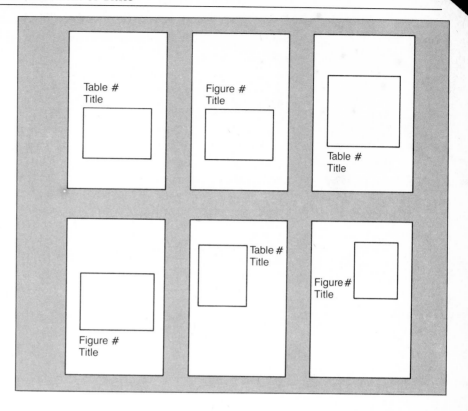

Modern: (*either above, below, or alongside the table*)
Table 1
1980–1985 Sales for Branches of Clover Department Stores in Chicago

(*either above, below, or alongside the figure*)
Figure 1
1980–1985 Sales for Branches of Clover Department Stores in Chicago

   Titles must be clear and descriptive. When appropriate, they should answer the questions who, what, where, when, why, and how. Of course, not every title needs to answer all of these questions. The title in the example for title placement answers the following: when (1980–1985), what (sales comparisons), and where (Chicago).

SOURCE NOTES

If the visual aid presents material drawn from a source other than your own primary research, you should credit that source in a **source note** placed immediately below it.

Sour...
The source note credits the secondary source of data.

FOOTNOTES

Footnote
The footnote in a visual aid is an explanatory note.

Footnotes to visual aids must be distinguished from footnotes to the text, which identify the source of material used in the text. Footnotes to tables and figures are clarifying comments. The report writer uses them to explain a specific point in the visual aid or when data is missing in the visual aid. If, for example, in a table depicting income figures for several countries not all figures are available, the writer may explain the omission in a footnote.

Footnotes for visual aids are indicated by symbols such as asterisks, daggers, double daggers, crosses, and lowercase letters, but rarely with Arabic numbers. Numbers might be confused with text footnote numbers or with numerical data in the table or figure itself.

Footnotes can precede or follow the source note. In Exhibit 13.29, it precedes.

DISCUSSION

Visual aids clarify the text. To be certain that the reader will make the best use of them, the writer should direct the reader to each visual aid at the most appropriate time. The writer's introduction should tell the reader what the visual aid does. A clear introduction might be, "As the following table illustrates, the sales figures have shown a steady increase during the last five years." It gives more information than "The following table shows the sales figures."

Ideally the writer introduces the visual aid, presents the visual aid, and then discusses it. In the final layout of the report, however, this arrangement is often not possible. For example, the introduction may fall so near the bottom of a page that it cannot be completed in the space that remains. In that case the writer places the table at the top of the next page and then continues the discussion below it. At other times, the remaining space on the page dictates that the entire discussion precede the table or figure. The report writer should not divide a table and present it on two different pages.

For a simple table or graph, a one-sentence discussion may be enough. More detailed tables and figures require more detailed discussion. To say that the data in the table is self-explanatory is not enough. The writer must summarize the information, point out trends, compare data, and in any way possible facilitate the reading of the report.

For More Need Table of illustrations Separate from table of Contents.

Exhibit 13.29 **Placement of Footnotes in Exhibits**

Estimated Quarterly Gross State Product by Industry Division
Seasonally Adjusted at Annual Rates (millions of U.S. dollars)

	1985p			
	I	II	III	IV
GROSS STATE PRODUCT	$187,556	$187,928		
GSP in Constant 1972 Dollars	(81,877)	(81,513)		
Private Nonfarm	167,270	168,994		
Mining	1,853	2,057		
Contract Construction	6,934	7,880		
Manufacturing	42,703	42,120		
Durable Goods	24,247	23,868		
Nondurable Goods	18,456	18,252		
Wholesale & Retail Trade	31,138	31,468		
Finance, Insurance and Real Estate	37,032	37,181		
Transportation	6,958	7,004		
Communication and Utilities	11,283	11,196		
Services	29,369	30,088		
Government	15,190	15,442		
Agriculture	5,096	3,492		

p - preliminary
Source: Illinois Department of Commerce and Community Affairs

COMPUTER GRAPHICS

Computer Graphics
Computer graphics are visual aids generated by a computer.

Computer graphics is one of the most rapidly expanding areas in computer science. Research in the fields of perceptual and cognitive psychology as well as computer and information science have helped in developing programs for the highly talented designer and the novice. Large companies often have departments that specialize in designing and producing visual material. Using their services may take considerable time, however. If you can make your own visual aids, you can have the graph or picture you want when you need it. For small businesses, which usually do not have special design people, computer graphics offer the opportunity to enhance reports with effective visual aids.

Computer graphics allow you to enhance the visual aids you want to use in your report. The computer also allows you to compare possible visual presentations. Traditionally, you would type the text part of the report and leave space for visual presentations. You then would decide which type of visual—line graph, bar graph, or pie chart, for example—would present the data best. Next you would draw the figure and paste it in the report. The page would then be reproduced to visually integrate the visual aid into the text. Now a computer can do the cut-and-paste work for you.

If you must prepare the figures manually, you usually will not draw several in order to compare them for effectiveness because making visual aids is time consuming and tedious. With the help of the computer, however, you can experiment. After producing several possible illustrations, you can choose the one that is clearest and best highlights the important points.

Complex tables can be generated with the help of spreadsheets. Spreadsheets then can transform the numeric information into graphic data. You can also create graphs from a database or other business programs that use a standard-data format or from numeric data entered by hand. Your computer and the particular program you use will influence how you enter the data.

Most graphics packages on the market today print the title, provide a legend, and combine symbols with lines. In many cases you can also supply special labels that can be moved anywhere in the graph. For example, you can label one group of bars *current expenses* and another one *predicted expenses*.

In the beginning computer graphics were restricted to line graphs, bar graphs, and pie charts. Today the opportunities are almost unlimited. With the help of computers you can draw two- and three-dimensional images. You can use the computer for flowcharts, block diagrams, product design, and space planning. Special programs have been developed for drawing and technical designs. The information can be entered either via the keyboard or a special device like a *mouse*.

For the printing of visual aids you can use dot matrix, ink-jet plotters, electrostatic plotters, or microfilm recorders. Some programs allow you to print the visual directly from the screen; some programs will print the visual only after it has been stored. The quality of the computer graph depends on the resolution of the computer and the printer. The higher the resolution, the better the quality will be.

The screen is made up of hundreds of horizontal and vertical lines that consist of dots or pixels. As the number of pixels increases, the clarity of the picture improves. A typical American television screen has about 250 rows and 500 columns, or about 125,000 pixels. In the future the screen will consist of about 4,000 rows by 4,000 columns, or 16 million pixels. This high resolution allows for almost photographic sharpness.

Computer graphics have truly revolutionized the use of visuals in reports. You can try many options, compare them, and then choose the best. Computer graphics save time and foster creativity, but they also have a potential danger.

Because it is so easy to produce the visuals and they are all so attractive, you may be reluctant to choose between them. Too many visual aids can confuse the reader and take away from the importance of the message. That the data can be presented in a table, bar graph, line graph, and pie chart does not mean all should be used or all are equally good. The conscientious report writer will carefully evaluate the options. The choice will depend on the purpose of the report. The computer can help you to do a better job, but it is a tool that you must manage carefully.

SUMMARY OF LEARNING OBJECTIVES

To Understand the Purpose of Visual Aids.
Visual aids are tools; they are not an end in themselves. Their purpose is to highlight, to summarize, to show patterns and trends, and to facilitate the understanding of complex processes and situations.

To Understand the Underlying Principles of Tables and Figures.
The report writer must know the basic principles of designing visual aids so data is not misrepresented. In the line graph the Y-axis is always the dependent variable, and the X-axis the independent variable. The Y-axis must start with zero. In the bar graph the dependent variable can be either on the X- or the Y-axis. Practical considerations often influence the decision.

The writer must pay special attention to the scale of the axes. Designing effective and correctly scaled visual aids involves an awareness of business ethics.

In tables the stubs and columns can be switched. The decision is based on the appearance of the finished table.

To Design Effective and Appropriate Tables and Figures.
Visual aids must be titled and numbered. They should be introduced and discussed in the text. Visual aids must be clear and easy to read to fulfill their purpose.

Tables are systematic arrangements of data in rows and columns. Tables present quantitative information.

Figure is an overall term that includes all visual aids except tables. Line graphs show trends and patterns over time. Bar graphs are effective for comparisons at a particular point in time. Pie charts illustrate the composition of a whole. Pictograms combine pictures and bar graphs. The statistical map is a combination of maps and line graphs, bar graphs, or pie charts. Other visual aids frequently used in business reports are the diagram, the organizational chart, and the flowchart. More and more businesses use the computer to design graphs.

To Understand the Role of Computer Graphics in Report Writing.
Computer graphics make it easy to convert numeric data into graphs. The report writer can compare several visual presentations of the same data and then choose the most effective one for the report.

QUESTIONS AND PROBLEMS

1. What are some of the problems of scaling data in a line graph?
2. Why must the bars in a bar graph be the same width?
3. When do you use a subdivided and when a multiple-line graph?
4. Discuss the ethical problems inherent in designing visual aids.
5. Name the major parts of a table.
6. Examine the visual aids in several annual reports and evaluate them. How effective are they?
7. Discuss the most appropriate location of visual aids in a report.
8. Examine the visual aids in your local newspaper or student paper. Are the figures mechanically correct? What is the visual impact?
9. Design a PERT chart for the course work in your major.
10. Present the following data visually. What types of graphs are possible? Justify your choices.

Per Capita Consumption of Major Food Commodities (in kilograms)

Commodity	United States	France	West Germany	Soviet Union
Beef	46.9	18.5	21.5	11.0
Pork	33.3	9.9	50.3	23.5
Poultry	27.7	17.2	9.6	6.0
Fresh Fruit	40.2	63.6	84.0	34.0
Sugar	38.0	15.0	35.6	42.2
Cheese	8.0	18.2	13.9	n.a.

Source: United States Department of Commerce, Bureau of the Census. *Statistical Abstracts of the United States,* 1985, p. 848.

11. Design appropriate graphs for presenting the data in the following table. Discuss your choices.

Veterans' Benefits—Expenditures by Programs (in millions of dollars)

Program	1978	1979	1980	1981	1982	1983
Compensation and Pension	9,630	10,540	11,257	12,492	13,348	13,881
Education	3,337	2,800	2,383	2,333	2,001	1,676
Medical Services	5,684	6,206	6,647	7,199	8,009	8,722

Source: United States Department of Commerce, Bureau of the Census. *Statistical Abstracts of the United States,* 1985, p. 349.

CHAPTER FOURTEEN

ORGANIZING THE LONG FORMAL REPORT

LEARNING OBJECTIVES

- To understand various organizational patterns.
- To become familiar with basic outlining systems.
- To construct effective headings.

Up to this point your work has been guided by the outline and organization of the report plan that you wrote at the beginning of the report process although along the way you have probably made a number of changes. You may have reorganized your approach as a result of talking to employees in other departments or researching company documents in depth. Your budget may have increased as top management strongly supported your study because of its potential to effect cost savings. Your budget may have decreased as the company experienced financial difficulties. As a result, you are not able to visit as many sites or conduct the in-depth surveys you had planned.

Time constraints may have changed. Because of competitive developments, management may need the report earlier than the original request indicated. New developments in your firm such as a takeover or internal reorganization may have caused a redefinition of the problem. You have adjusted as the need arose, but now you have to finalize your efforts.

Before starting the final outline of the report, you return to the questions you asked at the beginning of the planning process:

1. Who is the reader?
2. What is the purpose of the report?
3. What are the prejudices of the reader?
4. How many people will read the report?
5. What does the reader know about the topic?

At the beginning the answers to the questions helped you to focus your work. Now these questions will help you to write and present the final report.

ORGANIZATION PATTERNS

An effective organization of material will help the reader to understand it. The writer must shape the organization so that it will fit the problem and the needs and preferences of the reader.

This chapter is concerned about the order of presentation in the report, not the order in which the writer does the work. The writer summarizes the material only *after* all the research has been done and draws conclusions and makes recommendations only *after* a thorough examination of all the facts. In the actual report, however, the writer may want to use a different sequence and begin with the conclusions and recommendations.

Chapter 4 examined in detail the differences between inductive and deductive reports. This chapter will begin with a review of some of the major points, followed by an examination of data presentation in the body of the report. The organization patterns presented can be applied to either the inductive or the deductive report. They refer to the order of the presentation and discussion of facts within the report and not to the overall organization of the report.

INDUCTIVE PRESENTATION

The inductive report presents information in the sequence in which you did the work. The report leads the reader from the introduction to the presentation of facts, to the discussion of facts, and finally to conclusions and recommendations. You show the reader how you arrived at your conclusions and hope that the reader will agree with you.

The inductive approach is the best choice if you believe that the reader may resent the conclusions and recommendations. If you believe that the reader will accept the conclusions and recommendations, however, the inductive presentation may be too slow and time consuming.

DEDUCTIVE PRESENTATION

In the deductive presentation you introduce the problem and then move directly to conclusions and recommendations. The facts and the analysis follow. The deductive arrangement is faster and more direct. Many business people prefer the deductive organization of reports because it immediately gives the crucial parts of the report.

CHRONOLOGICAL PRESENTATION

The chronological presentation is used when the sequence of occurrences and the historical development of the problem are important. Minutes of meetings are usually arranged chronologically.

The meeting was called to order at 10:15 a.m. First item of business was. . . .

The meeting was adjourned at 10:45 a.m.

Closely related to the chronological presentation is the step-by-step presentation. Instructions fall into this category. Strictly speaking, the sequence of a process rather than time is important in the step-by-step approach. Steps have to be done in a certain order to achieve the desired outcome.

For example, imagine that your parents have purchased a computer. They know nothing about computers. The instructions are written for technicians, and they ask you for help because you have worked with computers. You write out step-by-step instructions on how to get the computer, an IBM PC, ready for using the program WordStar. Your instructions might read:

1. Insert the WordStar disk into the left drive, usually called drive *a*.

2. Insert the work disk into the right drive, usually called drive *b*.

3. Turn on the computer.

4. When you see A>, type "ws" for WordStar and press RETURN.

5. You will then see a list (called a *menu*) of commands with the heading EDITING NO FILE.

6. Type "L" to change the disk drive to *b*.

7. When the prompt NEW LOGGED DISK DRIVE? appears, type "b:" and press RETURN.

8. When the EDITING NO FILE MENU appears on the screen, press d to create a file.

9. Type the name of your file (the title you want to give your document) when the prompt NAME OF FILE TO EDIT? appears and press RETURN.

10. You are ready to type your message.

A business that wants to examine its collection procedures for overdue accounts could also use the chronological organization to present the steps in the collection process:

1. The customer receives a friendly reminder as soon as the deadline has passed. Emphasis is on the positive. The assumption is that the customer will pay.

2. The customer receives a request to pay the bill promptly. This note follows two weeks after the first one. The emphasis is on payment of the bill and the benefits of a good credit rating.

3. The customer is informed that, unless the money is paid within one week, the account will be turned over to a collection agency. This letter follows two weeks after the second note.

The chronological presentation facilitates a comparison with collection efforts of other companies. The writer can research how many notes similar businesses send out. The timing of notes can also be compared. Chronological presentation lends itself to flowcharting. A diagram of the steps in the process can help in identifying strong and weak points in the process, as in the following step-by-step presentation:

Due Date
  ↓ 4 weeks
Reminder 1
  ↓ 4 to 6 weeks
Reminder 2
  ↓ 3 weeks
Reminder 3
  ↓ 6 to 7 weeks
Turn Over to Collection Agency

PRESENTATION BY ORDER OF IMPORTANCE

You can present your data either by starting with the least important and building up to the most important point or by starting with the most important and ending with the least important point. Much depends on your analysis of the reader. If the reader is impatient, you may want to begin with the most important point. Chances are the reader will not read the entire report if you build up slowly. On the other hand, some readers may want to know about all the details. In that case, presenting the strongest point at the end may make more sense because readers will remember best the point that is made last.

Organization from least important to most important is illustrated in this example:

Advantages of proposed machine over present machine:
Less noise
10% lower electricity use
15% lower maintenance cost
30% higher productivity
Fewer workers (one rather than three operators)

A reversal of the order of the five advantages illustrates the most important to least important organization.

ORGANIZATION BASED ON COMPARISON

Your company may want to introduce computers into the office. After examining and analyzing three different computers, you will recommend one for adoption. In order to compare the computers, you have determined that the factors most important to your company are price, speed, complexity, and capacity.

In your report you could discuss each criterion for Computer A, then each for Computer B, and finally each for Computer C, but this would not facilitate comparisons. In your research you may have started that way, but in your analysis and in the presentation you may want to choose a different organization. The reader is more interested in finding out how the three computers rank under each criterion than in a detailed description of each computer. Your outline for the report would probably resemble the one at the left:

Outline 1	**Outline 2**
Cost	Computer 1
Computer 1	Cost
Computer 2	Speed
Computer 3	Capacity
	Complexity
Speed	
Computer 1	Computer 2
Computer 2	Cost
Computer 3	Speed
	Capacity
Capacity	Complexity
Computer 1	
Computer 2	Computer 3
Computer 3	Cost
	Speed
Complexity	Capacity
Computer 1	Complexity
Computer 2	
Computer 3	

ORGANIZATION BASED ON CAUSE–EFFECT RELATIONSHIP

If the major concern is, "What happens if. . . ?" then you are dealing with cause–effect organization patterns. Managers ask this type of question frequently because they must make decisions under uncertainty. They hope that an examination of cause–effect relationships will help in answering such questions as how the new training program will affect motivation, what the result or the effect of the new training program will be, and what effect the reorganization of the assembly line will have on productivity.

The cause–effect organization moves from a known factor to the unknown. The process is linked to the chronological and step-by-step organization. When you employ the cause–effect organization, you present the facts or options and then the possible outcomes. You want to show what might happen under certain circumstances. The cause–effect organization emphasizes future orientation and is useful in forecasting.

ORGANIZATION BASED ON EFFECT–CAUSE RELATIONSHIP

The effect–cause presentation is the exact opposite of the cause–effect presentation. Here you know the results. For example, productivity is low; sales are up; profits are down; absenteeism is down. You want to know the reasons or the cause behind certain phenomena that you have observed and examined. The organization pattern moves from the present to the past.

The relationship between cause–effect and effect–cause is shown in this diagram:

Past   *Present* *Future*

Cause◀——Effect

Cause——▶Effect

As the diagram illustrates, you must look into the future if you know the cause and want to examine possible effects. On the other hand, if you search for possible causes, you must look at the past. In both the cause–effect and effect–cause orders, a clear problem statement is important. Otherwise, the investigation cannot be directed well.

ORGANIZATION BY GEOGRAPHIC AREA

A sales manager may want to organize sales reports by districts. This order facilitates the comparison of sales performances in various territories. Multinational companies report their profits and losses by location of subsidiaries in other countries. Management can then see immediately whether investments in Southeast Asia have been profitable and how they compare to investments in Latin America or Europe.

Geographic organization can be combined with a number of other organizational patterns. The writer might present the historical development of the problem in each region and division. The writer might also arrange each region according to cause–effect relationships. The presentation within regions will depend on the nature of the problem and the needs of the reader.

OUTLINING SYSTEMS

If you choose a deductive order, it will be reflected in the outline of your report. The outline and the order of the presentation cannot be separated. The tentative outline that you put together in the proposal for the report may have undergone a number of changes as you progressed. It was a working outline. Now that you have completed the research, you are ready to complete the final outline. How detailed it will be depends on the complexity of the problem. A report of a few pages needs a less detailed outline than does a 30-page report. The two basic outline systems are (1) a combination of Roman numerals, Arabic numbers, and letters and (2) the decimal system.

THE COMBINATION SYSTEM

Combination System
The combination system uses both numbers and letters.

The **combination system** is the traditional system, and it is probably used most frequently even today. Traditionally, the system uses indentations; however, it can also use the blocked form, with all headings and paragraphs on the left margin. The basic pattern for the combination system is as follows:

[handwritten margin notes: NO 1 without a 2 / NO A without a B / Just these is O.K. / Can have]

First degree heading (usually the title)
I.   Second-degree heading
   A.   Third-degree heading
      1.   Fourth-degree heading
         a.   Fifth-degree heading
            (1)   Sixth-degree heading
               (a)   Seventh-degree heading
               (b)   Seventh-degree heading
            (2)   Sixth-degree heading
         b.   Fifth-degree heading
      2.   Fourth-degree heading
   B.   Third-degree heading
II.   Second-degree heading
   etc. . . .

The word *degree* refers to the level of importance of a heading.

THE DECIMAL SYSTEM

Decimal System
The decimal system uses only numbers. Decimal points identify the level of heading.

The **decimal system** uses either indented or blocked format. The basic pattern is as follows:

First-degree heading (usually the title)
1.   Second-degree heading

    1.1   Third-degree heading

        1.1.1   Fourth-degree heading

        1.1.2   Fourth-degree heading

           1.1.2.1   Fifth-degree heading

              1.1.2.1.1   Sixth-degree heading

              1.1.2.1.2   Sixth-degree heading

The system you choose will depend, to some extent at least, on company practice. If everyone in your company uses the combination system, you should use it too. The sciences tend to use the decimal system. If you work with scientists or in a chemical firm, you may want to use the decimal system.

Some writers argue that the decimal system is better because it allows an infinite division into subtopics. Although that is true, an infinite number of subdivisions is not necessary. In most cases four parts (I.A.1.a. or 1.1.1.1.) are sufficient. The purpose of the divisions is to help the reader understand the problem and the report. The divisions are not meant to draw attention to themselves. Too many headings can confuse and break the continuity of the report.

GUIDELINES FOR OUTLINES

In order to effectively outline your report, you should observe these three guidelines:

Balanced Outline
A balanced outline subdivides report parts into approximately the same number of subparts.

    1.   *The outline must be* **balanced**. Divisions should be fairly equal in length and all major parts should have approximately the same number of subparts. Of course, you must use good judgment when applying this guideline, as these three outlines will illustrate:

Outline 1	Outline 2	Outline 3
I. xxxxxxxxxx	I. xxxxxxxxxx	I. xxxxxxxxxx
A. xxxxxxx	A. xxxxxxx	A. xxxxxxx
1. xxxx	1. xxxx	1. xxxx
a. x	2. xxxx	a. xxxxx
b. x	a. x	b. xxxxx
2. xxxx	b. x	c. xxxxx
a. x	3. xxxx	d. xxxxx
b. x	B. xxxxxxx	e. xxxxx
B. xxxxxxx	1. xxxx	2. xxxx
1. xxxx	2. xxxx	B. xxxxxxx
a. x	II. xxxxxxxxxx	II. xxxxxxx
b. x	A. xxxxxxx	III. xxxxxxx
2. xxxx	1. xxxx	A. xxxxxxx
a. x	2. xxxx	B. xxxxxxx
b. x	3. xxxx	C. xxxxxxx

(Continued)

Outline 1	Outline 2	Outline 3

```
II.  xxxxxxxxxx           B.  xxxxxxx          D.  xxxxxxx
     A.  xxxxxxx               1.  xxxx         E.  xxxxxxx
         1.  xxxx              2.  xxxx         F.  xxxxxxx
             a.  x        C.  xxxxxxx
             b.  x            1.  xxxx
         2.  xxxx             2.  xxxx
             a.  x    III.  xxxxxxxxxx
             b.  x        A.  xxxxxxx
     B   1.  xxxx         B.  xxxxxxx
             a.  x            1.  xxxx
                             2.  xxxx
The same pattern
continues for
Chapter III.
```

Outline 1 is perfectly balanced. Every chapter has two divisions, and these, in turn, have two subdivisions each. It looks beautiful, but it is artificial, because few problems lend themselves to a perfect outline. The writer has probably forced the topic into this pattern. Outline 2 is more typical of a balanced outline that grows out of the material gathered for the report. The divisions are not even, but they are close. One chapter has two subdivisions, another has three. Differences exist, but they are not overwhelming.

Outline 3 has no balance at all. Point I.A.1. has been subdivided into five parts; I.A.2. has not been divided at all. Chapter II has no subdivisions, whereas Chapter III has six. A number of reasons may account for the imbalance. The writer may not have researched the material for Chapter II sufficiently. Perhaps Chapter II is not actually a separate chapter but a subdivision of Chapter I or Chapter III. Perhaps the writer had enough material for Chapter II but simply failed to show it in the outline. In any case, Outline 3 needs a lot of work. The entire approach to the problem might need to be rethought.

2. *A section, if divided, must have at least two subdivisions.* If you have an *A,* you need a *B.* You cannot divide Chapter I into *A* only because subdivisions divide a whole into parts. One part or one subdivision can never present the whole. If you discuss the workforce in your company, for example, you can use as a heading the word *workforce,* which you then can divide into *men* and *women.* The subheading *women* alone would not present the entire workforce. A single subdivision suggests carelessness on the part of the writer; it can also suggest that the writer has not thought the problem through properly.

3. *Titles and headings must be parallel in grammar and thought.* All chapter titles must be parallel in structure. If you use a sentence for one chapter title, you need sentences for all chapter titles. This rule applies to all levels in the outline; therefore, headings within each subdivision under

Chapter I must be parallel. This means that I.A. must be parallel with I.B. On the other hand, II.A. and II.B. need not be parallel with I.A. and I.B., nor must I.A. and I.B. be parallel with I. and II. The diagram below illustrates an acceptable outline:

I. Sentence
  A. Decapitated Sentence
  B. Decapitated Sentence
    1. Noun
    2. Noun
II. Sentence
  A. Noun Phrase
  B. Noun Phrase

The following section of an outline illustrates violations of the principle of parallel structure:

1. Productivity is decreasing (sentence).

2. Delivery of raw material becoming unreliable (decapitated sentence).

3. Increase in cost of raw materials (noun phrase).

The writer could change all headings to sentences, all to noun phrases, all to decapitated sentences, or all to another consistent grammatical form. The point is that all three headings must be grammatically parallel. Improved wordings for the example are illustrated by the following:

All noun phrases:
1. Decrease in productivity

2. Unreliability of delivery of raw materials

3. Increase in cost of raw materials

All sentences:
1. Productivity is decreasing.

2. The delivery of raw materials is unreliable.

3. The cost of raw materials is increasing.

All decapitated sentences:
1. Productivity decreasing

2. Delivery of raw materials becoming unreliable

3. Cost of raw materials increasing

All participial phrases:
1. Decreasing productivity

2. Growing unreliability of delivery of raw materials

3. Increasing cost of raw materials

THE WORDING OF HEADINGS

All headings appear both in the table of contents and in the body of the report. They provide guidelines for the reader and should therefore be informative and precise. Because the reader may decide after looking at the headings whether or not to read a particular section, the wording of headings is extremely important.

The two main types are topic headings and talking headings. Which one you use will depend on the nature of your report, on the reader, and on the format your company uses for reports.

TOPIC HEADINGS

Topic Headings
Topic headings tend to identify the function of the report parts.

Topic headings, in their most basic form, do not provide much information. The basic topic outline is abstract, as the following example illustrates:

>   Introduction
>   Presentation of Facts
>   Analysis of Facts
>   Conclusion
>   Recommendations

This outline does not tell the reader anything about the content of any of the parts. At best it would serve as a working outline for the writer. Some topic outlines are less abstract; for example, a writer examining difficulties in production might use headings such as:

>   Motivation
>   Workflow
>   Absenteeism
>   Training
>   Quality of Raw Materials
>   Working Conditions

This outline provides the reader at least with the major areas for discussion although it does not give any idea what the report will say about them.

TALKING HEADINGS

Talking Headings
Talking headings tend to emphasize the content of the report parts.

Talking headings, on the other hand, provide information about the content. The writer might expand the topic headings in the example to form these talking headings:

>   Problem of poor motivation
>   Inefficient workflow
>   Frequent absences of employees
>   Low level of training standards

> Poor quality of raw materials
> Outdated working conditions

The same headings could also be presented in sentence form:

> Employees lack motivation.
> The workflow is inefficient.
> Employees are absent too often.
> Training standards need improvement.
> The quality of raw materials is poor.
> Working conditions need improvement.

Talking headings help both the writer and the reader. After the writer has prepared a topic outline and completed the research, writing a talking outline might be a useful next step. The talking outline summarizes the major points of the discussion and may enable the writer to organize the report more effectively.

On the other hand, the writer must be careful not to provide the reader with too much information. Headings should be short and efficient. Too much information, as in the following example, may confuse the reader.

> Evaluation of motivational problems in Department Three of Subsidiary Midwest based on an examination of production records and interviews with employees and supervisors of the department

The reader must read this heading several times in order to comprehend the content. Perhaps the writer should rearrange the entire section, as follows:

> Evaluation of motivational problems of Department Three in Subsidiary Midwest
> A.   Interviews with employees and supervisors
> B.   Examination of production records

If the department and the subsidiary have already been identified, perhaps even in the title of the report, the information does not need to be repeated in the subheadings. The heading could therefore be shortened to:

> Evaluation of motivational problems
> A.   Interviews with employees and supervisors
> B.   Examination of production records

The development of talking headings can help some writers to overcome writer's block, where the writer sits at the desk with all the information but does not know how to start the writing process. Talking headings give the writer an opportunity to develop paragraphs and whole sections from the outline. The writer who chooses this approach, however, must be careful to reduce the final outline to an effective length for presentation in the table of contents.

SUMMARY OF LEARNING OBJECTIVES

To Understand Various Organizational Patterns.
The final organization of the report is based on a reevaluation of the reader and the problem at hand. The writer can present the information in deductive or inductive order. The choice will depend on company practice, reader bias, and preference. In inductive order the report progresses from problem presentation to presentation of data, analysis of data, conclusions, and recommendations. In the deductive report the writer presents the problem, conclusions, and recommendations first. The presentation and analysis come last.
Other organizational patterns are chronological presentation, presentation by order of importance, organization based on comparisons, organization based on cause–effect relationships, organization based on effect–cause relationships, and organization based on geographic area. For each report the writer must determine which organization presents the material most effectively.

To Become Familiar with Basic Outlining Systems.
The writer must complete the outline of the report based on the organizational pattern chosen, using a combination system or the decimal system. Headings must be consistent and grammatically parallel. Although headings are necessary to guide the reader through the report, the writer must take care not to use too many. Too many headings make the report choppy and destroy the flow of ideas.

To Construct Effective Headings.
Good headings are informative. The writer can use either topic or talking headings. Topic headings are shorter, but they do not provide much information about the material under the heading. When using talking captions, the writer should concentrate on the most important information. Headings must be concise and informative.

QUESTIONS AND PROBLEMS

1. Discuss the inductive and deductive organization patterns. What are advantages and disadvantages of each?
2. What are the characteristics of organization based on comparison, cause–effect relationships, effect–cause relationships, geographic area, chronological sequence, order of importance?
3. Describe the characteristics of a balanced outline.
4. Discuss the advantages and disadvantages of using the combination or the decimal system for outlining a report.
5. Discuss the necessity for parallel headings.
6. Discuss the difference between talking and topic headings.

7. Which of the following headings does not fit?
   a. Growing sales
   b. Decreasing labor cost
   (c.) Materials unfinished
   d. Declining absenteeism
8. Which of the following does not fit?
   a. Production is holding steady.
   b. Negotiations progress smoothly.
   (c.) Competition making inroads.
   d. Advertising has to be improved.
9. Evaluate the following outlines. Are they logical and proportional? What improvements would you make in them?

   I. The Ranch-Style House
      A. Advantages
         1. No stairs to climb
         2. Modern in design
         3. Large roof area adds to construction cost.
   II. B. The Cape Cod-Style House
         1. Utilized to a large extent in New England
         2. Utilizes space to excellent advantage
   III. The Colonial-Style House
      A. Advantages
         1. Two floors make for low construction cost.
         2. Limited lot-size needed
      B. Disadvantages

   I. Directions of Communication in Industry
      A. Upward
         1. Purposes
            a. To inform
            b. To suggest action
      B. Downward
         1. Purposes
            a. To direct
            b. To inform
            c. To issue orders
      C. Laterally
         1. Purposes
            a. To inform
            b. To suggest

   ---

   1. The engineer's liberal education
      1.1 Necessary courses in the humanities

CHAPTER FIFTEEN

PRESENTING THE

LONG FORMAL

REPORT

LEARNING OBJECTIVES

- To understand the role of the preliminary pages, the body of the report, and the supplementary parts.
- To present an attractive and effective long report.

Most long formal reports are special reports intended to help management in solving special problems and in making major decisions. The long report is the result of detailed work. It reveals to management how well you can organize your time, how up-to-date your research tools are, and how well you can analyze information, draw conclusions, and make recommendations.

All of your planning, research, analysis, and organization were preparation for synthesizing the material into a long report. The examples in this chapter and the sample report in the chapter appendix will guide you in writing your long report.

PARTS OF THE REPORT

The discussion of the parts will follow the order in which they will appear in the final report, although you will not necessarily write them in this order. In fact, you will write the report itself before you write most of the preliminary pages and supplementary parts. A long, formal report may include all of the following:

Preliminary Pages
Preliminary pages are at the beginning of the report.

Preliminary Pages
- Cover
- Title Fly
- Title Page
- Letter of Authorization *optional*
- Letter of Acceptance *optional* } *Do Both if Do one*
- Letter of Transmittal *pg 321*
- Acknowledgments *optional*
- Table of Contents *pg 323*
- Table of Illustrations *more than 4 you have to have one*
- Executive Summary

Body of the Report
The body of the report is the actual report.

Supplementary Parts
Supplementary parts support the report. They are helpful but not necessary for understanding the report.

Body of the Report

Supplementary Parts
Appendix *not needed*
Bibliography — *Works cited*
Index *no*

The length and the formality of the report will determine which parts to include. Formal and long reports may have all of them. Medium-length and short formal reports, which tend to be less formal, will have only some. Exhibit 15.1 illustrates the parts of typical long, medium, and short formal reports.

PRELIMINARY PAGES

The first pages of a report are called preliminary pages, preliminary parts, or prefatory pages because they precede the body of the report. They provide background information and give guidance to the reader.

Cover. The cover usually carries the title of the report. Depending on company policy, the cover may also carry the name of the writer. All important reports should have covers to set them off from less important documents and also to protect them. Your company may use a company cover and standard binding. If you can decide on the cover to use, choose one that is durable. Many people may read your report, and you want it to look as good when the tenth person receives it as when the first one reads it.

Exhibit 15.1 **Parts Included in Typical Formal Reports**

Long Report	Medium Report	Short Report
Cover	Cover	
Title Fly		
Title Page	Title Page	Title Page
Letter of Authorization		
Letter of Acceptance		
Letter of Transmittal	Letter of Transmittal	Letter of Transmittal
Acknowledgments		
Table of Contents	Table of Contents	Table of Contents
Table of Illustrations		
Executive Summary	Executive Summary	
Body of Report	Body of Report	Body of Report
Appendix	Appendix	Appendix
Bibliography	Bibliography	Bibliography
Index		

Title Fly. The title fly, which may be included in very long formal reports, carries only the title of the report. In order to reduce the number of pages, the writer can easily omit this page.

Title Page. The title should be concise (a maximum of 10 words) but descriptive, giving the purpose and subject of the report. As a guide to title content, reread your purpose and problem statements. Check that your title tells what, why, how, when, and where. If the title runs over to a second line, break the line at a logical place, center each line, and leave a double space between them.

The title page carries the title of the report, the name and title of the receiver, the name and location of the receiver's business, the name and title of the writer, and the date. It may also have the name and location of the writer's business. Exhibit 15.2 illustrates the title page of a formal report.

Letter of Authorization. The letter or memo of authorization is the original request for the report and may be included to provide justification for the particular report project. The letter of authorization may be particularly useful if the report is to be kept for future reference.

As illustrated in Exhibit 15.3, the letter of authorization makes clear what the final report should cover. This letter also indicates that Paul Meere was asked to write the report because of his knowledge of scanner systems. As guidance to the writer, it explains why the report is requested, when and how it will be used, and when the report is needed.

Letter of Acceptance. In the letter or memo of acceptance the writer accepts the task of writing the report. Few writers include it in the final report. If the letter of acceptance also summarizes the writer's understanding of the assignment, it gives the requestor an opportunity to clear up any misunderstandings. In the example in Exhibit 15.4 Paul Meere accepts the assignment, promises to complete the report on time, and mentions the topics the final report will cover.

Letter of Transmittal. The letter of transmittal, sometimes called the cover letter, submits the finished report to the reader. The letter is typed in regular business format and includes all the standard parts of a business letter: return address, date, inside address, salutation, body, complimentary close, and signature block. It is single-spaced even if the report is double-spaced. Traditionally paragraphs were indented, but more and more business writers now block paragraphs.

The letter of transmittal begins with transmitting the report. Sentences often used include the following:

Here is the evaluation of possible sites for Company A's new plant.

Here is the report that you requested on September 15, 19XX.

Exhibit 15.2   **Title Page**

AN EXAMINATION OF COMPUTER SCANNERS

FOR KREISNER FOODS

Prepared for
Ralph Kreisner
President
Kreisner Foods
240 College Avenue
Springdale, Colorado
73598

Prepared by
Paul Meere
Staff Analyst

Blooming Grove, Illinois
November 15, 19XX

The letter states the problem or purpose of the report and may also include its scope and limitations. How much of that information is included will depend on the formality of the report.

The letter of transmittal may include acknowledgments if the report has no separate section for them. In shorter and less formal reports, the letter might even contain a summary of the findings of the report. The short letter of transmittal in Exhibit 15.5 transmits the report but does not summarize it because the report has a separate summary at the end of the preliminary pages. The letter in Exhibit 15.6, on the other hand, provides a summary of the findings, conclusions, and recommendations; therefore, a separate summary in the preliminary pages is not necessary.

If additional work is necessary to solve the problem, the writer may want to mention that in the letter. It is possible that time and budget constraints did not allow for a complete investigation. It is also possible that new developments in the economy, the competition, or the organization of the firm would necessitate an update of the report within a certain time period.

The letter should end positively. The writer, if an outside consultant, may express appreciation for the opportunity to prepare the report and an interest in future assignments from the client.

Acknowledgments. Writers sometimes receive valuable help in the form of interviews, data, or verification of information. Acknowledging that help in the report is appropriate. The note of acknowledgment can be presented under a separate heading in the report or in the letter of transmittal.

Table of Contents. The table of contents is completed after the report is typed and the page numbers are known. All headings and subheadings in the report must appear in the table of contents, worded and capitalized exactly the same as they are in the report. The level of headings, that is, their degree of importance, should be apparent from their placement on the contents page. You may therefore either include the numbers and letters designating degree of importance, as shown in Exhibit 15.7, or you may omit them. Except for the executive summary or synopsis, preliminary pages do not appear in the table of contents.

The words *Contents* or *Table of Contents* appear at the top of the page in capital letters. The list of headings and subheadings may be single-spaced or double-spaced, depending on whether you are trying to fit a long table of contents onto a single page. Even if it is single-spaced, you may want to leave extra space between major sections. To make the page easier to read, you may use rows of periods, called *leaders,* between each heading and the corresponding page number.

Table of Illustrations. A table of illustrations is used only if the report has more than four illustrations or if the writer wants to call special attention to

Exhibit 15.3   **Letter of Authorization**

KREISNER FOODS
240 College Avenue
Springdale, CO 73598
(309) 438-7144

January 15, 19XX

Mr. Paul Meere, Staff Analyst
Kreisner Foods
1215 N. Main St.
Blooming Grove, IL 61761

Dear Mr. Meere:

Based on the December meeting of Kreisner managers, Kreisner Foods is considering installing scanners in its stores. You impressed me with your detailed knowledge of scanner systems, and I would like you to prepare a report on the feasibility of scanners for Kreisner Foods.

The report should cover information on the impact of the scanners on store operations, reactions of customers to the scanners, and the cost of a scanning system.

So that the report can be distributed before the April meeting, my office will need the report by March 25.

Please let me know if you have any questions.

Sincerely,

Ralph Kreisner

Ralph Kreisner, President

rw

Source: Reprinted by permission of Paul Meere.

Exhibit 15.4   **Letter of Acceptance**

KREISNER FOODS
1215 N. Main Street
Blooming Grove, IL 61761
(312) 555-6321

February 5, 19XX

Mr. Ralph Kreisner, President
Kreisner Foods
240 College Ave.
Springdale, CO 73598

Dear Mr. Kreisner:

I gladly accept the assignment to prepare a report on scanners in Kreisner supermarkets. Because I have been collecting material on scanners for the last few
months, I will have no difficulty completing the report by March 25.

I will examine the impact of scanners on such store operations as inventory control and shelving. To examine consumer reactions I plan to interview consumers
and checkout clerks. Obtaining figures on the cost of installing a scanning
system will be no problem. The possible savings for Kreisner will be more complicated to determine, but possible savings can be estimated based on the
experiences of other stores.

I am excited about the project and believe that the results will be helpful in
deciding whether Kreisner could benefit from the installation of scanning devices.

Sincerely,

Paul Meere

Paul Meere
Staff Analyst

jp

Source: Reprinted by permission of Paul Meere.

Exhibit 15.5   **Letter of Transmittal (no Summary)**

return address

KREISNER FOODS
1215 N. Main Street
Blooming Grove, IL 61761
(312) 555-6321

March 15, 19XX

Mr. Ralph Kreisner, President
Kreisner Foods
240 College Ave.
Springdale, CO 73598

Dear Mr. Kreisner:

Here is the report you requested concerning the feasibility of introducing
computer scanning devices into Kreisner supermarkets.

Based on the research presented in the report, I recommend that you go ahead with
installing a CSD system. The scanners would save the company money and help with
inventory control.

Sincerely,

Paul Meere

Paul Meere
Staff Analyst

jp

Source: Reprinted by permission of Paul Meere.

Exhibit 15.6   **Letter of Transmittal (with Summary)**

KREISNER FOODS
1215 N. Main Street
Blooming Grove, IL 61761
(312) 555-6321

March 15, 19XX

Mr. Ralph Kreisner, President
Kreisner Foods
240 College Ave.
Springdale, CO 73598

Dear Mr. Kreisner:

Here is the report you requested concerning the feasibility of introducing computer scanning devices into Kreisner supermarkets.

The impact of the scanners on the following aspects of operations was evaluated in detail: inventory control, marketing strategy, costs, customer satisfaction, and employee efficiency. The results are encouraging. With the exception of customer satisfaction all aspects are expected to be influenced positively.

Consumer reaction is mixed. Some prefer the new systems because they provide a detailed receipt, but others object to scanners because they make comparison of prices very difficult. However, stores that have introduced the system have had few complaints from consumers.

The system could save each store about $174,200 annually after the second year in operation.

Based on the research, I recommend that Kreisner Foods introduce computer scanners into its supermarkets.

Sincerely,

Paul Meere

Paul Meere
Staff Analyst

jp

Source: Reprinted by permission of Paul Meere.

Exhibit 15.7   **Table of Contents (with Heading Levels Designated)** the illustrations. The layout is the same as for the table of contents. Illustrations are listed in order of appearance in the report. As shown in Exhibit 15.8, the table gives illustration numbers, titles, and page numbers. If you have numbered figures and tables in two separate series, you may list them separately on the illustrations page.

Executive Summary. The executive summary or synopsis is a summary of the entire report. It emphasizes the results or findings but also briefly states the scope, problem, method, and background. In many companies the executive summary may not exceed one single-spaced page regardless of the length of the report. After reading the executive summary, the reader should have a clear understanding of the report content.

The summary may be written in deductive or inductive order. In deductive order it begins with the conclusions and recommendations, followed by a summary of the introduction, and finally by a summary of the findings and analysis. The executive summary in Exhibit 15.9 is arranged deductively. The writer gives the recommendation at the beginning. The reader is told how the data was collected. The summary of the findings highlights three areas of investigation: impact on store operations, reactions of consumers, and cost.

BODY OF THE REPORT

The report must have headings to guide the reader. If you center the major headings, the degrees of importance can be differentiated as follows:

FIRST-DEGREE HEADING

Usually the title of the report is the first-degree heading. It is typed in capital letters and underlined.

SECOND-DEGREE HEADING

Chapter titles in the long report are typed as second-degree headings. They are typed in capital letters but are not underlined.

Third-Degree Heading

This heading uses upper and lower case letters. It is underlined.

Fourth-Degree Heading

The fourth-degree heading uses upper and lower case letters. It is not underlined.

Exhibit 15.8   **Table of Illustrations**

TABLE OF ILLUSTRATIONS

Exhibit 15.9   **Executive Summary**

EXECUTIVE SUMMARY

Kreisner Foods should install computer scanning devices in all of its stores.

Studying the feasibility of installing the scanners involved the evaluation of the following factors: marketing strategy, inventory control, customer satisfaction, employee efficiency, and cost and savings of the system.

In marketing the scanners are invaluable for pricing and advertising strategies. Scanners help in the allocation of shelf space. They also assist management in relocating items and rearranging merchandise by brands and sizes.

Consumer reaction to the scanners is mixed. Some consumers prefer the detailed receipts provided by the system, but others complain that individual items are not priced. They argue that comparison shopping is difficult without individual pricing. However, stores that use scanners have not suffered a loss of customers. It seems that consumers will get used to the new system without any major problems.

The scanners help eliminate pricing errors that occur if prices are stamped on items manually. Discounting and couponing can be used more effectively and efficiently with the help of the scanners.

Inventory control is simplified, and manual counting of goods is almost completely eliminated.

Savings should amount to about 1 percent of sales. With sales of $20 million, a store could realize savings of $200,000. Considering leasing and maintenance costs of $25,000 per year, net savings of $175,000 can be expected.

Kreisner Foods would definitely benefit from installing computer scanners.

Source: Reprinted by permission of Paul Meere.

The Fifth-Degree Heading

This heading is on the left margin. It uses upper and lower case letters.

The Sixth-Degree Heading

It is typed the same way as the fifth-degree heading, but it is not underlined.

The Seventh-Degree Heading. This heading becomes part of the paragraph. It is no longer set off in a separate line.

If you block the entire report, including the headings, the levels will appear as follows:

FIRST-DEGREE HEADING

SECOND-DEGREE HEADING

Third-Degree Heading

Fourth-Degree Heading

Fifth-Degree Heading: This is part of the paragraph.

When deciding how to set up the headings in your report, remember that:

1. Centered headings are more important than headings on the margin.
2. Capitalized headings are more important than lowercase headings.
3. Underlined headings are more important than headings that are not underlined.

Introduction. The introduction serves as an orientation for the reader. The major parts of the introduction are background, problem and purpose, scope, method, limitations, and, where applicable, time and budget information. All those parts were discussed in detail in Chapter 6.

The introduction is the revised report plan. It contains all the information that was in the research plan with the exception of the tentative outline and the bibliography. The tentative outline for the report becomes the table of contents, and the bibliography appears at the end of the report. Another difference between the report plan and the introduction to the final report is that they are written in a different tense. The research plan is written in future tense because the writer plans to do certain things. In the report itself the writer has done all those things; therefore, the introduction is written either in present or past tense.

Writers sometimes feel that the introductory material is unnecessary because the reader probably has the information already. At this point, however, the writer has to understand that she is more thoroughly familiar with all aspects of the problem than the person who requested the report. The introduction refreshes the memory of the reader who is knowledgeable about the problem; it serves as orientation for the reader who is not.

A report is seldom read by only one person. Even if the requestor knows all of the background details, other readers may not. If the report is to be kept for future reference, the detailed introduction is absolutely necessary. In the future new employees who are not familiar with the situation may need to consult the report.

Findings and Analysis. The presentation of the findings and the analysis is the heart of the report and forms the basis for the conclusions and recommendations. The material is divided into chapters, and the chapters are again divided into subparts. Clear organization and logic are necessary to make the presentation effective. Chapters 7 through 13 of this book are devoted to secondary and primary research, the analysis of data with the help of statistics, and the presentation of the data with the help of visual aids. Their object was to prepare you to present your findings and analysis in the written report.

Conclusions and Recommendations. Conclusions and recommendations must be stated clearly and concisely. No new facts should be introduced at this point. Conclusions and recommendations are based on the presentation and analysis of the facts. For a detailed discussion of how to draw conclusions and make recommendations, you should check Chapter 12. The recommendation report has both conclusions and recommendations. Some analytical reports have conclusions but no recommendations. The writer may combine conclusions and recommendations or present them in separate sections. Informational reports, of course, have neither; they have only a summary.

SUPPLEMENTARY PARTS

Appendix. In the appendix you present supplementary material that is useful but not absolutely necessary for understanding the report. You may want to put copies of questionnaires or working papers in the appendix (Exhibit 15.10). Detailed statistical information may also be included.

Bibliography. The bibliography lists all the secondary sources that you used in writing the report and the interviews you conducted. Some writers include only those sources that they footnoted; others include those they used as references but did not footnote. Some writers put together an extensive bibliography of all sources relating to the report topic. In most cases the limited bibliography, listing only material that you actively used, is sufficient. The limited bibliography is also called *works cited.*

Exhibit 15.10 **Appendix**

APPENDIX

Manager Interview Questions

1. What brand of optical scanners does this store use?

2. How long have the scanners been in the store?

3. How do the scanners aid in this store's labor productivity?

4. How do the scanners help in terms of operating costs?

5. How does the system aid in inventory control?

6. Does this store use the system data for shelf-space allocation?

7. Does the information from the system help you make better decisions?

8. Do consumers complain about item price removal in your store?

9. Please describe any disadvantages you see with the system.

10. Do you believe that most stores will adopt scanning systems? If so, why?

For a detailed discussion on the compilation of a bibliography check Chapter 8.

Index. An index is a listing of all the key words in the report with the page numbers on which they occur. Business reports seldom use an index because of the time required to put together a good and functional index. Most reports depend on the clarity of the table of contents instead.

PHYSICAL PRESENTATION

APPEARANCE

A neat report indicates that you care about your work, just as a sloppy report with errors and poor page layout indicates that the work was not important to you. The report communicates to management how seriously you take your work. Because you are responsible for the work that goes out under your name, you should carefully proofread reports typed by your secretary or a secretary in the word-processing center. If it has your name on it, it is your report; you—not your secretary—will be blamed or praised for it.

Many companies tell the writer what paper to use for a particular purpose. The more formal and official the report, the higher quality the paper should be. The most important reports are on 20- or 16-pound bond paper.

If the report is to be bound on the left, the writer must leave about half an inch additional space on the typed page to allow for the binding. Otherwise, the left, right, and top margins should all be the same, usually about one inch in a double-spaced report. The bottom margin is somewhat larger, about an inch and a half. The bottom margin may vary slightly because visual aids, for example, may end above or below the normal margin. For the first page of the report body and for pages that start with major headings, the top margin is usually two inches rather than one inch. This treatment is called a *dropped head*. A frequently used page layout for business reports is illustrated in Exhibit 15.11. Special reports may require special layouts.

PAGE NUMBERING

Page numbers may appear at top center, top right, or bottom center. Whichever pattern is chosen, the placement must be consistent. The traditional placement pattern uses Arabic numbers at the top of the page for the report body. They may be either centered or flush with the right margin. A double-space separates the page number from the text. On pages with a dropped head, the number is at the bottom, separated by a double-space from the text.

The preliminary pages are numbered with lowercase Roman numerals. All pages are counted in the report, but the number does not appear on all

Exhibit 15.11 **Page Layout and Numbering**

AN EXAMINATION OF COMPUTER SCANNERS ← *14down ? 2 inches*

FOR KREISNER FOODS

ORIENTATION TO THE PROBLEM

Background of Computer Scanners

Many supermarkets have already installed computer scanning devices (CSDs).
As of May of this year, more than 40 percent of all supermarkets used CSDs. It is
estimated that more than 10,000 stores will be using scanner systems by the end of
the year. The scanners are designed to reduce errors in inventory records, the
waiting time in checkout lines, and pricing errors.

The CSDs utilize the Universal Product Code (UPC) to read information from
packaged goods. The UPC represents the product code, the manufacturer, and the
associated price and product class. The UPC has been in existence since 1973.
Most products in the Kreisner supermarkets carry the code, but so far Kreisner's
does not take advantage of the system.

The use of the CSDs is easy. The clerk simply slides the coded item over
the scanner's eye. The eye is a laser beam that reads the code and enters the
information into the computer. The clerk does not need to enter any information
manually except in cases where the code is not clearly marked on the product.
These products typically include produce, fresh meat, and fish.

CSDs can be used to generate data on advertising response rates and merchandising success rates.

Problem

How can computer scanning devices help Kreisner Foods to stay competitive?

1

Source: Reprinted by permission of Paul Meere.   (*continued*)

Exhibit 15.11 **Page Layout and Numbering** (*continued*)

2

Scope of the Study

In order to determine how Kreisner Foods can benefit from computer scanning devices, the report will examine the impact of scanners on productivity, inventory control, and marketing strategy at Kreisner Foods.

Once the possible savings in those areas have been determined, it will be possible to calculate the time required to recapture the initial investment. A cost-benefit analysis will help decide how profitable the scanners will be for Kreisner Foods.

Limitations

Because Kreisner has not used scanners in the past, no data on the impact of scanners at Kreisner was available. Some of Kreisner's competitors have been using scanners for some time, but their data, of course, is not available to Kreisner. A telephone survey of consumers in the area helped to establish the attitudes of consumers toward scanners; however, such a survey faces some serious limitations.

Methodology

Two hundred consumers in Central Illinois were interviewed by telephone. The respondents were divided into two groups: consumers who had been exposed to scanners and those who had not. Out of the sample, 150 consumers were familiar with scanners. The questionnaire used a Likert-type scale for responses.

The survey was conducted during the first week of March between 6:00 p.m. and 8:00 p.m. by four college students who had had a marketing research class. Before they called consumers, they received instruction in telephone etiquette and the purpose of the interview. The students then conducted several practice interviews.

of them. If you look at the beginning of this book, you will find that the first few pages are not numbered. In a formal report the first page that normally carries a number is the table of contents. The preliminary pages may be numbered at the bottom or in the upper right-hand corner. As in the body of the report, however, pages with dropped heads should have page numbers at the bottom. This would include the first page of both the table of contents and of the executive summary.

INDENTATION

If you single-space and block your report, you double-space between paragraphs. If you double-space the report, you should indent paragraph beginnings. Blocking a double-spaced report would require triple spacing between paragraphs to make clear where paragraphs begin. There is no definite rule by how many spaces a paragraph has to be indented. It is important, however, that you are consistent. Most report writers indent between four and ten spaces.

SUMMARY OF LEARNING OBJECTIVES

To Understand the Role of the Preliminary Pages, the Body of the Report, and the Supplementary Parts.
This chapter presented the parts of the most complete type of analytical report. Not all parts are necessary for each report. The decision as to which ones to include will depend on the nature of the topic, the purpose of the report, and the reader.

A formal report has three major sections: the preliminary pages, the body of the report, and the supplementary parts. The preliminary pages provide background information on the report. The reader can see who requested the report, why the report was written, and how much time and money were available for putting the report together. The preliminary pages put the report in perspective so that the reader can understand it better.

Preliminary pages are unnumbered except for the table of contents and the executive summary, which carry Roman numerals. The report proper carries Arabic numbers.

In formal reports, an executive summary or a synopsis is included in the preliminary pages.

The body of the report may be arranged inductively or deductively. The inductive order leads up to the conclusion and recommendation, whereas the deductive order gives the conclusion and recommendation at the beginning of the report.

The supplementary parts usually consist of the appendix and the bibliography. Copies of questionnaires or detailed statistical information are often presented in an appendix.

To Present an Attractive and Effective Long Report.
The specific format and page layout will depend on conventions in any given company and considerations for the use of the report. The writer must use good judgment and discretion in the choice of the final format of the report.

QUESTIONS AND PROBLEMS

1. What is the purpose of the preliminary pages, the body of the report, and the supplementary parts?
2. Discuss the role of the letter of transmittal. What information can appropriately be included?
3. Discuss the system for numbering pages in the formal report.
4. Discuss the advantages and disadvantages of a deductive or inductive arrangement of the report.
5. Discuss the role of the introduction in relation to the report planning process.
6. Discuss the role and format of the executive summary or synopsis.
7. Obtain a long business report and discuss its format.
8. Discuss the role of the appendix.
9. Discuss the role of the index.
10. Your company builds brakes for automobiles. Business is going well and management is considering purchasing a factory building to expand production. You are asked to write a report to examine the potential of the building for your company. You are also to recommend whether or not to purchase the building. What parts should your final report have? Would you arrange the report inductively or deductively? What supplementary parts might the report have?

COMMUNICATION STUDY OF THE WORD PROCESSING CENTER
COLLEGE OF EDUCATION
PRAIRIE STATE UNIVERSITY

Prepared for

Dr. John Smith

Dean, College of Education

Prepared by

Mary Modern

Supervisor, Word Processing Center

December 4, 19xx

December 4, 19XX

Dr. John Smith
Dean, College of Education
Prairie State University
Middletown, IL 65555

Dear Dr. Smith:

Here is the requested report assessing the communication flow of the Word Processing Center.

The report focuses on the present communication system. It includes a description
of the present system and its problems along with suggestions for improvements.

The information presented should help you in making a decision that can benefit
both the Center's staff and the faculty and staff members who use the Word Processing Center.

Please let me know if there is any further information that you may need.

Sincerely,

Mary Modern
Mary Modern
Supervisor, Word Processing Center

Enclosure

TABLE OF CONTENTS

iii

EXECUTIVE SUMMARY

This report provides an overview of the communication networks in the Word Processing Center located at the College of Education of Prairie State University. It addresses the limitations of the Center's physical layout, which has negatively influenced the Center's workflow. The formal and informal networks of communication between the clients (faculty and staff) and the Center's staff are also analyzed in terms of workflow and productivity.

The purpose of this report is to provide suggestions to improve the communication structure of the Center. Previous studies have shown that work environment and communication structure are two important elements that directly influence productivity. They may also affect job satisfaction.

Although the Center has relatively up-to-date and efficient equipment, noise and fumes produced by this machinery negatively affect the work environment. Improvements such as sound barriers and fans have not been previously considered a means to increase staff productivity. Another consideration is the placement of the equipment and workstations to facilitate a more effective flow of communication between the clients and the Center's staff.

The second area of analysis involves the present communication networks. The positive or negative effect of these networks influences the work environment and the quality of work. An increased demand for work produced by the Center's staff makes it necessary to study the Center's flow of communication to determine the most efficient communication structure, one which would lead to increased productivity and job satisfaction.

I recommend a better arrangement of equipment and furniture in the Center for two reasons: to reduce noise and distractions, and to create more effective communication channels between clients and staff. A detailed analysis of the strengths and weaknesses of the present communication channels indicates that the formal network can be restructured. Another suggestion involves cross-training the staff members to use all the equipment available in the Center as a means of increasing job satisfaction.

iv

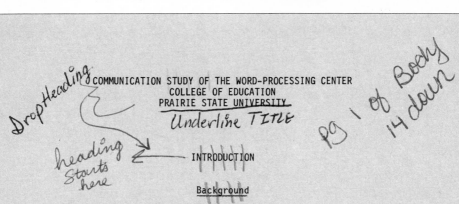

COMMUNICATION STUDY OF THE WORD-PROCESSING CENTER
COLLEGE OF EDUCATION
PRAIRIE STATE UNIVERSITY

Drop Heading

Underline TITLE

heading starts here

Pg 1 of Body 14 down

INTRODUCTION

Background

The Word-Processing Center is a special-services center for the College of
Education at Prairie State University. It provides services for the Departments of Elementary Education, Secondary Education, and Administration as well
as the administrative staff of the College. The services include word processing and reproduction of materials.

The word-processing area produces material needed for use in the classroom, in professional development, and for administrative use. The work is
done on five word processors and three printers. The word processors have recently been updated. A new scientific printer can provide faculty and staff
with typed and printed papers that contain complex scientific formulas and
Greek letters. A new microcomputer used with one of the word processors can
convert disk information to a configuration compatible with the word processor.

The reproduction services for classroom, professional, and administrative
needs include photocopying, offset printing, processing of transparencies, and
duplicating on copiers. All materials are collated and stapled on request.
Much of the reproduction work is given directly to the reproduction area with-

Don't Need to Number Pg. 1

2

out editing. The purchase of new equipment has substantially improved the quality and quantity of reproduction. University Printing Services recently installed a photocopying machine with enlargement and reduction capabilities. The demand for this new service has increased staff time spent on photocopying, and the time available to perform other services has greatly decreased.

The addition of the new equipment has caused many changes in workloads and work patterns. The result has been a lengthening of the time needed to complete each type of work. New schedules need to be circulated within the Center and with the clients. This has caused misunderstandings, and new guidelines need to be established and printed for the Center's staff and clients.

Problem Statement

How can communications between the College of Education Word Processing Center staff and its clients be enhanced in order to provide the best services possible for the College faculty and staff and also ensure a healthy and happy working environment for the Center's staff? What kinds of improvements can be made to facilitate better communications and increase work productivity?

Scope

The study is limited to the communication network that presently exists in the Center and the effect of that network on the work environment and work quality. This study does not include interpersonal relationships outside the Center and the formal organizational structure of the University.

Limitations

Several important factors influence the communication structure of the Center. Some of them cannot be changed, but they limit the number and types of

3

improvements that can be implemented.

1. The first-floor location on a busy hallway leads to excessive noise and student inquiries.

2. The present floor plan inhibits effective communication between Center staff members.

3. Noise produced by reproduction and printing equipment makes all communication difficult.

4. Clients are not fully aware of the proper use of the Center's services or even, in many cases, of the services available.

5. Equipment and furniture, often departmental castoffs, do not always match or meet Center needs.

6. Guidelines have not been updated to meet faculty/administrative needs or to determine the proper use of the Center.

Methodology

Primary and secondary sources were used for the data and information gathered for this report. Primary sources included personal observation and faculty/staff interviews. Secondary sources included research on organizational communication and behavior as well as the Center's procedures manual.

THE WORD-PROCESSING CENTER

Center Activities

The Center's communication activities were observed during six normal workdays. The supervisor collected the data and recorded it on a daily log sheet, kept at her desk. The observations included the names of both the client and the person who initiated the contact. The type of activity performed, the length of the contact, and the mode of communication were also recorded. The following table shows a portion of one day's log.

4

Table Daily Observation Log for Communication Study

Client's Name	Initiator of Contact	Activity Performed	Time Spent	Mode of Communication
Woolson	Woolson	Photocopying transparencies	8:10/8:20	Verbal/ in person
Jane	Mary	Discussing daily work activity	8:20/8:35	Verbal/ in person
Johnson	Mary	Clarifying directions	8:35/8:38	Verbal/ by phone
Evans	Evans	Clarifying directions	8:38/8:43	Verbal/ in person

From 8:10 to 8:20, for example, Mary provided Professor Woolson with the services of photocopying and making enlargements of book charts for classroom transparencies. This was a verbal request by Professor Woolson. The initiator's name is listed in Column 2.

Figure 1 summarizes the average number of daily contacts made by clients, Center staff members, and others with Mary in her capacity as word-processing supervisor.

Of the 99 daily contacts, 45 were with clients, 47 were with the Center's staff, and 7 were with outside people such as students and workmen. All contacts between clients and the Center's staff go through the supervisor. Much of the communication between the people in Word-Processing Services and Reproductive Services also goes through the supervisor. During the observation period the supervisor contacted Word-Processing Services an average of 48 times

5

<u>Figure 1</u> Daily Communication Patterns for Mary

                            Supervisor
                        Number of Contacts

                                              →25 Word-Processing Services
Clients   45 ◄──────────→20 Reproductive Services
                                              → 0 Other Services

Center's Staff   47 ◄──────────→23 Word-Processing Services
                                              →18 Reproductive Services
                                              → 6 Other Services

Outside People   7 ◄──────────→ 0 Word-Processing Services
                                              → 2 Reproductive Services
                                              → 5 Other Services

Total
Number of
Daily Contacts   99

---

daily and Reproductive Services an average of 40 times daily. Contact with

outside people was more limited. Two students came in daily with requests to

talk to student workers. Five students came into the center daily for general

information about office locations and directions.

Physical Layout of the Center

Communication can be thought of as an interpersonal process of sending and

receiving symbols with meanings attached to them (Schermerhorn 439). The pro-

cess of communication is in many ways difficult to understand. It is the most

basic of human processes and the most misunderstood (Hunt 28). The major parts

of the communication process are sender, channel, receiver, and feedback. Of

the many elements that affect these four major parts, some enhance communica-

6

tion and understanding and others inhibit communication. Physical surroundings affect people in many different ways. Effectiveness in communicating will often depend on whether the individual's surroundings are pleasant, unpleasant, calm and quiet, or noisy and confused.

This section of the report will focus on the effects of the physical properties and barriers as they relate to communication effectiveness within the Center and between the Center's staff and clients. Suggestions for improvements in the physical layout will also be discussed.

The current physical layout is shown in Appendix 1. One room is devoted to word-processing activities and the other to client reception and reproduction. Several problems exist because of this physical layout:

1. <u>Traffic Pattern in the Center</u>.

   The present traffic pattern is a problem because the main door is on a busy hallway. Visitors in the building and students seeking information cause disruptions. Clients wander into the word-processing area or reproduction area when the supervisor is absent from her desk or is busy.

2. <u>The Lack of Sound-Absorbing Material on the Walls</u>.

   Both rooms have high ceilings and plaster walls and are uncarpeted. A metal-and-glass divider between the reception and the reproduction areas does not absorb sound.

3. <u>The Location of the Photocopying Machine</u>.

   Presently, the photocopying machine is located in the word-processing room and is accessible to faculty. It was placed there by University Printing Services in December 1984. The capabilities of the machine have meant a need for more client assistance and less time for staff members to

7

do other work.

4. The Lack of Bafflers on the Word-Processing Printers.

When the four printers in the word-processing room are all operating,
the noise is deafening. The sound echos and is often combined with noise
from the reproduction equipment in the adjoining room.

5. The Lack of Sufficient Lighting for Word Processors.

Lights in the word-processing room are not directly over the individual workstations. Because of the high ceilings, lighting is a great distance from the machines and the work.

6. The Lack of Space in the Reproduction Area.

A new printer and a new collator have made the reproduction area
cramped. This equipment is larger than the old equipment it replaced.

7. The Fumes from the Offset Press.

Fumes from the offset printing press create a problem. Even short
runs on the press produce fumes that rise to the third floor. The trap-
ping of fumes in the Center is hazardous to the health of the people who
work in the Center.

Formal Communication Network

The present formal communication network is shown in Figure 2. This type
of network, called the Star Communication Network, maintains a high degree of
centralization. The number of possible communication channels is low, leader-
ship predictability is high, group satisfaction is low, and individual satisfaction is high.

8

Figure 2   Present Formal Communication Network

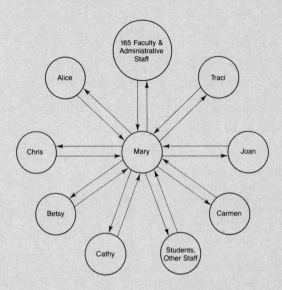

The desired formal communication network suggested in Figure 3 would allow for effective and productive communication between clients and Center staff members. Questions regarding work status, new work, and other scheduling and planning matters would still be directed through the supervisor. Center staff would be able to directly contact clients about details on a specific job. Figure 3 shows a breakdown of the five major groups in the network: clients, the Center supervisor, word-processing staff, reproduction staff, and miscellaneous others. This type of communication network would help ease tensions and still maintain control.

9

Figure 3   Desired Formal Communication Network

<u>Informal Communication Network</u>

The present informal network in Figure 4 shows the supervisor at the center with word-processing and reproduction services on either side. Strong
channels of communication exist within each work area, with weaker channels
between work areas and between the supervisor and the Center's staff. A change
in physical layout will help to improve these communication channels.

10

Figure 4   Present Informal Communication Network

Key:
Regular ————————
Occasional ——————

CONCLUSIONS

The problem presented in this report involves three areas: the physical layout, the work environment, and the formal/informal communication structure. Ineffective and unproductive communication between the Center's staff and clients can be improved by changing the physical layout and improving the work environment. Communication barriers could be removed and communication improved by careful planning and implementation of the following recommendations.

RECOMMENDATIONS

The following recommendations should be considered for solving the problems caused by physical layout and the communication structure.

11

1. Move the photocopying machine from the word-processing room into the reception/reproduction room.

2. Rearrange both rooms as shown in the floor plans.

3. Apply sound-absorbing material to all walls.

4. Install bafflers on each of the word-processing printers.

5. Adjust lighting to be beneficial and flexible for word processors.

6. Move the wall dividing the reception and reproduction areas to allow for more reproduction space.

7. Install a fan on the outside wall of the reproduction area to draw out fumes.

Some of these recommendations can be carried out easily and inexpensively; others will require some planning and budgeting.

12

APPENDIX 1: FLOOR PLAN

APPENDIX 2: NEW FLOOR PLAN

13

WORKS CITED

Goldhaber, G. M. Organizational Communication, 3rd. ed. Dubuque, IA:
    Wm. C. Brown, 1983.

Hunt, G. T. Communication Skills in the Organization. Englewood Cliffs, NJ:
    Prentice-Hall, 1980.

Schermerhorn, J. R., J. G. Hunt, and R. N. Osborn. Managing Organizational
    Behavior. New York: John Wiley, 1982.

Users' Procedures Manual. Middletown, IL: Prairie State University, College
    of Education Word Processing Center, 1981.

CHAPTER SIXTEEN

ORAL REPORTS

ORAL REPORTS

LEARNING OBJECTIVES

- To prepare a good oral presentation.
- To prepare effective visual aids.
- To evaluate strengths and weaknesses of a speaker.
- To deliver an informative speech.
- To analyze the audience and adapt the speech to the audience.
- To evaluate the presentation objectively.

Writing is only one way of communicating. In business you will not only write reports but will also present them orally. You may talk with one person, present your findings to a small group for discussion, or speak before a large audience. Oral reports can range from an informal exchange of ideas to a very formal presentation. This chapter will concentrate on the more formal oral reporting settings rather than on the informal one-on-one exchanges of ideas.

COMPARISON OF ORAL AND WRITTEN REPORTS

Like written reports, oral reports can be short or long, formal or informal, informational or analytical. Some of the basic characteristics are also the same. Good oral reports require planning, organization, and effective delivery.

AUDIENCE ANALYSIS

The report writer, carefully analyzing the audience for the report, must answer these questions:

1. Who is the reader?
2. What are the needs of the reader?
3. How is the reader going to use the report?

The oral reporter conducts the same analysis but must be even more aware of the audience. A speaker analyzes the audience both during the planning of the speech and during the delivery. Unlike the reader of a report, the listener to an oral presentation provides immediate feedback, and the speaker must be able to adapt the speech on the basis of the feedback received.

The oral report must be instantly understandable because the audience cannot reread it. The reader of a written report can think about it, make notes, and compare it to other reports. The listener in oral reporting must keep up with the speaker; therefore, the speaker has to pay special attention to clarity and the use of examples.

USE OF VISUAL AIDS

Visual aids play an important role in written and oral reports. In both they clarify and emphasize data. Visual aids in oral reports, however, must be simple. They should concentrate on some key points rather than all of the details. At the beginning of a presentation the speaker may outline the topics he will discuss in a visual aid. Complex arguments and conclusions may be effectively summarized in a table that presents the most important points.

NONVERBAL COMMUNICATION

In written reports nonverbal communication is limited. In oral reporting, on the other hand, nonverbal communication influences the response of the audience and the delivery of the speech. The intonation of the speaker, the appearance of the speaker, the lighting, the gestures, and facial expressions all have an impact on the effectiveness of the oral report. The nonverbal aspects of oral communication will be discussed in detail later in this chapter.

PLANNING OF ORAL REPORTS

As you plan your oral report, you should answer the following questions:

1. What is the purpose of the oral report?
2. What is the occasion for the speech?
3. Under what conditions will you deliver the report?
4. Who is the audience? *Can tell them who they are*
5. What visual aids will help you to make a good presentation?
6. What are your characteristics as a speaker?

WHAT IS THE PURPOSE OF THE ORAL REPORT?

Purpose of the Oral Report
The purpose of the oral report may be different from that of the written report.

You must determine whether you are to present information, analyze information, draw conclusions and make recommendations, or persuade the audience to a particular viewpoint. A good request for an oral report will tell you what is expected, but the request you receive may not be specific. If you have any doubts about what you are expected to do, you must ask. As an example, assume that you have written a 50-page evaluation of production costs in your plant. If you are asked to present the evaluation orally to a group of top managers, you must determine the **purpose of the oral report**. It might be one of the following:

1. To give an overview of your findings
2. To give a summary of your recommendations on how to cut waste
3. To analyze the impact of inflation on production costs

As you begin your planning, you should write down the purpose of the oral presentation. If it will be based on a written report, you may also want to list the differences between the purpose of the written and the oral reports as in the following example:

Purpose of Written Report:
To analyze the reasons for the increase in production costs

Purpose of Oral Report:
To summarize the reasons for production cost increases to upper management.

The writing of the purpose will guide you in your preparation of the oral report. You will not always write a formal report before making an oral presentation. If you are asked to give only an oral report, you still should write down a precise purpose statement. The purpose is related to the audience. If you talk about the subject to a group of production workers, for example, you may want to concentrate on their role in cutting costs. Presenting detailed findings and management's role in cutting costs might be useless and irrelevant.

In summary, the purpose of the oral and written report can be identical, but it may also be different. The purpose of the speech is influenced by the audience, the situation, and the time you are given to deliver it. In ten minutes you could give only an overview of how to keep down production costs. In an hour you could go into detail.

WHAT IS THE OCCASION FOR THE SPEECH?

Occasion for the Speech
The occasion influences the tone.

The **occasion for the speech** will influence the tone, the style of delivery, the examples you use, and the amount of detail you include. If you give an oral report to the same group under different circumstances, your report will be different. Assume that you talk to managers about the influence of the economy on company performance. For a dinner speech you use a somewhat lighter approach than for a workday session on policy formulation. The purpose of the dinner speech is not only to inform but also to entertain.

UNDER WHAT CONDITIONS WILL YOU DELIVER THE SPEECH?

Conditions
The speaker must examine the physical environment for the speech.

The good speaker determines the answers to many questions during the planning stage. You need to know whether you will be one member of a panel, one of many speakers, or the only presenter. Will you speak in a large lecture hall or give your report in a small seminar room? What equipment will be available? Is there a projector, a blackboard, a podium? Must you bring your own projector, extension cords, and spare projector bulbs? You need to know whether you will stand on a stage removed from the audience or whether you will be on the same level. In small groups you may use different visual aids than in a large hall. If the audience will sit around a table, your delivery style will be different. The **conditions** under which you will deliver your speech will influence what you say and how you say it.

WHO IS THE AUDIENCE?

Audience Analysis
Knowledge of the audience helps in effective planning.

Audience analysis is essential. The speaker must know who the audience is. The occasion and the situation will serve as indicators, but the speaker should get as much information as possible about the audience, both as individuals and as a group. These are some questions you may want to ask about the audience:

1. How large is the audience?
2. How old is the audience? Are there notable age differences within the group?
3. What is the background of the audience?
4. Do the listeners have the same educational background?
5. Do the listeners have common work experiences?
6. What are the political beliefs of the audience? (This question may not be important for all reports.)
7. Does the audience hold certain beliefs about your topic?
8. Is the audience conservative or liberal?
9. What are the interests of the audience?
10. What does the audience expect?

The more you know about your audience, the better you will be able to adapt your oral report to the audience. If you know that your audience is suspicious of environmentalists and government regulation of industrial waste, for example, you will use a different approach for your report on the effects of industrial waste than if your audience is convinced that industrial waste is harmful and endorses legislation to deal with the problem. The substance of your report is the same, but your introduction, your examples, and your visual aids may be different. One audience has recognized the problem, whereas the other audience has to still be convinced that a problem exists.

WHAT VISUAL AIDS WILL HELP YOU MAKE A GOOD PRESENTATION?

Visual Aids
Visual aids in speeches have to be clear and simple.

Visual aids in oral and written reports have different functions. In oral reports visual aids are often used to let the audience know what the speaker will emphasize. They are also used to summarize important facts and conclusions. In a written report the summary is in paragraph form, but a speaker may find that a verbal summary is not clear enough. The speaker may therefore decide to highlight the key points with a visual aid.

For example, the conclusions in Exhibit 16.1 concentrate on savings in three areas: elimination of credit cards, reduction of direct-dial calls, and reduction of long-distance calls. The reader of the report can think about these conclusions. In an oral report, however, the listener may have difficulty remembering all three areas. A summary like the one in Exhibit 16.2 can make the conclusions much clearer. The speaker can point to each conclusion as it is discussed.

Exhibit 16.1   **Conclusions and Recommendations in Written Report**

Conclusions and Recommendations

The Illinois Valley Library System has successfully controlled telephone costs during the last three years; however, with rising costs additional efforts are needed. At the same time we must continue to provide quality service to member libraries. The analysis suggests the following:

Elimination of credit cards would save $683 annually.
Reduction in direct-dial calls would save $514 annually.
Reduction in length of calls would save $514 annually.

In addition, a special committee should examine alternative telephone systems for the library so that we can increase our service to member libraries and stay within the limits of our budget.

Exhibit 16.2   **Conclusions and Recommendations in Oral Report**

ELIMINATE CREDIT CARDS	$ 683.00
REDUCE DIRECT CALLS	514.00
REDUCE LENGTH OF CALLS	514.00
SAVINGS	$1,711.00

The speaker may find that visual aids from a written report must be adapted for use in the oral presentation. Although they were effective in the written report, they may contain too much detail for the oral presentation. Exhibit 16.3 shows a detailed income statement for Walgreens for three years. The speaker who wants to show the company's performance during

Exhibit 16.3   **Visual Aid in Written Report**

Eleven-Year Summary of Selected Financial Data (1)

Walgreen Co. and Subsidiaries
(Dollars in Thousands, except per share data)

	Fiscal Year	1985	1984	1983
Net Sales	Drugstores	$3,028,034	$2,614,265	$2,238,217
	Food Services	122,322	119,411	112,815
	Other Sales	11,579	10,949	9,582
	Total Net Sales	3,161,935	2,744,625	2,360,614
Costs and Deductions	Cost of sales	2,192,367	1,900,703	1,637,133
	Selling, occupancy and administration	791,697	691,139	601,623
	Other expense (income)	4,171	2,800	1,309
		2,988,235	2,594,642	2,240,065
Earnings	Earnings from U.S. operations before income taxes	173,700	149,983	120,549
	Income taxes	79,531	69,340	53,873
	Earnings from U.S. operations	94,169	80,643	66,676
	Equity in net earnings of Mexican operations	—	1,205	3,113
	Gain on sale of equity investments in Mexican operations, net of income taxes	—	3,598	—
	Net Earnings	$ 94,169	$ 85,446	$ 69,789
Net Earnings per Share(2)	Assuming full dilution	$ 1.53	$ 1.39	$ 1.13
	Assuming no dilution	1.53	1.39	1.14
Per Share(2)	Dividends Declared	$ .44	$ .36	$ .30
	Shareholders' Equity	7.83	6.76	5.74
Long-Term Obligations	Debt	$ 44,336	$ 24,472	$ 24,821
	Capital Leases	27,604	28,725	29,142
Assets and Equity	Total Assets	$ 961,938	$ 840,803	$ 718,022
	Shareholders' Equity	$ 480,974	$ 414,618	$ 351,705
	Return on Average Shareholders' Equity	21.0%	22.3%	21.4%

(1) Excludes the operations of the Globe Discount Department Store Division discontinued in fiscal 1978.
(2) Per share data have been adjusted for two-for-one stock splits in 1985, 1983 and 1982.

Source: *Annual Report*, Walgreen Co. and Subsidiaries, 1985.

the past year should simplify the information and highlight only major points, as Exhibit 16.4 does.

You can present your visual aids in many different ways. You may choose flipcharts, blackboards, opaque projectors, overhead projectors, slide projectors, or handouts. Your choice will depend on the availability of material, the size of the audience, the formality of the situation, your artistic ability, and your handwriting.

Flipcharts.
You will need a supply of colored pens and the flipchart, which is cumbersome to transport. If you use a flipchart, you can make your visual aids as you speak. Your handwriting must be neat, of course, and your creativity sufficient to make meaningful drawings on the spot. The result is usually less neat and not as attractive as other forms of visual aids.

Flipcharts are most effective in small groups during genuine discussions. If the speaker makes a formal presentation, the visual aids should be prepared ahead of time. Because the flipchart is small, people sitting in the back of a large room might not be able to see the illustrations.

Blackboards.
The blackboard has many of the same characteristics as the flipchart. The speaker can create visual aids on the spot. A drawback is that the speaker, while writing on the board, turns his back to the audience. If the audience is large, the viewers in the back of the room may not be able to see the visual aid. The speaker who counts on using a blackboard must make sure that a blackboard, colored chalk, and an eraser will be available.

Opaque Projectors.
The advantage of the opaque projector is that no special transparencies need to be prepared because it projects printed material. By moving the projector, the presenter can adjust the size of the projection. An opaque projector requires a dark room; as a result, the speaker has no eye contact with the audience. Opaque projectors are large, and few convention centers or hotels have them.

Exhibit 16.4   **Visual Aid in Oral Report**

Walgreens' 1985 Performance (thousands of dollars, except per share data)	
Net Sales	3,161,935
Costs	2,988,235
Earnings before Taxes	173,700
Net Earnings	94,169
Net Earnings per Share	$1.53
Return on Equity	21%

Overhead Projectors. The overhead projector, which projects transparencies, is probably the most widely used machine for showing visual aids. The visual aid can be produced ahead of time. It will be neat and can be multicolored. With the help of a thermofax machine the visual aid can be transferred from a written report to a transparency.

An advantage of the overhead projector is that you can use overlays. By placing one transparency over another, you can show developments over time. By using a special pen, you can also make notations on the visual aid as you talk. The overhead projector combines the advantages of the flipchart and the opaque projector.

By moving the machine, you can adapt the size of the projection to the size of the room. When you are talking to an audience about a transparency, you should face the audience and not the screen. Stand by the projector only if you do not block someone's view. While you explain a transparency, point with a pen or pointer to each area as you discuss it, and keep eye contact with the audience.

Most businesses, convention centers, and hotels have overhead projectors. Still, before making your decision, you should check to see whether the necessary equipment will be there for your use.

Slide Projectors. A slide presentation can be very effective. The slides can be prepared professionally and can be used many times. Some speakers combine slides with taped music and a recorded script. Slide presentations can be creative and of high quality, but the production of slides is more costly than the production of overhead transparencies. Unless you will use the slides a number of times, the expense may not be justifiable. In addition, because the lights must be turned off when you show slides, you will lose eye contact with the audience. You will need to weigh advantages and disadvantages of slide presentations carefully.

Handouts. The handout is useful because listeners can follow the material on the handout while you explain it. The disadvantage is that the audience may get ahead of you and concentrate on the handout rather than on your presentation. Some speakers, to overcome this problem, give handouts at the end of the oral report. The result is that the audience does not have the material available when it would be most useful. In general, if you do not use any other visual aids and if the presentation is rather technical, you should give the handouts at the beginning of the presentation.

WHAT ARE YOUR CHARACTERISTICS AS A SPEAKER?

In order to give a good speech, you should know your strengths and weaknesses as a speaker. You should also know what helps you give a good speech and what makes you nervous. In the examination of your characteristics you can draw on your evaluation of past performances. The better your evaluation was then, the better your preparation can be. You may want to pay particular attention to timing, use of examples, nervousness, and actual preparation or practice of a speech.

Timing. Do you have difficulty staying within a given time limit? If you are asked to speak for ten minutes, are you still talking after 30 minutes? **Timing** difficulties can be caused by lack of organization and preparation. If you have ten minutes, you should practice your speech to see whether you can deliver it in ten minutes. You must determine the essential points so that you will not spend too much time on unimportant details. With experience you will develop a better sense for timing, but in the beginning practice may be the only way to find out how well you manage your time.

Timing
The speaker has to consider the length of the entire speech and of the parts.

Timing is also an element of delivery style. A speaker who delivers an entire speech without a change in tempo will be boring. A speaker should slow down to explain difficult material and perhaps speed up at a climax. After an important point a speaker may pause for reflection. The speed of delivery must match the content.

Use of Examples. Some speakers can think of example after example, whereas others are hard pressed to think of one. If you notice that the audience is puzzled, you may need more examples to make your point. In the middle of a speech, however, you will not have time to search your mind for examples; you must have them ready. Chances are that with experience this aspect of speaking will become easier for you, but in the beginning you should prepare more examples than you think you will use. You should write down the key points of all the examples and have them ready.

Nervousness. People react differently to nervousness. Some people sweat, some tremble, some suffer a dry throat. You know how nervousness affects you, and you should prepare accordingly. If you may need a glass of ice water, request it. Even if you do not drink it, simply having the water available may help. If you have a tendency to sweat, you may want to wear lightweight clothing. In most cases nervousness decreases once the speaker has started the presentation. The most important factor in overcoming nervousness is the confidence that comes from knowing your material and being thoroughly prepared.

Preparation of Your Speech. Most speakers speak from cards. Some write out their complete speeches verbatim, and some memorize them.

Note Cards
Note cards have to be readable and contain key words.

Note Cards. Unless you have a complete speech ready (perhaps as a previously written report), writing one out may be too time consuming. **Note cards** will give you the key words and the outline of your speech. With the notes your speech will be well organized, and you will not need to carry a stack of paper with you. An audience that sees 50 pages of material may worry about the length of your speech. Note cards are less conspicuous.

Note cards do not hold a lot of information. They do not give you the exact formulation for every idea. Some speakers, worried that note cards are not detailed enough, begin to write complete sentences on every card. That practice destroys the concept of the note card by tempting the speaker to look at the cards too often. If you use note cards, you should only write key words and quotations on them. The quotations should be marked so that you can find them easily.

Entire Speech on Paper
If the entire speech is on paper, the speaker may be tempted to read and, as a result, lose eye contact.

Complete Written Report. The biggest advantage of having the **entire speech on paper** is that you know everything is there. Because you cannot forget anything, you may relax more. The biggest problem is that you may concentrate on your paper and forget the audience in front of you. It is tempting to read the speech if it is in front of you. But when you read, you will not look at the audience and may lose control. Without eye contact you may miss important feedback.

In some situations a business person must read a speech or large portions of a speech because of technical details, possible litigation, and briefings. The following guidelines may help you if you must read your presentation:

1. Have the entire speech printed in large print.
2. Read the speech ahead of time and know the material thoroughly.
3. Highlight key points and use them as guides through the presentation.
4. If at all possible, have the podium high enough so that you do not have to lean down and forward to read your speech.
5. Establish eye contact.
6. Work on timing and intonation. Many read speeches are ineffective because the speaker does not vary the speed of delivery and has a monotonous intonation.

Memorized Speech
Memorized speeches are delivered in a monotonous voice.

Memorized Speech. In most business settings, speaking without notes is not effective. The speaker must provide precise numbers and facts, and memorizing them is pointless. Moreover, **memorized speeches** have a tendency to sound monotonous and boring. The speaker may mentally concentrate on a perfect recitation rather than on an effective delivery of the speech. The speaker who loses his concentration may forget the rest of the speech. As in the case of a read speech, the establishment of contact with the audience is difficult.

You must determine which approach works best for you. Your past experience will help you to prepare. If you know that you will be tempted to read a complete report, you should not take the complete report with you.

If you know that you are nervous about the opening and transitions, you may want to prepare those parts more carefully and practice them more often than other parts of your speech.

Practice of Your Speech. If you feel childish practicing a speech, it may help you to know that many speakers **practice** in front of a mirror. They time their speeches and practice the precise wording of key elements. They may even practice the nonverbal elements of their speeches. Once you are in business, you will not have enough time to practice every speech, but in the beginning you may benefit by practicing the actual delivery.

Practice
Practicing a speech
builds confidence.

Rather than memorize the introduction, key points, and important transitions verbatim, you may be better off to practice those sections several times. Each time you may vary the wording slightly, and that is good. This way you do not concentrate on the exact wording which you might forget during delivery. Good and meaningful practice can help you to relax by building your confidence.

DELIVERY OF ORAL REPORTS

During the delivery of your speech you will repeat the same evaluation process that was part of your preparation. You must examine the situation, your style, and the audience.

SITUATION ANALYSIS

If you have given any speeches at all, you know that the situation, in spite of careful preparation, may not always be what you expected. The room may be smaller or larger than you anticipated. Perhaps you were one of two scheduled speakers, but the second speaker did not arrive. Perhaps you anticipated a small group and audience participation instead of 100 people and a podium.

In any case, you must adapt your delivery to the new situation. Obviously you cannot prepare for all eventualities, but you should make some contingency plans in case something goes wrong or differs from your expectations. In your preparation you might want to think about how you would change your presentation for a large or a small group.

SELF-ANALYSIS

The analysis of your delivery goes hand in hand with the audience analysis discussed in the next section. Already aware of your strengths and weaknesses, during the delivery you must be aware of your presentation. You can only analyze your presentation, however, if you are thoroughly familiar with the material you are presenting. As a report presenter you must give a speech that is informative, factually correct, well organized, and interesting. At the same time, you must be aware of style of delivery, because the effectiveness of a speech depends on more than content and organization.

Self-Confidence
A confident speaker presents a positive image to the audience.

Confidence. The more you speak, the more **self-confidence** you will develop. Beginning speakers often are nervous because they are not sure how they will do. They may be worried about the topic, their delivery, and the audience reception. Although preparation is important for all speakers, the beginning speaker, who often is nervous and unsure of himself, must know the topic inside out. If the delivery is not perfect, at least the content will be organized. Of course, even experienced speakers are not all relaxed. Many suffer stage fright before large audiences.

What can you do to overcome the fear and apprehension? Most important is to realize that nervousness is not all bad. In fact, you may not want to eliminate all of your anxiety. You simply want to get rid of the excess and the crippling fear. Some anxiety can be beneficial in starting your adrenalin to flow; it readies you for the speech. In a completely relaxed state you might give a thorough talk but probably not an inspiring or exciting one. You must realize the difference between being scared and simply being nervous in anticipation.

If you are truly afraid of speaking to groups, the following suggestions may help you overcome your fear:

1. **Be positive.** The worst thing you can do is to "psyche yourself out" by telling yourself that your speech will most definitely be a failure. Instead, contemplate the positive aspects. You know the material and have practiced your speech. Your transparencies are clear and well designed. You have every reason to be confident. Concentrating on your preparation may help you to forget your fear.

2. **Be excited about your speech.** Enthusiasm can build your confidence. After all, you are talking about something that is of interest to you and of importance to the audience.

3. **Think of the audience as an ally rather than an enemy.** The audience is there to get information. In a weekly sales meeting, for example, the salespeople want to know how to improve their performance. They want encouragement. They need your suggestions.

   At a convention, delegates will come to hear you because you have researched a particular topic that they are interested in. They want to learn how they can apply your findings or how your research relates to their work. They are there because they need you.

   Most audiences are friendly. They show goodwill and want the speaker to succeed. People are willing to listen, and they are not there to see you fail.

4. **Look at your audience.** The audience is not one big mass. It consists of individuals. Picture how they might use your information.

5. **Be confident of your ability.** You have a message to deliver and, in order for that message to reach your audience, you adapt to that audience just as you adapt to friends and colleagues. The basics of good communication remain the same for a more formal talk.

Sincerity
Sincerity has to be genuine to be convincing.

Sincerity. You must believe in what you say, and you must be **sincere** in your delivery. The audience will detect quickly if you yourself do not have confidence in your findings. As an example, assume you are speaking on business ethics. In your speech you examine ways of improving the ethical conduct of business people. If your voice, your examples, and your nonverbal signals tell the audience that you yourself think the whole subject is blown out of proportion and that no problem exists, you are not sincere. The audience will detect your attitude and react to it. In any case, the audience will not learn much about how to improve ethical conduct. Sincerity cannot be faked.

Friendliness. As a speaker, you want to be friendly rather than aloof. A smile as you approach the podium, the establishment of eye contact as you address the audience, and nonthreatening gestures as you speak tell the audience that you are friendly. Like sincerity, friendliness must be real. The audience will respond to a friendly speaker.

NONVERBAL COMMUNICATION

Nonverbal Signals
Nonverbal signals must support the words.

Although the most important part of a speech is its content, the success of a speech is not determined by content alone. The content may be factual and well organized, and yet the audience may be confused and puzzled because of distracting or inappropriate **nonverbal signals**. On the other hand, a speech may be judged excellent because the speaker used effective gestures and facial expressions to highlight key points. Nonverbal communication is not an adjunct to a presentation; it is an integral part. Appearance, gestures, posture, facial expressions, and eye contact are elements of nonverbal communication.

Appearance
The speaker must plan her appearance to fit the occasion and the purpose for the speech.

Appearance. Your **appearance** will reflect confidence or lack of confidence, sincerity or lack of sincerity. You may argue that your appearance has nothing to do with the content of your speech, which the audience should judge on its own merit. You may be right, but that is seldom what happens. Inappropriate clothing will draw attention to itself. If you want the audience to concentrate on your speech, you must dress to support what you say by underlining your friendliness, sincerity, self-confidence, and your authority.

If you are a male in upper management, you will wear a conservative business suit for most of your presentations. If you speak to workers as the boss, the business suit is appropriate. If, on the other hand, you want to talk to workers as a manager who seeks their cooperation and suggestions, the suit may be too intimidating. You may decide to wear slacks and a shirt. If you visit an oil rig or a farm, you may wear overalls or jeans.

Your attire will also depend on what you want to communicate. Do you want to project an image of authority, friendliness, or technical competence? And what is the purpose of your speech? The two must be combined. For example, a few years ago the coal miners were on strike. In a television report the miners first voiced their grievances, and then the chief executive spoke. The CEO did not sit behind his executive desk in a dark business suit. He talked in the yard with a mine shaft as backdrop. He wore slacks and a flannel shirt and a hard hat. Clearly, the company wanted to project an image of management concern and understanding.

John T. Molloy, a clothing consultant, describes appropriate and successful dress for men and women in his book, *The Woman's Dress for Success Book*.[1] He advocates business suits in basic colors and conservative tailoring. While some business people accept his advice, others find his recommendations too narrow and stifling. Women face an additional problem when choosing business dress. For centuries women have been the target of the fashion industry. Women's clothing is generally more colorful, stylish, and trendy than men's. And women may ask why they should wear suits and boring colors just because they advanced to management ranks.

The issue is not what is most comfortable but what is most effective in communicating. A woman speaking to an audience on fashion merchandising and style will wear something different from the woman who presents her recommendations for the purchase of a new computer system to upper management. This may not be fair, but the two speeches have different audiences and functions. If the woman recommending computers is wearing the latest styles with flashy colors and gaudy costume jewelry, her recommendations might not be taken seriously. Although her recommendations may be excellent, the perception of her as insincere and unbusinesslike may influence their reception.

If you prepare for a television presentation, the producers may tell you which colors and styles are most appropriate. Some colors are better for television than others. You will need to get expert advice.

Gestures
Gestures must be in harmony with the words.

Gestures. Confidence, apprehension, or nervousness can be indicated by **gestures**. The experts do not always agree on what specific gestures mean. Much depends on content and circumstances. Gestures, nevertheless, are important in effective communications. A speaker who stands behind the podium with arms straight down does not look relaxed. A speaker who grasps the podium with white-knuckled hands does not inspire confidence. A speaker who taps his note cards throughout the speech will appear nervous, although the habit can also indicate a lack of concentration. Hand movements that support what you say, on the other hand, will help the audience understand your speech better. Taking a few steps can underscore a point you are making.

Gestures are culture related. Americans are more restrained in their gestures than people from Latin America, Southern Europe, or the Middle East. Northern Europeans and the Japanese, on the other hand, are more reserved than Americans. The degree of gesturing and arm movements will be influenced by a careful audience analysis.

During a formal speech walking could be perceived as informal and inappropriate. In a less formal setting the speaker may walk, for example, from the podium to the overhead projector to point out specific data on the transparency.

Posture. The speaker must be relaxed and comfortable without slouching. Posture not only will communicate to the audience, but it also will influence the speaker's self-perception. Because posture is a personal trait, absolute rules are difficult to set. Good posture proclaims confidence. Slumped shoulders can mean insecurity. Those are general statements, however, that do not always hold.

Posture is a component of the entire image the speaker presents. Posture can underscore the speaker's words but can also negate them. Good posture will help the speaker with a delivery of the presentation because it facilitates breathing. Many excellent speakers take instruction in posture and breathing so that they do not become tired during a long speech.

Facial Expressions. Facial expressions, more than any of the other nonverbal components, show sincerity. Because the audience looks mostly at the speaker's face, the speaker must be aware of facial expressions. They can underline or contradict words and give away the true feelings of the speaker. They can show friendliness and respect or disdain for the audience. Facial expressions also must be synchronized with the content of the speech. A broad smile is not appropriate when discussing the harmful effects of pollution.

Eye Contact
Eye contact provides feedback to the speaker and helps in audience adaptation.

Eye Contact. Part of facial expression is **eye contact**, one of the most powerful tools for holding an audience's attention. Eye contact also signals to the speaker how the audience feels and reacts. Is the audience becoming bored? Is the audience agreeing or disagreeing? Does the audience understand? The feedback is crucial in adjusting the delivery of the speech. Long before the audience begins to fidget, the speaker can determine restlessness through eye contact. A good speaker will adapt his speech, change his voice, or shorten the speech to keep the audience's interest.

To elicit feedback, you must look at the audience. This means that you look at people; you do not simply glance. You look directly at individuals in all parts of the room. If you look at people, they will feel personally addressed, and they will respond personally.

QUESTION-AND-ANSWER SESSIONS

At the end of many speeches the audience is given the opportunity to ask questions. Listeners may ask for clarifications of remarks in the speech. They may want to know more about the method for data collection. Some may ask about related topics that were not specifically addressed in the speech. As the speaker, you must be prepared to answer questions. You should reflect beforehand on what types of questions the audience might ask and bring supporting material, such as statistics. If you do not know the answer to a question, you should say so. The audience will not expect you to have every detail committed to memory.

Most audiences are friendly, but occasionally you may face a hostile audience or hostile individuals in an audience. If you have delivered a speech on your company's advertising, you expect questions related to advertising. If your company has been in the news because of pollution problems, however, someone may ask you about those problems even though pollution is not your area. If the pollution problem was "big news," you should have anticipated that someone might ask. You should be familiar with your company's position and be able to make a brief statement. You can also point out that you simply are not familiar enough with that area to talk about it. You can suggest the name of a person to contact for more detailed information.

Whatever you do, you should avoid being pulled into an argument. When only a few hostile persons are in the audience, the rest of the audience often comes to the speaker's aid by asking friendly and topic-related questions. During question-and-answer periods you can show how well you know your area and how well you can handle pressure.

AUDIENCE ANALYSIS

Responsibilities of the Speaker. Even though you carefully analyzed your audience before the presentation, you must also analyze the audience during your presentation so that you can adapt your speech. Based on feedback—from eye contact, for example—you may need to delete or add examples, provide additional background information, or cut part of the background. You may want to emphasize some points more than others. In any case, you must respond to the audience.

You must make it easy for the audience to listen. This means you have to get their attention at the beginning and hold it throughout your speech. The following guidelines will help you to keep the interest of listeners:

1. Tell the audience at the beginning what you are going to talk about. Give the necessary background information. Describe exactly what you will cover.

2. Lead the audience through your presentation. Let them know where you are. If you have finished point three and are ready to start point

four, say so. Summarize complicated or long parts so that the audience can remember the important points.

3. Summarize the speech at the end. You may want to itemize the crucial points in order to emphasize them.

Communication is a two-way process in which the audience is actively involved and has obligations and responsibilities. All of you will not only be speakers but also listeners. Let us examine some of the aspects of a good and responsible audience.

Responsibilities of the Audience. The following guidelines will help you to become a better member of an audience:

1. Come prepared. If you know the topic ahead of time, think about it. If you are expected to read material related to the presentation, you must prepare. The speaker will base his presentation on the assumption that you have read the material.

2. Provide feedback. You play an active role. Even good speakers have difficulty giving a good presentation if the audience does not participate. Theater people can testify to that. An excellent performance can fall flat if the audience does not become involved, that is, if the audience does not respond, applaud, or react in some manner. Actors need feedback. Many actors find it difficult to act without an audience. A speaker is in the same situation as the actor. As a member of the audience, you are essential to the success of the presentation.

3. Be attentive. Your posture, facial expressions, and attitudes should tell the speaker that you are listening actively. In most business settings you are not there to be entertained but to obtain information. You spend your time and the company's money to listen to that speech. You have an obligation to learn all you can.

Listening
Effective listening requires concentration and an open mind.

Listening is not always easy. Experts say that the brain can process up to 500 words a minute but that a speaker can deliver only about 250 words per minute. That allows you plenty of time to daydream. While your mind wanders, you may miss important points, and you may have difficulty picking up the train of thought. A good speaker takes those occurrences into account and will organize the speech accordingly. The speaker can give summaries, itemize points, and give clear objectives for every section; however, the task of communicating is shared with the audience. Good listening requires determination and discipline. The suggestions below can help you to become an effective listener:

1. Limit distractions.

2. Look at the speaker. Looking at the speaker rather than staring into space will help you to follow the speech.

3. Avoid being critical of the delivery of the speech, that is, the voice, the appearance, or the nonverbal skills of the speaker. Control your emotions.

4. Concentrate on the content of the speech. What does the speaker say? What is the central theme?

5. Listen for ideas and patterns of reasoning.

6. Imagine that you must summarize the speech for someone else several hours after you have heard it.

7. Listen actively rather than passively. Summarize material and points in your mind as you listen.

8. Be open minded. Do not make up your mind beforehand that the topic is boring.

EVALUATION OF ORAL REPORTS

Evaluation
The evaluation of the speech must be thorough and systematic to be of any use in the future.

Part of every presentation is an **evaluation** of your strengths and weaknesses. You must be honest with yourself as you go through that process. Glossing over problems will not improve your skills as a speaker. You must determine what went particularly well and what went less well, and you will also want to find out the reasons. A checklist like the one in Exhibit 16.5 might be a good place to write down the main points in your evaluation. You can use this feedback in preparing for your next presentation.

Exhibit 16.5   **Form for Speech Evaluation**

	Good	Average	Weak	Comments
1. Organization				
2. Summary				
3. Transitions				
4. Examples				
5. Visual aids				
6. Eye contact				
7. Ability to adapt to audience				
8. Confidence of speaker				
9. Nervousness				
10. Effectiveness of preparation				
11. Effective adaptation to time constraints				
12. Summary of material				
13. Overall evaluation of speech				

ADAPTATION TO GROUP SIZE AND SETTING

A presentation to a large group requires different skills, techniques, and preparation than a presentation to a small group. The following points may help you in giving an effective speech to groups of different sizes and in different settings.

LARGE GROUPS

1. Your presentation to a large group must be more formal than to a small group.
2. You are removed from the audience; usually you will stand behind a podium, probably on a stage.
3. Your visual aids must be large enough so that people sitting in the back of the room can see them.
4. In a large group people may feel uncomfortable asking questions; therefore, you must sense whether people understand what you say. You must watch the audience closely for feedback.
5. You may ask the audience to hold questions until the end of your presentation.

SMALL GROUPS

1. A group of 20 to 40 people is relatively intimate. You may stand close to the audience. This provides you with better feedback, but the audience can also look more closely at you.
2. In a small group you may accept questions during your presentation, but you can also ask your audience to hold questions until the end.
3. Whether you invite an open discussion or maintain a more formal atmosphere will depend on the topic and the group. If you give a presentation to colleagues on a topic that has already been discussed at length, you might decide in favor of a dialogue. However, the danger with a dialogue or discussion is that you lose control of the presentation. The audience may jump ahead and bring up points that you prefer to bring up later. Unless everyone is well informed, the organization of the material may suffer with too much audience participation. The relationship between facts may be lost as a result.

CONFERENCE SETTING

1. In a conference setting people usually sit around a table. The group is closed.

2. You may stand or sit for your presentation. Your decision will depend on the group and on the material. Some groups may resent it if you sit. Others may prefer that you sit so that the presentation is more personal.

3. If you have visual aids, you may need to stand.

4. In small conference groups, you must be aware of political currents. Your personal relationship with group members may influence the acceptance of your presentation.

5. The place on the agenda and the time allotted for your presentation are key factors in your presentation.

6. To save time, you may use handouts.

7. The conference setting is usually goal oriented. Your presentation will not be simply a general overview or a pep talk. In a conference setting you present specific issues about which many group members may be knowledgeable. You must therefore be able to support your presentation with data and facts.

SUMMARY OF LEARNING OBJECTIVES

To Prepare a Good Oral Presentation.
In the preparation you must determine the purpose and the situation of the speech. You must determine who the audience is and what visual aids to use. You must also evaluate your strengths and weaknesses as a speaker.

To Prepare Effective Visual Aids.
Many ways are available to present material visually. You may choose a slide projector, an opaque projector, an overhead projector, a flipchart, a blackboard, or a handout. Size of the audience, size of the room, and purpose of the presentation will influence the method of visual presentation.

To Evaluate Strengths and Weaknesses of a Speaker.
You must determine what makes you comfortable and what makes you nervous. Do you prefer note cards or the complete report? Do you read your speech or memorize it? Do you have a tendency to speak longer than you were asked to speak? Honest answers to these questions will help you prepare and deliver your speech.

To Deliver an Informative Speech.
You should use audience feedback to adapt your speech to the audience. You must show confidence, friendliness, and sincerity.

To Analyze the Audience and Adapt the Speech to the Audience.
Audience analysis is an ongoing process. You must read the nonverbal signals the audience sends you to adapt to your audience. Most audiences are friendly and show goodwill.

To Evaluate the Presentation Objectively.
After you have given your speech, you must evaluate your performance and use the feedback to improve future speeches.

QUESTIONS AND PROBLEMS

1. What are the characteristics of a good oral presentation?
2. How can you overcome nervousness before and during a speech?
3. Discuss the role of nonverbal communication during a speech.
4. Discuss the role of appearance when giving a speech.
5. What role does the audience play during a speech?
6. What is the role of eye contact?
7. Listen to a speech and try to write down the most important points afterward.
8. The next time you listen to a speech, evaluate the performance of the speaker.
9. Discuss the three delivery styles—reading of a speech, reciting from memory, and using note cards.
10. Discuss the elements of good listening.

NOTES

1 John T. Molloy, *The Woman's Dress for Success Book* (Chicago: Follett Publishing, 1977).

CHAPTER SEVENTEEN

WRITING WITH

THE COMPUTER

LEARNING OBJECTIVES

- To become aware of the influence of technology on report writing functions in the office.
- To understand the principles underlying word processing.
- To understand the influence of word processing on the planning, writing, and editing process.
- To become familiar with the use of software to check style and spelling.
- To realize the potential of databases and spreadsheets in report writing.
- To understand the principles of electronic mail.

THE ROLE OF
THE MANAGER IN A MODERN ORGANIZATION

During the past 100 years production processes have changed tremendously. Many workers have been replaced by machines, and robots have become commonplace on assembly lines. As a result, production costs have decreased while blue-collar productivity has increased. Changes in offices have come more slowly. Until recently telephones, typewriters, carbon paper, and mimeograph machines were the major equipment in many offices and, as a result, white-collar productivity has not increased significantly during the past 50 years. The table in Exhibit 17.1 shows when important new types of supplies and equipment were introduced into offices.

Today, word-processing equipment and microcomputers are changing the work of the secretary, but the influence of the technology does not stop there. The new equipment is beginning to influence the structure of the organization and to change the role of both the manager and the secretary.

Traditionally a businessperson wrote reports in longhand and gave them to a secretary. At the beginning of his career he might share a secretary with several other people, but as he advanced in the corporation, he might ultimately have his own private secretary. The private secretary's many functions included typing, editing, and proofreading. In other instances secretaries wrote reports from rough notes. It was generally understood that a

Exhibit 17.1 **Office Innovations**

Carbon paper	1806
Typewriters	1872
Mimeograph machines	1875
Telephones	1877
Ballpoint pens	1938
Electric computers	1946
Dry-duplicating machines	1950
Mass-produced computers	1951
Word-processing equipment	1976
Local area networks	1979
Integrated office automation	1982

Source: Stanley Rothman and Charles Mosman. *Computer Uses and Issues.* Chicago: Science Research Association, 1985, p. 243.

manager's time was too valuable to be spent typing. A manager did not need keyboarding skills. If the manager decided to make any changes in the final copy, the secretary retyped the entire report.

Self-correcting cartridges and memory typewriters brought significant changes and made life easier for the secretary. Now the secretary did not have to retype an entire page because of a typographical error, although even a memory typewriter did not permit the rearrangement of material once it had been typed. The new typewriters did improve the appearance of reports and letters and saved some time. They did not, however, change the roles of the manager and the secretary in any significant way.

The traditional division of work was not questioned until the arrival of microcomputers, which are beginning to have a significant impact on many business organizations. As an example, Jeff Johnson, a manager in a large insurance company, no longer has a private secretary. He abolished that position shortly after he began using a microcomputer. He decided that the time of his former secretary, now an administrative assistant, was too valuable to be spent typing reports from longhand drafts. He now keys in his own reports, which a secretary will later finish and proofread. The report is typed only once.

The time that was formerly spent on retyping an entire report can now be used to make corrections and improvements. Of course, to write efficiently on the computer, the manager needs computer and keyboarding skills. In the future more and more businesses will probably look for good keyboarding skills in the people they hire. Research indicates that managers with poor keyboarding skills are reluctant to use the computer, and a computer assigned to a manager who does not use it is a waste of money. If you think that keyboarding wastes a manager's valuable time, consider that reports composed on the microcomputer require less time than those written out in longhand.

Writing with a microcomputer requires an understanding of word processing, which can be done on either a free-standing word processor or on a microcomputer with a word-processing software package. If the equipment is to be used strictly for typing and editing texts, a word processor may be the best choice because it is faster. If it will also be used for statistical calculations, graphs and tables, then a microcomputer is the best choice.

Free-standing, or dedicated, word processors are mostly used in word-processing centers. The word-processing center in that sense has replaced the typing pool. The report writer may bring the rough copy to the word-processing center, where secretaries type it and then return it for revision. The writer may also dictate the report into the word-processing center. The difference between this and the old typing pool is that corrections are easier to make. The report does not need to be retyped when the manager decides to rearrange paragraphs, change a phrase, or change a word. A word-processing center increases productivity, but it does not change the roles of people in the organization.

HARDWARE AND SOFTWARE FOR REPORT WRITING

Hardware
Hardware includes computer, monitor, and printer.

Managers usually work with microcomputers rather than with free-standing word processors. The **hardware** components of a microcomputer system for report writing are the central unit, keyboard, monitor, disks, disk drive, and printer. The actual **computer** is a minute but sophisticated microchip inside the central unit. The size of this tiny component determines the memory capacity of the system.

Computer
The computer is the central unit in the system.

Memory capacity is given in Ks. One K represents 1,000 bytes; a 64K computer has 64,000 bytes. One byte is roughly equal to one alphabet character or numeral. Thus, if you type one letter or one period, you use up one byte. The first personal computers had an 8K capacity. Today, many microcomputers have more than 250K, and this can be increased by installing a card with additional Ks.

Software
Computer programs are software.

Not all of a 64K computer's 64,000 bytes are available for entry, however. Some are needed for the **word-processing software package**—that is, whatever computer program you use for writing reports. You can develop your own programs, but for most report-writing tasks you will be better off purchasing commercial ones. To do word processing on a microcomputer, you would begin by loading into it one of the good available word-processing programs, such as WordStar, EasyWriter, VisiWord, or Perfect Writer.

Keyboard
The keyboard is the data-entry device.

The **keyboard** is the device for entering material into the computer. It often resembles a typewriter keyboard. Most older microcomputers have stationary keyboards built into the central unit, an arrangement that allows little flexibility. Newer ones, with detached keyboards, allow more flexibility in arranging the hardware on the desk. Today, data entry does not always occur via a keyboard. Some computers can read text and enter it into memory. Some computers have voice recognition capabilities, allowing the writer to speak directly into the memory of the computer.

Monitor
The monitor is the data-display unit.

The **monitor** displays on a screen the material in memory. The report writer can see the text as it is being typed. Monitors are available in black and white or color. Sometimes the monitor and the computer are one unit. The Macintosh has a built-in monitor; the monitor for the IBM PC is separate. The new monitors tend to be smaller than the old ones but are easier on the eyes because they produce clearer, high-resolution images on the screen.

Disk
The disk stores information.

Software is on **disks**, and you can also use disks to store your work. Material on disks is stored in circles called *tracks*. When the number of circles is increased, the storage capacity increases. Capacity can also be increased by using both sides of the disk.

Most microcomputers can use either hard or floppy disks for storage. Floppy disks are less expensive but hold much less data. About 28 floppy disks are needed to hold ten megabytes of hard-disk data. Hard disks rotate about ten times faster than floppy disks, speeding up overall operations.

Material can also be stored on inexpensive tape or cartridges. Data stored on both types of disks is in sections that can be accessed randomly. Material on tapes or cassettes, on the other hand, is stored sequentially and therefore takes longer to find. Although tapes have a high storage capacity and are the most mechanically reliable computer storage medium, they are very slow.

Disk Drive
The disk drive houses the disk.

The **disk drives** hold the disks. Sometimes the disk drive(s) is built in, as in the IBM PC and the Macintosh; sometimes the disk drives are separate, as with the Apple II+. The number of disk drives needed is determined by the complexity of the task you perform and by the software you use. The word-processing package WordStar, for example, sometimes requires two disk drives. The software package must remain in the disk drive in order to use the functions of the word-processing package. In order to save your material, you need a disk that goes into a second disk drive. Software that must stay in the disk drive is called a resident package. Applewriter, in contrast to WordStar, can be removed from the disk drive as soon as it has been loaded into memory. When you are ready to save your report, the disk for storing the material can be put into the same disk drive.

Printer
The printer prints the data from the computer.

Two basic types of **printers** are the letter quality and the dot matrix. The letter-quality produces printed material comparable in quality to an electronic typewriter. Printwheels are available with a variety of scripts. If you use your printer mostly for correspondence, a letter-quality printer is probably the best choice. Dot-matrix printers print material in a sequence of dots rather than solid lines. By using a high-quality ribbon and making a photocopy of the final copy, you can achieve results that approach letter quality. Graphics require a dot-matrix printer or ink-blot printer.

STEPS IN WORD PROCESSING

Some basic steps in word-processing are the same, regardless of the type of computer system or software package you use:

1. Load the package into the memory of the computer. To do this insert the word-processing disk into the designated disk drive and turn on the computer. You may have to answer a sequence of questions to bring the opening menu on the screen. A menu is a list of options. For example, the opening menu may give you the options of printing a file, exiting the system, or opening a file. If you want to open a file, follow the necessary commands to call up the main menu.

    Word-processing packages all differ. WordStar, for example, provides the main menu at the top of the screen. The main menu tells what controls you need in order to perform certain functions. Applewriter, on the other hand, does not display the main menu on the screen, but you can call it up if you need the information. The specific commands are different and the specific capabilities are different from package to package, but the basic elements are the same.

    Most word-processing packages provide basic information in the data line at the top of the screen. The data line gives the name of the file you are working on. Some packages tell you what page you are on; some list the amount of space left in memory, the length of the paragraph on which you are working, and the position of the cursor (pointer) in relation to the entire document.

2. Key in your report. When you use WordStar, you must name a new file before you can start working on it; if you use Applewriter, you name the file when you save it on the disk. As you type, the text appears on the monitor. You can correct mistakes as you go along or wait until you have finished your rough draft.

3. Periodically save your text on the disk.

4. Edit the draft. You can edit shorter documents directly on the screen. For longer documents you may want to print out a **hard copy** on which to edit, especially if you think you may want to reorganize material. With practice, you will find that you can do more editing on the screen.

5. Print the edited report.

6. Save the final copy on the disk, so that you can refer to it later.

7. Make a backup copy for all important reports.

Hard Copy
A hard copy is a printed output from a computer.

WORD-PROCESSING FUNCTIONS

With a word-processing package you can perform the following tasks:

Locate Any Point in the Text. No matter where you are or how long your text is, you can easily move to the end or the beginning. You can either move the cursor in increments of 12 lines or scroll the text up or down. *Scrolling* means to roll the text as if it were a scroll.

Delete and Add Letters, Words, and Paragraphs. All word-processing packages allow you to delete and add text. The specific steps for this process vary from program to program, but in most cases the task is easy.

Reorganize Material. If you want to exchange your second and third paragraphs, for example, you can switch them easily. The specific commands vary, but all packages allow you to move paragraphs. If you know that you will frequently use this function to move large chunks of text, you should pay attention to that feature when you choose software. Some packages allow you to move larger chunks than others.

Indent. Whole sections are easy to indent and, until you change the command, they remain indented.

Underline. You can automatically underline words or sentences.

Highlight. Most word-processing packages allow you to print material in boldface type for emphasis.

Vary the Print Type. You may use italics, German script, or Gothic script. The special capabilities will depend on the compatability of your computer, the software, and the printer. Special commands may be necessary to access particular capabilities.

Print Foreign Characters. More and more packages allow you to easily print Greek and Russian letters, as well as German umlauts and French accents above letters. If you use foreign characters frequently, you may want to make the ease with which you can obtain them a major criterion for selecting the package.

Find Words or Strings of Words and Replace Them. Assume, for example, that you use the company name a number of times in a report about Quaker Oats. Rather than write the name out each time, you choose to write the letter Q instead. After you finish your report, you command the computer to find each Q and replace it automatically with the full company name.

THE INFLUENCE OF TECHNOLOGY ON THE PLANNING AND WRITING PROCESS

In order to use the microcomputer to its fullest potential, you must compose on it. If you use it simply as a fancy typewriter, you waste time and the opportunity to key in your ideas as they occur. If you write your report in longhand and revise it before dictating to a secretary or keying in the report yourself, you defeat the purpose of the system.

PLANNING ON THE MICROCOMPUTER

Planning takes time. The report writer may write many drafts of an outline, either using the cut-and-paste method, or retyping the outline until she has it the way she wants it. The outlining task can be much more efficient with the computer. Planning programs designed especially for outlining include MaxThink, ThinkTank, and Framework. Such programs are sometimes called idea processors. Of course, programs cannot process ideas; people do. However, the programs can help in organizing the ideas.

In the early stage of planning you can use the programs to record your brainstorming results by making lists of concepts, facts, and tentative approaches to solving the problem. In the second stage you can begin to process the list. You can organize, categorize, and establish hierarchical relationships between ideas. In the third stage you can develop paragraphs of text under each heading and thus actually write the report.

Planning programs allow you to view the entire outline, a single major heading with all the related subheadings, or only the major headings. For example, when you are working on a detailed outline of one section of a report, you can collapse the material so that you have only the major outline on the screen. If you are considering whether to rearrange material, you can examine the outline to see where it might fit best. The planning programs encourage experimenting with the arrangement of material and examining the relationship between ideas. As a result, they help you to focus on the problem.

WRITING ON THE MICROCOMPUTER

Writing with a computer requires a different kind of memory and imagination from the traditional writing process. When composing on the screen you never see an entire page. You cannot place three or four pages side by side. You must therefore remember what you have written. Of course, you can reread a section, and a split screen will enable you to view two sections simultaneously. You can check consistent use of terminology. You can check for contradictions. You can decide where a text segment fits best. Given the size of the screen, however, the sections are fairly small. Looking at a split screen is not the same as looking simultaneously at different sections of a report on sheets of paper spread out in front of you. You must therefore keep in mind how the parts fit together and how a particular section fits into the whole.

Writing with a computer also requires a special visual imagination because you do not see the entire page on the screen. Regardless of whether you type solid text or design tables and graphs, you must be able to imagine how the whole page will look when it is printed.

The writing process itself changes, too. The writer still must plan well, but the computer can help in developing a more improvisational view of writing. The act of writing can help the writer to discover what he should be saying. As long as the writer writes with pen and paper, this discovery process is hindered by the impossibility of writing as fast as the ideas flow. Even a typewriter fails to keep up with the thought process for a number of reasons. The writer must return the carriage. The amount of time this takes may appear insignificant, but it does add up. Each carriage return also tends to interrupt the flow of ideas. The awareness that typing errors mean retyping the page further slows down the writing process.

Although matching the speed of writing with the flow of ideas is probably not possible, good keyboarding skills and a microcomputer help to record ideas quickly. The speed also increases because the writer does not have to dread revisions. Errors can be easily corrected, and the automatic wraparound makes the carriage return superfluous. In automatic wraparound the cursor automatically moves from the right side of the screen to the left side of the next line. The only time the writer must push the return button is to start a new paragraph.

Many writing instructors in the past emphasized deliberate and careful writing. Revisions were often seen as punishment for not doing an acceptable job the first time. With the microcomputer revision takes on a different dimension. The clear distinction between various drafts disappears unless you print out a hard copy. From planning to final copy the drafts flow into each other.

When you first key your ideas into the computer, you should concentrate on the content and the flow of ideas. You need not be particularly careful about sequences, spelling, grammar, or style because you can easily correct any mistakes. Revision and editing of mechanics, content, and style become essential, but revision is not seen as punishment for failing the first time. Revision is seen as an essential part of the writing process.

It does not matter how you start the report. You do not have to wait for the perfect beginning. If you are not certain of a transition, you may simply type in the word *transition* to flag the spot so that you can go back to it later. Because you can start at any point in the report, writing with a microcomputer may help you to overcome writer's block. Because revision does not include the frustration of recopying the same material, the microcomputer encourages more substantive changes and improvements.

Revision is so easy that writers may more readily give and accept criticism and suggestions for change. Let us assume that a manager looking over the third draft of a long report would like to add a few words on the second page and omit a sentence on page four. These minor changes would enhance clarity but would require the secretary to retype several pages, if not the entire report. The manager decides against the change, rationalizing that the report is good enough and that the additional time required could be used better. If the same report were on a word processor, the last minute revisions would be so easy to make that the manager might go ahead with them and thus improve the report.

Revision cannot be an endless process. Business rarely ever permits enough time to reach absolute perfection in a report. A business writer must judge when to stop revising. Not only does revision reach a point of diminishing returns, but reports must be finished and submitted to meet deadlines.

Exhibit 17.2 illustrates the writing process when using a computer. After keying in the report, the writer edits it on the screen and makes necessary corrections. Next she checks the report for spelling and format. Then she prints the report and edits it. She keys in the changes and again checks for spelling and format. Then she once more prints and checks the report. If there are no errors, she can submit it; otherwise, she must key additional corrections into the computer. All reports should go through at least one hard copy for editing before the final copy is printed.

Writing with the microcomputer has many advantages, but it also creates some problems. Computers make the report look so perfect that

Exhibit 17.2 **Writing with a Micro Word Processor**

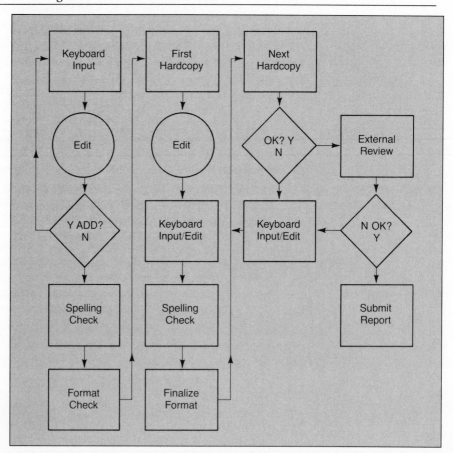

Source: Reprinted with permission of William James Buchholz, Bentley College, Waltham, MA.

problems in content and meaning might be overlooked. Visually, a computer-produced report is appealing. The centered headings, the footnotes in proper form, the justified margins, the freedom from spelling and grammatical errors—all of these can lull the writer into overlooking other important elements.

Using software properly is important. You can use programs to check for mechanics. Freed from the drudgery of proofreading for certain types of errors, you can use the time gained to polish elements of content, meaning, and organization. These elements are essential to a report's effectiveness.

EDITING SOFTWARE

A number of software packages on the market will check spelling, grammar, punctuation. A writer may, of course, edit and proofread without this additional software; however, as you may know from experience, typographical errors are easy to miss. A spelling error made because you do not know how to spell is impossible to catch. If you are at all uncertain, you must consult a dictionary, which takes time.

Spell checkers are available in a variety of sizes. For example, the Word Plus and the Random House Proofreader contain dictionaries ranging from 20,000 to 83,000 words. A small dictionary may not find all errors; on the other hand, the larger the dictionary, the longer time the computer takes to search the material for errors. For most purposes a dictionary of about 50,000 words should be sufficient. Most dictionaries can be amended. If the checker does not have words you frequently use, you can add them.

Spell checkers have difficulty with proper names, abbreviations, prefixes, and combination words. Random House Proofreader and Word Plus allow the user to turn off the search for words that start with capital letters. Spell checkers flag potential errors, but they cannot decide whether the writer wants to use the word *accept* or *except*. By questioning the spelling, however, they will require the writer to evaluate word usage in the report. You should proofread your report carefully even after you have used a spell checker because not all of your words may be in the dictionary.

Style evaluators, such as Grammatik, examine writing style and punctuation. They go beyond the spell checkers, but many also perform the spell check function. They often check for problems in the following categories:

Informal usage of a word
Archaic usage
Capitalization errors
Gender-specific terms
Jargon
Awkward usage
Overworked phrases

Commonly misspelled words
Punctuation errors
Vague adverbs
Wordy phrases

Style evaluators do not uncover all true errors, and they may flash some words that are correct. When a writer uses the word *affect* correctly, the computer may ask whether the writer meant *affect* or *effect.*

Most packages are easy to use. The writer can decide whether the computer is to show each error on the screen or whether errors should be corrected when printing the document later. In all cases the writer decides whether to make a change. Some programs provide a summary of the style analysis. For example, they may indicate whether a writer overuses certain words and phrases or overuses passive voice. Some also calculate average sentence length. This is useful information because sentence length influences the readability of a text. Some programs identify these problems with phrases:

Awkward phrases
Clichés
Erroneous phrases
Folksy phrases
Muddy phrases
Pompous phrases
Redundant phrases
Wordy phrases

Although style programs cannot correct the overuse of passive voice, they can help the writer to identify passive voice each time it occurs.

SOFTWARE SUPPORT SYSTEMS

Reports are composed not only of words but also of charts and tables used to illustrate relationships between data. A number of software programs on the market help the report writer to organize and present data visually. Database management programs, graphics packages, and **spreadsheets** are invaluable tools for the report writer. Computer graphics were discussed in detail in Chapter 13. This section will concentrate on database management and spreadsheets.

Spreadsheet
A spreadsheet is a program for entering, manipulating, and displaying data in table form.

DATABASE MANAGEMENT

A database is an organized collection of facts. An example is the card catalog in a library, which is an inventory report. It enables the user to know whether a particular book is owned by the library. Traditionally a librarian wrote a new card for each acquisition and added it to the catalog. Adding a vast number of titles every year made the upkeep of the catalog difficult and time consuming.

A computer system speeds up the process of cataloging, and the catalog itself takes up less space. In addition, several databases can be linked. The result is an integrated database. For example, the catalog of a Chicago library can be linked to the catalogs of other libraries around the country, enabling the user to determine which one has a specific book.

Database management helps store, organize, and retrieve information. For example, XYZ Car Company may want to send information on new cars to everyone who owns an XYZ car. Another company may need to find information on past product-development decisions or to update product and customer lists. Still another company may want to add categories to its employee-evaluation systems; it may want to establish an employee profile. For all these tasks the companies need information. The material in the system can be used as research data for an in-depth report and also may form a report in itself. A printout of customer lists, for example, is an informational report.

In the past, even though needed information was often in the company files, it was difficult to find and organize. In many cases redoing a survey was easier than searching through disorganized files. With database management the management of information is much easier. With a computerized database management system, for example, an inventory manager can shift and centralize inventory and at the same time generate up-to-date inventory reports. If Store X sells a ski jacket, the computer will decrease the inventory at the central inventory control. If Store X only has small and medium jackets, the clerk can find out from the computer which store in the area has large jackets in stock and can order one.

Ideally each company would have its own tailor-made database management system. Because of the expense, however, users adapt a number of standard systems on the market to their particular needs. For report writers a database management system is helpful in the research stage. As an example, for a report on production costs the writer can retrieve past cost figures, production volume, quality-control statistics, cost of raw materials, and inventory. Rather than read through old files, the writer can use the computer to obtain answers quickly.

SPREADSHEETS

A spreadsheet organizes information into rows and columns. Each row, or line, represents a single item or class of items. The columns in a line are subgroups of the item. The sum of all columns for an item add up to the total for that particular item. The first spreadsheet for microcomputers was Visacalc. Later came Supercalc, Magicalc, Lotus, and Lotus 1-2-3.

Exhibit 17.3 **Organization of a Spreadsheet**

Budget Items	Jan.	Feb.	March	April	May	June
Sales	10,000	12,000	9,000	14,000	14,000	16,000
Expenses						
Production	3,000	3,600	2,700	4,200	4,200	4,800
Advertising	500	600	550	600	650	700
Personnel	5,000	5,600	5,000	6,000	6,000	6,000
Rent	500	540	480	580	580	620
Taxes	400	480	360	560	560	640
Utilities	200	250	300	200	200	300
Total Expenses	9,600	11,070	9,390	12,140	12,190	13,060
Balance	400	930	(390)	1,860	1,810	2,940

A spreadsheet answers the question, "What if?" It helps in making predictions, planning alternatives, analyzing trends, graphing results, and producing reports. A manager putting together a budget for the coming year could enter relevant budget information like that in Exhibit 17.3 onto a spreadsheet. The budget includes such items as sales, production, advertising, personnel costs, rent, taxes, and utilities, which are all related. For example, production influences sales and personnel costs. Sales and production influence advertising costs. Taxes are dependent partially on production and revenue. Utilities are influenced by production and weather. Rent may be a function of profit.

In the past year, total sales for the business illustrated in Exhibit 17.3 were $169,000, and total expenses were $145,860. The business earned a profit of $23,140. Based on past records, the manager can establish the relationship between various budget items. If, for example, rent is composed of a base figure and a percentage of sales, the manager can enter the formula rather than the absolute figure for rent into the cell. The computer will calculate the exact amount. If sales increase in January, rent will increase. If rent is $300 plus 2 percent of sales, the manager can either figure the rent or enter the formula. The entering of the formula makes more sense because the computer can easily calculate the rent if the other variables change.

The manager can ask the computer what will happen to rent if sales triple, quadruple, or are cut in half. The computer can also calculate what would happen if the cost of raw materials rose by ten percent. When the price of the product is raised, sales may decline. Once the relationships between the variables have been established and entered, the computer can project a budget. As key components in the budget change, the final budget changes. The manager can experiment with the budget and develop several different approaches.

July	Aug.	Sept.	Oct.	Nov.	Dec.	Total
16,000	16,000	15,500	16,500	15,000	15,000	169,000
4,800	4,800	4,650	4,950	4,500	4,500	50,700
800	750	750	750	750	750	8,150
6,500	6,000	6,000	6,000	6,000	6,000	70,100
620	620	610	630	600	600	6,980
640	640	620	660	600	600	6.760
300	300	250	250	300	320	3,170
13,660	13,110	12,880	13,240	12,750	12,770	145,860
2,340	2,890	2,620	3,260	2,250	2,230	23,140

In the first microcomputers it was not possible to combine word-processing and spreadsheet functions. Until recently the writer could not integrate the spreadsheet directly in the report and move freely back and forth between word processing and spreadsheet. To use the spreadsheet in a report, the writer had to abandon the word-processing package. To use information created with a word-processing package, the writer had to abandon the spreadsheet.

Integrated Software
Integrated software combines the functions of several programs.

Today, a number of **integrated software** packages allow an easy switch from spreadsheet to database to word processing. In most cases the commands are integrated also. In an integrated package the same command will delete information from the spreadsheet, the word-processing program, and the database. The writer can copy information from one application to another. For example, numbers from a spreadsheet can go into a report in the word processor, and addresses in the database can be copied into a letter. Some of the most popular integrated software packages are Symphony, Jazz, and Appleworks. Because these integrated packages use from 150K to 250K, the computer must be powerful.

ELECTRONIC MAIL

Electronic Mail
Electronic mail consists of messages sent via computer.

Electronic mail, which is a logical extension of word processing, can improve the collection, routing, storage, and retrieval of interoffice communication. Its efficiency and speed result from the delivery of messages without first printing them. Electronic mail will not replace written reports, but it may to some extent replace routine memos and messages.

The central computer can be programmed so that everyone who has access to a terminal can read messages that are generated anywhere in the company. To cut down on information overflow, users should receive only information that is important to them. With electronic mail a section of the computer's memory is allocated for each user. The segment, reserved for a user, becomes that user's mailbox. Access is by a password, which ensures privacy and confidentiality. Incoming messages are stored in the mailbox until the user wants to read them.

Let us assume Lupe Gallardo works for a company that uses electronic mail for interoffice communication. As she checks her mailbox for any messages, she finds a request for information on the evaluation of Jesse Hurtado. Because she wants to have a record of the request for Hurtado's file, she prints out a hard copy. The evaluation took place the day before, and the file is still at her desk. She can enter and send the message electronically to John Lauger who requested the information.

Also in her mailbox she finds a notice of a meeting scheduled for the next day on personnel evaluation procedures. She enters the time on her calendar and deletes the message from the mailbox. She then enters and sends some ideas she wants to share with some colleagues before the meeting.

Electronic mail allows users to send and read messages at their convenience. They need not page coworkers for discussions or interrupt their own work to take calls. Electronic mail reduces paper handling and waste. Because of its impersonal nature, however, users sometimes prefer a telephone call or a face-to-face discussion. Electronic mail is not a substitute for all interpersonal communication, but it can facilitate the flow of communications.

Electronic mail also provides an efficient and effective way of communicating with people outside the company. This requires sending messages through the company's computer to outside computers.

SUMMARY OF LEARNING OBJECTIVES

To Become Aware of the Influence of Technology on Report Writing Functions in the Office.
The regular use of microcomputers in businesses will change the traditional roles of the secretary and the manager. Managers will increasingly need good keyboarding skills.

To Understand the Principles Underlying Word Processing.
With the help of a word-processing package writers can reorganize material, delete and add material, underline, highlight, use foreign characters, and find and replace words or strings of words.

To Understand the Influence of Word Processing on the Planning, Writing, and Editing Process.
Idea-processing programs can help the writer to plan and organize a report outline.

Because making changes and reorganizing the text material is so easy, the microcomputer may help the writer to overcome writer's block. Once the material is on the screen, the writer can concentrate on improvements rather than on retyping. The microcomputer allows concentrating on content and meaning.

To Become Familiar with the Use of Software to Check Style and Spelling. A number of software packages on the market will check the text for spelling, grammar, and style. Programs can flag spelling errors and possible style problems, but they cannot make decisions. The report writer still must proofread and carefully edit the report.

To Realize the Potential of Databases and Spreadsheets in Report Writing. Spreadsheets allow the writer to produce appropriate tables and graphs to enhance the meaning of the report. Spreadsheets are helpful in examining options as conditions change. Integrated software combines the functions of several programs such as word processing, spreadsheet, and database.

To Understand the Principles of Electronic Mail.
Electronic mail transmits reports via the computer and thus reduces the use of paper. Special passwords protect access to information.

QUESTIONS AND PROBLEMS

1. What is hardware? What is software?
2. What major hardware pieces do you need for a functional microcomputer system?
3. What are the basic functions of word-processing packages?
4. Discuss some of the advantages and disadvantages of composing text on a microcomputer.
5. What are some potential disadvantages of using a word processor for writing?
6. Discuss computer memory as it relates to report writing.
7. Compile an annotated bibliography on spell checkers.
8. Read and summarize four or more articles dealing with the impact of the microcomputer on the writing process.
9. Read and summarize two or more articles on the impact of electronic mail on business communication.
10. If you have the opportunity to write on a microcomputer, describe how it affects your style and your writing process. What do you like about it? What do you dislike?

CHAPTER EIGHTEEN

INTERNATIONAL

COMMUNICATIONS

LEARNING OBJECTIVES

- To understand the influence of language and cultural differences in international reporting.
- To be aware of the impact of organizational structures on reporting in international business.
- To become knowledgeable about the impact of technology on international reporting.
- To be aware of different communication conventions.

Columbus took 70 days to make the trip from Spain to the Americas. Because transportation was slow, communications were slow. The exchange of goods also took much time. A ship might be gone for several years before returning with spices from India or silk from China. All this has changed. Today a letter from New York takes no longer to reach Frankfurt, Germany, than Austin, Texas. A manager in Chicago can call a partner in Tokyo or Sydney to discuss business opportunities. Telex makes even instant written communication possible. Contact with foreign businesses is faster, cheaper, and more frequent than at any other time in history.

If you are not interested in working overseas or for an international company, you may ask what this has to do with you and with report writing. The answer is that business will in all likelihood be even more international during the next 40 years than it is now, and you may work in **international business** whether you want to or not. Some experts predict that all business will someday be international. Even today an increasing number of medium and small companies are engaging in importing and exporting. To work in international business you do not have to work overseas. With the revolution in transportation and communications, you can do business with any business person in the world without leaving your desk.

Many banks are involved in international loans to help finance projects of foreign companies in this country or to provide money to American companies wishing to expand overseas. Even the investment departments of insurance companies look at overseas opportunities because, at present, one half of all equity investments are overseas.

International Business
Companies of all sizes are involved in international business.

If you plan a career in banking or insurance, you may therefore communicate with people from other countries and cultures. Your success will depend not only on your technical expertise but also your ability to communicate successfully with these people.

COMMUNICATION BACKGROUND

The more different the cultures and the languages, the more difficult it becomes to communicate effectively. An American of European descent and a European share a common Western heritage. Their histories are related, and they have common ancestors. Both America and Europe look to Greece and Rome as the cradles of their civilization. The American of European descent has much less in common with someone from Asia. Their languages, their histories, and their outlooks on life are different. They show their emotions in different ways. Americans, for example, show their joy and sorrow more openly than the Japanese.

Not every American is boisterous, of course, and not every Japanese is reserved and quiet. Individuals have their own characteristics. Yet, generalizations help in communicating with people from other cultures because the generalizations bring out some of the major differences.

Some people emphasize that all people are human beings and individuals. They resent the discussion of differences and prefer to concentrate on similarities. Although the orientation toward similarities may be very well meant, it can also lead to a false sense of security and cultural understanding. Superficial similarities between cultures can be deceptive and lead to serious misunderstandings.

A number of business managers, apprehensive about expanding to other cultures, begin their international ventures in Great Britain. They feel more comfortable doing business in Great Britain than in France because the language is the same and many customs are similar. They feel secure and are surprised when plans do not always work out. They would be well advised to remember Churchill's comment that we are two people divided by a common language.

As an example, assume that representatives of British and American business firms have met to negotiate a contract. The Americans would like to drop one point from the discussion, or, at the least, postpone discussion on this point until a later time. They suggest to the British tabling that particular point, and the British accept the suggestion. As the negotiations begin, however, the Americans are astonished as the British bring up that very point. To the Americans *tabling* means postponing or dropping a point, whereas to the British it means bringing a point to the table for discussion. Both sides understand the words, but they do not share a common meaning.

LANGUAGE PROBLEMS

The language problems in international business communication are obscured by statements such as "Everyone speaks English" or "English is the language of international business" or "One can always go to Berlitz and pick up a language in a few weeks."

International Language
Even though it is an international language, English is not spoken and understood by everyone.

It is true that students in many countries do learn English; in some, such as Germany, the study of English is compulsory. Many Japanese, Chinese, Indians, and Koreans study English. English is an **international language**. Because neither the English nor the Americans have ever been particularly protective of their language, English has absorbed words from many other languages. At the same time, English business terms have been absorbed into other languages. Business managers in many other countries, for example, speak of *marketing, stress, management,* and *training.* Computer terminology used around the globe is almost exclusively in English. The language in airport control towers is English. Given that so many people speak and understand English, the question becomes, Why should Americans bother to learn a foreign language?

First, having studied English does not mean that the speaker understands it perfectly. The knowledge of business terminology may be rudimentary and insufficient for contract negotiations. Second, cultural pride is a factor. Many business people in other countries resent always having to accommodate Americans. By speaking only English, Americans convey the message that other languages are not important. Finally, monolinguism is an expensive way of doing business. As a buyer you may be able to conduct business entirely in English, because the other person is eager to sell. If you are the seller, however, you must adapt. The Japanese say that the most important language in international business is the language of the customer.

A French businessman in the wool industry, for example, refused to see an English salesman who was unable even to make the appointment in French. Another French businessman refused to do business with an American manufacturer of components for printing equipment, even though he was interested in the product, because he believed that business is too personal a relationship to be conducted entirely through interpreters. He himself spoke English but was not willing to accommodate the American by always speaking and writing in English.

Knowledge of Culture
Effective international communication requires a knowledge of language and culture.

The mastery of a language goes beyond the mastery of mechanics; it includes a **knowledge of the culture**—particularly business conventions and practices. Americans tend to be informal. Moreover, the English language lacks the distinction of a familiar and polite form of the personal pronoun *you.* Whether addressing friends, a customer, a colleague, or the president of a company, the speaker uses the same word, *you.* Most other languages have a familiar and polite form—in German *Du* and *Sie,* in French *tu* and *vous,* and in Spanish *tu* and *usted.*

If Eric Vanderveer, an American, greets a German business person by saying "Hallo, Kurt. Wie geht es Dir?" he may have lost a business deal. The greeting, "Hello, Kurt. How are you?" is correct grammatically but incorrect culturally. Until they know each other well and have specifically agreed to say *Du* and to use first names, Eric Vanderveer should never call Mr. Miller by his first name or address him as *Du*. Even close friends in Europe are often on a last-name basis. Almost all other cultures are more formal than the American. Wanting to be friendly, Americans may alienate people from more formal backgrounds. What is appropriate and good business in Denver may not be good business in Frankfurt or Singapore.

Monolingual business people in an American firm have difficulty communicating with foreign subsidiaries. For example, the president of an American subsidiary in Mexico could not speak Spanish. One of his four vice presidents spoke good English; two spoke conversational English; one spoke little English. No one below the level of vice president could communicate in English. All reports, however, had to be sent in English to corporate headquarters in Chicago.

The vice presidents collected information in Spanish from their subordinates. They wrote their reports in Spanish and then translated them into English. Because the president did not speak Spanish, he could not judge if all the necessary data had been included or whether the reports were accurate. The vice presidents tended to be selective about what they told him. The process was frustrating and time consuming.

The president, not comfortable in Mexico, left after a short time and was replaced by someone who spoke both English and Spanish. This person collected the material and the reports from the vice presidents in Spanish and checked them for accuracy. He then wrote the reports in English. Because he was fluent in both languages, he understood the nuances of each. He could discuss production not only with the vice presidents but also with workers and supervisors on the shop floor.

Translation is a way of life in an international company. To overcome some of the language problems in international business, some multinational companies require all managers in a subsidiary to be fluent in English. Someone must be able to communicate with workers, customers, suppliers, and government agencies.

In most countries correspondence with the government and reports for the government must be prepared in the language of the country. In Saudi Arabia correspondence with the tax department must be in Arabic, for example. The French government expects reports in French; the Germans want them in German; the Chinese want them in Chinese. Some countries will accept material relating to international business in the local language and in English. Poland, for example, will accept documents in Polish and English. As a result, even Japanese business people will write in English when they transact business in Poland. India has two official languages, English and

Hindi. Americans should check the language policy of a country carefully before submitting final documents.

Interpreters
Translations are influenced by the culture of the interpreter.

Many companies employ **interpreters** and translators. Competent interpreters can solve most problems, but a Japanese interpreter brings his Japanese background to the translation, just as an American translator brings his American cultural background to the translation. The possibility of bias and error always exists.

Organize a Report
The organization of reports depends on the cultural background of the writer.

A writer may **organize a report** in many different ways. Depending on the purpose and the reader, it can be arranged deductively or inductively, chronologically, by geographic area, or by cause–effect or effect–cause relationships. However, different cultures approach reports differently. The Japanese tend to organize all reports in chronological order. They do not agree with our rearranging of the sequence of events. The Germans tend to have detailed discussions of background material regardless of the reader's needs or knowledge. A report without a detailed introductory section would be considered incomplete. An American who knows that the reader is familiar with the problem, on the other hand, will give little background information. The French begin with a presentation and discussion of the theory underlying the problem and then proceed to a discussion of the past. They tend to go from the abstract to the concrete. An American manager might be impatient with the slow start of the report and the seemingly irrelevant information at the beginning.

In Latin countries, subordinates are reluctant to pass along bad news. As a result, bad news may be sometimes omitted from a report or presented in such positive and misleading language that it would be difficult to base a decision on it. A manager might believe that the production department is performing well, for example, when in reality the company faces major problems. A manager who does not understand and learn to compensate for this cultural trait, especially one who cannot communicate with other managers and production workers in Spanish, may not be aware of the problem for quite some time.

COMMUNICATION CHANNELS AND ORGANIZATIONAL STRUCTURES

Organizational structures in most multinational corporations complicate the sharing of ideas even among associates with common understandings and backgrounds. Traditionally companies have had an international division in charge of all international activities including marketing, finance, accounting, and management. This **organizational structure** has sometimes interfered with important and necessary communication.

Organizational Structure
Many international businesses are changing their structures to facilitate international operations.

As an example, Laura Bozich has worked in marketing at her company's headquarters in Chicago for five years. She knows the marketing people well and is familiar with the company's overall marketing strategy, marketing philosophy, and advertising practices. Laura speaks Portuguese, and she is assigned to work in Brazil. She now reports to the manager in charge of South American operations in São Paulo. He, in turn, is responsible to the vice president of the international division in Chicago. As Laura considers a marketing problem in Brazil, should she go through channels or directly contact her friends in Chicago? From Chicago she may receive a quick answer; at least she can discuss the problem with marketing people she knows. Going through channels may require waiting for an answer. However, the manager in charge of Latin America has experience solving Latin American marketing problems, and in any case Laura needs to keep him informed of what she does so that he can develop a unified approach to marketing in Latin America.

More and more multinational companies are reorganizing. They are internationalizing all areas of the company by abolishing the international divisions. With the new arrangement marketing people from the subsidiary contact marketing people at headquarters; finance people contact finance people rather than the international division. As a result, more people must be familiar with international operations.

TECHNOLOGY IN INTERNATIONAL COMMUNICATIONS

American values and attitudes have led to an increase in written reports. Americans are number oriented. They want to know where they stand and want to have records of decisions and recommendations. Advances in technology have made it ever easier to write, type, print, duplicate, and store reports. Whether on paper or on disk, reports are usually saved.

Not all cultures share this desire for detailed records and multiple copies. People in Japan and the Middle East, for example, see business as a personal relationship. To request or provide detailed specifications or detailed records for all transactions might be seen as cold and impersonal. It would hinder the development of trust.

In the Middle East contracts are often confirmed with a handshake. Even if a contract is in writing, it may not be considered binding. As the business climate changes, it is assumed that the terms of the contract will change. An American firm that submits a proposal for a joint venture or a production facility may find that, even after the proposal has been formally accepted, the terms of the proposal are subject to renegotiation. Americans who insist on the terms of the contract do not understand local business practices. They should have studied both customs and contract law in order to avoid misunderstandings.

In Japan and China the writing of reports is much more time consuming and cumbersome than in America, another reason why **Oriental cultures**

Oriental Cultures
Cultures with complex languages and writing systems write fewer reports.

do not emphasize written reports. Written Chinese uses characters that stand for complete words, expressions, or even short sentences. Chinese does not have an alphabet. In addition, Chinese is written from top to bottom or right to left. This system does not lend itself to the use of typewriters.

A Chinese or Japanese typewriter needs 4,000 to 5,000 characters to be of any practical use in business. Such a typewriter takes up much space and is difficult to use. For example, Taiwan Normal University in Taipei, Taiwan, has only one Chinese typewriter, which is used for important and official occasions. One secretary in the university knows how to operate it. All memos within the university and most reports and correspondence to the outside are written by hand. Writing by hand is faster and more economical, although it takes much longer than typing a memo in English. Computers, even though they simplify the process, are still complex.

Even languages that use the Latin alphabet cannot always use the same computer hardware. One difficulty is keying in the German umlauts or the French accents. Some computer manufacturers are working on the problem of foreign letters. The number of strikes to produce a foreign letter depends on the computer, the software, and the printer. A writer who uses an Apple II+ computer, an Epson MX-80 printer, and the Applewriter word-processing package performs eleven strikes to write the German letter ä. A writer using foreign characters on a regular basis should examine the hardware and software for ease of entry.

The approach to filing differs from culture to culture. In America documents remain in the department that receives them. If Doug Dubois, for example, is transferred from production to personnel, the production reports that he wrote or received, while he worked in production, stay in the production department. This is not true in traditional Indian companies. In India, Doug would take the reports with him to his new position. Anyone who later needed to refer to a production report from that period would first have to determine that Doug was the production manager at that time.

Filing Practices
Traditional filing systems in some countries make it difficult to retrieve reports.

Filing practices also differ from country to country. In the Middle East files are traditionally stored vertically. Folders are simply stacked on top of one another. In a government office in Baghdad, for example, all the files containing visa applications and records were in piles about three feet high on the floor. When a foreign traveller applied for an extension of the visa, the official checked the passport to see when the visa was granted. A clerk then checked one of the piles to locate the file. After the official prepared the necessary documents for the extension, the clerk returned the folder to the pile. It is hardly surprising that files are not checked often and that only the most necessary documents are kept.

Americans use reports in planning and making business decisions. Americans are goal oriented, accustomed to looking ahead and shaping the future in their favor. In Islamic countries planning is frowned upon. The future is in Allah's hands. To plan is considered presumptuous and equated to playing God. Any planning documents must take Islamic attitudes toward planning into consideration.

COMMUNICATION CONVENTIONS

Communication Conventions
In order to avoid miscommunication, the international business writer must know how other cultures write dates and numbers.

Communication conventions differ among countries. Although some of the differences are simple, others are not. Europeans write the date in the following sequence: day, month, year. Americans use the sequence: month, day, year. For international business a new sequence is suggested: year, month, day. The Fourth of July could be written in the following ways:

American	European	International
7/4/19XX	4.7.19XX	19XX, 7, 4

Until all countries adopt the same format for writing dates, dates should always be spelled out in any international correspondence and contracts to avoid misunderstandings.

Times are written differently. Europeans use the 24-hour clock. A meeting at 4:30 p.m. takes place at 16:30 hours. Timetables for buses, planes, and trains are written on the 24-hour basis. Americans doing business with countries in the Far East must also take into account the international dateline. The 24 time zones around the world were established by Europeans at a time when most international traffic and commerce was across the Atlantic Ocean. The dateline where the first and twenty-fourth zones meet was therefore put in the middle of the Pacific.

With increasing business among the Pacific countries, the dateline poses a problem. For example, when it is March 3 in San Francisco, it is already March 4 in Tokyo. Contracts must stipulate exactly when they are to be fulfilled. The parties should agree on whether goods are to be delivered on March 3 in San Francisco or March 3 in Tokyo. When scheduling a meeting in Seoul, Korea, the manager from headquarters in Los Angeles must take into consideration the day that will be lost on the trip to Seoul. On the other hand, a business person traveling from Tokyo to San Francisco gains a day and may, if not careful, arrive one day earlier than necessary.

Conventions for writing numbers vary. Americans separate decimal fractions from whole numbers with a period. To facilitate reading large numbers, they use commas to set off thousands. In most other countries, the decimal fractions are set off by commas and the thousands by periods. The sum of three hundred and thirty-three thousand dollars and sixty-six cents could be written as follows:

American	European
$333,000.66	333.000,66$

Business partners must be aware of differing conventions. If necessary, large numbers should be spelled out.

Measurements for weights and distances vary. Most countries by now follow the metric system, and a number of business people argue that the traditional English system of ounces, gallons, pints, inches, feet, yards, miles, and bushels puts the United States at a competitive disadvantage in foreign markets. Therefore, many businesses in the United States have already converted to the metric system. The way measurements are communicated can differ also. For example, Americans measure fuel efficiency in miles per gallon. The Germans, on the other hand, measure it in terms of gasoline consumption per 100 kilometers. The conversion of miles per gallon into kilometers per liter is meaningless to a German.

Both German and American texts for business communication emphasize clarity, conciseness, and simple and direct language. A closer examination, however, will show that they use the terms differently. What a German considers a direct and straightforward opening may strike an American as stilted and unnatural. Perceptions of what is simple, concrete, direct, formal, and informal vary from culture to culture. Allowances for cultural differences must be made when either writing a report for a person in another country or reading one written by a foreign business person.

The following guidelines should help you in writing effective reports in international business:

1. Carefully examine whether the report is actually needed. This should be done for any report but is especially important for international business. You do not want to burden someone with reading or writing an unnecessary report in a foreign language.

2. Use even more simple and concrete English words than when writing to an American. Do not try to impress the foreign business person with your vocabulary. You want to get your message across. An exception to this rule might be when you write to a French person, because many difficult English words are derived from French and Latin. A Frenchman might more easily understand *ascend* and *descend* than *going up* and *going down*.

3. Keep paragraphs short and simple, with only one major idea in each one. Not all languages use paragraphs and punctuation. The Chinese and Japanese system of writing from top to bottom, for example, does not lend itself to forming paragraphs.

4. Pay attention to organization. The French want a presentation and discussion of theory before they consider practical applications. Germans want to know what a new machine can do for them and how they can use it before they read the engineering theory. The Japanese prefer a chronological arrangement of data.

5. Stick to the truth and avoid superlatives. Use words you can justify. Do not describe your product as the best unless you can prove that it is. You will need to be familiar with local laws as they apply to

superlatives and comparisons of products. Germany, for example, does not allow the comparison of specific products.

6. Know the technology. Your report must show that you understand the technical aspects of your subject. Chinese buyers, for example, are not interested in advertising slogans and the public-relations aspects of a product. They want to know the technical features of the product. They want numbers, graphs, charts, and detailed technical descriptions.

7. Use figures, pictures, graphs, and tables to make your point. The reader who has trouble with the text may still be able to understand the visual presentation.

8. Avoid idioms based on sports. Americans probably use more sports metaphors than the people in any other country. Even Americans who have never played sports understand and may use such phrases and expressions as *home run, the bases are loaded, third down and seven to go, Monday-morning quarterbacking,* and *touchdown.* The person from Germany, Saudi Arabia, or Korea may understand the separate words but not the idea expressed.

9. Avoid slang and buzzwords. Because they change frequently, they are usually not familiar to those for whom English is a second language. Reports should be in standard English.

10. Use plenty of white space. Wide margins make reading easier and, in addition, can be used for notations and translations.

11. When it really counts, use an interpreter. Your Spanish may be good enough for social conversations but not for business. Although you may speak Japanese, you might not want to negotiate a contract in Japanese. You should know your limits.

12. Be courteous and prompt. Observe the conventions of formality. Write your letters and reports with the cultural background of the reader in mind.

SUMMARY OF LEARNING OBJECTIVES

To Understand the Influence of Language and Cultural Differences on International Reporting.

The growth in international business directly affects business communication and report writing. The report writer must be aware of cultural differences and communication practices. What is considered a good and effective report in America may not be effective in Japan or France.

The organization of reports changes from culture to culture. Americans are direct and to the point. The American manager does not want to read material that is not relevant to the problem. The Germans and the French provide much more background information.

To be successful in international business, a report writer must be sensitive and willing to adapt the principles of good writing to a different environment.

To Be Aware of the Impact of Organizational Structures on Reporting in International Business.
If the company has an international division, the international business person is expected to contact the international division concerning any problems before contacting people in the functional areas. As international business expands, many companies are abolishing the international division and integrating international affairs into the appropriate functional areas.

To Become Knowledgeable about the Impact of Technology on International Reporting.
One of the reasons Oriental people prefer face-to-face communication to written reports is that writing Chinese and Japanese is complex. It remains to be seen how computers will change the Oriental attitude toward written reports. Filing systems act as a deterrent to writing and storing reports in some countries.

To Be Aware of Different Communication Conventions.
The report writer who must send reports to foreign companies or to subsidiaries must know the conventions for writing numbers, dates, and times. A literal translation is not always meaningful. In many cases the business person must rethink material to be presented to someone with a different cultural background.

QUESTIONS AND PROBLEMS

1. Discuss some of the language problems a person in international business encounters.
2. Discuss some of the problems related to planning and writing international business proposals.
3. Discuss the organization of reports and relate the organization to culture.
4. How does technology influence international business communication and report writing?
5. Discuss some of the implications of the different conventions for writing dates and numbers.
6. How do different measuring systems for distance and volume affect American business?
7. Discuss some of the channel problems in communicating in international business.

8. Discuss how you might prepare for writing in an international environment.

9. Examine *The Wall Street Journal, Business Week,* and *Time* for one week and note the number of articles on international business.

10. Check telephone rates and postage rates to Germany, Great Britain, France, Saudi Arabia, Singapore, Australia, Japan, and Brazil. Find out how long a letter from your city or town would take to reach each of those countries. Given the time difference, determine by how many hours the business day in each of those countries overlaps with the business day in your time zone. Also consider the impact of different work weeks.

CHAPTER NINETEEN

ETHICAL

ASPECTS OF

WRITING

LEARNING OBJECTIVES

- To acquire a framework for ethics.
- To become aware of the ethical dimensions of organizations.
- To understand the ethical implications of word choice.
- To distinguish between factual and ethical data presentation.
- To examine questions of confidentiality and the law in report writing.

In order to discuss the ethical aspects of writing, we must first examine ethics. Ethics is one of the concepts we all think we know a great deal about, but when put to the test of defining the term precisely, we may not know where to begin.

To act ethically means to do the right thing. An ethical person's behavior could be written about in the newspaper for neighbors and friends to read, and the person would have nothing to be ashamed of. Ethical behavior is characterized by honesty, fairness, and good judgment. Some people argue that ethics are universal. What is ethical in Des Moines, Iowa, is ethical in Cairo and Singapore as well. What is not ethical here is not ethical anywhere else either. Others believe that ethical behavior depends on place and circumstance. According to this viewpoint, what is ethical in New York may be unethical in Berlin or Hong Kong.

In a way both groups are right. Most cultures agree to certain underlying principles of human behavior. For example, murder is considered unethical behavior in almost all cultures. On the other hand, ethical norms also change from culture to culture. Religion, history, and cultural values influence the definition of ethical behavior. Norms for ethical behavior in America, based on Christianity, Western philosophy, and Western values, have also been shaped by the environment of a new continent and life on the frontier. Moslems and Buddhists, who have different traditions, do not share all of our views on ethics.

For example, the United States government has declared that bribes are unethical, illegal, and punishable under the Foreign Corrupt Practices Act. In the Middle East and Latin America, on the other hand, bribes are an accepted cultural practice. People in those cultures have a feeling for the right time, place, and appropriate amount for a bribe. Outsiders, on the other hand, usually do not have that feeling because they did not grow up with the practice. They may go through the motions without really understanding the cultural underpinnings of bribes.

Most of us understand that people in business must make many decisions that involve ethics. We associate ethics with problems of bribery, shady deals, poor quality of products, lies about product performance, and false advertisements. However, we usually do not think of ethics in connection with writing.

Although we often think of writers as simply presenting facts objectively, writers cannot escape the political pressures and realities. How should they handle the demand to "fix" data so that the details of questionable expenses do not show up? How should they phrase recommendations for employees who are lazy or unreliable? Is a good recommendation for a mediocre employee ethical?

Ethical behavior is a part of writing. Writing does not take place in a vacuum. A company does not hire some people as managers and others as writers. Writing is directly tied to actions. The personnel manager writes a performance appraisal; the production manager writes the production report; the advertising manager writes or evaluates the advertising copy. In a management course students concentrate on how to make decisions; the focus of this chapter is on how to communicate those decisions in writing.

A FRAMEWORK FOR ETHICS

Ethical decisions always involve judgment. A model or guide is needed to help people avoid the problem of circumstantial ethics. However, the several theories that scholars have developed are not prescriptions for ethical behavior; they are merely different ways of looking at a complicated concept. What may be ethical under one may not be ethical under another. The three most important are the utilitarian, the rights, and the justice theories. They help to determine answers in three areas of ethics: Is the action or decision good for the community (company)? Does the decision protect basic rights of all affected parties? Is the decision just?

UTILITARIAN THEORY

Utilitarian Theory
Utilitarian theory considers as just that which serves the greatest good for the greatest number.

The **utilitarian theory** maintains that actions should be judged by their consequences; that means, if the outcome is good, the action is good. The utilitarian theory is also reflected in the statement that "the end justifies the means" and the concept of "the greatest good to the most people." If more people benefit from a questionable action than suffer from an ethical decision, the action is just. For example, if not promoting George means that harmony and, therefore, productivity in the department will be maintained, George should not be promoted.

As the example indicates, the utilitarian theory does not necessarily take individual justice into account. If George has worked much harder than anyone else and if he has the necessary qualifications for the position, one could argue that he should be promoted. The utilitarian theory does not necessarily concern itself with George's promotion; it concentrates on whether George's promotion is best for the welfare of the whole.

THE THEORY OF RIGHTS

Theory of Rights
Theory of rights emphasizes rights rather than obligations.

Due Process
Due process requires fair procedures and fair laws.

The **theory of rights** puts the issues of privacy, freedom of conscience, free speech, and **due process** at the center of ethical behavior. For example, free speech is a basic right, and, therefore, the exercise of free speech does not violate ethical principles. The right to due process is also a basic right and therefore, some argue, never violates ethical principles. As an example, assume that Pam Black finds out that Margery Rodway, who is a pillar in the community, was convicted of petty theft 20 years ago. She begins to spread the news to discredit Margery. Pam, under the theory of rights, could argue that she is simply exercising her right to free speech.

The difficulty with the theory of rights is that the emphasis on rights neglects to consider duties and obligations. The theory of rights does not pay enough attention to issues of social welfare and the benefit to others. It may result in an egotistic and selfish interpretation of ethical norms.

THE THEORY OF JUSTICE

Theory of Justice
Theory of justice concerns itself with fairness and justice rather than profitability.

The **theory of justice** emphasizes equity, objectivity, fairness, and impartiality. Concern for the well being of the other person enters the picture. The question is not so much whether an action is profitable but whether it is fair. For example, special training programs for minorities may not be profitable in the short run, but they may be fair because they provide opportunities for employees who have been discriminated against in the past.

Stressing the principles of fairness, equity, and impartiality too much may lessen the incentive to produce and to do well. The theory of justice raises the question of whether equity and fairness require equity of opportunities or equity of results. For example, in addition to providing the opportunity for all students to attend high school, does the obligation exist to graduate all those who have attended regardless of level of achievement and credits earned?

THE INTEGRATION OF THE THEORIES

Ideally an ethical decision would be in agreement with all three theories. However, this is rarely the case. A decision may be just, for example, but may violate the utilitarian theory or the rights theory. A business person must test each possible decision against all three theories, one by one. If it violates the principles under one theory, the question becomes whether justifiable reasons exist for still going ahead with the decision.

For example, management by asking to keep confidential a discussion on new-product development may violate the right of free speech (rights theory). Management might argue that the exercise of free speech would hurt the company in the competitive environment. Another argument might be that keeping the discussion confidential will benefit the employees (utilitarian theory) and therefore the request to curtail free speech is ethical.

In negotiations between countries secrecy is often necessary to achieve results. If the details of negotiations between two countries are published in newspapers, the parties may be reluctant to engage in any meaningful discussions.

The model in Exhibit 19.1 may help you in making ethical decisions and in communicating those decisions. Ethical decisions are, of course, more complex than the model indicates. In making ethical decisions, you must examine yourself and your motives to root out rationalizations and false justifications. Related to motives are values, judgments, behaviors, and attitudes.

The model implies that people will always think in terms of the well-being of others; however, what people invariably do is first decide what is good for themselves. The reality of self-interest is usually at the center and, therefore, a prime determinant in moral and ethical decisions. Self-interest does not necessarily mean selfishness; it also means the natural inclination toward self-preservation. Few people will sacrifice themselves for the betterment of a company or community—and, after all, only rarely will an act that benefits an individual clearly harm the company (except in cases of theft or embezzlement).

ETHICAL DIMENSIONS OF ORGANIZATION

After spending many weeks on a report, you want the reader to agree with your conclusions and recommendations. If you doubt this will happen, but you are convinced that your recommendations will ultimately benefit the company, the solution may lie in the organization of the material. Taking the reader through the inductive process—presentation of facts, analysis of facts, conclusions, recommendations—may result in acceptance of the recommendation. On the other hand, presenting the recommendation first might cause the reader to reject the report before even reading the analysis. In this case you would be wise to choose the inductive arrangement. Is this ethical? Yes, if you believe in the soundness and truth of your conclusions and recommendations. You are in compliance with all three theories. The arrangement may benefit the future of the company. The presentation is fair. You have not changed anything; all you have done is rearrange the

Exhibit 19.1   **Model for Making Ethical Decisions**

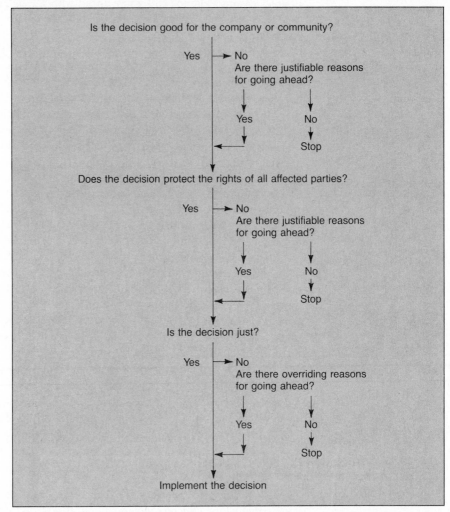

Source: Adapted from Gerald F. Cavanaugh, Dennis J. Moberg, and Manuel Velasquez, "The Ethics of Organizational Politics." Unpublished paper presented at 40th Annual Meeting of the Academy of Management, Detroit, Mich., August 9–13, 1980.

information. The reader is still free to agree or disagree with you. You are not trying to influence the reader by manipulation of the data itself.

When you organize material in a particular way, you must ask yourself why you are doing so. Do you choose an arrangement in order to further understanding or to manipulate? A fine line divides persuasion from manipulation. Persuasion presents the data in an arrangement that will help the reader see the facts in a certain order. Manipulation tries to influence the reader through a particular interpretation of the data, through editing and word choice, and even manipulation of the data itself.

As a report writer, you must realize that data is nothing per se. Most people do not know what to do with it. Businesses need people who place data in context, who signify its possible meanings, who hypothesize and project. Data only gains meaning when its patterns are perceived and interpreted. These two steps present a great challenge to the report writer.

Organization and presentation of information are closely related. For example, a company that is losing money still wants to present itself in a positive light to stockholders. The letter to stockholders in the annual report may begin with a positive element, such as reorganization of the firm for future growth. Based on the first sentence the reader might get the impression that the past year was actually good. Not until later in the letter may the stockholder realize that the company lost money or experienced a sharp decline in earnings. The following example illustrates the point:

> This is the year we celebrate the completion of the. . .mine. . . . It was completed on time, close to budget and in a manner consistent with current environmental perceptions. It will be a profitable operation. Our stockholders will be the richer for it.

Several paragraphs later the letter continues:

> Net earnings for 1981 were $50,038,000, or $1.54 per common share, compared with $237,388,000, or $8.02 per share, in 1980. The reduction in earnings reflects the sharp deterioration in prices for. . . principal products.

Is this approach ethical? Some people argue that the facts are all somewhere in the report and that the figures must be correct to meet legal requirements. That may be true but, by starting as it does with very positive information, the report may also be misleading. Many stockholders may not look at the figures. They may simply glance at the opening of the letter and some of the graphs in the annual report. If the letter is positive, and if the lines in the graph go up, many will consider the performance satisfactory, if not excellent.

The presentation covered up negative news. The company wanted to present a positive image in order to attract and keep investors. The company acted out of narrow self-interest rather than in the interest of the stockholders and investors. Some will argue that the company manipulated the arrangement of data to present an image that did not reflect the whole truth, and that therefore the company acted unethically.

ETHICAL DIMENSIONS OF WORD CHOICE

 The organization of material cannot be completely separated from the presentation and wording of the material. Word choice can influence the meaning of a message. Words like *outstanding, major, large majority, by a wide*

margin, enthusiastic, best, inferior, bargain, and *special offer* are used to create a special impression. Although these words can describe a product or a person correctly, they may also be misleading.

Let us take the example of *special offer.* Intuitively you interpret the term to mean a large price cut, a substantial cut. Your supplier has lowered the price of an item from $100 to $99 for one month. In an advertisement the supplier refers to substantial savings to be gained by taking advantage of the special offer. You will indeed save money, but the question is whether the one-dollar reduction truly is a special offer.

If you read in a union report that the new union representatives were elected by a large majority, you have to ask what constitutes a large majority? To most people it is over 60 percent. Yet, in some elections, the terms *large majority* and *wide margin* are used when the candidate won by 52 percent. Fifty-one percent is a majority but does not constitute a win by a wide margin. Actually, the margin is very small.

Some words have more positive connotations than others with similar meanings. A research study showed that even a small change in the tone of a written communication directly affects a reader's perceptions of the material presented. To illustrate, an announcement of a company policy relating to social welfare, labor relations, and employment climate was written in two versions varying only in tone. One was intended to give the impression of a flexible company, the other of a strict company. Seven sentences distributed evenly throughout the material were selected for modification. In each of the seven sentences a nonsubstantive word was chosen for modification. Nonsubstantive words change only the climate of the text and not the factual content.

The seven word pairs used to present the strict–flexible image were:

Asked—required
Trying—driving
Hesitant—willing
Should—must
Agreeable—forceful
Offering—pushing
Insightful—shrewd

The words on the left were considered more positive. The readers felt that the company described by using the words on the left was more flexible and responsive to people. The company described by the words on the right was seen as more authoritarian and strict.[1] The important point is that the facts were the same in both versions.

The example shows how much influence word choice can have on perceptions of the reader. This knowledge can be used positively to help present a positive image. It can also be used to manipulate perception. Management can use words to present a company as it is, as they perceive it, or as they want others to see it. The difficulty is that the three overlap and cannot always be separated.

A strict company can be presented as flexible, and a flexible company can be presented as strict by changing some key words in the description. The writer must be aware of the impact of certain words and also the overall climate of the text as the following example illustrates.

A university student who will graduate in May has applied for a job in your department. You look over the application and decide the student's credentials are impressive, but you have no openings. Remembering your difficulty in finding a job when you graduated, you do not want to discourage the student. After the interview you write a letter praising the resumé, adding that you do not have an opening now but will keep the application on file. You are absolutely certain that nothing will open up in the next few months, but you do not have the heart to say no.

Is your action ethical? Not completely. Someone who is familiar with the hiring process and with the style of rejection letters may recognize "keeping the application on file" as meaningless. Most readers understand the true meaning. Someone who is new to the job market may not, although no student is likely to expect to hear from you.

Now assume a different set of facts. You receive in the mail an application from a student who will graduate in May. You look at the resumé and the cover letter. The letter has numerous spelling and grammar errors, and the student is below average in academic performance. You would not hire that student under any circumstances. Your reply is the same letter that you wrote to the first student.

Is the behavior ethical? No. In this case you are lying. You may argue that the student can more easily take a polite and positive *maybe* rather than a definite *no,* but you are taking the easy way out. You may argue that it is not your responsibility to let that student know that his achievements are simply not sufficient to find a job with your company, but the point is that your message is deliberately wrong and untruthful. Your message violates the utilitarian and justice theories. Your message is not in the interest of your company or the student, and by being dishonest it also is unfair.

Ethical behavior takes courage. Writing a positive message is much more fun than writing a negative message; saying *yes* is much more fun than saying *no.* The conscientious report writer must strive for ethically acceptable reports.

ETHICAL DIMENSIONS OF FACTUAL PRESENTATION

Many people believe that a report meets ethical standards if the facts are correct. Some even say, "Let the facts speak for themselves." They believe that facts by themselves will present a true picture. Of course, the facts should be correct. However, situations are not usually that simplistic.

In a report on the financial performance of your company you cannot present every piece of financial information. You must summarize and concentrate on the major figures, which means you must select data for presentation. Everyone may agree that cost of raw materials, sales price, sales volume, and wages should be identified. However, you may feel pressure not to identify other costs. Do you identify what it costs the company to have a rejection rate of two percent? Do you include the cost of cars provided for executives? Do you itemize fringe benefits for executives, or do you lump them under "cost of doing business"? These costs may not look good to stockholders, investors, or employees. You must decide whether failing to identify them is ethical.

Deciding what to do is only part of the problem. Central to the decision is the consequence of the action, and again self-interest is involved. In deciding, you take into account the personal, social, and corporate effects of your actions. Once the decision has been made, you must act on it. Otherwise, you have not behaved ethically at all. Ethical behavior takes courage.

As you collect information for your report, you must be careful not to concentrate on facts that present a particular viewpoint. Reading only material that supports your views is tempting. Chapter 12 discussed the problem of objective and unbiased analysis. Obviously the analysis can be unbiased only if your facts are correct and unbiased and complete.

Even if the facts are correct and all the important ones are included, the presentation still may not meet all ethical requirements. For example, a few years ago a national magazine carried the following article:

> The juvenile reading habits of American GIs stationed in West Germany have local authorities worried. It seems, according to the magazine *Der Spiegel,* that our soldiers have gone ape over World War II comic books that are published in New York and sold through army outlets abroad. The Germans depicted in these lurid publications are bestial and anti-American, and authorities fear that too many GIs are confusing these fictional characters with the present-day German public.
>
> The deplorable impression such war comics are making on lonely young GIs is evident even to casual observers. The youngsters are especially attracted to simplistic cartoon books because, *Der Spiegel* says, reading comprehension levels among post-Vietnam American recruits are so low: of 200,000 volunteers who signed up with the army, just 78,000 had a high school education.
>
> But whatever the reasons for the craze, war comics are a big business. *Der Spiegel* claims that 500,000 war-oriented comic books are sold yearly to American soldiers in European army installations. By contrast, *Playboy* sells 28,500 copies a month, and *Time* and *Newsweek* between them account for only 8,500 sales a week.

The two messages *Der Spiegel* wanted to convey were that GIs are poorly educated and have an incorrect picture of Germany and the Germans. How did *Der Spiegel* get this message across?

The article depicts the GIs as poorly educated in that few have a high-school diploma. As a result, they can read and comprehend little above the level of a comic book. The issue of comic books also brings out a cultural prejudice. Germans are convinced that comic books foster illiteracy. Comic books are read only by people who cannot read well. In Germany educators are opposed to their sale.

As the magazine presents the story, the material that GIs read reinforces stereotypes of soldiers: (1) they are not very bright, (2) they are interested in sex—they read *Playboy,* and (3) few are interested in politics or anything else worth knowing.

The comparative popularity of the reading material supports the stereotype of the uneducated soldier. However, closer examination (Exhibit 19.2) shows that the sales figures are not presented objectively. They are in three different units: per year, per month, and per week. Are the figures correct? We have no reason to doubt the numbers. In that sense the facts are correct. However, they are neither unbiased nor presented fairly. They are presented to support a particular viewpoint. The impact of the numbers changes when they are converted to comparable units, that is, sales per year.

People reading a paper do not study every word. They assume that the bases of comparison are the same. After reading that GIs are buying 500,000 comic books per year, they skip to the next figure. Because the figures coincide with the perception of the reader, the reader sees no need to check more carefully.

The facts may be correct, but the presentation is unethical. The writer manipulated the information to support a particular viewpoint. The presentation violates the utilitarian and the justice theories, and possibly the rights theory. The article does not foster the common good, the cooperation between the two countries. It violates the rights of GIs to fairness. The misrepresentation also violates the principle of due process.

A United Press International news column on unemployment provides another example of unethical presentation of data:

Exhibit 19.2 **Unethical Presentation of Facts**

	As Presented	**Revised**
Comic Books	500,000 annually	500,000 annually
Playboy	28,500 monthly	342,000 annually
Time and *Newsweek*	8,500 weekly	442,000 annually

JOBLESS RATE UP IN 42 STATES

Washington (UPI)—Unemployment increased in 42 states during January, according to raw data released Tuesday by the Labor Department, with 17 states suffering double-digit unemployment.

The largest over-the-month jump was in Indiana, where unemployment went from December's 8.9-percent level to 12 percent in January, a rise of 3.1 percentage points.

West Virginia, which leads the nation in unemployment, increased to 17 percent from December's 15.1-percent level but was below the 20.8 percent rate of a year ago.

Besides West Virginia, states with double-digit unemployment in January were: Alabama, 13.5 percent; Alaska, 13.3 percent; Michigan, 12.8 percent; Washington, 12.3 percent; Indiana, 12 percent; Kentucky, 11.7 percent; Oregon, 11.6 percent; Tennessee, 11.1 percent; Mississippi, 11 percent; Arkansas and Illinois, both 10.7 percent; Louisiana and Montana, both 10.4 percent; Ohio, 10.3 percent; Missouri, 10.2 percent; and Pennsylvania, 10.1 percent.

In addition, Puerto Rico had a 23-percent rate, and the District of Columbia, 12.2 percent.

The data was not adjusted for seasonal factors and compares to an unadjusted national rate dropped to 8.4 percent in February.

The seasonally adjusted national rate was 8 percent in January and dropped to 7.8 percent in February.

In addition to Indiana and West Virginia, six other jurisdictions had increases of 2 percentage points or more - Kentucky, Puerto Rico, Alaska, North Dakota, Alabama, and Arkansas.[2]

What does the article really report? A careful reading reveals that the national unemployment rate dropped from 8 percent to 7.8 percent—a substantial drop for one month. This information is hidden, and the headline gives a different impression—unemployment has increased dramatically.

Again, no cause exists to doubt the basic accuracy of the data, but the reporting is selective and confusing. For example, the article does not give the adjusted and unadjusted national rate for December. In order to put the figures for January and February in perspective, those figures would be helpful. Most of the article concentrates on the 17 states worst hit, and only at the end is the reader told that all the figures are seasonally unadjusted. The article was published in March. The headline implies that the latest figures show a tremendous increase in unemployment, yet the article reports toward the end that the adjusted rate for February dropped from the January rate. The first four paragraphs discuss the increase, the final paragraph discusses increases in unemployment, and the information on the drop in February is buried in the middle.

The article does not present the information in perspective. The reason could be either incompetent reporting or willful confusion of information. In any case, the reader will have the impression that unemployment took a turn for the worse. The presentation is not fair and does not serve the common good; therefore, it violates utilitarian and justice theories.

As a final example, supermarkets in many states are required by law to provide **unit pricing** of items. The reason is to make comparison shopping easier for the consumer. Comparing prices is very difficult if one tall, thin bottle costs 65 cents; a short, stubby bottle costs 55 cents; and a cylinder-shaped bottle costs 57 cents. One approach is to consider the volume, but the first bottle might contain 12 ounces, the second 10 ounces, and the third 15 ounces. Most consumers would have difficulty calculating the cost per ounce for each bottle while shopping.

Unit Pricing
Unit pricing breaks down the price of an item to show the amount per unit, such as an ounce or a quart.

In the supermarkets that are required to provide unit price, the units of comparison are often different. The unit price is not helpful under those circumstances. For example, if one unit is 5 cents per ounce, another is 10 cents per pint, and a third is 3 cents per quart, the consumer cannot easily determine the least expensive one. The supermarket has complied with the law but has willfully twisted the intent of the law. The unjust practice does not help the consumer.

ETHICAL DIMENSIONS OF WRITING IN DECISION MAKING

You will always need to evaluate the political climate in an organization when you make decisions. You should examine how much the political pressures can, will, and should influence both the decisions you make and how you communicate them. If you think you are by nature totally objective, accept that all people at times have hidden agendas. They are after power, control, protectionism, or favoritism, and this influences their decisions and actions. As a first step in dealing with your own preferences and fears, you must recognize them. If you admit that you want a promotion and are afraid that you will put it in jeopardy by taking a stand against your supervisor, you at least know the factors that will influence your decisions. Once you have recognized them, you can deal with them.

The case study in Exhibit 19.3 involves an employee evaluation in which you are a supervisor. The evaluation process will require two stages: you must evaluate the employee and then communicate your conclusion. Although the communication takes place after reaching the conclusion, you may begin considering how you want to communicate some aspects of the evaluation as you evaluate.

At first glance you may not recognize the ethical ramifications of the process, but they are clearly present. In fact, all three theories of ethics are

Exhibit 19.3 Ethics and Employee Evaluation

You are a first-line supervisor in a department in a large corporation. You and Lee each supervise ten clerks. One of the men you supervise is Jack.

Job Performance:

Jack is, in your opinion, ready for promotion to Clerk II. He does the same amount of work as the other clerks in your unit. He is an efficient employee producing high-quality work. Because he has been with the company two years, he is eligible for 20 days of paid and 20 days of unpaid sick leave per year.

Problem:

You recommend Jack for promotion. Ruth reviews your request and informs you that his absentee rate exceeds the informal standard for the department of ten days per year. Jack has been absent 15 days—one and two days at a time. In addition Jack has been given time off for doctor's appointments. You do not feel Jack's absences are excessive but Ruth will not okay the promotion.

Situation:

It is time for Jack's performance review and you know the absences must be brought up.

1. How would you fill out the appraisal form?

2. Do you document Jack's absentee record?

3. What are the ramifications of documenting the file?

4. What are the ramifications of not documenting the file?

Appraisal Form:

1. List several strengths displayed on the job.

2. List several limitations to advancement.

3. Employee
   _____ At present is ready for advancement
   _____ Has potential for advancement
   _____ Needs further development

4. Additional Comments

Source: This case was developed by Patricia Marcum Grogg, Professor of Business Communication, Illinois State University, and Beth Kranz, Personnel Communications.

involved. The ethical questions relate to the good of the company, Jack's rights, and the issue of fairness and due process. Some of the factors you must weigh in making your decision are the following:

1. Formal versus informal absentee standards. According to written guidelines, Jack is ready for advancement. The question is whether an informal standard, which is tougher than the formal standard, can be applied. A complicating factor is that Jack may not even know about the informal standard. You might therefore conclude that Ruth is acting unethically in applying the informal standard.

    At the same time, you may want to find out why Jack was absent. Was he usually absent either on Monday or Friday? Was there any other pattern? You would also need to compare his record with that of other employees. In order to use the information against Jack, you need proof that he abused the sick-day policy. If he did, you might argue that his behavior is not in the best interest of the company and the other employees. In that case Jack acted unethically.

2. Quality of Jack's work. Based on the criterion of work quality, the promotion is in order.

3. Quantity of Jack's work. He produces the same quantity as others. On the other hand, if he were not absent so much, he might produce more.

4. Opinion of your supervisor. Ruth is against the promotion. Officially she bases her decision on the informal standard, but she may simply be using it to hide her real motives. She may realize that her insistence on standards will be perceived as laudable whereas the real motives might not. Ruth may have a hidden agenda, and so may you. Neither of you may be fully aware of the real motives of your actions; nevertheless, you must make a decision. Are you going to take a stand against Ruth on this issue? This question is related to the next factor.

5. Your own advancement in the company. What will happen to your own promotion if you defy Ruth? Does that concern enter into your decision? Should it? You must recognize and deal with the fact that it will be part of your decision process. Will you accept Ruth's decision? At first, making the decent decision appears to mean support of Jack's promotion. Suppose you find out that Jack was not sick at all but simply took the days off. Although he did not violate the allowable limit of absences, will the fact change your decision?

    As a further complication, two people in your area may be considered for promotion at the same time. You must do some persuading in both cases. Knowing Ruth's feeling about Jack, should you concentrate on John's promotion? Ruth does not seem to be as concerned about it. If you support Jack, Ruth may block both promotions. Would it be better to settle for one than to risk both?

You may be tempted to dismiss this case study as capricious and unrealistic, believing that situations within companies are not that unfair. Actually, such situations do occur, and usually employees have a difficult time deciding what to do. Political power plays are a reality. The fact exists that you cannot divorce your own job completely from the situation. You have your career goals and wishes, and they will enter into the decision-making process.

You must weigh the alternatives and the implications of each. You must be honest with yourself about your reasons for choosing a certain alternative and then willing to accept the consequences of your actions. After you have evaluated the situation and filled out the appraisal form, you must still decide whether to document Jack's absences even though they did not exceed the allowed limit. If any reason exists to believe that Jack abused the sick-day privilege, his absences should be documented and he should be informed of the documentation. This case study points out the importance of keeping records of the absences of all employees so that no one will appear singled out. Fairness, honesty, and tact are the most important elements in evaluating employees. Standards must be uniform, and they must be enforced.

WRITING AND CONFIDENTIALITY

When you write reports, your research will often involve confidential information. It might relate to personnel, marketing, competitors, production runs, or product research. Secretaries, supervisors, and managers are all at one time or another entrusted with confidential information that somehow becomes generally known. Even the White House has problems with leaks of confidential material to unauthorized people, such as the press. Indeed, the people who give out the information know that they are not authorized to talk about it to outsiders.

Confidentiality is basically ethical. It protects the right to privacy and can be fair and just. Secrecy and confidentiality that are used to mislead and to harm require careful examination. On the other hand, confidentiality and secrecy are often important to the future of a company. A classic example is the company that has just developed a new product. A competitor that learns about it could copy and sell it without spending money on research and development. Keeping new-product information confidential will encourage more research and will reward the company that develops new products.

Some companies encourage employees to report the wrongdoings of other employees. Is whistle blowing ethical? Do you do it in writing? Do you do it anonymously or do you give your name? Reporting the actions of another employee would seem to violate that person's right to privacy, but other issues are also at stake. If a crime is involved, the answer is easier because an employee who steals money from the company hurts the company and, therefore, other employees. The employee has clearly violated ethical and legal norms and should be held responsible.

Some decisions are obvious. An employee who sees safety violations in an atomic-energy plant has an obligation to the public to report them. The lives of many people may be at stake. In your everyday business the results of your decisions probably will be much less dramatic. The ethical issues may seem to be negligible in many cases, but they exist. Your duty as a writer is to present reports that can meet ethical standards. You will always need to weigh the issues of rights, public welfare, and justice.

LEGAL ISSUES IN WRITING

 Many companies have codes for ethical conduct. If you examine these codes, you will find that most codes actually concentrate on legal rather than ethical issues, but the law and ethics are not the same. The law represents a base for acceptable behavior. An action that does not break the law is not necessarily ethical.

In report writing the legal issues will become important when you write proposals, contracts, employee evaluations, and job descriptions. The law gives you clear guidelines on what is permissible and what is not.

For example, the law addresses the following questions: What questions can an employer legally ask in a job interview? Is it legal to provide unsolicited information in a personnel report? Although you may want to leave the final decisions to company lawyers, you as report writer must be aware of the basics. You must be knowledgeable enough about the legal issues in report writing and business communication to know when to ask for expert legal advice. When preparing job descriptions or interview questions, you should check the law.

An important question the law addresses is, *What can an employer legally ask in a job interview?* The civil rights law prohibits discrimination in hiring on the basis of race, color, religion, sex, or national origin. Based on the law, questions per se are not illegal; discrimination is illegal. Because the information gained from certain questions can be used to discriminate, the interviewer must be careful about the questions asked.

An interviewer who asks about marital status and children might use the information to discriminate against women with small children, but discrimination must be proved. Courts will take all facts and circumstances into consideration in a case. Let us assume that a company has a job opening for a traveling salesperson. The job requires the employee to be on the road 35 weeks a year, 3 to 4 weeks at a time. Under these circumstances, a company could refuse to hire persons with small children or single parents with children at home. The interviewer asking applicants about children must ask all applicants. To ask women about their marital status and small children and not to ask men the same questions would be illegal discrimination. To give the job to a man with small children and refuse even to consider a woman with small children would also be illegal. Questions asked in a job interview must relate to the job and not expose the company to a charge of discrimination.

A second question of importance is, *Can report writers legally provide unsolicited information in personnel reports?* In writing a letter of recommendation or a personnel report, your moral duty is to state honestly what you know about an employee. If you provide unsolicited information, you should be sure that you speak the truth; otherwise you may be sued for libel. Even the truth does not necessarily protect you from a lawsuit if you acted maliciously in speaking the truth.

In one case, for example, a person was held liable for speaking the truth. The facts of the case show that the person had sent a letter to a supplier warning him not to sell goods to a competitor because the competitor was a bad credit risk. The court ruled that the writer had acted maliciously and for personal gain.

If you are asked for information about employees, you should basically have no fear of saying what you know and adding unsolicited information as long as you act in good faith. Good faith is the standard normally applied. When you are seeking information about an employee or potential employee, you, of course, want to know everything important and necessary. At the end of your inquiry you should ask whether the person would like to add anything else that you should be aware of.

If you understand some basic legal principles, you can avoid legal problems in report writing and business communication. For special cases you should, of course, consult a lawyer; however, an awareness of the law will help you understand when you need a lawyer and when you can solve the problem yourself.

SUMMARY OF LEARNING OBJECTIVES

To Acquire a Framework for Ethics.
In order to write reports that are ethical, a report writer must understand the principles of ethics and the framework of ethical theory. The writer must answer three questions before making and communicating a decision:

1. Does the report protect the interest of the parties involved?
2. Does the report protect the rights of people?
3. Is the report fair and just?

The writer must weigh the answers and decide whether any special circumstances would allow a violation of any one of the three.

After answering the basic questions, the writer can concentrate on the particulars of the presentation, which will require an examination of the organization, the word choice, and the facts.

To Become Aware of the Ethical Dimensions of Organizations.
The report writer must be aware that decisions and implementations of decisions take place in complex reality. People have hidden agendas, are after power, and act out of self-interest. Although many people are capable of recognizing the ethical decision in a case, many are not willing or capable of following through with action. Ethical conduct takes courage.

To Understand the Ethical Implications of Word Choice.
The writer must be aware that word pairs such as *asked–required, trying–driving,* and *should–must* create a climate in the presentation even though they do not change the factual presentation of the material.

To Distinguish between Factual and Ethical Data Presentation.
Facts must be not only correct but also presented objectively and fairly.
Both the decision-making process and the presentation of the decision are influenced by the political pressures and realities of an organization. The report writer must be aware of and must understand those pressures.

To Examine Questions of Confidentiality and the Law in Report Writing.
A report writer should know the legal ramifications of reporting. The law and ethics are not the same, but the law does provide a basis for acceptable behavior.

QUESTIONS AND PROBLEMS

1. Discuss the utilitarian theory, the rights theory, and the justice theory in terms of ethics.
2. When are inductive and deductive orders of presentation not ethical?
3. Discuss the statement that "the facts speak for themselves."
4. Discuss some of the legal issues in report writing.
5. How does word choice influence the presentation in a report?
6. Discuss how a nonsubstantive word can influence the perception of the reader.
7. Examine letters to stockholders in several annual reports and discuss the presentation and organization of the letters in terms of ethics.
8. Examine the codes of conduct of several companies. What are the major concerns of the companies? How do the companies try to solve ethical problems? To whom are the codes addressed? How do the codes define ethical behavior?
9. Select a newspaper or magazine article that violates the ethical norms of presentation of information. Write a brief discussion of the article.

10. Discuss the following:
    a. Is it ethical to have someone proofread a report for you that you must turn in for a grade?
    b. Mary is presenting a report on which she has worked a long time. The report is good, but you notice some minor mistakes. Should you speak up in the meeting and interrupt her presentation or wait until after the meeting?
    c. You are asked to write a recommendation for Ivan, who is an average employee at best. You do not think he will be able to do a good job in the position he has applied for, but you would like to get rid of him. You know that a good recommendation may get him the job. What do you do?

NOTES

[1] Raymond W. Kulhavy and Neil H. Schwartz, "Tone of Communication and Climate Perceptions," *Journal of Business Communication* 18 (Winter 1981): 25–34.
[2] "Jobless Rate Up in 42 States," *Vidette* 21 March 1984: 2.

CASES

The cases are divided into two groups, those that do not require further research and those that do. Cases 1 to 17 provide all of the information necessary to write a report. You can add more detail and additional information, but you should not change the data provided. Cases 18 to 35 give background information, along with a description of the audience of the report and the position of the writer. Assembling the necessary data to write the report will require secondary research, primary research, or both.

One word of caution: the cases are not perfect. Both wording and organization should be improved; therefore, you should avoid copying the case verbatim for your report.

1. BUSINESS ORGANIZATIONS AND MANAGEMENT

All business students at Central State University must take Business Organizations and Management. Last year Dr. Feldstein, a management professor, reorganized the course. Up to that point four sections of the course with 45 students each were taught every semester.

Now all 180 students meet in the same class once a week. During that time the professor lectures and introduces new material. Twice a week the class is broken up into lab sections of about 15 students. Lab managers, who are in charge of the lab sections, are undergraduate students with a minimum grade point average of 3.5. During the lab sessions the lecture material is discussed. The lab managers also must supervise group projects. For the purpose of the projects students are divided into groups of five students. The group projects provide some problems because not all students work equally hard.

You are a graduate assistant to Dr. Feldstein. Your job is to supervise the lab managers. Based on your discussions with the lab managers and with students who take the course, you are concerned about the effectiveness of the course organization.

You have formulated the following hypotheses and have decided to test them.

1. Lab material is repetitious and not challenging enough.
2. Lab section managers do not possess the necessary teaching skills to motivate students.
3. The written group report causes students to withdraw from lab activities.

You administer a questionnaire to two lab sections, one with 16 students, the other with 15 students. You have tabulated the results of the survey in the following table. Now you must evaluate the responses. Analyze the material to determine whether the findings support the hypotheses. Write a report of the results for Dr. Feldstein.

QUESTIONNAIRE

Please circle the appropriate responses.

Number of students in both sections	Percent of students in both sections	Number of students in section 03	Percent of students in section 03	Number of students in section 04	Percent of students in section 04	
1.		**What**	**section**	**are you**	**in?**	
		16				Section 03
				15		Section 04
2.		**What**	**sex are**	**you?**		
16	52	9	56	7	47	Male
15	48	7	44	8	53	Female
3.		**What**	**year are**	**you in**	**college?**	
						Freshman
						Sophomore
23	74	10	63	13	87	Junior
7	23	5	31	2	13	Senior
1	3	1	6			Graduate
4.		**How would you rate the level of class participation in lab activities?**				
7	22	4	25	3	20	Excellent participation
21	68	9	56	12	80	Good participation
3	10	3	19			Average participation
						Below-average participation
						Poor participation
5.		**How clear are the objectives and purpose of lab-experience material?**				
5	16	1	6	4	27	Consistently clear
17	55	8	50	9	61	Generally clear
5	16	4	25	1	6	Inconsistently clear
4	13	3	19	1	6	Seldom clear
						Never clear
6.		**Does your lab manager create interest in the lab material?**				
13	42	6	38	7	47	Stimulates interest to a high degree
13	42	8	50	5	33	Stimulates interest at times
5	16	2	12	3	20	Neither stimulates nor reduces interest
						Reduces interest
						Destroys interest
7.		**What is the level of the lab-experience material?**				
3	10	2	13	1	7	Course material too easy, no challenge
11	35	6	37	5	33	Course material at right level, no challenge
14	45	5	31	9	60	Course material at right level, challenge exists
						Course material too difficult, too much of a challenge
3	10	3	19			Course material merely a repeat of material from other courses

8. How enthusiastic is your lab manager?

12	39	8	50	4	27	Highly enthusiastic
18	58	8	50	10	67	Generally enthusiastic
1	3			1	6	Occasionally enthusiastic
						Rarely enthusiastic
						Never enthusiastic

9. How would you rate the overall effectiveness of your lab instructor?

13	42	7	44	6	40	Excellent
18	58	9	56	9	60	Good
						Fair
						Poor
						Very poor

10. Do you participate in group activities?

21	68	11	69	10	67	I always participate.
5	16	3	19	2	13	I generally participate.
5	16	2	12	3	20	I occasionally participate.
						I almost never participate.
						I never participate.

11. Does written group work encourage you to participate in lab activities?

1	3	1	6			It always encourages me to participate.
7	23	2	13	5	33	It encourages rather than discourages me to participate.
21	68	12	75	9	60	It does not affect my participation.
2	6	1	6	1	7	Written group work always discourages me from participating.

12. Have any of your previous classes discussed the material being presented in lab experiences?

13	42	4	25	9	60	None of my previous classes covered this material.
8	26	4	25	4	26	One previous class covered this material.
5	16	3	19	2	14	Two previous classes covered this material.
2	6	2	12			Three previous classes covered this material.
3	10	3	19			Four or more previous classes covered this material.

13. What areas, in your opinion, need the most change?

1	3	1	6			Lab-manager preparation
3	10	1	6	2	13	Student participation
11	36	6	38	5	34	Lab material
14	45	8	50	6	40	Written group work
2	6	1	6	1	7	Do not know

Which Fast Food Entreés Are the Most Nutritious?

	Nutritional Factors					
Fast Food Entreés	Serving Size oz.	Calories #	Fat gm.	Carbohydrates gm.	Total Sugars gm.	Sodium mg.
Hamburgers						
Burger King Whopper	9	660	41	49	9	1083
McDonald's Big Mac	7.5	591	33	46	6	963
Wendy's Old Fashioned	6.5	413	22	29	5	708
Hamburger Group Average	8	555	32	41	7	918
Fish						
Long John Silver's	7.5	483	27	27	0.1	1333
Arthur Treacher's Original	5.25	439	27	27	0.3	421
McDonald's Filet-O-Fish	4.5	383	18	38	3	613
Burger King Whaler	7	584	34	50	5	968
Fish Group Average	6	472	27	36	2	834
Chicken						
Kentucky Fried Chicken	6.75	405	21	16	0	728
Arthur Treacher's Original Chicken	5.5	409	23	25	0	580
Chicken Group Average	6	407	22	21	0	654
Pizza						
Pizza Hut Pizza Supreme[2]	7.75	506	15	64	6	1281

[1]Recommended Daily Allowance for an adult woman, as set by the National Academy of Sciences/National Research Council.
[2]One-half of a 15½-oz. 10-in. Pizza Supreme Thin and Crispy.
Source: Adapted from "Fast-Food Chains," *Consumer Reports* (September 1979):509.

2. NUTRITION CONSULTANTS

Nancy Redgrave, the owner of Nutrition Consultants, is receiving an increasing number of requests for nutritional information on fast food. After the local papers ran several articles on the link between a high-fat, high-salt diet and heart disease and high blood pressure, people seem to be more concerned about what they eat. Furthermore, an article by the diet center Trim-Slim emphasized the fact that most Americans consume too many calories. Nancy Redgrave feels that it is time to have a systematic nutrition evaluation of fast foods to answer questions of clients. She asks you to collect the data on fast food in town and report the findings to her in a standard memo report.

You have assembled the material in the above table.

			Nutritional Factors							
			Percentage of RDA Requirements[1]							
	Vitamin			**Vitamin**	**Vitamin**					**Average**
Protein	**A**	**Thiamine**	**Riboflavin**	**B$_6$**	**B$_{12}$**	**Niacin**	**Calcium**	**Phosphorus**	**Iron**	**Total**
%	**%**	**%**	**%**	**%**	**%**	**%**	**%**	**%**	**%**	**%**
57	12	51	30	19	67	55	9	29	26	35.5
59	5	52	33	13	63	55	23	44	23	37.0
52	8	36	26	13	83	45	8	24	27	32.2
56	8	46	30	15	71	52	13	32	25	34.8
72	5	17	12	16	133	24	3	46	3	33.1
46	3	11	6	10	27	18	2	32	3	15.8
35	3	39	19	6	23	25	14	27	9	20.0
48	3	38	20	7	60	31	8	50	12	27.7
50	4	26	14	13	61	25	7	39	7	24.6
78	4	21	25	19	40	72	6	35	14	31.4
57	3	12	10	24	10	87	2	23	4	24.2
68	4	17	18	22	25	80	4	34	9	28.1
61	36	59	40	17	43	49	41	46	24	41.6

3.   ST. MARK CHURCH

The congregation of St. Mark faces a problem. The church was built in two phases. The first part was constructed during a time when asbestos was widely used; the new part does not have any asbestos. The asbestos in the older part is restricted to the ceilings in the basement under the fellowship hall. The four rooms in that area are used one hour a week for Sunday-school classes for grades 1 to 4. The rooms are not used during the week.

As soon as the announcement was made that asbestos was in the ceilings, parents of the children who are affected became very concerned. The church had tests run that showed some particles in the air, but the particles were not identified as asbestos. The concern is that the ceilings might begin to disintegrate with age. An additional problem is that the results of the asbestos exposure in the Sunday school classes will not be known for many years.

The church faces possible liability suits from parents and their children but also from workers who would be involved in removing the asbestos. The church has three options:

1. Do nothing. A number of people argue that one hour is not sufficient exposure to cause any harm. Research has only examined high-level exposure over long periods of time.

2. Encase the asbestos. In that process a material is sprayed over the ceiling to ensure that the asbestos will not flake off. That process would cost about $9,000. Any crack in the coating, however, would expose the asbestos again. A number of people insist on the removal of the asbestos.

3. Remove the asbestos. The removal would solve the problem, but this alternative is very costly. The church has asked three firms for bids on the cost of the removal of the asbestos and the installation of new ceilings.

    The bids were as follows:

Firm A:	$25,000
Firm B:	$38,000
Firm C:	$33,000

All three companies seem to be reputable.

Currently the church does not have the money to pay for Option 3. It would have to be raised either through bonds or special donations. Before this problem surfaced, the Finance Committee had decided to have a special fund drive for a sister congregation in Central America. During an earthquake the church of that congregation was badly damaged. The roof collapsed, and the furniture was destroyed. The congregation of that church has asked for support from St. Mark. The committee in charge of special projects at St. Mark feels that the congregation will be hard-pressed to finance both projects.

Write a report to the membership explaining the situation and making recommendations on what to do. The ultimate decision lies with the congregation.

4. TOOLS, INC.

Your company, Tools, Inc., has plans to expand into Western Europe. Tools, Inc. will face tough competition, but management thinks that with good planning Tools, Inc. will be able to establish itself in the market. Tools, Inc. specializes in tools for the do-it-yourself person. Over the past five years the do-it-yourself market has grown tremendously in Western Europe. Tools,

Inc. is considering manufacturing tools in Europe rather than just exporting them from the United States. Ron Houston, Vice President for Sales, has asked you to collect information on the cost of labor and inflation rates in selected countries. Of course, additional information will be necessary before any decision can be made, but Ron Houston believes that the information on labor costs and inflation can help in narrowing down the number of countries under consideration for production of your tools.

Organize the data you found and analyze your findings in a memo to Ron Houston.

Cost of Labor (in U.S. dollars)

	Direct Cost Per Hour	Indirect Cost Per Hour
United States	$26.09	$10.36
Switzerland	20.18	9.89
West Germany	15.63	12.69
Netherlands	14.64	11.86
Belgium	14.38	11.14
Denmark	18.76	4.24
Italy	11.71	11.01
France	11.89	9.69
Austria	10.83	10.29
Great Britain	12.70	5.27

Rate of Inflation

United States	3.4%
Switzerland	3.0
West Germany	1.8
Netherlands	2.3
Belgium	4.6
Denmark	4.1
Italy	9.5
France	5.6
Austria	2.6
Great Britain	6.2

5. ELECTRONIC INSTRUMENTS, INC.

You are the public-relations manager for Electronic Instruments, Inc. Your company has decided to expand production into Korea. Management feels that the expansion into Korea is the only way the company can stay competitive. Plans are to have production and routine assembly of basic components done in Korea. The finished components will then be shipped to the plant in Freemont, Iowa. Freemont has a population of 30,000. Currently the company employs 1,000 people. As a result of the move, 500 people will be laid off. The company hopes that the move will increase sales by 15 percent after the second year and profits by 20 percent after five years. The company also thinks that employment in Freemont will slightly rise as production in Korea expands. The jobs in Freemont will become more sophisticated. The move by Electronics, Inc., will have an impact on the community.

It is your task to write a press release for the local paper, *The Freemont Star*. Keep in mind that you write as a company spokesperson.

6. IMPROVING LIFE

You work for Improving Life, a nonprofit organization. The organization has as its goal the improvement of the quality of life in developing countries. The organization believes that the developed nations have a moral obligation to support the less-fortunate countries. Most governments publish how much aid they give. Your organization, however, thinks that many governments do not give nearly enough. In an effort to lobby for more foreign aid and to appeal to the representatives of the national governments in the United Nations, you have assembled the following data:

Foreign Aid

	Millions of U.S. dollars	Percentage of GNP
United States	8,698	.24
Japan	4,319	.35
France	3,790	.77
Saudi Arabia	3,310	3.29
West Germany	2,782	.45
Soviet Union	2,450	.18
Canada	1,625	.50
Great Britain	1,432	.33
Netherlands	1,268	1.02
Kuwait	1,020	3.81
Australia	773	.45
Sweden	741	.80
Norway	526	.99
Denmark	449	.85
Belgium	434	.56
Switzerland	268	.30
Austria	181	.28

Analyze the information and write a letter report presenting your appeal for more help.

7. SWEET GRAIN, INC.

You work in the personnel department of Sweet Grain, Inc. It is your job to regularly evaluate absentee rates at your various plants. The company has 15 plants all over the United States. Every three months the plants send in the absentee data for hourly and salaried employees. The company is concerned about unscheduled absences because they disrupt production and cost the company a considerable amount of money every year.

You have organized the data for the past four periods in the table entitled *Quarterly Summary Report of Job-Absence Rates* (see pages 436–437). Now you must evaluate the information and write a report to Frank McDonald, Vice President for Personnel.

8. SUNBELT MUTUAL INSURANCE COMPANY

You are an accounting supervisor for Sunbelt Mutual Insurance Company. Two weeks ago you attended a seminar on time management and the importance of effectively organizing the workday. The seminar really stirred you up, and you have resolved to translate some of what you learned into reality. As a first step you have decided to keep a detailed record of what you do during the day. You hope that this knowledge will help you set priorities and organize your schedule better.

On a sheet you have recorded the time of each activity, the type of activity (phone, one-on-one meeting, small group interaction, large group interaction), and the content of the activity for several days. You have assembled the data in the table entitled *Record of Communication Activity* (see pages 438–439). You are ready to analyze your daily patterns and develop a plan for your day.

Quarterly Summary Report of Job-Absence Rates: Sweet-Grain, Inc.

	JUNE 30, 19XX						SEPTEMBER 30, 19XX					
	Hourly		Salaried		Total		Hourly		Salaried		Total	
	1–4 Total	All Total	1–4 Total	All Total	1–4 Total	All Total	1–4 Total	All Total	1–4 Total	All Total	1–4 Total	All Total
Bedford	2.7%	2.7%	1.6%	8.4%	2.3%	4.8%	2.9%	2.9%	2.4%	6.9%	2.7%	4.3%
Clinton	4.3	7.0	1.3	2.2	3.7	6.1	4.8	7.4	1.2	1.9	4.1	6.4
Cleveland	3.0	5.3	1.1	1.7	2.6	4.4	2.9	4.9	1.2	1.8	2.5	4.1
Charleston	2.4	5.9	1.3	3.2	2.0	4.9	2.1	7.1	1.2	3.0	1.8	5.6
Dallas	4.1	7.7	1.1	2.0	3.0	5.7	4.3	7.5	1.0	1.9	3.0	5.4
Danville	2.1	3.4	1.1	1.2	1.9	2.9	2.2	3.7	1.0	1.2	2.0	3.1
Frankfort	3.3	5.0	2.3	5.3	2.9	5.1	3.6	5.8	1.8	3.8	2.9	5.0
Jackson	1.1	2.7	1.6	1.8	1.2	2.5	1.2	2.8	1.6	2.2	1.3	2.7
Lexington	1.2	1.5	2.1	2.4	1.5	1.8	1.2	1.6	1.9	2.2	1.4	1.8
Milford	3.3	6.3	1.3	3.0	2.8	5.4	3.4	6.7	1.4	3.0	2.9	5.6
Oakbrook	2.3	2.9	1.2	1.2	2.1	2.6	2.0	2.5	1.7	1.7	2.0	2.3
Winston	1.3	1.9	1.0	1.0	1.2	1.7	2.1	3.3	.8	.8	1.9	2.8
Rockford	2.9	5.0	2.1	3.4	2.7	4.7	2.9	5.3	1.9	3.1	2.7	4.8
Salem	2.9	5.6	1.5	2.4	2.6	4.9	2.8	5.7	1.3	2.3	2.4	4.8
Seattle	3.6	6.4	1.4	1.7	3.0	5.1	3.7	6.6	1.1	1.3	3.0	5.2
National Average* (B.N.A.)					1.8						1.8	

*Note: The criteria of the Bureau of National Affairs (B.N.A.) for measuring job-absence averages is to count *only the first four days* of any *unscheduled* absences. Therefore, the B.N.A. National Average should be compared *only* to "1–4 Total" rates in the TOTAL Section for each quarterly period. (The "All Total" rates reflect all absences.)

	DECEMBER 31, 19XX						MARCH 31, 19XX					
	Hourly		Salaried		Total		Hourly		Salaried		Total	
	1–4 Total	All Total	1–4 Total	All Total	1–4 Total	All Total	1–4 Total	All Total	1–4 Total	All Total	1–4 Total	All Total
	3.0%	3.0%	2.0%	5.4%	2.6%	3.9%	3.2%	3.2%	.4%	.4%	2.2%	2.2%
	4.9	7.4	1.2	2.0	4.2	6.4	4.4	6.7	1.1	2.6	3.8	5.9
	3.0	4.9	1.1	1.6	2.5	4.1	2.8	4.3	1.0	1.2	2.3	3.5
	1.9	7.7	1.2	3.4	1.7	6.2	.7	6.5	.8	2.5	.7	5.2
	4.4	7.0	1.3	2.0	3.2	5.0	1.6	2.3	1.1	7.7	1.4	4.4
	2.2	3.7	1.0	1.2	2.0	3.1	2.3	2.3	1.4	1.4	2.1	2.7
	3.3	5.0	1.8	3.8	2.9	4.6	3.3	5.1	1.6	1.6	2.8	4.0
	1.1	2.7	1.6	2.3	1.2	2.6	1.0	2.4	1.6	1.9	1.1	2.3
	1.2	1.8	1.8	2.6	1.4	2.0	.8	2.5	2.1	5.3	1.1	3.3
	3.5	7.1	1.3	2.7	2.9	5.9	3.5	8.0	1.3	3.4	3.0	6.9
	2.1	2.8	1.8	2.0	2.0	2.5	2.7	2.8	2.0	6.5	2.6	3.7
	2.3	3.6	.7	.7	2.0	3.0	1.4	1.4	1.0	3.9	1.4	1.9
	2.9	5.2	1.9	3.4	2.7	4.8	2.1	2.9	1.6	1.8	2.0	2.6
	2.8	5.9	1.3	2.1	2.5	5.0	2.2	4.4	1.4	3.1	2.0	4.1
	3.8	6.7	1.1	1.2	3.1	5.2	3.6	5.8	1.6	1.6	3.0	4.6
					1.9						N/A	

Record of Communication Activity: Sunbelt Mutual Insurance Company

Time	Phone	1-on-1	Small Group	Large Group	Writing	Initial	Comments
Sept. 26:							
7:45– 8:00		X				ME	Non-bus/Good mornings
8:00– 8:10					X		Bus/Prep for 2:30 MBO session w/employee
8:10– 8:20		X				JW	Questions re his trng.
8:20– 8:35		X				MG	Discuss his wrtg. assgmt.
8:35–10:55			X			BK	Boss's staff mtg.
10:55–11:30		X				DG	Questions re methodology and format of 9/27 mtg.
11:30–11:45		X				MG	We have 2 problems!
11:45–11:50			X			ME	Discuss resolutions to above problems.
11:50–11:55		X				ME	Compliment SC/Good job!
11:55–12:10					X		Prep. for 12:30 mtg.
Lunch							
12:20–12:30					X		Revisions (ATS Handout)
12:30– 3:45			X			ME	ATS walkthru.
3:45– 4:05		X				MG	? re a job posting and MBO documentation
4:05– 4:20			X			ME	Bus & non-bus (SJ & LH)
4:25– 4:30		X				ME	Confirm Fla trip (SZ)
4:30– 4:40		X				DG	How'd 12:30 mtg. go?
4:40– 4:55		X				ME	Start date set for CR?
Sept. 27:							
8:00– 8:10		X				ME	Good mornings.
8:10– 8:15		X				ME	Typing instructions (MU)
8:15– 8:30			X			ME	Status/What needs to be done for 9/28 mtg.
8:30– 9:50		X				ME	MBO session w/LH.
9:50–10:00					X		Misc. administrative duties/approvals
10:00–10:10		X				ME	Status of ISS project
10:10–10:20		X				ME	Non-bus. (VB)
10:20–10:45	X					ME	CR, have you set a start date?
10:45–10:55	X					ME	United Way Report.
10:55–11:00	X					NM	Lunch invitation.

Record of Communication Activity (*Continued*)

Time	Phone	1-on-1	Small Group	Large Group	Writing	Initial	Comments
11:00–11:10	X					BD	9/28 meeting place?
11:10–11:45		X				AP	Congrats on promotion.
						LH	Schedule mtg. for MDT project. . .when?
						DD	Discuss ATS diagram, OK?
						DV	Chat; set 3:30 mtg.
						SC	Any special requirements for photocopy request?
11:45–11:50					X		Revisions (ATS handout)
Lunch							
12:15–12:30		X				WL	Congrats & presentation skills class
12:30– 1:00			X			LH	Graduation of trainee.
1:05– 1:10		X			X	ME	United Way call/write while on hold.
1:10– 1:20		X				NP	Question re procedure for discovery response
1:20– 1:25			X			DD/MG	Suggested revisions re ATS handout
1:30– 3:15				X		BK	Divn. mtg/1985 plans
3:15– 3:45		X				NP	Questions re div. mtg.
3:45		X				DW	Got a min? NO! Later.
3:46– 4:30		X				ME	Would you be interested in a job? (DV)
3:55	X					BD	(Interruption) Ok to bring 3 to 9/28 mtg?
4:00		X				BK	(Interruption) Did CR set a start date?
4:05		X				DD	(Interruption) Here's copies of ATS handouts.
4:10		X				DG	(Interruption) Can you attend a 10:00 on 9/28?
4:30– 4:45		X				ME	Ready for 9/28 mtg?
4:45– 5:00					X		Review/send terminal messages.
5:00– 5:15		X				ME	Comments re software we are piloting? (SC)
5:15– 6:00					X		Outline/key points for 9/28 mtg.

Record of Communication Activity   (*Continued*)

Time	Phone	1-on-1	Small Group	Large Group	Writing	Initial	Comments
Sept. 28:							
8:00– 8:05	X					ME	PC Are you coming to 8:30 mtg today?
8:05– 8:07		X				ME	LH How do diagrams look?
8:08		X				SJ	Congrats on promotion.
8:09– 8:15	X					ME	DW Invited to party Sat.
8:20	X					ME	Invite BD for coffee
8:30–10:00			X			ME	ATS project status mtg.
10:00–10:10		X				BK	Comments re 8:30 mtg.
10:15	X					ME	Credit union requirements for sig. loan?
10:18		X				LH	Did BK give response re Rockford seminar—no.
10:20		X				SJ	Will you have time later?
10:20–11:30			X			DD	Walkthru proposed ATS
11:30–12:30			X			ME	Business luncheon
12:30	X					ME	Return call to husband
Oct. 2:							
8:00– 8:04		X				LC	MG Called in sick
8:05		X				ME	Good mornings
8:06		X				NT	Good morning
8:10– 8:15		X				ME	Explained completed loan forms to credit union
8:15– 8:30					X	ME	Review terminal messages and route on
8:30–11:00			X			DD	Walkthru entrex/ATS
11:05	X					ME	Return call to credit u.
11:07	X					ME	Return call to LB
11:10		X				ME	LH Where did check come from/reason?
11:15		X				ME	SC, Status of work?
11:17			X			DD	8:30 mtg. impressions
11:30–11:40							Thinking!
11:40–11:48	X					LB	JW's training plan
Lunch							

9. ANNA REED MUSEUM

You have just left a stormy meeting with the trustees of the Anna Reed Museum. Last spring the Friends of the Arts in your town approached you with a request to schedule an exhibit of the young avant-garde artist René Tremblay. The contacts with the artist were made, and he seemed to be excited about the possibility of showing his multimedia exhibit of man's environment in the past, the present, and the future. The past and future environment components were safe enough, but the present posed a problem. Mr. Tremblay was planning to include live members of a street gang in the exhibit. It took a lot of effort to convince him to drop that idea. But one problem remained. Mr. Tremblay has insisted on showing about 20 photographs of the city's worst tenements. The photographs include revolting scenes from the slums. Each photograph is carefully labeled with the name of the owner. Some of the owners are prominent business people in town. They have given much money to local charities and the arts. During the past year, in fact, they gave about $100,000 to help with the remodeling of the museum. Without their generous help the museum would not have been able to finance the needed structural work.

You have talked to the artist, but he insists that the names are an integral part of his work and that any attempt to influence him to leave off the names infringes on his right as an artist. He has made it clear that he will not change his mind. The board of trustees, on the other hand, argues that the exhibit will alienate museum goers, not to mention the business leaders. The trustees are worried about a libel suit. They want the exhibit canceled.

You must decide what to do. Will you go on with the exhibit or will you cancel it? You are torn because you can see the viewpoints of both sides. In an effort to be as objective as possible, you draw up lists for and against each side. If you decide to hold the exhibit, write to the trustees explaining your decision. If you decide to cancel the exhibit, write to the artist explaining your decision. In order to avoid similar problems in the future, draw up guidelines.

10. GREEN THUMB, INC.

You have just received the figures for last month's manufacturing personnel expenses. As production manager of Green Thumb, Inc., you must analyze and summarize the information in a report to Ross Klinger, your supervisor. You are aware that the organization of the information in a table does not have the same impact as a graph. You, therefore, decide also to present the data in a graph.

Green Thumb, Inc., June 19XX

| | Current Month | | | |
| | | | Actual Better (Worse) | Better |
Expense Classification	Plan	Actual	Plan	(Worse)
Salaried Payroll	$ 5,092	$ 5,463	$ (371)	(7.29)%
Illness–Accident	2,500	2,551	(51)	(2.04)
Income Security, Full	0	0	0	.00
Income Security, Partial	334	728	(394)	(117.96)
Miscellaneous Tools and Supplies	43	4	39	90.70
Sundry Expense	447	46	401	89.71
Workman's Comp Insurance	3,980	2,473	1,507	37.86
Workman's Comp Supplement	282	276	6	2.13
Employee Acty-train	3,843	3,039	804	20.92
Personnel Telephone	34	43	(9)	(26.47)
Travel	668	74	594	88.92
Uniforms–Laundry	150	12	138	92.00
Fringe Benefits	2,053	2,036	17	.83
Total	19,426	16,745	2,681	13.80

		Year-to-Date	
Plan	Actual	Actual Better (Worse) Plan	Better (Worse)
$ 61,104	$ 64,086	$ (2,982)	(4.88)%
30,000	36,462	(6,462)	(21.54)
0	0	0	.00
4,000	5,456	(1,456)	(36.40)
500	521	(21)	(4,20)
6,350	2,390	3,960	62.36
47,760	39,781	7,979	16.71
3,386	1,548	1,838	54.28
27,900	21,609	6,291	22.55
400	393	7	1.75
5,000	2,362	2,638	52.76
1,800	1,851	(51)	(2.83)
23,636	23,817	(181)	(.77)
211,836	200,276	11,560	5.46

11. GAHR GLASS, INC.

As EEO officer it is your job to regularly analyze the composition of the workforce at Gahr Glass, Inc. Since you were hired five years ago, you have actively tried to recruit women and minorities. Your company is committed to affirmative action, but in spite of all your efforts you have not been too successful. You have just assembled the data for the quarterly status report, potential promotions, and applications received. You are ready to analyze the information and examine the possibilities of hiring more women for management positions. Address your report to Robert Galyen, President of Gahr Glass, Inc.

Gahr Glass, Inc.
Period Ending August 31, 19XX
Quarterly Status Report

| | | | | Minority Employees | | | |
| | All Employees | | | Male | | | |
EEO-1 Job Category	Total	Male	Female	B	A/A	A/I	S/A
Officials and Managers	9	9					
Salaried Foremen	9	7	2				
Professionals	4	3	1				
Technicians	10	4	6				
Sales Works	2	2					
Office and Clerical	9	2	7				
Craftsmen (skilled)	67	65	2			1	
Operatives (semi-skilled)	36	27	9				
Laborers (unskilled)	122	48	74		1		
Service Workers	4	3	1				
Total	272	170	102		1	1	

B–Black.
A/A–Asian American.
A/I–American Indian.
S/A–Spanish American.

| Minority Employees | | | | Job Openings to fill through | | Female | | |
| Female | | | | | | | | |
B	A/A	A/I	S/A	Recalls	New Hires	Current %	Avail. %	Goals
							12.6	1
						22.2	14.8	
						25.0	62.7	1
						60.0	25.3	
							8.2	
	1					77.8	70.9	
						3.0	14.9	2
						25.0	24.7	
1				3		60.7	40.5	
						25.0	69.0	1
1	1					37.5	43.0	5

Gahr Glass, Inc.
Current Employee Profile

EEO-1 Category	Current Period Data as of Sept. 1, 19XX										
	All Employees			Minority Employees							
				Male				Female			
	Total	M	F	B	A/A	A/I	S/A	B	A/A	A/I	S/A
EEO-1 Job Classifications											
Officials and Managers	9	9									
Salaried Foremen	9	7	2								
Professionals	4	3	1								
Technicians	10	4	6								
Sales Workers	2	2									
Office and Clerical	9	2	7						1		
Craftsmen (skilled)	67	65	2			1					
Operatives (semi-skilled)	36	27	9								
Laborers (unskilled)	122	48	74	1				1			
Service Workers	4	3	1								
Total	272	170	102	1	1			1	1		

*In the absence of other bonafide criteria, the preceding year's record of activity should be used.

Timetable Period From Sept. 1, 19XX to Feb. 28, 19XX							
Percent		*Anticipated Vacancies	Job Openings				
			To Be Filled By				
M	F		Recalls	Transfer	Promotions	New Hires	Total
100							
78	22	1			1		1
75	25	1			1		1
40	60	1			1		1
100							
22	78	2			2		2
97	3	2			2		2
75	25	3			3		3
39	61	3	3				3
75	25						
62	38	13	3		10		13

Gahr Glass, Inc.
Applicant Flow Summary

	Total Applicant Flow		
Job Categories	Total Applicants	Total Male	Total Female
Officials and Managers	5	5	
Professionals			
Technicians			
Sales Workers			
Office and Clerical	15		15
Craftsmen (skilled)	2	2	
Operatives (semi-skilled)			
Laborers (unskilled)	208*	150	58
Service Workers			
Total	230	157	73

*Includes applications for temporary summer positions.

12. DILUTED OIL COMPANY

As a junior executive in charge of site selection for the Diluted Oil Company, you must select one of three sites that have been recommended for a new service station in Utopia, California. You have collected the following information:

Hill Avenue and 37th Street: This is a commercial area. The lot is 150 × 100 feet. It is a corner location. The lot costs $25,000. Traffic count per day is 4,200 cars. Distance from the nearest company station is 3.1 miles.

311 Belmont Street: This is a commercial area. Lot size is 200 × 100 feet. It is a noncorner location. It costs $24,000. Traffic count is 9,000 per day. Distance from the nearest company station is 3.9 miles.

Avenue at Independence Street: This is a commercial area. The lot size is 150 × 150 feet. It is a corner location, and the site costs $30,000. Traffic count per day is 6,000 cars. The distance from the nearest company station is 2.1 miles.

Minority-Group Applicant Flow									
Male				Female				Percentage	
B	A/A	A/I	S/A	B	A/A	A/I	S/A	Minority	Female
			1					20	
									100
1	1		1					1.4	27.9
1	1		2					1.7	31.7

All of the above sites have relatively the same amount of competition in the immediate area. Each has a competitive station within five blocks. Your task is to analyze the data and rank the sites. Present your analysis and recommendation in a memorandum report to Dennis Maine. Use deductive organization and include an appropriate table.

13. TEXAS BIG
TIME OIL EQUIPMENT COMPANY

As assistant to the personnel director of international affairs at Texas Big Time Oil Equipment Company, write a memo to the director evaluating and ranking the three finalists for an opening in Nigeria. There were 20 people who applied for the job. After examination of the résumés and references, three are left for the final selection process.

Nigeria is the largest country in Africa. The country has many different tribes. There are 84 million people who speak 250 different dialects. English is the language of business and commerce and the basis for communication between the tribes.

Job Description: Texas Big Time Oil Equipment Company looks for a Director of Sales in Nigeria. The major business for the company comes from government contracts. The Director of Sales will have to deal with government officials at many different levels and at many stages of negotiations. The person hired for the job will be in charge of making initial contacts. The director will have public-relations responsibilities to develop a positive company image. Social contacts and interactions will be important. The company is looking for someone with international experience, preferably in sales. The finalists are Mohamed Aljanabi, Susan Gessler, and Okie Johnson.

> Mohamed Aljanabi is from Kenya. He is married and 30 years old. He has four years of experience in the United States and Kenya selling agricultural equipment on established routes. He speaks French and English. His references say that he gets along well with people. He is a hard worker along established lines.

> Susan Gessler is from the United States. She is 32 years old, is single, and has an M.B.A. She has worked for six years for U.S. banks on international loans. In that job she frequently dealt with government officials from Africa. Susan Gessler speaks English, French, and some Arabic. Her references say that she is very ambitious. She works hard and expects her subordinates to work hard as well. She is fair and well respected.

> Okie Johnson is from the United States. He is 40 years old, is married, and has two teenaged children. He has a B.S. He worked for 10 years as a petroleum engineer in Texas. He was in Saudi Arabia for two months eight years ago. He has no sales experience. His references say that he is congenial and easygoing. He gets along well with people.

14. METROLINE (A)

Your business, Metroline, has decided to centralize all word-processing activities into a word-processing center. Ten secretaries will work in the center. Some of these secretaries have been with the company for many years, and they are not very excited about the change.

The center will have ten word processors, three microcomputers, four printers, and two copying machines. One of the copying machines has the capability to enlarge or reduce documents. Managers have three options in submitting their work. They can submit a handwritten or typed copy, they can submit a tape, and they can dictate their material over the phone.

The company needs someone to supervise the center. The supervisor will report to the vice president of personnel. You are looking for someone who can develop guidelines and procedures for the center. The person must be familiar with modern office equipment. In addition the supervisor must have managerial and supervisory skills. The supervisor will have to coordinate and schedule the work for each secretary.

It is your task to write a job description for the position.

15. METROLINE (B)

Assume you have written the job description requested in Case 14. You received a number of applications and have selected three finalists. Analyze the credentials of the three finalists and rank them in order of preference. Send your report to Caleb Woodyard, Vice President of Personnel. Following are qualifications of the finalists.

Joanne Right: She is 22 years old and married with two children. She graduated with an office administration major from Central University. She has a GPA of 3.7. During her last year she had an internship in office administration with a large company. Mrs. Right is familiar with modern office equipment. Her recommendations say she is organized, hard working, and well liked.

Anne Hanson: Anne Hanson is 30 years old and single. She attended two years of college where she took mostly secretarial courses. She has worked as a secretary for ten years, the last five at Metroline. For the last three years she has used a word processor. She is a conscientious worker. References say she is easygoing and gets along well with coworkers. She is an excellent typist and secretary.

Robert Green: Mr. Green is 26 years old. He has a degree in management and has gone through a management-training program for an office-equipment firm. He did very well in his training program. Mr. Green is an excellent programmer. References say that he has good technical skills. He is hard working, and people respect him.

16. AROUND THE GLOBE

Around the Globe, the student newspaper at Great Lakes University, wants to examine how many students regularly read the student paper or other newspapers and magazines. The editor of *Around the Globe* also wants to determine what types of information students concentrate on when reading a newspaper. You were asked to conduct a survey of students. You designed a questionnaire and administered it in the library, in lounges at the union, and in dorms. Here are your findings.

Students and the News
(Results are in %)

	Total	Male	Female	Senior	Nonsenior
Percentage of students who read a newspaper other than *Around the Globe* daily	62	73	50	53	71
Percentage of students who subscribe to a newspaper	30	42	17	63	85
Percentage of students who subscribe to a periodical	57	68	44	52	50
Sections of newspapers students concentrate on (multiple answers were possible)					
World News	51	58	55	37	57
U.S. News	57	58	44	37	71
Community News	48	47	50	58	57
Sections of radio/TV broadcasts students focus on (multiple responses were possible)					
World News	54	63	44	37	71
U.S. News	65	79	50	63	64
Community News	39	32	44	37	42

17.   PROFESSOR HINSBERGER

You are Professor Hinsberger's assistant. Professor Hinsberger teaches business communication. This semester he decided to give all his students a writing-apprehension test at the beginning of the semester. The test was developed by Daly and Miller. Scores for the test range from 26 (low writing apprehension) to 130 (high apprehension). The test asks students to indicate whether they strongly agree, agree, are uncertain, disagree, or strongly disagree with statements about writing. Some examples of these statements are "I avoid writing," "I look forward to writing," and "I am afraid of writing when I know I will be evaluated."

Professor Hinsberger hopes that the results will help him in adapting the course material to the specific needs of the students.

You have supervised the test for two classes and calculated the scores for each student. You have arranged the data in the following table. Now you are ready to evaluate the findings. Present the results and your analysis in a memo to Dr. Hinsberger.

Results of Writing Apprehension Test

Scores	Section 1		Section 2		Total	
	F	M	F	M	F	M
52	1				1	
55				1		1
56	1				1	
57		1	1	1	1	2
58				1		1
59	1	1	1	2	2	3
61		1		1		2
64				1		1
66	1		1		2	
68		2	1	1	1	3
69	2				2	
71				1		1
73				1		1
74		1				1
75	1				1	
76	1	1		1	1	2
78		1				1
79				1		1
81		1	1		1	1
82	1	2			1	2
84		1				1
85		1				1
86				2		2
89			2		2	
91		1				1
94				1		1

18. ACCOUNTING SOCIETY

Prepare a report for the Accounting Society at your university about beginning jobs in accounting with large accounting firms. Cover aspects such as salary, hours, fringes, and promotion.

19. NATIONAL CEREAL, INC.

Your company, National Cereal, Inc., is headquartered in Chicago. The company has plants in Memphis, Tennessee; Marion, Ohio; Rockford, Illinois; and Jackson, Mississippi. Currently the company is considering building or acquiring a plant in Dallas, Phoenix, Seattle, or Philadelphia. In order to make a good decision Clayton Shriver, who is in charge of the project, has asked you to prepare a report comparing the four cities in the following areas: unemployment, cost of living, unionization, transportation, cultural activities, schools, and quality of life. Present your report to Clayton Shriver.

20. WOMEN IN BUSINESS

You are the president of Women in Business in your community. Your group is quite concerned about the image of women in print advertising. You have decided to examine the issue in more detail and prepare a report to be sent to major advertising firms and corporations. You will select advertisements from at least five magazines published during the last year and compare them with ads from five years ago.

21. INTERNATIONAL ADVERTISEMENT

You work for an advertising company that designs ads for the international market. International advertisement is a very sensitive area, and it is important that you understand the culture in which you market a product. Religion, values, and traditions influence what is acceptable and not acceptable. Your boss has asked you to examine the image of women in advertisements in several countries. (You will find copies of international magazines and newspapers in your library.) Select ads from at least three different foreign magazines and compare the way women are portrayed in the ads.

22. LINDGREEN INSURANCE

You work for Lindgreen Insurance. Lindgreen Insurance employs 3,000 people at headquarters. It has offices in every state. A number of the corporate employees have requested that the company implement a daycare center for the children of the employees. Management is aware that daycare is a problem in town. There are not enough places, and the quality of care varies. Charles Geigner, Vice President of Personnel, has asked you to examine the possibilities of corporate daycare and feasible alternatives. You should examine aspects of cost, space, stockholder reaction, branch-office reaction, and impact on employee satisfaction.

23. QUALITY CIRCLES

Your company produces parts for automobiles. A few months ago your boss, manager in charge of production, visited similar companies in Japan. He came back all excited about quality circles, and he would like to implement quality circles in your plant. He has asked you to research the topic in more detail before he approaches upper management with the idea. In your report you should examine quality circles in view of Japanese culture. You should address the changes that would have to be made to use quality circles successfully in the United States.

24. SUCCESSFUL WOMEN

Over half of all women are in the workforce. Some people argue that women have made rapid progress in advancement, while others maintain there has been very little progress. Research the progress of women into managerial and executive positions. Develop a profile of successful women and make recommendations to women business majors on how to prepare for climbing the corporate ladder.

25. CAFETERIA-FOOD STUDY (A)

For one week, record the food served in the cafeteria of your dorm. Document variety, overall quality, freshness, temperature, and appearance. Assemble your findings in a table and discuss them. Present your results and recommendations for improvement to the cafeteria manager.

26. CAFETERIA-FOOD STUDY (B)

The President for Student Affairs has received a number of complaints about the food in the cafeteria, and he has asked you to research the problem. Prepare a questionnaire to evaluate attitudes of students about cafeteria food. Address issues of waiting time, variety of food, temperature, freshness, and quality of service. Because you want to know whether there are differences in the opinions of women and men, freshmen and seniors, you will need to ask for selected personal demographics. Prepare a report and send it to the cafeteria manager.

27. ACCOUNTING-FIRM ADVERTISING

Even though advertising for accounting firms has been legal for several years, many companies still shy away from advertising. They consider advertising unprofessional. Examine the status of advertising of accounting firms and design an ad campaign for a firm that currently does not advertise.

28. WORLD BANK

You are an employee of the World Bank. During the past few years many developing countries have run into problems with repaying the loans they took from private banks and the International Monetary Fund. The inability to pay the loans back as scheduled is threatening the stability of banks in industrialized countries. In addition, some countries with outstanding loans have threatened to stop payment completely. You are asked to prepare a report on the loan status of selected countries (your choice). You should examine where the money was borrowed and how it was used. You will also have to analyze the countries' past record of paying back debts, the attitude of the countries toward the debts, and the outlook for the future. Write your report to the President of the World Bank.

29. CLUBS ON CAMPUS

Incoming freshmen are confused by the variety of extracurricular activities in your Business College. You remember that it took you quite some time to become familiar with the variety of clubs. Now that you are on the committee representing all the clubs in the college, you have decided to do something about the problem. You will prepare a pamphlet for all incoming freshmen. The pamphlet will have the following information on each club:

> Name of each club
> Purpose of the club
> Names of officers
> Dues
> Frequency of meetings
> Sample program titles for previous year

30. KISSINGER AND THOMPSON

Kissinger and Thompson is a very successful law firm. During the past ten years the office has grown tremendously, and the number of clients has doubled. The firm started out with two secretaries. As time went on, two more were hired. Lynn Hayes has been in the office for ten years. She works very hard, but she is not open to changes. She likes her typewriter and manual files and considers computers and word processors a waste of money. Jackie Meldahl has been with the firm for five years, Rose Parkins for three years, and Sue Johnsen for one year. Only Sue has been exposed to modern office technology. At a professional seminar Mr. Kissinger talked to a number of colleagues and friends, all of whom are into computers. The presenter in one session emphasized the importance of hiring an office manager so that lawyers can concentrate on their legal work rather than on administrative details. The partners discussed the matter and decided to hire Sarah Grady as office manager. Sarah is an office-administration graduate. She had hoped to manage a modern office, but she thought things over and decided to accept the challenge to modernize Kissinger and Thompson. She would be able to select equipment and design the entire office.

Imagine you are Sarah. After you have thoroughly familiarized yourself with current procedures, you decide to write an equipment proposal for approval by the partners. You would like to get micros for correspondence, accounting, and filing. You will also need a copying machine. You will have to evaluate appropriate software and hardware for cost and usefulness in a law firm. Address your proposal to the partners.

31. BRADY INVESTMENTS

You are an investment consultant with Brady Investments. One of the many sources you use in making investment decisions is annual reports. In the past you have found that many of your clients barely look at the financial information in the annual reports. Particularly, older clients tend to read the letter to the stockholders and the graphs. You have decided to examine how well this material reflects the financial performance of the company. You will examine at least four annual reports, two of companies that were profitable last year and two from companies that had losses. Analyze the letter to stockholders and the visual aids in view of the financial performance. How did the companies present bad news and good news? What was the focal point of the letter to the stockholders? Address the report to John Brady, the President of Brady Investments. You believe that the information will be useful for all investment consultants.

32. SAVINGS & LOAN ASSOCIATION

For many years home buyers would get a fixed-rate mortgage when purchasing a home. The mortgage used to be for 30 years. As inflation increased and interest rates rose, mortgage rates changed. Homeowners now face a variety of options. They can take mortgages with variable interest rates, increasing interest rates, fixed rates, and several others. You work for a Savings & Loan Association and are in charge of the department for mortgages. Because there are so many options and the whole area is very confusing, you think it is very important that all loan officers are familiar with the options home buyers have. Write a report discussing the available options and evaluate the advantages and disadvantages of each.

33. BUSINESS CLIMATES OVERSEAS

Your company is considering going international. Before any detailed discussion, the president has asked you to prepare a report on the business climate in the foreign country. She wants you to examine the areas of government regulation of business, management practices, marketing strategies, transportation, and value structures as they influence your product.

Some suggestions for products and countries:

1. Cosmetics Unlimited is considering entering the Middle East.
2. Pleasure Burger is considering entering Italy.
3. Cornchunks is considering introducing its breakfast cereal in France.
4. Hotplate Company is considering entering the Japanese market with household appliances.
5. Tractor Company is considering entering India with agricultural machines.
6. Oklahoma Oil is considering entering China with its petroleum-extraction equipment.

34. GUNNING FOG INDEX

Your grandmother just bought a new car, a Mercedes. She wants to make certain that she gets the appropriate insurance policy for the car. Because you studied business communication and finance in college, she asks you to examine the policy with her. As you start reading the policy, you are getting very frustrated. The insurance jargon is difficult to understand, and the small print is almost impossible to read. After you have struggled through, you decide to write to the insurance company.

You determine the readability level of the policy. You examine two random samples and calculate the Gunning Fog Index. Of course, you are aware that other factors than the ones the index measures influence the readability also. You evaluate layout, print, etc. Tell the insurance firm what you found, and make recommendations for improvement. (You can do the same with policies for health insurance, home insurance, or any other policy.)

35. SAMPLE INVESTMENT PORTFOLIOS

You work for an investment firm. You supervise investment counselors who have been recently hired. From experience you know that new counselors can be overwhelmed by the number of combinations and portfolio options in investments. You have talked to your boss about putting together sample portfolios that could be used as guides by the new people. Your boss thinks the idea is very good, and he encourages you to go ahead.

You know that personal preferences and risk attitudes influence investment decisions. In the initial interview with a client the counselor can establish a profile of the client concerning risk and investment goals. Once the profile is established, the counselor can refer to the sample portfolio. You are convinced that sample portfolios would be a great help.

Develop three sample portfolios (each for $200,000). In your report you must explain how to use the samples. They are guidelines rather than investment blueprints. And they do have to be updated regularly. In your report you must address various types of investment possibilities, return on equity, purchasing price, and tax implications. Distribute your report to the people you supervise and to your boss.

INDEX